Complete report on the organization and campaigns of the Army of the Potomac.

George Brinton McClellan

Sold at 13 Park Row, New York, and at all Democratic Newspaper Offices, at $1 per 1,000 pages.

COMPLETE REPORT

ON THE

ORGANIZATION AND CAMPAIGNS

OF THE

ARMY OF THE POTOMAC,

BY

GEORGE B. McCLELLAN,

MAJOR-GENERAL UNITED STATES ARMY.

FIRST PERIOD
NEW YORK, August 4th, 1863.
BRIG.-GENERAL L. THOMAS, *Adjutant-General U. S. Army.*

SIR:—I have the honor to submit herein the Official Report of the operations of the Army of the Potomac, while under my charge. Accompanying it are the reports of the corps, division and subordinate commanders, pertaining to the various engagements, battles, and occurrences of the campaigns, and important documents connected with its organization supply and movements. These, with list of maps and memoranda submitted, will be found appended, duly arranged and marked for convenient reference.

Charged, in the spring of 1861, with the operations in the department of the Ohio, which included the States of Illinois, Indiana, Ohio, and latterly, Western Virginia, it had become my duty to counteract the hostile designs of the enemy in Western Virginia which were immediately directed to the destruction of the Baltimore and Ohio Railroad and the possession of the Kanawha Valley, with the ultimate object of gaining Wheeling, and the control of the Ohio River. The successful affairs of Philippi, Rich Mountain, Carrick's Ford, etc., had been fought, and I had acquired possession of all Western Virginia, north of the Kanawha Valley, as well as of the lower portion of that valley.

I had determined to proceed to the relief of the upper Kanawha Valley, as soon as provision was made for the permanent defense of the mountain passes leading from the east into the region under our control, when I received, at Beverly, in Randolph County, on the 21st July, 1861, intelligence of the unfortunate result of the battle of Manassas, fought on that day.

On the 22d, I received an order by telegraph, directing me to turn over my command to Brig.-General Rosecrans, and repair at once to Washington.

I had already caused reconnoissances to be made for intrenchments at the Cheat Mountain Pass, also on the Huntersville road, near Elkwater, and at Red House, near the main road from Romney to Grafton. During the afternoon and the night of the 22d, I gave the final instructions for the construction of these works, turned over the command to Brig.-Gen. Rosecrans, and started, on the morning of the 23d, for Washington, arriving there on the afternoon of the 26th. On the 27th, I assumed command of the Division of the Potomac, comprising the troops in and around Washington, on both banks of the river.

With this brief statement of the events which immediately preceded my being called to the command of the troops at Washington, I proceed to an account from such authentic data as are at hand, of my military operations while commander of the Army of the Potomac.

The subjects to be considered, naturally arrange themselves as follows: The organization of the Army of the Potomac, the military events connected with the defenses of Washington, from July, 1861, to March, 1862; the campaign on the Peninsula and that in Maryland.

The great resources and capacity for powerful resistance, of the South, at the breaking out of the rebellion, and the full proportions of the great conflict about to take place, were sought to be carefully measured, and I had also endeavored, by every means in my power, to impress upon the authorities the necessity for such immediate and full preparation as alone would enable the government to prosecute the war on a scale commensurate with the resistance to be offered.

On the 4th of August, 1861, I addressed to the President, the following memorandum, prepared at his request:

MEMORANDUM.—The object of the present war differs from those in which nations are usually engaged, mainly in this: That the purpose of ordinary war is to conquer a peace, and make a treaty on advantageous terms. In this contest it has become necessary to crush a population sufficiently numerous, intelligent and warlike to constitute a nation. We have not only to defeat their armed and organized forces in the field but to display such an overwhelming strength as will convince all our antagonists, especially those of the governing, aristocratic class, of the utter impossibility of resistance. Our late reverses make this course imperative. Had we been successful in the recent battle (Manassas), it is possible that we might have been spared the labor and expense of a great effort, now we have no alternative. Their success will enable the political leaders of the rebels to convince the mass of their people that we are inferior to them in force and courage, and to command all their resources. The contest began with a class, now it is with a people, our military success can alone restore the former issue.

By thoroughly defeating their armies, taking their strong places, and pursuing a rigidly protective policy as to private property, and unarmed persons, and a lenient course as to private soldiers, we may well hope for a permanent restoration of a peaceful Union. But, in the first instance, the authority of the government must be supported by overwhelming physical force.

Our foreign relations and financial credit also imperatively demand that the military action of the government should be prompt and irresistible.

The rebels have chosen Virginia as their battle-field, and it seems proper for us to make the first great struggle there. But while thus directing our main efforts, it is necessary to diminish the resistance there offered us, by movements on other points, both by land and water.

Without entering at present into details, I would advise that a strong movement be made on the Mississippi, and that the rebels be driven out of Missouri.

As soon as it becomes perfectly clear that Kentucky is cordially united with us, I would advise a movement through that State into Eastern Tennessee, for the purpose of assisting the Union men of that region, and of seizing the railroads leading from Memphis to the east.

The possession of those roads by us, in connection with the movement on the Mississippi would go far towards determining the evacuation of Virginia by the rebels. In the meantime all the passes into Western Virginia, from the east, should be securely guarded; but I would advise no movement from that quarter toward Richmond, unless the political condition of Kentucky renders it impossible, or inexpedient for us to make the movement upon Eastern Tennessee, through that State. Every effort should however, be made to organize, equip and arm as many troops as possible in Western Virginia, in order to render the Ohio and Indiana regiments available for other operations. At as early a day as practicable, it would be well to protect and re-open the Baltimore and Ohio Railroad.

Baltimore and Fort Munroe should be occupied by garrisons sufficient to retain them in our possession. The importance of Harper's Ferry and the line of the Potomac, in the direction of Leesburg, will be very materially diminished so soon as our force in this vicinity becomes organized, strong and efficient, because no capable general will cross the river, north of this city, when we have a strong army here, ready to cut off his retreat.

To revert to the West, it is probable that no very large additions to the troops now in Missouri, will be necessary to secure that State.

I presume that the force required for the movement down the Mississippi, will be determined by its commander and the President. If Kentucky assumes the right position, not more than 20,000 troops will be needed, together with those that can be raised in that State and Eastern Tennessee, to secure the latter region and its railroads, as well as ultimately to occupy Nashville.

The Western Virginia troops, with more than 5,000 to 10,000 from Ohio and Indiana, should, under proper management, suffice for its protection. When we have reorganized our main army here, 10,000 men ought to be enough to protect the Baltimore and Ohio Railroad and the Potomac. Five thousand will garrison Baltimore, 3,000 Fort Monroe, and not more than 20,000 will be necessary, at the utmost, for the defense of Washington.

For the main army of operations, I urge the following composition:

250 Regiments of Infantry, say	225,000 men.
100 Field Batteries, 600 guns	15,000 "
28 Regiments Cavalry	25,500 "
5 " Engineer troops	7,500 "
Total	273,000

The force must be supplied with the necessary engineer and pontoon trains, and with transportation for everything save tents. Its general line of operations should be so directed that water transportation can be availed of from point to point, by means of the ocean and the rivers emptying into it. An essential feature of the plan of operations, will be the employment of a strong naval force, to protect the movements of a fleet of transports intended to convey a considerable body of troops from point to point of the enemy's sea-coast, thus either creating diversions, and rendering it necessary to detach largely from their main body, in order to protect such of their cities as may be threatened, or else landing and forming establishments on their coast at any favorable places that opportunity might offer. This naval force should also co-operate with the main army, in its efforts to seize the important sea-board town of the rebels.

It cannot be ignored that the construction of railroads, has introduced a new and very important element into war, by the great facilities thus given for concentrating at particular positions, large masses of troops from remote sections and by creating new strategic points and lines of operations. It is intended to overcome this difficulty by the partial operations suggested, and such other as the particular case may require. We must endeavor to seize places on the railways, in the rear of the enemy's points of concentration, and we must threaten their sea-board cities, in order that each State may be forced, by the necessity of its own defense to diminish its contingent to the Confederate army.

The proposed movement down the Mississippi, will produce important results in this connection. That advance and the progress of the main army at the East, will materially assist each other by diminishing the resistance to be encountered by each. The tendency of the Mississippi movement upon all questions connected with cotton, is too well understood by the President and Cabinet, to need any illustration from me. There is another independent movement which has often been suggested and which has always recommended itself to my judgment. I refer to a movement from Kansas and Nebraska through the Indian Territory upon Red River and Western Texas, for the purpose of protecting and developing the latent Union and free state sentiment, well known to predominate in Western Texas, and which, like a similar sentiment in Western Virginia, will, if protected, ultimately organize that section into a free state. How far it will be possible to support this movement by an advance through New Mexico from California, is a matter which I have not sufficiently examined to be able to express a decided opinion. If at all practicable, it is eminently desirable, as bringing into play the resources and warlike qualities of the Pacific States, as well as identifying them with our cause, and cementing the bond of Union between them and the General Government.

If it is not departing too far from my province, I will venture to suggest the policy of an intimate alliance and cordial understanding with Mexico; their sympathies and interests are with us; their antipathies exclusively against our enemies, and their institutions. I think it would not be difficult to obtain from the Mexican government the right to use, at least during the present contest, the road from Guaymas to New Mexico. This concession would very materially reduce the obstacles of the column moving from the Pacific. A similar permission to use their territory for the passage of troops between the Panuco and the Rio Grande, would enable us to throw a column of troops, by a good road from Tampico or some of the small harbors north of it, upon and across the Rio Grande, without risk, and scarcely firing a shot. To what extent, if any, it would be desirable to take into service and employ Mexican soldiers, is a question entirely political, on which I do not venture to offer an opinion.

The force I have recommended is large, the expense is great. It is possible that a smaller force might accomplish the object in view; but I understand it to be the purpose of this great nation to re-establish the power of its government, and to restore peace to its citizens, in the shortest possible time. The question to be decided is simply this; shall we crush the rebellion at one blow, terminate the war in one campaign, or shall we leave it for a legacy to our descendants?

When the extent of the possible line of operations is considered, the force asked for the main army under my command cannot be regarded as unduly large. Every mile we advance carries us further from our base of operations, and renders detachments necessary to cover our communications, while the enemy will be constantly concentrating as he falls back. I propose with the force which I have requested, not only to drive the enemy out of Virginia and occupy Richmond, but to occupy Charleston, Savannah, Montgomery, Pensacola, Mobile and New Orleans; in other words to move into the heart of the enemy's country, and crush out the rebellion in its very heart.

By seizing and repairing the railroads as we advance, the difficulties of transportation will be materially diminished. It is perhaps, unnecessary to state, that in addition to the forces named in this memorandum, strong reserves should be formed, ready to supply any losses that may occur.

In conclusion, I would submit that the exigencies of the treasury may be lessened by making only partial payments to our troops, when in the enemy's country, and by giving the obligations of the United States for such supplies as may there be obtained.

GEO. B. McCLELLAN,
Major-General.

I do not think the events of the war have proved these views, upon the methods and plans of its conduct, altogether incorrect. They certainly have not proved my estimate of the number of troops and scope of operations too large. It is probable that I did under-estimate the time necessary for the completion of arms and equipments. It was not strange, however, that by many civilians intrusted with authority there should have been an exactly opposite opinion held in both these particulars.

The result of the first battle of Manassas had been almost to destroy the morale and organization of our army, and to alarm government and people. The national capital was in danger. It was necessary, besides holding the enemy in check, to build works for its defense, strong and capable of being held by a small force.

It was necessary also to create a new army for active operations, and to expedite its organization, equipment, and the accumulation of the material of war, and to this not inconsiderable labor all my energies for the next three months were constantly devoted

Time is a necessary element in the creation of armies, and I do not therefore think it necessary to more than mention the impatience with which many regarded the delay in the arrival of the new levies though recruited and pressed forward with unexampled rapidity—the manufacture and supply of arms and equipments, or the vehemence with which an immediate advance upon the enemy's works directly in our front was urged by a patriotic but sanguine people

The President too was anxious for the speedy employment of our army, and although possessed of my plans through frequent conferences, desired a paper from me upon the condition of the forces under my command, and the immediate measures to be taken to increase their efficiency Accordingly, in the latter part of October, I addressed the following letter to the Secretary of War

To THE HON SIMON CAMERON,

Secretary of War :

SIR,—In conformity with a personal understanding with the President, yesterday, I have the honor to submit the following statement of the condition of the army under my command, and the measures required for the preservation of the government and the suppression of the rebellion :

It will be remembered that, in a memorial I had the honor to address to the President soon after my arrival at Washington, and in my communication addressed to Lieut-General Scott, under date of 8th of August; in my letter to the President authorizing him, at his request, to withdraw the letter written by me to General Scott, and in my letter of the 8th of September, answering your note of inquiry of that date, my views on the same subject are frankly and fully expressed

In these several communications I have stated the force I regarded as necessary to enable this army to advance with a reasonable certainty of success, at the same time leaving the capital and the line of the Potomac sufficiently guarded not only to secure the retreat of the main army in the event of disaster, but to render it out of the enemy's power to attempt a diversion in Maryland

So much time has passed, and the winter is approaching so rapidly, that but two courses are left to the government, viz., either to go into winter quarters, or to assume the offensive with forces greatly inferior in numbers to the army I regarded as desirable and necessary.

If political considerations render the first course unadvisable the second alone remains. While I regret that it has not been deemed expedient or perhaps possible to concentrate the forces of the nation in this vicinity, (remaining on the defensive elsewhere,) keeping the attention and efforts of the government fixed upon this as the vital point, where the issue of the great contest is to be decided, it may still be that by introducing unity of action and design among the various armies of the land, by determining the courses to be pursued by the various commanders under one general plan transferring from the other armies the superfluous strength not required for the purpose in view and thus re-inforcing this main army whose destiny it is to decide the controversy, we may yet be able to move with a reasonable prospect of success before the winter is fully upon us. The nation feels, and I share that feeling, that the army of the Potomac holds the fate of the country in its hands. The stake is so vast, the issue so momentous, and the effect of the next battle will be so important throughout the future, as well as the present, that I continue to urge, as I have ever done since I entered upon the command of this army, upon the government to devote its energies and its available resources towards increasing the numbers and efficiency of the army on which its salvation depends.

A statement, carefully prepared by the chiefs of engineers and artillery of this army, gives as the necessary garrison of this city and its fortifications 33,795 men—say 35,000. The present garrison of Baltimore and its dependencies is about 10,000 I have sent the chief of my staff to make a careful examination into the condition of these troops and to obtain the information requisite to enable me to decide whether this number can be diminished or the reverse. At least 5,000 men will be required to watch the river hence to Harper's Ferry and its vicinity; probably 8,000 to guard the lower Potomac

As you are aware, all the information we have from spies, prisoners &c , agree in showing that the enemy have a force on the Potomac not less than 150,000 strong, well drilled and equipped, ably commanded and strongly intrenched. It is plain, therefore, that to ensure success, or to render it reasonably certain, the active army should not number less than 150,000 efficient troops, with 400 guns, unless some material change occurs in the force in front of us

The requisite force for an advance movement by the army of the Potomac may be thus estimated :

Column of active operations 150,000 men, 400 guns,
Garrison of city of Washington 35,000 " 40 "
To guard Potoc'c to Hrp's Ferry 5,000 " 12 "
To guard lower Potomac 8,000 " 24 "
Garrison for Balt. and Annapolis 10,000 " 12 "

Total effective force required 208,000 men, 488 guns.

Or an aggregate, present and absent, of about 240,000 men, should the losses by sickness. &c , not rise to a higher per-centage than at present.

Having stated what I regard as the requisite force to enable this army to advance, I now proceed to give the actual strength of the army of the Potomac.

The aggregate strength of the army of the

Potomac by the official report on the morning of the 27th inst was 168,318 officers and men of all grades and arms. This includes the troops at Baltimore and Annapolis, on the upper and lower Potomac, the sick, absent, &c.

The force present for duty was 147,695. Of this number 4,268 cavalry were completely unarmed, 3,163 cavalry only partially armed, 5,979 infantry unequipped, making 13,410 unfit for the field, (irrespective of those not yet sufficiently drilled) and reducing the effective force to 134,285 and the number disposable for an advance to 76,285. The infantry regiments are to a considerable extent, armed with unserviceable weapons—quite a large number of good arms, which had been intended for this army, were ordered elsewhere, leaving the army of the Potomac insufficiently and, in some cases, badly armed.

On the 30th of September there were with this army 228 field guns ready for the field so far as arms and equipments are concerned; some of the batteries are still quite raw, and unfit to go into action. I have intelligence that eight new batteries are en route hither, two others are ready for the field. I will still (if the New York batteries have six guns each) be 112 guns short of the number required for the active column, saying nothing for the present of those necessary for the garrisons and corps on the Potomac, which would make a total deficiency of 200 guns.

I have thus briefly stated our present condition and wants. It remains to suggest the means of supplying the deficiencies.

First. That *all* the cavalry and infantry arms, as fast as procured, whether manufactured in this country or purchased abroad, be sent to this army, until it is fully prepared for the field.

Second. That the two companies of the 4th artillery, now understood to be en route from Fort Randall to Fort Monroe, be ordered to this army, to be mounted at once; also that the companies of the 3d artillery, en route from California be sent here. Had not the order for Sinead's battery to come here from Harrisburgh to replace the battery I gave General Sherman, been so often countermanded, I would again ask for it.

Third. That a more effective regulation may be made, authorizing the transfer of men from the volunteers to the regular batteries, infantry and cavalry; that we may make the best possible use of the invaluable regular "skeletons."

Fourth. I have no official information as to the United States' forces elsewhere; but from the best information I can obtain from the War Department, and other sources, I am led to believe that the United States troops are,

In Western Virginia about	30,000
In Kentucky about	40,000
In Missouri about	80,000
In Fortress Monroe about	11,000
Total,	161,000

Besides these, I am informed that more than 100,000 are in progress of organization in other northern and western states.

I would therefore recommend that not interfering with Kentucky, there should be retained in Western Virginia and Missouri a sufficient force for defensive purposes, and that the surplus troops be sent to the army of the Potomac, to enable it to assume the offensive, that the same course be pursued in respect to Fortress Monroe, and that no further outside expeditions be attempted until we have fought the great battle in front of us.

Fifth. That every nerve be strained to hasten the enrollment, organization, and armament of new batteries and regiments of infantry.

Sixth. That all the battalions now raised for the new regiments of regular infantry be at once ordered to this army, and that the old infantry and cavalry en route from California, be ordered to this army immediately on their arrival in New York.

I have thus indicated in a general manner, the objects to be accomplished and the means by which we may gain our ends.

A vigorous employment of these means will in my opinion, enable the army of the Potomac to assume successfully this season, the offensive operations which, ever since entering upon the command, it has been my anxious desire and diligent effort to prepare for and prosecute. The advance should not be postponed beyond the 25th of November, if possible to avoid it.

Unity in councils, the utmost vigor and energy in action, are indispensable. The entire military field should be grasped as a whole, and not in detatched parts.

One plan should be agreed upon and pursued, a single will should direct and carry out these plans.

The great object to be atcomplished—the crushing defeat of the rebel army [now] at Manassas—should never for one instant be lost sight of, but all the intellect and means and men of the government poured upon that point. The loyal States possess ample force to effect all this, and more. The rebels have displayed energy, unanimity, and wisdom worthy of the most desperate days of the French Revolution—should we do less?

The unity of this nation, the preservation of our institutions, are so dear to me that I have willingly sacrificed my private happiness, with the single object of doing my duty to my country. When the task is accomplished I shall be glad to return to the obscurity from which events have drawn me.

Whatever the determination of the government may be, I will do the best I can with the army of the Potomac, and will share its fate, whatever may be the task imposed upon me.

Permit me to add, that on this occasion as heretofore, it has been my aim neither to exaggerate nor underrate the power of the enemy, nor fail to express clearly the means by which, in my judgment, that power may be broken Urging the energy of preparation and action, which has ever been my choice, but with the fixed purpose by no act of mine to expose this government to hazard by premature movement, and requesting that this communication may be laid before the President,

I have the honor to be, very respectfully,
Your obedient servant G B McC Maj -Gen.

When I assumed command in Washington on the 27th of July, 1861, the number of troops in and around the city was about 50,000 infantry, less than 1,000 cavalry, and 650 artillery men, with nine imperfect field-batteries of thirty pieces

On the Virginia bank of the Potomac the brigade organization of General McDowell still existed, and the troops were stationed at and in rear of Fort Corcoran, Arlington, and Fort Albany, at Fort Runyon, Roach's Mills, Cole's Mill, and in the vicinity of Fort Ellsworth, with a detachment at the Theological Seminary.

There were no troops south of Hunting Creek, and many of the regiments were encamped on the low grounds bordering the Potomac,—seldom in the best positions for defense, and entirely inadequate in numbers and condition to defend the long line from Fort Corcoran to Alexandria.

On the Maryland side of the river, upon the heights overlooking the Chain Bridge, two regiments were stationed, whose commanders were independent of each other.

There were no troops on the important Tenallytown road, or on the roads entering the city from the south

The camps were located without regard to purposes of defense or instruction, the roads were not picketed, and there was no attempt at an organization into brigades

In no quarter were the dispositions for defense such as to offer a vigorous resistance to a respectable body of the enemy either in the positions and numbers of the troops, or the number and character of the defensive works. Earthworks in the nature of "tetes-de-pont" looked upon the approaches to the Georgetown aqueduct and ferry, the Long Bridge, and Alexandria by the Little River Turnpike and some simple defensive arrangements were made at the Chain Bridge. With the latter exception, not a single defensive work had been commenced on the Maryland side.

There was nothing to prevent the enemy shelling the city from heights, within easy range, which could be occupied by a hostile column almost without resistance. Many soldiers had deserted, and the streets of Washington were crowded with straggling officers and men, absent from their stations without authority, whose behavior indicated the general want of discipline and organization.

I at once designated an efficient staff, afterwards adding to it, as opportunity offered and necessity required, who zealously co-operated with me in the labor of bringing order out of confusion, reassigning troops and commands, projecting and throwing up defensive works, receiving and organizing, equipping and providing for the new levies arriving in the city.

The valuable services of these officers in their various departments, during this and throughout the subsequent periods of the history of the army of the Potomac, can hardly be sufficiently appreciated Their names and duties will be given in another part of this report, and they are commended to the favorable notice of the War Department

The restoration of order in the city of Washington was effected through the appointment of a provost marshal, whose authority was supported by the few regular troops within my command. These troops were thus in position to act as a reserve, to be sent to any point of attack where their services might be most wanted.

The energy and ability displayed by Col. A. Porter, the provost marshal and his assistants, and the strict discharge of their duty by the troops, produced the best results, and Washington soon became one of the most quiet cities in the Union

The new levies of infantry, upon arriving in Washington, were formed into provisional brigades, and placed in camp in the suburbs of the city for equipment, instruction and discipline. As soon as regiments were in fit condition for transfer to the forces across the Potomac, they were assigned to the brigades serving there.

Brig.-Gen. F J. Porter was at first assigned to the charge of the provisional brigades. Brig-Gen A. E Burnside was the next officer assigned to this duty, from which, however, he was soon relieved by Brig -Gen S. Casey, who continued in charge of the newly arriving regiments until the army of the Potomac departed for the Peninsula, in March, 1862. The newly arriving artillery troops reported to Brig.-Gen. Wm F Barry, the Chief of Artillery, and the cavalry to Brig -Gen. Geo. Stoneman, the Chief of Cavalry.

By the 15th of October, the number of troops in and about Washington, inclusive of the garrison of the city and Alexandria, the city guard, and the forces on the Maryland shore of the Potomac, below Washington, and as far as Cumberland above, the troops under the command of Gen. Dix at Baltimore, and its dependencies, was as follows:

```
Total present for duty .............. 133,201
   "    sick     ..................     9,290
   "    in confinement ..............   1,156

Aggregate present  ........... 143 647
   "    absent       ...........   8,404

Grand aggregate............. 152,051
```

The following table exhibits similar data for the periods stated including the troops in Maryland and Delaware:

	PRESENT			ABSENT	PRESENT AND ABSENT
	For Duty	Sick	In Confinement		Grand Aggregate
1861					
Dec 1	169,452	15,102	2,189	11,470	198,213
1862					
Jan 1	191,480	14,790	2,260	11,707	219,707
Feb 1	190,806	14,373	2,917	14,110	222,196
Mch. 1	193,142	13,167	2,108	13,570	221,987

For convenience of reference, the strength of the army of the Potomac at subsequent periods is given:

1862	PRESENT						ABSENT		Grand Aggregate present and absent
	For Duty		Sick		In Arrest or Confinement		By Authority	Without Authority	
	Officers	Men	Officers	Men	Officers	Men	Aggregate			
April 30	4,725	104,610	233	5,385	41	356	115,350	11,037		126,387
June 20	4,665	101,160	496	10,541	44	320	117,226	27,700	887	145,813
July 10	3,834	85,715	685	15,959	60	213	106,466	34,638	3,782	144,886

In organizing the army of the Potomac, and preparing it for the field, the first step taken was to organize the infantry into brigades of four regiments each, retaining the newly arrived regiments on the Maryland side, until their armament and equipment were issued, and they had obtained some little elementary instruction, before assigning them permanently to brigades.

When the organization of the brigades was well established, and the troops somewhat disciplined and instructed, divisions of three brigades each were gradually formed.

As is elsewhere stated in this report, although I was always in favor of the organization into army corps as an abstract principle, I did not desire to form them until the army had been for some little time in the field, in order to enable the general officers first to acquire the requisite experience as division commanders on active service, and that I might be able to decide from actual trial who were best fitted to exercise those important commands.

For a similar reason, I carefully abstained from making any recommendations for the promotion of officers to the grade of Major-General.

When new batteries of artillery arrived, they also were retained in Washington until their armament and equipment were completed, and their instruction sufficiently advanced, to justify their being assigned to divisions.

The same course was pursued in regard to the cavalry. I regret that circumstances have delayed the Chief of Cavalry, Gen Geo. Stoneman, in furnishing his report upon the organization of that arm of service. It will, however, be forwarded as soon as completed, and will, doubtless, show that the difficult and important duties intrusted to him were efficiently performed. He encountered and overcame, as far as it was possible, continual and vexatious obstacles arising from the great deficiency of cavalry arms and equipments, and the entire inefficiency of many of the regimental officers first appointed; this last difficulty was, to a considerable extent, overcome in the cavalry, as well as in the infantry and artillery, by the continual and prompt action of courts-martial and boards of examination.

As rapidly as circumstances permitted, every cavalry soldier was armed with a sabre and revolver, and at least two squadrons in every regiment with carbines.

It was intended to assign at least one regiment of cavalry to each division of the active army, besides forming a cavalry reserve of the regular regiments, and some picket regiments of volunteer cavalry. Circumstances beyond my control rendered it impossible to carry out this intention fully, and the cavalry force, serving with the army in the field, was never as large as it ought to have been.

It was determined to collect the regular infantry to form the nucleus of a reserve. The advantage of such a body of troops at a critical moment, especially in an army constituted mainly of new levies, imperfectly disciplined, has been frequently illustrated in military history, and was brought to the attention of the country at the first battle of Manassas. I have not been disappointed in the estimate formed of the value of these troops. I have always found them to be relied on; whenever they have been brought under fire, they have shown the utmost gallantry and tenacity.

The regular infantry, which had been collected from distant posts, and which had been recruited as rapidly as the slow progress of recruiting for the regular service would allow, added to the small battalion with McDowell's army, which I found at Washington, on my arrival, amounted, on the 30th of August, to 1040 men; on the 28th of February, 1862, to 2682, and on the 30th of April, to 4608.

On the 17th of May, 1862, they were assigned to Gen Porter's corps, for organization as a division with the 5th regiment of New York Volunteers, which joined May 4th, and the 10th New York Volunteers, which joined subsequently. They remained from the commencement, under the command of Brig.-Gen. Geo. Sykes, Major 14th Infantry, U. S. Army.

ARTILLERY.

The creation of an adequate artillery establishment, for an army of so large proportions, was a formidable undertaking; and had it not been that the country possessed, in the regular service, a body of accomplished and energetic artillery officers, the task would have been almost hopeless

The charge of organizing this most important army was confided to Major (afterwards Brig.-Gen.) W. M. F. Barry, Chief of Artillery, whose industry and zeal achieved the best results. The report of Gen. B. is appended among the accompanying documents. By referring to it, it will be observed that the following principles were adopted as the basis of organization:

"1st. That the proportion of artillery should be in the ratio of at least 2½ pieces to 1,000 men, to be expanded, if possible, to 3 pieces to 1,000 men.

"2d. That the proportion of rifled guns should be restricted to the system of the U. S. Ordnance Department, and of Parrott, and the smooth bores (with the exception of a few howitzers for special service) to be exclusively the 12-pounder gun, of the model of 1857, variously called the 'gun-howitzer,' the 'light 12-pounder,' or the 'Napoleon.'

"3d. That each field-battery should, if practicable, be composed of 6 guns, and none to be less than 4 guns, and in all cases the guns of each battery should be of uniform calibre.

"4th. That the field-batteries were to be assigned to divisions, and not to brigades, and in the proportion of 4 to each division, of which one was to be a battery of regulars, the remainder of volunteers, the captain of the regular battery to be the commandant of artillery of the division. In the event of several divisions constituting an army corps, at least one-half of the divisional artillery was to constitute the reserve of the corps.

"5th. That the artillery reserve of the whole army, should consist of 100 guns, and should comprise, besides a sufficient number of light 'mounted batteries,' all the guns of position, and until the cavalry was massed, all the horse artillery.

"6th. That the amount of ammunition to accompany the field batteries, was not to be less than 400 rounds per gun.

"7th. A siege train of 50 pieces. This was subsequently expanded—for special service at the siege of Yorktown—to very nearly 100 pieces, and comprised the unusual calibres, and enormously heavy weight of metal of 2 200-pounders; 5 100-pounders, and 10 thirteen-inch sea-coast mortars."

As has been before stated, the Chief of Artillery reports:

"The whole of the field-artillery of the army of the Potomac, July 28th, 1861, was comprised of 9 imperfectly equipped batteries of 30 guns, 650 men, and 400 horses. In March, 1862, when the whole army took the field, it consisted of 92 batteries of 520 guns, 12,500 men, and 11,000 horses, fully equipped, and in readiness for active field service. Of the whole force, 30 batteries were regulars, and 62 batteries volunteers. During the short period of seven months, all of this immense amount of material was issued by the Ordnance Department, and placed in the hands of the artillery troops after their arrival in Washington.

"About one-fourth of all the volunteer batteries brought with them from their respective States a few guns and carriages, but they were nearly all of such peculiar calibre, as to lack uniformity with the more modern and more serviceable ordnance, with which the other batteries were armed, and they, therefore, had to be withdrawn and replaced by more suitable material. While about one-sixth came supplied with horses and harness, less than one-tenth were apparently fully equipped for service when they reported, and every one of these required the supply of many deficiencies of material, and very extensive instruction in the theory and practice of their special arm.

* * * * *

"The operations on the Peninsula by the army of the Potomac, commenced with a full field-artillery force of 52 batteries of 299 guns. To this, must be added the field-artillery of Franklin's division, of McDowell's corps, which joined a few days before the capture of Yorktown, but was not disembarked from its transports for service until after the battle of Williamsburg; and the field-artillery of McCall's division, of McDowell's corps—4 batteries, 22 guns—which joined in June, a few days before the battle of Mechanicsville, (June 26th, 1862), making a grand total of field-artillery, at any time with the army of the Potomac of 60 batteries, of 343 guns. With this large force serving in six corps-d'armée of eleven divisions, and the artillery reserve, the only general and field-officers were 1 brigadier-general, 4 colonels, 3 lieutenant-colonels, and 3 majors; a number obviously insufficient, and which impaired, to a great degree, in consequence of the want of rank and official influence of the commanders of corps and division artillery, the efficiency of the arm. As this faulty organization can be suitably corrected only by legislative action, it is earnestly hoped that the attention of the proper authorities may be at an early day invited to it.

"When there were so many newly organized volunteer field-batteries, many of whom received their first and only instruction in the intrenched camps covering Washington, during the three or four inclement months of the winter of 1861-62, there was, of course, much to be improved. Many of the volunteer batteries, however, evinced such zeal and intelligence, and availed themselves so industriously of the instructions of the regular officers, their commanders and the example of the regular batteries, their associates, that they made rapid progress, and attained a degree of proficiency highly creditable."

The zeal and services of Major A. S. Webb, assistant to General Barry, entitle him to especial praise. At the close of the Peninsula campaign, General Barry assumed the duties of chief of artillery of the defenses of Washington, and was relieved in his former position by Col. H. J. Hunt, who had commanded the artillery reserve with marked skill, and brought to his duties as chief of artillery the highest qualifications. The services of this distinguished officer in re-organizing and re-fitting the batteries prior to and after the battle of Antietam, and his gallant and skillful conduct on that field, merit the highest encomiums in my power to bestow. His assistant, Major Doull, deserves high credit for his services and gallantry throughout both campaigns.

[Detailed statement of the distribution of various regiments and batteries, as they arrived in Washington at this period, and, also, an account of the composition of the army on the 15th of October, 1862, which are given in Sheldon's edition of the Report, are omitted in this edition.]

ARMY CORPS.

On the 8th of March 1862, the President directed, by the following order, the organization of the active portion of the Army of the Potomac, into four army corps, and the formation of a fifth corps, from the divisions of Banks and Shields. The following is the text of the President's order.

Executive Mansion,
Washington, March 8th, 1862.
President's General War Order, No. 2.

Ordered 1st. That the Major-General commanding the Army of the Potomac, proceed, forthwith, to organize that part of said army designed to enter upon active operations, (including the reserve, but excluding the troops to be left in the fortifications about Washington), into four army corps, to be commanded according to seniority of rank, as follows:

1st Corps. To consist of four divisions, and to be commanded by Maj.-Gen. I. McDowell.

2d Corps. To consist of three divisions, and to be commanded by Brig.-Gen. E. V. Sumner.

3d Corps. To consist of three divisions, and to be commanded by Brig.-Gen. S. P. Heintzelman.

4th Corps. To consist of three divisions, and to be commanded by Brig.-Gen. E. D. Keyes.

2d. That the divisions now commanded by the officers above assigned to the commands of army corps, shall be embraced in and form part of their respective corps.

3d. The forces left for the defense of Washington, will be placed in command of Brig.-Gen. James Wadsworth, who shall also be Military Governor of the District of Columbia.

4th. That this order be executed with such promptness and dispatch, as not to delay the commencement of the operations already directed to be undertaken by the Army of the Potomac.

5th. A fifth army corps to be commanded by Maj.-Gen. N. P. Banks, will be formed from his own, and General Shields', late Gen. Lander's, division.
A. LINCOLN.

The following order, which was made as soon as circumstances permitted, exhibits the steps taken to carry out the requirements of the President's War Order, No. 2:

Headquarters, Army of the Potomac,
Fairfax Court House, Va., March 13, 1862.
General Orders, No 101.

In compliance with the President's War Order, No. 2, of March 8th, 1862, the active portion of the army of the Potomac is formed into corps, as follows.

1st Corps, Major-Gen. Irwin McDowell, to consist, for the present, of the divisions of Franklin, McCall, and King.

2d Corps, Brig.-Gen. E. V. Sumner, divisions, Richardson Blenker and Sedgwick.

3d. Corps, Brig.-Gen. S. P. Heintzelman, divisions, F. J. Porter, Hooker, and Hamilton

4th Corps, Brig.-Gen. E D. Keyes, divisions, Couch, Smith, and Casey.

5th Corps Maj.-Gen. N. P. Banks, divisions, Williams and Shields.

The cavalry regiments attached to divisions, will, for the present remain so, subsequent orders will provide for these regiments, as well as for the reserve artillery, regular infantry, and regular cavalry.

Arrangements will be made to unite the divisions of each army corps, as promptly as possible. The commanders of divisions will at once report in person, or where that is impossible, by letter to the commander of their army corps. By command of

MAJ.-GEN. McCLELLAN,
A. V COLBURN, Ass't. Adjt.-Gen'l.

[The details of the organization of the army, April 1, 1862, are omitted in this edition

THE STAFF.

In a staff charged with labors so various and important as that of the army of the Potomac, a chief was indispensible to supervise the various departments, and to relieve the commanding general of details. The office of chief-of-staff, well known in European armies, had not been considered necessary in our small peace establishment. The functions of the office were not defined, and, so far as exercised, had been included in the adjutant-general's department. The small number of officers in this department, and the necessity for their employment in other duties, have obliged commanding generals during this war to resort to other branches of the service to furnish suitable chiefs-of-staff

On the 4th of September, 1861, I appointed Colonel R. B Marcy, of the inspector-general's department, chief-of-staff, and he entered upon service immediately, discharging the various and important duties with great fidelity, industry, and ability, from this period until I was removed from command at Rectortown.

Many improvements have been made during the war in our system of staff administration; but much remains to be done.

Our own experience and that of other armies

agree in determining the necessity for an efficient and able staff. To obtain this, our staff establishment should be based on correct principles and extended to be adequate to the necessities of the service, and should include a system of staff and line education.

The affairs of the adjutant-general's department, while I commanded the army of the Potomac, were conducted by Brig.-Gen. S. Williams, assisted by Lieut.-Col. James A. Hardie, A. D. C.

Their management of the department during the organization of the army, in the fall and winter of 1861, and during its subsequent operations in the field, was excellent.

They were during the entire period, assisted by Capt. Rd. B. Irwin, A. D. C., and during the organization of the army by the following named officers.

Capt. Jos. Kirkland, A. D. C., Capt. Arthur McClellan, A. D. C.; Capt. M. T. McMahon, A. D. C.; Capt. W. P. Mason, A. D. C., Capt. W. F. Biddle, A. D. C.

My personal staff, when we embarked for the peninsula, consisted of—

Col. T. M. Key, additional A. D. C.; Col. E. H. Wright, do., and Major 6th U. S. Cavalry, Col. T. T. Gantt, add. A. D. C.; Col. J. J. Astor, Jr., volunteer aid-de-camp, Lieut.-Col. A. V. Colburn, add. A. D. C., and Captain in adjutant-general's department, Lieut.-Col. N. B. Sweitzer, add. A. D. C., and Capt. 1st U. S. Cavalry, Lieut.-Col. E. M. K. Hudson, add. A. D. C. and Capt. 14th U. S. Infantry; Lieut. Col. Paul Von Radowitz, add. A. D. C.; Maj. H. Von Hammerstein, add. A. D. C., Maj. W. W. Russell. U. S. Marine Corps; Maj. F. Lecompte, of Swiss army, volunteer aid-de-camp; Capt. Jos. Kirkland, add. A. D. C.; Capt. Arthur McClellan, add. A. D. C.; Capt. L. P. D'Orleans, do.; Capt. R. D'Orleans, do., Capt. M. T. McMahon, do.; Capt. W. P. Mason, Jr., do.; Capt. W. F. Biddle, do., Catp. E. A. Raymond.

To this number I am tempted to add the Prince de Joinville, who constantly accompanied me through the trying campaign of the peninsula, and frequently rendered important service.

Of these officers, Capt. McMahon was assigned to the personal staff of Brig.-Gen. Franklin, and Capts. Kirkland and Mason to that of Brig.-Gen. F. J. Porter during the siege of Yorktown: they remained subsequently with those general officers.

Major Le Compte left the army during the siege of Yorktown; Col. Gantt, Col. Astor, Maj. Russell, Capts. L. P. D'Orleans, R. D'Orleans and Raymond, at the close of the Peninsula campaign.

Before its termination, Capts. W. S. Abert and Chas R. Lowell, of the 6th U. S. Cavalry and Capt. G. A. Custer, 1st Lieut. 5th U. S. Cavalry, joined my staff as aids-de-camp, and remained with me until I was relieved from the command of the army of the Potomac.

All of these officers served me with great gallantry and devotion, they were ever ready to execute any service, no matter how dangerous, difficult or fatiguing.

INSPECTOR GENERAL'S DEPARTMENT.

The highly important duties of this department were performed by Col. D. B. Sacket and Major N. H. Davis, to my entire satisfaction, They introduced many valuable changes in the system of inspections and in the forms of reports, and so systematized the labors of the inspectors of corps and divisions that excellent results were obtained. The intelligent and energetic performance of their duties by these officers enabled me to keep myself well informed of the condition of the troops and correct evils promptly.

ENGINEERS

When I assumed command of the Army of the Potomac, I found Major J. G. Barnard, U. S. Engineers, subsequently Brig.-Gen. of volunteers, occupying the position of chief engineer of the army. I continued him in the same office, and at once gave the necessary instructions for the completion of the defences of the capital, and for the entire reorganization of the department.

Under his direction the entire system of defences was carried into execution. This was completed before the army departed for Fort Monroe, and is a sufficient evidence of the skill of the engineers and the diligent labor of the troops.

For some months after the organization of the army of the Potomac was commenced, there were no engineer troops with it; at length, however, three companies were assigned. Under the skillful management of Capt. J. C. Duane, U. S. Engineers, these new companies rapidly became efficient, and, as will be seen, rendered most valuable service during the ensuing campaigns.

The number of engineer troops being entirely inadequate to the necessities of the army, an effort was made to partially remedy this defect, by detailing the 15th and 50th New York Volunteers, which contained many sailors and mechanics, as engineer troops. They were first placed under the immediate superintendence of Lieut.-Col. B. S. Alexander, U. S. Engineers, by whom they were instructed in the duties of pontooneers, and became somewhat familiar with those of sappers and miners. Previous to the movement of the army for the Peninsula, this brigade was placed under the command of Brig.-Gen. D. P. Woodbury, Major U. S. Engineers.

The labor of preparing the engineer and bridge trains devolved chiefly upon Capt. Duane, who was instructed to procure the new model French bridge train, as I was satisfied that the India-rubber pontoon was entirely useless for the general purposes of a campaign.

The engineer department presented the following complete organization when the army moved for the Peninsula:

Brig.-Gen. J. G. Barnard, Chief Engineer; 1st Lieut. H. L. Abbott, Top Engineers, A D C; Brigade Vol. Engineers, Brig.-Gen. Woodbury, comm'g; 15th Col. McLeod Murphy; 50th do., Col. C. B. Stewart, Battalion 3 Cos U S Engineers, Capt. J. C. Duane, comm'g.

Companies respectively commanded by 1st Lieut. C B Reese, U S Engineers, 1st C. E. Cross, do; 1st Lieut O E Babcock do

The chief engineer was ably assisted in his duties by Lieut.-Col B S Alexander U. S Engineers, 1st Lieut. C R. Comstock, do, 1st Lieut M D McAlester, do., 1st Lieut. Merrill, do

Capt C S Stewart, and 2d Lieut. F U Farquhar, U. S. Engineers, joined after the army arrived at Fort Monroe

The necessary bridge equipage for the operations of a large army had been collected, consisting of batteaux with the anchors and flooring material, (French model) trestles and engineers' tools, with the wagons for their transportation.

The small number of officers of this corps available rendered it impracticable to detail engineers permanently at the headquarters of corps and divisions

The companies of regular engineers never had their proper number of officers, and it was necessary, as a rule, to follow the principle of detailing engineer officers temporarily where ever their services were required

TOPOGRAPHICAL ENGINEERS.

To the corps of Topographical Engineers was intrusted the collection of topographical information and the preparation of campaign maps. Until a short time previous to the departure of the army for Fort Monroe, Lieut.-Col John W. Macomb, was in charge of this department, and prepared a large amount of valuable material. He was succeeded by Brig.-Gen A. A Humphreys, who retained the position throughout the peninsular campaign

These officers were assisted by Lieut H L Abbot, Topographical Engineers, Lieut O G Wagner, do; Lieut N Bowen, do; Lieut John M. Wilson, do.; Lieut. James H. Wilson, do

This number, being the greatest available, was so small that much of the duty of the department devolved upon parties furnished by Professor Bache, Superintendent of Coast Survey, and other gentlemen from civil life.

Owing to the entire absence of reliable topographical maps, the labors of this corps were difficult and arduous in the extreme. Notwithstanding the energy and ability displayed by General Humphreys, Lieut.-Col. Macomb and their subordinates, who frequently obtained the necessary information under fire, the movements of the army were sometimes unavoidably delayed by the difficulty of obtaining knowledge of the country in advance. The result of their labors has been the preparation of an excellent series of maps, which will be invaluable to any army traversing the same ground

During the campaign it was impossible to draw a distinct line of demarcation between the duties of the two corps of engineers, so that the labors of reconnoissances of roads, of lines for trenches, of fields for battle, and of the positions of the enemy, as well as the construction of siege and defensive works, were habitually performed by detail from either corps as the convenience of the service demanded

I desire to express my high appreciation of the skill, gallantry, and devotion displayed by the officers of both corps of engineers under the most trying circumstances

During the Maryland campaign I united the two corps under Captain J C Duane, U. S. Engineers, and found great advantages from this arrangement

MEDICAL DEPARTMENT

For the operations of the medical department I refer to the reports transmitted herewith, of Surgeon Chas S. Tripler, and Surgeon Jonathan Letterman, who, in turn, performed the duties of medical director of the army of the Potomac: the former from August 12, 1861, until July 1, 1862, and the latter after that date.

The difficulties to be overcome, in organizing and making effective the medical department, were very great, arising principally from the inexperience of the regimental medical officers, many of whom were physicians taken suddenly from civil life, who, according to Surgeon Tripler, "had to be instructed in their duties from the very alphabet," and from the ignorance of the line officers as to their relations with the medical officers, which gave rise to confusion and conflict of authority.

Boards of examination were instituted, by which many incompetent officers were removed, and by the successive exertions of Surgeons Tripler and Letterman the medical corps was brought to a very high degree of efficiency.

With regard to the sanitary condition of the army while on the Potomac, Dr Tripler says, that the records show a constantly increasing immunity from disease "In October and November, 1861, with an army averaging 130,000 men, we had 7,932 cases of fever of all sorts; of these about 1,000 were reported as cases of typhoid fever I knew that errors of diagnosis were frequently committed, and therefore this must be considered as the limit of typhoid cases If any army in the world can show such a record as this. I do not know when or where it was assembled"

From September, 1861, to February, 1862, while the army was increasing, the number of sick decreased from 7 per cent. to 6 18 per cent.; of these, the men sick in the regimental and general hospitals, were less than one-half, the remainder were slight cases under treatment in quarters "During this time, so far as rumor was concerned, the army was being decimated by disease every month."

Of the sanitary condition of the army during the peninsular campaign, up to its arrival at Harrison's Landing, Dr. Tripler says:

"During this campaign the army was favored with excellent health. No epidemic disease appeared. Those scourges of modern armies—dysentery, typhus, cholera—were almost unknown We had some typhoid fever, and more malarial fevers, but even these never prevailed to such an extent as to create any alarm. The sick reports were sometimes larger than we cared to have them, but the great majority of the cases reported were such as did not threaten life, or permanent disability. I regret that I have not before me the retained copies of the monthly reports, so that I might give accurate statistics. I have endeavored to recover them, but have been unsuccessful My recollection is that the whole sick report never exceeded 8 per cent. of the force, and this included all sorts of cases—the trivial as well as the severe. The army of the Potomac must be considered to have been the most healthy army in the service of the United States."

His remarks at the conclusion of his report upon our system of medical administration, and his suggestions for its improvement, are especially worthy of attention.

The severe labors and privations of the troops during the seven day's battles, had of course a great effect on the health of the army after it reached Harrison's Landing, increasing the number of sick to about 20 per cent. of the whole force.

The nature of the military operations had also unavoidably placed the medical department in a very unsatisfactory condition. Supplies had been almost entirely exhausted, or necessarily abandoned; hospital tents abandoned or destroyed, and the medical officers deficient in numbers and broken down by fatigue

All the remarkable energy and ability of Surgeon Letterman were required to restore the efficiency of his department, but before we left Harrison's Landing he had succeeded in fitting it out throughout with the supplies it required, and the health of the army was vastly improved by the sanitary measures which were enforced at his suggestion.

The great haste with which the army was removed from the Peninsula, made it necessary to leave at Fort Monroe, to be forwarded afterwards, nearly all the baggage and transportation, including medical stores and ambulances, all the vessels being required to transport the troops themselves and their ammunition, and when the army of the Potomac returned to Washington, after General Pope's campaign, and the medical department came once more under Surgeon Letterman's control, he found it in a deplorable condition.

The officers were worn out by the labors they had performed, and the few supplies that had been brought from the Peninsula had been exhausted or abandoned, so that the work of reorganization and resupplying had to be again performed, and this while the army was moving rapidly and almost in the face of the enemy. That it was successfully accomplished is shown by the care and attention which the wounded received after the battles of South Mountain and Antietam

Among the improvements introduced into his department by Surgeon Letterman, the principal are, the organization of an ambulance corps, the system of field-hospitals, and the method of supplying by brigades; all of which were instituted during the Maryland campaign, and have since proved very efficient.

QUARTER-MASTER'S DEPARTMENT.

On assuming command of the troops in and about Washington, I appointed Captain S. Van Vliet, A. Q. M., (afterwards Brigadier-General,) Chief Quarter-master to my command, and gave him the necessary instructions for organizing his department, and collecting the supplies requisite for the large army then called for

The disaster at Manassas had but recently occurred, and the army was quite destitute of quarter-masters' stores.

General Van Vliet, with great energy and zeal, set himself about the task of furnishing the supplies immediately necessary, and preparing to obtain the still larger amounts which would be required by the new troops which were moving in large numbers towards the capital.

The principal depot for supplies in the city of Washington was under charge of Col D. H. Rucker, A. Q. M, who ably performed his duties.

Lieut.-Col. R. Ingalls, A. Q M., was placed in charge of the department on the south side of the Potomac. I directed a large depot for transportation to be established at Perryville, on the left bank of the Susquehanna, a point equally accessible by rail and water. Capt. C. G. Sawtelle, A. Q. M, had immediate charge of the transportation in and about Washington, as well as of the large number of horses purchased for the use of the artillery and cavalry The principal difficulties which Gen. Van Vliet had to encounter arose from the inexperience of the majority of the officers of his department in the new regiments and brigades The necessity of attending personally to minor details rendered his duties arduous and harassing in the extreme. All obstacles, however, were surmounted by the untiring industry of the chief-quarter master and his immediate subordinates, and when the army was prepared to move, the organization of the department was found to be admirable.

When it was determined to move the army to the peninsula, the duties of providing water transportation were devolved, by the Secretary of War, upon his assistant, the Hon J. Tucker. The vessels were ordered to Alexandria, and Lieut.-Col. Ingalls was placed in immediate charge of the embarkation of the troops, transportation, and material of every description Operations of this nature on so extensive a scale had no parallel in the history of our country.

The arrangements of Lieut.-Col Ingalls were perfected with remarkable skill and energy, and the army and its material, were embarked and transported to Fort Monroe in a very short space of time, and entirely without loss.

During the operations on the Peninsula, until the arrival of troops at Harrison's Landing, Gen. Van Vliet retained the position of Chief Quartermaster, and maintained the thorough organization and efficiency of his department. The principal depots of supplies were under the immediate charge of Lieut.-Col. Ingalls and Sawtalle.

On the 10th of July, 1862, Gen. Van Vliet, having requested to be relieved from duty with the army of the Potomac, I appointed Lieut.-Col. Ingalls Chief Quartermaster, and he continued to discharge the duties of that office during the remainder of the Peninsular and the Maryland campaigns, in a manner which fully sustained the high reputation he had previously acquired

The immense amount of labor accomplished, often under the most difficult circumstances, the admirable system under which the duties of the department were performed, and the entire success which attended the efforts to supply so large an army, reflect the highest credit upon the officers upon whom these onerous duties devolved The reports of Gen. Van Vliet, and Lieut.-Col Ingalls, with the accompanying documents, give, in detail, the history of the department, from its organization until I was relieved from the command of the army of the Potomac.

SUBSISTENCE DEPARTMENT

On the 1st of August, 1861, Colonel H. F. Clarke, C S, joined my staff, and at once entered upon his duties as Chief Commissary of the army of the Potomac. In order to realize the responsibilities pertaining to this office, as well as to form a proper estimate of the vast amount of labor which must necessarily devolve upon its occupant, it is only necessary to consider the unprepared state of the country to engage in a war of such magnitude as the present, and the lack of practical knowledge on the part of our officers, with reference to supplying and subsisting a large, and, at that time, an unorganized army. Yet, notwithstanding the existence of these great obstacles, the manner in which the duties of the commissary department were discharged, was such as to merit, and call forth the commendation of the entire army. During the stay of the army of the Potomac in the vicinity of Washington, prior to the Peninsular campaign, its subsistence was drawn chiefly from the depots which had been established by the commissary department at Washington, Alexandria, Forts Corcoran and Runyon In the important task of designating and establishing depots of supplies, Colonel Clarke was ably seconded by his assistants, Col. Amos Beckwith, C S., U S A., Lieut.-Col. Geo Bell, C S, U S A, Lieut.-Col. A P. Porter, C S, U S A, Capt Thomas Wilson, C. S, U S A, Capt Brownell Granger, C.S, U. S Vols, Capt W. H Bell, C S, U S A, Capt I H Woodward, C S, U. S Vols., and Captain W R Murphy, C S U S Vols For a full knowledge of the highly creditable manner in which each and all of the above mentioned officers discharged their duties, I invite attention to the detailed report of Col Clarke. The remarks and suggestions contained in this report are worthy of attention, as affording valuable rules for the future guidance of the subsistence department, in supplying armies in the field The success of the subsistence department of the army of the Potomac, was, in a great measure, attributable to the fact, that the subsistence department at Washington made ample previous provision for sending supplies to the peninsula, and that it always exercised the most intelligent foresight. It moreover gave its advise and countenance to the officers charged with its duties and reputation in the field, and those officers, I am happy to say, worked with it and together, in perfect harmony, for the public good.

During the entire period that I was in command of the army of the Potomac there was no instance within my knowledge, where the troops were without their rations from any fault of the officers of this department.

ORDINANCE DEPARTMENT.

This very important branch of the service was placed under the charge of Capt C P. Kingsbury, ordnance corps, Colonel and A.D C. Great difficulty existed in the proper organization of the department, from the want of a sufficient number of suitable officers to perform the duties at the various headquarters and depots of supply. But far greater obstacles had to be surmounted, from the fact that the supply of small arms was totally inadequate to the demands of a large army, and a vast proportion of those furnished, were of such inferior quality, as to be unsatisfactory to the troops, and condemned by their officers. The supply of artillery was more abundant, but of great variety. Rifled ordnance was just coming into use for the first time in this country, and the description of gun and kind of projectile, which would prove most effective, and should therefore be adopted, was a mere matter of theory.

To obviate these difficulties, large quantities of small arms of foreign manufacture were contracted for; private enterprise in the construction of arms and ammunition was encouraged; and by the time the army was ordered to move to the peninsula, the amount of ordnance and ordnance stores was ample.

Much, also, had been done to bring the quality both of arms and ammunition, up to the proper standard. Boards of officers were in session continually during the autumn and winter of 1861, to test the relative merits of new arms and projectiles. The reports of these boards, confirmed by subsequent experience in the field, have done much to establish the respective claims of different inventions and manufactories. During the campaigns of the Peninsula and Maryland, the officers connected with the department, were zealous and energetic, and kept the troops well supplied, notwithstanding the perplexing and arduous nature of their duties. One great source of perplexity, was the fact, that it had been necessary to issue arms of all varieties and calibres giving an equal diversity in the kinds of ammunition required. Untiring watchfulness was therefore incumbent upon the officers in charge to prevent confusion and improper distribution of cartridges. Colonel Kingsbury discharged the duties of his office with great efficiency, until the —— of July, 1862, when his health required that he should be relieved. 1st Lieut. Thomas G. Baylor, ordnance corps, succeeded him, and peformed his duty during the remainder of the Peninsular and Maryland campaigns, with marked ability and success. The want of reports from Colonel Kingsbury and Lieut. Baylor, renders it impossible for me to enter at all, into the details of the organization of the department.

PROVOST-MARSHAL'S DEPARTMENT.

Immediately after I was placed in command of the "Division of the Potomac" I appointed Col. Andrew Porter, 16th U. S. Infantry, Provost-Marshal of Washington. All the available regular infantry, a battery, and a squadron of cavalry, were placed under his command; and by his energetic action, he soon corrected the serious evils which existed, and restored order in the city.

When the army was about to take the field, General Porter was appointed Provost-Marshal General of the army of the Potomac, and held that most important position until the end of the Peninsular campaign, when sickness, contracted in the untiring discharge of his duties compelled him to ask to be relieved from the position he had so ably and energetically filled. The provost-marshal general's department had the charge of a class of duties, which had not before, in our service, been defined and grouped under the management of a special department. The following subjects indicate the sphere of this department:

Suppression of marauding and depredations and of all brawls and disturbances.

Preservation of good order and suppression of drunkenness beyond the limits of the camps.

Prevention of straggling on the march.

Suppression of gambling-houses, drinking-houses, or bar-rooms and brothels.

Regulation of hotels, taverns, markets, and places of public amusement.

Searches, seizures and arrests.

Execution of sentences of general courts martial, involving imprisonment or capital punishment.

Enforcement of orders prohibiting the sale of intoxicating liquors, whether by tradesmen or sutlers, and of orders respecting passes.

Deserters from the army.

Prisoners of war taken from the enemy.

Countersigning safe-guards.

Passes to citizens, within the lines and for purposes of trade.

Complaints of citizens as to the conduct of the soldiers.

General Porter was assisted by the following named officers:

Major W. H. Wood, 17th U. S. Infantry; Capt. James McMillan, A. A. A. G., U. S. Infantry; Capt. W. T. Gentry, 17th U. S. Infantry; Capt. J. W. Forsyth, 18th U. S. Infantry; Lieut. J. W. Jones, 12th U. S. Infantry; Lieut. C. F. Trowbridge, 16th U. S. Infantry; Lieut. C. D. Mehaffey, 1st U. S. Infantry.

The provost guard was composed of the 2d U. S. Cavalry, Major Pleasonton and a battalion of the 8th and 17th U. S. Infantry, Major Willard.

After General Porter was relieved, Major Wood was in charge of this department, until after the battle of Antietam, when Brigadier-General Patrick was appointed Provost Marshal General

COMMANDANT OF GENERAL HEAD-QUARTERS

When the army took the field, for the purpose of securing order and regularity in the camp of headquarters, and for facilitating its movements, the office of commandant of general headquarters was created, and assigned to Major G. O. Haller, 7th U. S. Infantry. Six companies of infantry were placed under his orders for guard and police duty. Among the orders appended to this report, is the one defining his duties, which were always satisfactorily performed.

JUDGE-ADVOCATE

From August, 1861, the position of judge-advocate was held by Col. Thos. Gantt, A. D. C., until compelled by ill health to retire, at Harrison's Landing, in August, 1862. His reviews of the decisions of courts-martial during this period, were of great utility in correcting the practice in military courts, diffusing true notions of discipline and subordination, and setting before the army a high standard of soldierly honor.

Upon the retirement of Colonel Gantt, the duties of judge-advocate were ably performed by Col. Thomas M. Key, A. D. C.

SIGNAL CORPS.

The method of conveying intelligence and orders, invented and introduced into the service by Maj. Albert J. Myer, signal officer, U. S. A., was first practically tested in large operations, during the organization of the army of the Potomac.

Under the direction of Major Myer, a signal corps was formed by detailing officers and men from the different regiments of volunteers, and instructing them in the use of the flags by day, and torches by night.

The chief signal officer was indefatigable in his exertions to render his corps effective, and it soon became available for service, in every division of the army.

In addition to the flags and torches, Major Myer introduced a portable insulated telegraph wire, which could be readily laid from point to point, and which could be used under the same general system.

In front of Washington, and on the lower Potomac, at any point within our lines not reached by the military telegraph, the great usefulness of this system of signals was made manifest. But it was not until after the arrival of the army upon the Peninsula, and during the siege and battles of that, and the Maryland campaign, that the great benefits to be derived from it on the field, and under fire, were fully appreciated.

There was scarcely an action or skirmish in which the signal corps did not render important services. Often, under heavy fire of artillery, and not unfrequently while exposed to musketry, the officers and men of this corps gave information of the movements of the enemy, and transmitted directions for the evolutions of our own troops.

The report of the chief signal officer, with accompanying documents, will give the details of the services of this corps, and call attention to those members of it who were particularly distinguished.

TELEGRAPHIC.

The telegraphic operations of the army of the Potomac were superintended by Major Thos. J. Eckert, and under the immediate direction of Mr. —— Caldwell, who was with the corps of operatives attached to my headquarters during the entire campaigns upon the peninsula and in Maryland.

The services of this corps were arduous and efficient. Under the admirable arrangements of Major Eckert they were constantly provided with all the material for constructing new lines, which were rapidly established whenever the army changed position; and it was not unfrequently the case that the operatives worked under fire from the enemy's guns, yet they invariably performed all the duties required of them with great alacrity and cheerfulness, and it was seldom that I was without the means of direct telegraphic communication with the War Department, and with the corps commanders.

From the organization of the army of the Potomac, up to Nov. 1, 1862, including the Peninsular and Maryland campaigns, upwards of 1,200 miles of military telegraph lines had been constructed in connection with the operations of the army, and the number of operatives and builders employed was about 200.

To Professor Lowe, the intelligent and enterprising aeronaut, who had the management of the balloons, I was greatly indebted for the valuable information obtained during his ascensions.

I have more than once taken occasion to recommend the members of my staff, both general and personal, for promotion and reward. I beg leave to repeat these recommendations, and to record their names in the history of the army of the Potomac as gallant soldiers, to whom their country owes a debt of gratitude, still unpaid, for the courage, ability and untiring zeal they displayed during the eventful campaigns in which they bore so prominent a part.

POSITION OF THE ARMY, OCT. 1862.

On the 15th of October, the main body of the army of the Potomac was in the immediate vicinity of Washington, with detachments on the left bank of the Potomac as far down as Liverpool Point, and as far up as Williamsport and its vicinity. The different divisions were posted as follows:

Hooker, at Budd's Ferry, lower Potomac; Heintzelman, at Fort Lyon and vicinity; Franklin, near the Theological Seminary; Blenker, near Hunter's Chapel; McDowell, at Upton's Hill and Arlington; F. J. Porter, at Hall's and Miner's Hills; Smith, at Mckall's Hill; McCall, at Langley; Buell, at Tenallytown, Meridian Hill, Emory's Chapel, &c., on the left bank of the river; Casey at Washington; Hunt's Artillery, do., Banks, at Darnstown, with Detachments at Point of Rocks, Sandy Hook, Williamsport, &c., Stone at Poolesville; Dix, at Baltimore, with detachments on the eastern shore.

THE AFFAIR AT BALL'S BLUFF.

On the 19th of October, 1861, Gen. McCall marched to Drainesville with his division, in order to cover reconnoissances to be made in all directions the next day, for the purpose of learning the position of the enemy, and of covering the operations of the topographical engineers in making maps of that region.

On the 20th acting in concert with Gen. McCall, Gen. Smith pushed strong parties to Freedom Hill, Vienna, Flint Hill, Peacock Hill, &c., to accomplish the same purpose in that part of the front.

These reconnoissances were successful.

On the morning of the 20th I received the following telegram from Gen. Banks' headquarters:

DARNESTOWN, Oct. 20, 1861.

GEN. MARCY:

SIR,—The signal station at Sugar Loaf telegraphs that the enemy have moved away from Leesburg. All quiet here.

R. M. COPELAND, A. A. G.

Whereupon I sent to Gen. Stone, at Poolesville, the following telegram:

CAMP GRIFFIN, Oct. 20, 1861.

Brig.-Gen. C. P. STONE, Poolesville:

Gen. McClellan desires me to inform you

that Gen McCall occupied Drainesville, yesterday, and is still there Will send out heavy reconnoissances to-day in all directions from that point. The general desires that you keep a good lookout on Leesburg, to see if this movement has the effect to drive them away. Perhaps a slight demonstration on your part would have the effect to move them.

A. V. COLBURN, Ass'-Adj Gen

Deeming it possible that Gen. McCall's movement to Drainesville, together with the subsequent reconnoissances, might have the effect of inducing the enemy to abandon Leesburg, and the dispatch from Sugar Loaf appearing to confirm this view, I wished Gen Stone, who had only a line of pickets on the river, the mass of his troops being out of, and beyond range from the Virginia bank, to make some display of intention to cross, and also to watch the enemy more closely than usual I did not direct him to cross, nor did I intend that he should cross the river in force for the purpose of fighting.

The above dispatch was sent on the 20th, and reached Gen Stone as early as 11 A. M. of that day. I expected him to accomplish all that was intended on the same day, and this he did, as will be seen from the following dispatch received at my headquarters in Washington, from Poolesville, on the evening of October 20th.

To MAJ-GEN. McCLELLAN:

Made a feint of crossing at this place this afternoon, and at the same time started a reconnoitring party towards Leesburg from Harrison's Island. The enemy's pickets retired to intrenchments Report of reconnoitring party not yet received. I have means of crossing 125 men once in ten minutes at each of two points. River falling slowly.

C P. STONE, Brig Gen.

As it was not foreseen or expected that Gen McCall would be needed to co-operate with Gen Stone in any attack, he was directed to fall back from Drainsville to his original camp near Prospect Hill, as soon as the required reconnoissances were completed. Accordingly he left Drainesville on his return at about 8 1-2 A M of the 21st, reaching his old camp at about 1 P. M.

In the meantime I was surprised to hear from Gen. Stone that a portion of his troops were engaged on the Virginia side of the river, and at once sent instructions to Gen. McCall to remain at Drainesville if he had not left before the order reached him.

The order did not reach him until his return to his camp at Langley He was then ordered to rest his men, and hold his division in readiness to return to Drainesville at a moments notice, should it become necessary.

Similar instructions were given to other divisions during the afternoon

The first intrusion I received from Gen Stone of the real nature of his movements was in a telegram as follows:

Edward's Ferry, 11 10 A M Oct. 21.
Maj.-Gen McClellan,—

The enemy have been engaged opposite Harrison's Island. Our men are behaving admirably.

C. P. STONE, Brigadier-Gen.

At 2 P. M. Gen. Banks' adjutant-general sent the following:

Darnstown, Oct. 21, 1861, 2 P. M.
Gen: R. B. Marcy,—

Gen. Stone safely crossed the river this morning. Some engagements have taken place on the other side of the river; how important is not known.

R. M COPELAND, A A A G.

Gen. Stone sent the following dispatches on the same day at the hours indicated:

Edwards' Ferry, Oct. 21, 1861, 2. P M.
Maj.-Gen. McClellan,—

There has been sharp firing on the right of our line, and our troops appear to be advancing there under Baker. The left under Gorman, has advanced its skirmishers nearly one mile, and if the movement continues successful will turn the enemy's right

C P STONE, Brigadier-General.

Edward' Ferry, Oct. 21st. 1861, 4 P. M.
Gen. McClellan,—

Nearly all my force is across the river. Baker on the right, Gorman on the left, right sharply engaged.

C P STONE, Brigadier-General.

Edward's Ferry, Oct. 21, 1861, 9 30 P M.
Maj.-Gen. McClellan,—

I am occupied in preventing further disaster, and trying to get into position to redeem. We have lost some of our best commanders— Baker dead, Cogswell a prisoner, or secreted. The wounded are being carefully and rapidly removed, and Gorman's wing is being cautiously withdrawn. Any advance from Drainesville must be made cautiously. All was reported going well up to Baker's death, but in the confusion following that, the right wing was outflanked. In a few hours I shall, unless a night attack is made, be in the same position as last night, save the loss of many good men.

C. P. STONE, Brigadier-General.

Although no more fully informed, of the state of affairs, I had, during the afternoon, as a precautionary measure, ordered Gen. Banks to send one Brigade to the support of the troops at Harrison's Island, and to move with the other two, to Seneca Mills, ready to support Gen. Stone if necessary. The 9.30 P. M. dispatch of Gen Stone did not give me an entire understanding of the state of the case. Aware of the difficulties, and perhaps fatal consequences of recrossing such a river as the Potomac after a repulse, and from these telegrams supposing his whole force to be on the Virginia side, I directed Gen. Stone to intrench himself, and hold the Virginia side at all hazards until re-enforcements could arrive, when he could safely withdraw to the Maryland side or hold his position on the Virginia side, should that prove advisable.

Gen Banks was instructed to move the rest of his division to Edward's Ferry, and to send over as many men as possible before daylight, to reinforce Stone. He did not arrive in time to effect this and was instructed to collect all the canal boats he could find, and use them for crossing at Edwards' Ferry in sufficient force to enable the troops already there to hold the opposite side.

On the 22d I went to the ground in person, and reaching Poolesville learned for the first time the full details of the affair.

The following extracts from the evidence of Gen Stone before the "Committee on the Conduct of the War," on the 5th of January, 1862, will throw further light on this occurrence.

Gen Stone says he received the orders from my headquarters, to make a slight demonstration, at about 11 o'clock A M of the 20th, and that in obedience to that order he made the demonstration on the evening of the same day.

In regard to the reconnoissance on the 21st, which resulted in the battle of Ball's Bluff, he was asked the following questions:

"*Question* Did this reconnoissance originate with yourself, or had you orders from the General-in-Chief to make it?"

To which he replied "It originated with myself—the reconnoissance."

"*Question* The order did not proceed from General McClellan?"

"*Answer* I was directed the day before, to make a demonstration. *That demonstration was made the day previous.*"

"*Question* Did you receive an order from the General-in-Chief to make the reconnoissance?"

"*Answer* No, sir."

Making a personal examination on the 22d I found that the position on the Virginia side at Edward's Ferry was not a tenable one, but did not think it wise to withdraw the troops by daylight. I therefore caused more artillery to be placed in position on the Maryland side, to cover the approaches to the ground held by us, and crossed the few additional troops that the high wind permitted us to get over, so as to be as secure as possible against any attack during the day. Before night-fall, all the precautions were taken to secure an orderly and quiet passage of the troops and guns. The movement was commenced soon after dark, under the general supervision of Gen Stone, who received the order for the withdrawal at 7 15 P M. By 4 A.M of the 24th every thing had reached the Maryland shore in safety.

A few days afterwards I received information, which seems to be authentic, to the effect that large bodies of the enemy had been ordered from Manassas to Leesburg, to cut off our troops on the Virginia side. Their timely withdrawal had probably prevented a still more serious disaster. I refer to Gen Stone's Report of this battle furnished to the War Department, and his published testimony before the "Committee on the Conduct of the War" for further details.

THE NORTH CAROLINA EXPEDITION.

The records of the War Department show my anxiety and efforts to assume active offensive operations in the fall and early winter. It is only just to say, however, that the unprecedented condition of the roads and Virginia soil would have delayed an advance till February had the discipline, organization and equipment of the army been as complete at the close of the fall as was necessary and as I desired and labored, against every impediment, to make them. While still in command only of the army of the Potomac, namely, in early September, I proposed the formation of a corps of New Englanders for coast service in the bays and inlets of the Chesapeake and Potomac to co-operate with my own command, from which most of its material was drawn.

On the 1st of November, however, I was called to relieve Lieut.-Gen Scott in the chief and general command of the armies of the Union. The direction and nature of this coast expedition, therefore, were somewhat changed, as will soon appear in the original plan submitted to the Secretary of War, and the letter of instructions later issued to Gen. Burnside, its commander. The whole country indeed had now become the theatre of military operations from the Potomac to and beyond the Mississippi, and to assist the Navy in perfecting and sustaining the blockade, it became necessary to extend those operations to points on the sea-coast, Roanoke Island, Savannah, and New Orleans. It remained also to equip and organize the armies of the West, whose condition was little better than that of the army of the Potomac had been.

The direction of the campaigns in the West, and of the operations upon the sea-board enabled me to enter upon larger combinations, and to accomplish results the necessity and advantage of which had not been unforeseen, but which had been beyond the ability of the single army formerly under my command, to effect.

The following letters and a subsequent paper addressed to the Secretary of War sufficiently indicate the nature of those combinations to minds accustomed to reason upon military operations.

HEADQUARTERS, ARMY OF THE POTOMAC,
WASHINGTON, Sept. 6, 1861.

Hon. SIMON CAMERON, *Secretary of War.*

SIR: I have the honor to suggest the following proposition, with the request that the necessary authority be at once given me to carry it out, to organize a force of two brigades of five regiments each of New England men, for the general service—but particularly adapted to coast service. The officers and men to be sufficiently conversant with boat service to manage steamers, sailing vessels, launches, barges, surf boats, floating batteries, &c. To charter or buy for the command a sufficient number of propellers or tug-boats for transportation of men and supplies, the machinery of which should be amply protected by timber the vessels to have permanent experienced officers from the merchant service, but to be manned by details from the command. A naval officer to be attached to the staff of the commanding officer. The flank companies of each regiment to be armed with Dahlgren boat guns and carbines with water-proof cartridges, the other companies to have such arms as I may hereafter designate, to be uniformed and equipped as the Rhode Island regiments are. Launches and floating batteries, with timber parapets of sufficient capacity to land or bring into action the entire force.

The entire management and organization of the force to be under my control, and to form an integral part of the army of the Potomac.

The immediate object of this force is for operations in the inlets of Chesapeake Bay and the Potomac, by enabling me thus to land troops at points where they are needed—this force can also be used in conjunction with a naval force operating against points on the sea-coast. This coast division to be commanded by a general officer of my selection. The regiments to be organized as other land forces. The disbursements for vessels, &c., to be made by the proper department of the army, upon the requisitions of the general commanding the division, with my approval.

I think the entire force can be organized in thirty days and by no means the least of the advantages of this proposition is the fact, that it will call into the service a class of men who would not otherwise enter the army.

You will immediately perceive that the object of this force is to follow along the coast, and up the inlets and rivers the movements of the main army when it advances.

I am, very respectfully, your obedient servant,
G. B. McCLELLAN, Maj.-Gen. Comdg.

Owing chiefly to the difficulty in procuring the requisite vessels and adapting them to the special purposes contemplated, this expedition was not ready for service until January, 1862.

Then in the chief command I deemed it best to send it to North Carolina with the design indicated in the following letter:

Head-quarters of the army, Washington, Jan 7 1862 Brig.-Gen. A. E. Burnside, *Commanding Expedition*

GENERAL.—In accordance with verbal instructions heretofore given you—you will, after uniting with flag-officer Goldsborough, at Fort Monroe, proceed under his convey to Hatteras Inlet, where you will in connection with him, take the most prompt measures for crossing the fleet over the bulkhead into the waters of the sound. Under the accompanying general order constituting the Department of North Carolina you will assume command of the garrison at Hatteras Inlet, and make such dispositions in regard to that place, as your ulterior operations may render necessary—always being careful to provide for the safety of that very important station in any contingency.

Your first point of attack will be Roanoke Island and its dependencies.

It is presumed that the navy can reduce the batteries on the marshes, and cover the landing of your troops on the main island by which, in connection with a rapid movement of the gun-boats to the northern extremity—as soon as the marsh battery is reduced—it may be hoped to capture the entire garrison of the place. Having occupied the Island and its dependencies, you will at once proceed to the erection of the batteries and defenses necessary to hold the position with a small force. Should the flag-officer require any assistance in seizing or holding the debouches of the canal from Norfolk—you will please afford it to him.

The commodore and yourself having completed your arrangements in regard to Roanoke Island, and the waters north of it, you will please at once make a descent on Newbern, having gained possession of which, and the railroad passing through it you will at once throw a sufficient force upon Beaufort, and take the steps necessary to reduce Fort Macon and open that port. When you seize Newbern, you will endeavor to seize the railroad as far west as Goldsborough—should circumstances favor such a movement. The temper of the people, the rebel force at hand, &c., will go far towards determining the question as to how far west the railroad can be occupied and held. Should circumstances render it advisable to seize and hold Raleigh—the main north and south line of railroad passing through Goldsborough, should be so effectually destroyed for considerable distances north and south of that point, as to render it impossible for the rebels to use it to your disadvantage. A great point would be gained in any event, by the effectual destruction of the Wilmington and Weldon Railroad.

I would advise great caution in moving so far into the interior as upon Raleigh. Having accomplished the objects mentioned—the next point of interest would probably be Wilmington, the reduction of which may require that additional means shall be afforded you. I would urge great caution in regard to proclamations. In no case would I go beyond a moderate joint proclamation with the naval commander, which should say as little as possible about politics or the negro, merely state that the true issue for which we are fighting is the preservation of the Union, and upholding the laws of the general government, and stating that all who conduct themselves properly, will as far as possible be protected in their persons and property.

You will please report your operations as often as an opportunity offers itself.

With my best wishes for your success.
I am, &c. &c., G. B. McCLELLAN
Maj. Gen. Com'g. in Chief

OPERATIONS IN THE WEST AND SOUTH

The following letters of instructions were sent to Generals Halleck, Buell, Sherman and Butler, and I also communicated verbally to these officers my views in full, regarding the field of operations assigned to each, and gave them their instructions as much in detail as was necessary at that time.

Head-Quarters of the Army
Washington, D C, November 11, 1861.
Maj-Gen H W. Halleck, U. S A.
Comd g. Dept. of Missouri.

GENERAL:—In assigning you to the command of the Department of Missouri, it is probably necessary for me to state that I have intrusted to you a duty which requires the utmost tact and decision

You have not merely the ordinary duties of a military commander to perform, but the far more difficult task of reducing chaos to order, of changing probably the majority of the personnel of the staff of the department, and of reducing to a point of economy consistent with the interests and necessities of the state, a system of reckless expenditure and fraud perhaps unheard of before in the history of the world

You will find in your department many general and staff-officers holding illegal commissions and appointments not recognized or approved by the President or Secretary of War, you will please at once inform these gentlemen of the nullity of their appointment, and see that no pay or allowances are issued to them until such time as commissions may be authorized by the President, or Secretary of War.

If any of them give the slightest trouble you will at once arrest him and send him under guard, out of the limits of your department, informing them that if they return they will be placed in close confinement You will please examine into the legality of the organization of the troops serving in the department. When you find any illegal, unusual, or improper organizations you will give to the officers and men an opportunity to enter the legal military establishment under general laws and orders from the War Department; reporting in full to these head-quarters any officer or organization that may decline.

You will please cause competent and reliable staff officers to examine all existing contracts immediately, and suspend all payments upon them until you receive the report in each case. Where there is the slightest doubt as to the propriety of the contract, you will be good enough to refer the matter with full explanation to these head-quarters, stating in each case what would be a fair compensation for the services or materials rendered under the contract. Discontinue at once the reception of material or services under any doubtful contract. Arrest and bring to prompt trial all officers who have in any way violated their duty to the government. In regard to the political conduct of affairs, you will please labor to impress upon the inhabitants of Missouri and the adjacent States, that we are fighting solely for the integrity of the Union, to uphold the power of our national government and to restore to the nation the blessings of peace and good order

With respect to military operations, it is probable, from the best information in my possession, that the interests of the government will be best served by fortifying and holding in considerable strength, Rolla, Sedalia and other interior points, keeping strong patrols constantly moving from the terminal stations, and concentrating the mass of the troops on or near the Mississippi, prepared for such ulterior operations as the public interests may demand.

I would be glad to have you make, as soon as possible, a personal inspection of all the important points in your department and report the result to me I cannot too strongly impress upon you the absolute necessity of keeping me constantly advised of the strength, condition, and location of your troops, together with all facts that will enable me to maintain that general direction of the armies of the United States which it is my purpose to exercise I trust to you to maintain thorough organization, discipline and economy throughout your department. Please inform me, as soon as possible, of everything relating to the gunboats now in process of construction, as well as those completed.

The militia force authorized to be raised by the State of Missouri for its defence, will be under your orders I am, General, &., &c..

GEO B McCLELLAN, M G Com U. S
Headquarters of the Army, Washington,
BRIG-GEN D C. BUELL · Nov 7, 1861.

General,—In giving you instructions for your guidance, in command of the department of the Ohio, I do not design to fetter you. I merely wish to express plainly the general ideas which occur to me in relation to the conduct of operations there. That portion of Kentucky west of the Cumberland River is, by its position, so closely related to the States of Illinois and Missouri that it has seemed best to attach it to the Department of Missouri. Your operations, then, in Kentucky will be confined to that portion of the State east of the Cumberland River I trust I need not repeat to you that I regard the importance of the territory committed to your care as second only to that occupied by the army under my immediate command And it is absolutely necessary that we shall hold all the State of Kentucky; not only that, but that the majority of its inhabitants shall be warmly in favor of our cause, it being that which best subserves their interests. It is possible that the conduct of our political affairs in Kentucky is more important than that of our military operations I certainly cannot over estimate the importance of the former You will please constantly bear in mind the precise issue for which we are fighting—that issue is the preservation of the Union and the restoration of the authority of the general government over all portions of our territory. We shall most readily suppress this rebellion and restore the authority of the government by religiously respecting the constitutional rights of all. I know that I express the feelings and opinions of the President when I say that we are fighting only to preserve the integrity of the Union and the constitutional authority of the general government.

The inhabitants of Kentucky may rely upon it, that their domestic institutions will in no manner be interfered with, and that they will receive at our hands every constitutional protection. I have only to repeat that you will in all respects, carefully regard the local institutions of the region in which you command, allowing nothing but the dictates of military necessity to cause you to depart from the spirit of these instructions.

So much in regard to political considerations. The military problem would be a simple one, could it be entirely separated from political influences; such is not the case. Were the population among which you are to operate, wholly or generally hostile, it is probable that Nashville should be your first and objective point. It so happens that a large majority of the inhabitants of Eastern Tennessee are in favor of the Union, it therefore seems proper that you should remain on the defensive on the line from Louisville, while you throw the mass of your forces, by rapid marches, by Cumberland Gap, or Walker's Gap on Knoxville, in order to occupy the railroad at that point, and thus enable the loyal citizens of Eastern Tennessee to use, while you at the same time cut off the railway communication between eastern Virginia and the Mississippi.

It will be prudent to fortify the pass, before leaving it in your rear. I am, &c.,

Geo B McClellan, M G Com, U S A

Headq's of the Army Washington, Nov. 12 '61
Brig-Gen D C Buell, Com Dep. of the Ohio:

General,—Upon assuming command of the department, I will be glad to have you make, as soon as possible, a careful report of the condition of your command. The main point to which I desire to call your attention is the necessity of entering eastern Tennessee as soon as it can be done with reasonable chances of success, and I hope that you will, with the least possible delay, organize a column for that purpose, sufficiently guarding, at the same time, the main avenues by which the rebels might invade Kentucky. Our conversations on the subject of military operations have been so full, and my confidence in your judgment is so great, that I will not dwell further on the subject, except to urge upon you the necessity of keeping me fully informed as to the state of affairs, both military and political, and your movements.

In regard to political matters, bear in mind that we are fighting only to preserve the integrity of the Union, and to uphold the general government, as far as military necessity will permit, religiously respect the constitutional rights of all. Preserve the strictest discipline among the troops, and while employing the utmost energy in military movements, be careful so to treat the unarmed inhabitants as to contract, not widen, the breach existing between us and the rebels. I mean by this, that it is the desire of the government to avoid unnecessary irritation by causeless arrests and persecution of individuals. Where there is good reason to believe that persons are actually giving aid, comfort, or information to the enemy, it is, of course, necessary to arrest them; but I have always found it is the tendency of subordinates to make vexatious arrests on mere suspicion. You will find it well to direct that no arrest shall be made except by your order, or that of your generals, unless in extraordinary cases, always holding the party making the arrest responsible for the propriety of his course. It should be our constant aim to make it apparent to all, that their property, their comfort, and their personal safety, will be best preserved by adhering to the cause of the Union.

If the military suggestions I have made in this letter prove to have been founded on erroneous data, you are, of course, perfectly free to change the plan of operations. I am, &c., &c., G. B McClellan, M G Com, U S A

Headq's of the Army, Washington, Feb 14 '62
B-Gen. P. W Sherman, C'g. at Port Royal, &c.:

General,—Your dispatches, in regard to the occupation of Daluskie Island, &c, were received to-day. I saw also to-day, for the first time, your requisition for a siege train for Savannah.

After giving the subject all the consideration in my power, I am forced to the conclusion that, under present circumstances, the siege and capture of Savannah do not promise results commensurate with the sacrifices necessary. When I learned that it was possible for the gun-boats to reach the Savannah River above Fort Pulaski, two operations suggested themselves to my mind, as its immediate results.

First. The capture of Savannah by a 'coup de main,' the result of an instantaneous advance and attack by the army and navy.

The time for this has passed, and your letter indicates that you are not accountable for the failure to seize the propitious moment, but that, on the contrary, you perceived its advantages.

Second. To isolate Fort Pulaski cut off its supplies, and at least facilitate its reduction by a bombardment.

Although we have a long delay to deplore, the second course still remains open to us; and I strongly advise the close blockade of Pulaski, and its bombardment as soon as the 13-inch mortars and heavy guns reach you. I am confident you can thus reduce it. With Pulaski, you gain all that is really essential, you obtain complete control of the harbor, you relieve the blockading fleet, and render the main body of your force disposable for other operations

I do not consider the possession of Savannah worth a siege, after Pulaski is in our hands. But the possession of Pulaski is of the first importance. The expedition to Fernandina is well, and I shall be glad to learn that it is ours

But, after all, the greatest moral effect would be produced by the reduction of Charleston and its defences. There the rebellion had its birth; there the unnatural hatred of our government is most intense; there is the centre of the boasted power and courage of the rebels. To gain Fort Sumter, and hold Charleston, is a task well worthy of our greatest efforts, and considerable sacrifices. That is the problem I would be glad to have you study. Some time must elapse before we can be in all respects ready to accomplish that purpose. Fleets are en route, and armies in motion, which have certain preliminary objects to accomplish before we are ready to take Charleston in hand. But the time will before long arrive when I shall be prepared to make that movement. In the mean time, it is my advice and wish that no attempt be made upon Savannah, unless it can be carried with certainty by a coup de main.

Please concentrate your attention and forces upon Pulaski, and Fernandina. St. Augustine might as well be taken by way of interlude, while awaiting the preparations for Charleston. Success attends us everywhere at present. Very truly yours, G B McC., Maj. G C. U. S A.

Head-Quarters of the Army, Washington, Feb 23, 1862. Maj.-General B F. Butler, *U. S. Volunteers.*—

GENERAL —You are assigned to the command of the land forces destined to co-operate with the navy, in the attack upon New Orleans. You will use every means to keep your destination a profound secret, even from your staff officers, with the exception of your chief of staff, and Lieut Weitzel, of the engineers. The force at your disposal, will consist of the first 13 regiments named in your memorandum handed to me in person, the 21st Indiana, 4th Wisconsin, and 6th Michigan, (old and good regiments from Baltimore.)

The 21st Indiana, 4th Wisconsin, and 6th Michigan, will await your orders at Fort Monroe.

Two companies of the 21st Indiana, are well drilled as heavy artillery. The cavalry force already en route for Ship Island, will be sufficient for your purposes

After full consultation with officers well acquainted with the country in which it is proposed to operate, I have arrived at the conclusion that (2) two light batteries fully equipped, and (1) one without horses, will be all that are necessary

This will make your force about 14,400 infantry, 275 cavalry, 680 artillery, total 15 255 men

The commanding general of the Department of Key West, is authorized to loan you, temporarily, 2 regiments; Fort Pickens can probably give you another, which will bring your force to nearly 18,000.

The object of your expedition is one of vital importance, the capture of New Orleans. The route selected is up the Mississippi River, and the first obstacle to be encountered, (perhaps the only one), is in the resistance offered by Forts St Philip and Jackson. It is expected that the navy can reduce these works, in that case, you will, after their capture leave a sufficient garrison in them to render them perfectly secure; and it is recommended, that on the upward passage, a few heavy guns and some troops, be left at the Pilot Station, (at the forks of the river), to cover a retreat in the event of a disaster. These troops and guns, will, of course, be removed as soon as the forts are captured

Should the navy fail to reduce the works, you will land your forces and siege train, and endeavor to breach the works, silence their fire, and carry them by assault.

The next resistance will be near the English Bend, where there are some earthen batteries; here it may be necessary for you to land your troops and co-operate with the naval attack, although it is more than probable, that the navy, unassisted, can accomplish the result. If these works are taken the city of New Orleans necessarily falls. In that event, it will probably be best to occupy Algiers with the mass of your troops, also, the eastern bank of the river above the city, it may be necessary to place some troops in the city to preserve order, but if there appears sufficient Union sentiment to control the city, it may be best for purposes of discipline, to keep your men out of the city

After obtaining possession of New Orleans, it will be necessary to reduce all the works guarding its approaches from the east, and particularly to gain the Manchac Pass. Baton Rouge, Berwick Bay, and Fort Livingston will next claim your attention.

A feint on Galveston may facilitate the objects we have in view. I need not call your attention to the necessity of gaining possession of all the rolling stock you can on the different railways, and of obtaining control of the roads themselves. The occupation of Baton Rouge by a combined naval and land force, should be accomplished as soon as possible after you have gained New Orleans. Then endeavor to open your communication with the northern column by the Mississippi, always bearing in mind the necessity of occupying Jackson Mississippi, as soon as you can safely do so, either after, or before you have effected the junction. Allow nothing to divert you from obtaining full possession of all the approaches to New Orleans. When that object is accomplished to its fullest extent, it will be necessary to make a combined attack on Mobile, in order to gain possession of the harbor and works, as well as to control the railway terminus at the city.

In regard to this, I will send more detailed instructions as the operations of the northern column develop themselves.

I may briefly state that the general objects of the expedition are *First*, The reduction of New Orleans and all its approaches; then Mobile and its defenses; then Pensacola, Galveston, &c. It is probable that by the time New Orleans is reduced it will be in the power of the government to reinforce the land forces sufficiently to accomplish all these objects; in the meantime you will please give all the assistance in your power to the army and navy commanders in your vicinity, never losing sight of the fact, that the great object to be achieved is the capture and firm retention of New Orleans. I am, &c., G. B. McC., M. G. C. U. S. A.

THE ARMY OF THE POTOMAC

The plan indicated in the above letters comprehended in its scope the operations of all the armies in the Union—the army of the Potomac as well. It was my intention, for reasons easy to be seen, that its various parts should be carried out simultaneously, or nearly so, and in co-operation along our whole line. It this plan was wise, and events have failed to prove that it was not, then it is unnecessary to defend any delay which would have enabled the army of the Potomac to perform its share in the execution of the whole work.

But about the middle of January, 1862, upon recovering from a severe illness, I found that excessive anxiety for an immediate movement of the army of the Potomac had taken possession of the minds of the administration.

A change had just been made in the War Department, and I was soon urged by the New Secretary, Mr. Stanton, to take immediate steps to secure the reopening of the Baltimore and Ohio Railroad, and to free the banks of the lower Potomac from the rebel batteries which annoyed passing vessels.

Very soon after his entrance upon office, I laid before him, verbally, my designs as to the part of the plan of campaign to be executed by the army of the Potomac, which was to attack Richmond by the lower Chesapeake.

He instructed me to develop it to the President, which I did. The result was, that the President disapproved it, and by an order of January 31, 1862, substituted one of his own.

On the 27th of January, 1862, the following order was issued without consultation with me.

Executive Mansion, Washington, Jan. 27, 1862. President's General War Order, No. 1.

Ordered: That the 22d day of February, 1862, be the day for a general movement of the land and naval forces of the United States against the insurgent forces. That, especially the army at and about Fortress Monroe, the army of the Potomac, the army of Western Virginia, the army near Mumfordsville, Kentucky, the army and flotilla at Cairo, and a naval force in the Gulf of Mexico, be ready to move on that day.

That all other forces, both land and naval, with their respective commanders obey existing orders for the time, and be ready to obey additional orders when duly given.

That the heads of departments, and especially the Secretaries of War and of the Navy, with all their subordinates, and the General-in-Chief, with all other commanders and subordinates of land and naval forces, will severally be held to their strict and full responsibilities for prompt execution of this order.

ABRAHAM LINCOLN.

The order of January 31, 1862, is as follows:

Executive Mansion, Washington, Jan. 31, 1862.

President's Special War Orders, No. 1.

Ordered: That all the disposable force of the army of the Potomac, after providing safely for the defense of Washington, be formed into an expedition for the immediate object of seizing and occupying a point upon the railroad southwestward of what is known as Manassas Junction, all details to be in the discretion of the Commander-in-Chief, and the expedition to move before or on the 22d day of February next.

ABRAHAM LINCOLN.

I asked his excellency whether this order was to be regarded as final, or whether I could be permitted to submit, in writing, my objections to his plan, and my reasons for preferring my own. Permission was accorded, and I therefore prepared the letter to the Secretary of War which is given below. Before this had been submitted to the President, he addressed the following note:

Executive Mansion, Washington, Feb. 3, 1862.

Maj.-Gen McClellan—My Dear Sir: You and I have distinct and different plans for a movement of the army of the Potomac. Yours to be done by the Chesapeake, up the Rappahannock to Urbana, and across and to the terminus of the railroad on the York River; mine to move directly to a point on the railroad southwest of Manassas.

If you will give me satisfactory answers to the following questions, I shall gladly yield my plan to yours.

1st. Does not your plan involve a greatly larger expenditure of *time* and *money* than mine? 2d. Wherein is a victory *more certain* by your plan than mine? 3d. Wherein is a victory *more valuable* by your plan than mine? 4th. In fact, would it not be *less* valuable in this, that it would break no great line of the enemy's communications, while mine would? 5th. In case of disaster, would not a retreat be more difficult by your plan than mine? Yours truly, A. LINCOLN.

These questions were substantially answered by the following letter of the same date to the Secretary of War

Headquarters of the Army, Washington Feb 3, 1862. Hon. E. M. STANTON, *Sec't'y of War*

Sir,—I ask your indulgence for the following paper rendered necessary by circumstances

I assumed command of the troops in the vicinity of Washington on Saturday, July 27, 1861, six days after the Battle of Bull Run. I found no army to command, a mere collection of regiments, cowering on the banks of the Potomac, some perfectly raw, others dispirited by the recent defeat. Nothing of any consequence had been done to secure the southern approaches to the capital by means of defensive works—nothing whatever had been undertaken to defend the avenues to the city on the northern side of the Potomac. The troops were not only undisciplined, undrilled, and dispirited, they were not even placed in military positions—the city was almost in a condition to have been taken by a dash of a regiment of cavalry

Without one day's delay I undertook the difficult task assigned to me; that task the Hon Secretary knows was given to me without my solicitation or foreknowledge. How far I have accomplished it will best be shown by the past and the present. The capital is secure against attack, the extensive fortifications erected by the labor of our troops enable a small garrison to hold it against a numerous army, the enemy have been held in check, the State of Maryland is securely in our possession; the detached counties of Virginia are again within the pale of our laws—and all apprehension of trouble in Delaware is at an end. the enemy are confined to the positions they occupied before the disaster of the 21st July; more than all this, I have now under my command a well drilled and reliable army, to which the destinies of the country may be confidently committed. this army is young and untried in battle—but it is animated by the highest spirit, and is capable of great deeds. That so much has been accomplished and such an army created, in so short a time, from nothing, will hereafter be regarded as one of the highest glories of the administration and the nation. Many weeks, I may say many months ago, this army of the Potomac was fully in condition to repel any attack, but there is a vast difference between that and the efficiency required to enable troops to attack successfully an army elated by victory and intrenched in a position long since selected, studied and fortified. In the earliest papers I submitted to the President, I asked for an effective and movable force far exceeding the aggregate now on the banks of the Potomac. I have not the force I asked for. Even when in a subordinate position, I always looked beyond the operations of the army of the Potomac. I was never satisfied in my own mind with a barren victory—but looked to combined and decisive operations. When I was placed in command of the armies of the United States, I immediately turned my attention to the whole field of operations, regarding the army of the Potomac as only *one*, while the most important, of the masses under my command. I confess that I did not then appreciate the total absence of a general plan which had before existed—nor did I know that utter disorganization and want of preparation pervaded the Western armies. I took it for granted that they were nearly, if not quite, in condition to move toward the fulfillment of my plans, I acknowledge that I made a great mistake. I sent at once, with the approval of the Executive, officers I considered competent to command in Kentucky and Missouri—their instructions looked to prompt movements—I soon found that the labor of creation and organization had to be performed there, transportation, arms, clothing, artillery discipline, all were wanting. these things required time to procure them. The generals in command have done their work most creditably—but we are still delayed. I had hoped that a general advance could be made during the good weather of December; I was mistaken. My wish was to gain possession of the Eastern Tennessee Railroad as a preliminary movement—then to follow it up immediately by an attack on Nashville and Richmond, as nearly at the same time as possible. I have ever regarded our true policy as being that of fully preparing ourselves, and then seeking for the most decisive results. I do not wish to waste life in useless battles—but I prefer to strike at the heart. Two bases of operations seem to present themselves for the advance of the army of the Potomac. 1st. That of Washington, its present position, involving a direct attack upon the intrenched positions of the enemy at Centreville, Manassas, &c, or else a movement to turn one or both flanks of those positions or a combination of the two plans. The relative force of the two armies will not justify an attack on both flanks, an attack on his left flank alone involves a long line of wagon communication, and cannot prevent him from collecting for the decisive battle all the detachments now on his extreme right and left. Should we attack his right flank by the line of the Occoquan and a crossing of the Potomac below that river and near his batteries, we could, perhaps, prevent the junction of the enemy's right with his centre (we might destroy the former), we would remove the obstructions to the navigation of the Potomac, reduce the length of wagon transportation by establishing new depots at the nearest points of the Potomac, and strike more directly his main railway communication

The fords of Occoquan, below the mouth of Bull Run, are watched by the rebels, batteries are said to be placed on the heights in rear, (concealed by the woods) and the arrangement of his troops is such that he can oppose some considerable resistance to a passage of that stream. Information has just been received, to the effect that the enemy are intrenching a line of heights extending from the vicinity of Sangsters, (Union Mills), towards Evansport. Early in January Sprigg's Ford was occupied by Gen Rhodes, with 3,600 men and eight guns. There are strong reasons for believing that Davis's Ford is occupied. These circumstances indicate, or prove, that the enemy anticipates the movement in question, and is prepared to resist it. Assuming, for the present, that this operation is determined upon, it may be well to examine briefly its probable progress. In the present state of things, our columns (for the movement of so large a force must be made in several columns at least five or six,) can reach the Accotink without danger; during the march thence to the Occoquan, our right flank becomes exposed to an attack from Fairfax Station, Sangsters and Union Mills. This danger must be met by occupying, in some force, either the two first-named places, or, better, the point of junction of the roads leading to the village of Occoquan. This occupation must be sustained so long as we continue to draw supplies by the roads from this city, or until a battle is won.

The crossing of the Occoquan should be made at all the fords from Wolf's Run to the mouth, the points of crossing not being necessarily confined to the fords themselves. Should the enemy occupy this line in force we must, with what assistance the flotilla can afford, endeavor to force the passage near the mouth, thus forcing the enemy to abandon the whole line, or be taken in flank himself.

Having gained the line of the Occoquan, it would be necessary to throw a column, by the shortest route, to Dumfries, partly to force the enemy to abandon his batteries on the Potomac, partly to cover our left flank against an attack from the direction of Acquia, and, lastly, to establish our communication with the river by the best roads, and thus give us new depots. The enemy would by this time have occupied the line of the Occoquan above Bull Run, holding Brentsville in the force, and perhaps extending his lines somewhat further to the south-west.

Our next step would be to prevent the enemy from crossing the Occoquan between Bull Run and the Broad Run, to fall upon our right flank while moving on Brentsville. This might be effected by occupying Bacon Race Church and the cross-roads near the mouth of Bull Run or still more effectually, by moving to the fords themselves, and preventing him from debouching on our side.

These operations would possibly be resisted, and it would require some time to effect them. As nearly, at the same time, as possible we should gain the fords necessary to our purposes above Broad Run. Having secured our right flank, it would become necessary to carry Brentsville at any cost, for we could not leave it between our right flank and the main body. The final movement on the railroad must be determined by circumstances existing at the time.

This brief sketch brings out in bold relief the great advantage possessed by the enemy in the strong central position he occupies, with roads diverging in every direction, and a strong line of defence, enabling him to remain on the defensive, with a small force on one flank, while he concentrates everything on the other for a decisive action.

Should we place a portion of our force in front of Centreville, while the rest crosses the Occoquan, we commit the error of dividing our army by a very difficult obstacle, and by a distance too great to enable the two parts to support each other, should either be attacked by the masses of the enemy, while the other is held in check.

I should, perhaps, have dwelt more decidedly on the fact that the force left near Sangsters must be allowed to remain somewhere on that side of the Occoquan, until the decisive battle is over, so as to cover our retreat, in the event of disaster; unless it should be decided to select and intrench a new base somewhere near Dumfries, a proceeding involving much time.

After the passage of the Occoquan by the main army, this covering force could be drawn in to a more central and less exposed position, say Brimstone Hill, or nearer the Occoquan.

In this latitude the weather will, for a considerable period, be very uncertain, and a movement commenced in force on roads in tolerably firm condition, will be liable, almost certain, to be much delayed by rains and snow. It will, therefore, be next to impossible to surprise the enemy or take him at a disadvantage by rapid manœuvres. Our slow progress will enable him to divine our purposes, and take his measures accordingly. The probability is, from the best information we possess, that the enemy has improved the roads leading to his line of defence, while we will have to work as we advance.

Bearing in mind what has been said, and the present unprecedented and impassable condition of the roads it will be evident that no precise period can be fixed upon for the movement on this line. Nor can its duration be closely calculated; it seems certain that many weeks may elapse, before it is possible to commence the march. Assuming the success of this operation, and the defeat of the enemy as certain the question at once arises, as to the importance of the results gained. I think these results would be confined to the possession of the field of battle, the evacuation of the line of the upper Potomac by the enemy, and the moral effect of the victory; important results, it is true, but not decisive of the war, nor securing the destruction of the enemy's main army, for he could fall back upon other positions and fight us again and again, should the condition of the troops permit. If he is in no condition to fight us again out of range of the intrenchments at Richmond, we would find it a very difficult and tedious matter to follow him up there, for he would destroy his railroad bridges, and otherwise impede our progress through a region where the roads are as bad as they well can be, and we would probably find ourselves forced, at last, to change the whole theatre of war, or to seek a shorter land route to Richmond, with a smaller available force, and at an expenditure of much more time than were we to adopt the short line at once. We would also have forced the enemy to concentrate his forces, and perfect his measures at the very point where it is desirable to strike him when least prepared.

II. The second base of operations available for the army of the Potomac, is that of the lower Chesapeake Bay, which affords the shortest possible land route to Richmond, and strikes directly at the heart of the enemy's power in the east.

The roads in that region are passable at all seasons of the year.

The country now alluded to is much more favorable for offensive operations than that in front of Washington, (which is very unfavorable,) much more level, more cleared land, the woods less dense, the soil more sandy, the spring some two or three weeks earlier. A movement in force on that line obliges the enemy to abandon his intrenched position at Manassas, in order to hasten to cover Richmond and Norfolk. He must do this, for should he permit us to occupy Richmond, his destruction can be averted only by entirely defeating us in a battle, in which he must be the assailant. This movement, if successful, gives us the capital, the communications, the supplies of the rebels, Norfolk would fall; all the waters of the Chesapeake would be ours, all Virginia would be in our power, and the enemy forced to abandon Tennessee and North Carolina. The alternative presented to the enemy would be to beat us in a position selected by ourselves; disperse or pass beneath the Caudine Forks.

Should we be beaten in a battle, we have a perfectly secure retreat down the Peninsula upon Fort Monroe, with our flanks perfectly covered by the fleet. During the whole movement our flank is covered by the water, our right is secure, for the reason that the enemy is too distant to reach us in time, he can only oppose us in front, we bring our fleet in full play.

After a successful battle, our position would be, Burnside forming our left, Norfolk held securely, our centre connecting Burnside with Buell, both by Raleigh and Lynchburg, Buell in Eastern Tennessee and Northern Alabama, Halleck at Nashville and Memphis.

The next movement would be to connect with Sherman on the left, by reducing Wilmington and Charleston, to advance our centre into South Carolina and Georgia, to push Buell either towards Montgomery, or to unite with the main army in Georgia, to throw Halleck southward to meet the naval expedition from New Orleans.

We should then be in a condition to reduce at our leisure, all the southern seaports, to occupy all the avenues of communication, to use the great outlet of the Mississippi, to reestablish our government and arms in Arkansas, Louisiana and Texas, to force the slaves to labor for our subsistence, instead of that of the rebels, to bid defiance to all foreign interference. Such is the object I ever had in view, this is the general plan which I hope to accomplish.

For many long months, I have labored to prepare the army of the Potomac to play its part in the programme; from the day when I was placed in command of all our armies, I have exerted myself to place all the other armies in such a condition, that they too could perform their allotted duties.

Should it be determined to operate from the lower Chesapeake, the point of landing which promises the most brilliant results, is Urbana, on the lower Rappahannock. This point is easily reached by vessels of heavy draught, it is neither occupied nor observed by the enemy, it is but one march from West Point, the key of that region, and thence but two marches to Richmond. A rapid movement from Urbana, would probably cut off Magruder in the Peninsula, and enable us to occupy Richmond before it could be strongly reinforced. Should we fail in that, we could, with the co-operation of the navy, cross the James and show ourselves in rear of Richmond, thus forcing the enemy to come out and attack us, for his position would be untenable, with us on the southern bank of the river.

Should circumstances render it not advisable to land at Urbana we can use Mob Jack Bay—or the worst coming to the worst, we can take Fort Monroe as a base, and operate with complete security, although with less celerity and brilliancy of results, up the Peninsula.

To reach whatever point may be selected as a base, a large amount of cheap water transportation must be collected, consisting mainly of canal-boats, barges, wood-boats, schooners, &c, towed by small steamers, all of a very different character from those required for all previous expeditions. This can certainly be accomplished within thirty days from the time the order is given. I propose as the best possible plan that can, in my judgment, be adopted to select Urbana as a landing-place for the first detachments. To transport by water four divisions of infantry with their batteries, the regular infantry, a few wagons, one bridge train, and a few squadrons of cavalry, making the vicinity of Hooker's position the place of embarkation for as many as possible. To move the regular cavalry and reserve artillery the remaining bridge trains and wagons to a point somewhere near Cape Lookout, then ferry them over the river by means of North River ferry-boats, march them over to the Rappahannock (covering the movement by an infantry force near Heathsville) and to cross the Rappahannock in a similar way. The expense and difficulty of the movement will thus be very much diminished (a saving of transportation of about 10,000 horses) and the result none the less certain.

The concentration of the cavalry, &c., in the lower counties of Maryland, can be effected without exciting suspicion, and the movement made without delay from that cause.

This movement, if adopted, will not at all expose the city of Washington to danger.

The total force to be thrown upon the new line would be, according to circumstances, from 110 to 140,000. I hope to use the latter number by bringing fresh troops into Washington, and still leaving it quite safe. I fully realize that in all projects offered, time will probably be the most valuable consideration. It is my decided opinion, that in that point of view, the second plan should be adopted. It is possible, nay highly probable, that the weather and state of the roads, may be such as to delay the direct movement from Washington, with its unsatisfactory results and great risks—far beyond the time required to complete the second plan. In the first case we can fix no definite time for an advance. The roads have gone from bad to worse—nothing like their present condition has ever been known here before; they are impassable at present, we are entirely at the mercy of the weather. It is by no means certain that we can beat them at Manassas. On the other line, I regard success as certain by all the chances of war. We demoralize the enemy by forcing him to abandon his prepared position for one which we have chosen, in which all is in our favor, and where success must produce immense results.

My judgment as a general, is clearly in favor of this project. Nothing is certain in war, but all the chances are in favor of this movement. So much am I in favor of the southern line of operations that I would prefer the move from Fort Monroe as a base—as a certain though less brilliant movement, than that from Urbana—to an attack upon Manassas.

I know that his Excellency the President, you and I, all agree in our wishes, and that those wishes are to bring the war to a close, as promptly as the means in our possession will permit. I believe that the mass of the people have entire confidence in us. I am sure of it. Let us then look only to the great result to be accomplished, and disregard everything else. I am, very respectfully, your obedient servant, G. B. McC., M. G. C.

This letter must have produced some effect upon the mind of the President, since the execution of his order was not required, although it was not revoked as formally as it had been issued. Many verbal conferences ensued, in which among other things, it was determined to collect as many canal-boats as possible, with a view to employ them largely in the transportation of the army to the lower Chesapeake. The idea was at one time entertained by the President to use them in forming a bridge across the Potomac, near Liverpool Point, in order to throw the army over at that point, but this was subsequently abandoned. It was also found by experience, that it would require much time to prepare the canal-boats for use in transportation to the extent that had been anticipated.

Finally, on the 27th of February, 1862, the Secretary of War, by the authority of the President, instructed Mr. John Tucker, Assistant Secretary of War, to procure at once the necessary steamers and sailing craft to transport the army of the Potomac to its new field of operations.

The following extracts from the report of Mr. Tucker, dated April 5th, will show the nature and progress of this well-executed service:

* * * * * *

"I was called to Washington by telegraph on 17th January last, by Assistant-Secretary of War Thomas A. Scott. I was informed that Maj.-Gen. McClellan wished to see me. From him I learned that he desired to know if transportation on smooth water could be obtained, to move at one time, for a short distance, about 50,000 troops, 10,000 horses, 1,000 wagons, 13 batteries and the usual equipment of such an army. He frankly stated to me, that he had always supposed such a movement entirely feasible until two experienced quarter-masters had recently reported it impracticable, in their judgment. A few days afterwards, I reported to Gen. McClellan that I was entirely confident the transports could be commanded, and stated the mode by which his object could be accomplished. A week or more afterwards, I had the honor of an interview with the President and Gen. McClellan, when the subject was further discussed, and especially as to the time required.

I expressed the opinion, that as the movement of the horses and wagons would have to be made chiefly by schooners and barges, that as each schooner would require to be properly fitted for the protection of the horses, and furnished with a supply of water and forage, and each transport for the troops provided with water, I did not deem it prudent to assume that such an expedition could start within thirty days from the time the order was given.

The President and Gen. McClellan both urgently stated the vast importance of an earlier movement. I replied that if favorable winds prevailed, and there was great dispatch in loading, the time might be materially diminished.

On the 14th of February, [Secretary of War] advertised for transports of various descriptions, inviting bids. On the 27th February I was informed that the proposed movement by water was decided upon That evening the quarter-master-general was informed of the decision. Directions were given to secure the transportation, and my assistance was tendered.

"He promptly detailed to this duty two most efficient assistants in his department. Col. Rufus Ingalls was stationed at Annapolis, where it was then proposed to embark the troops, and Capt. Henry C. Hodges was directed to meet me in Philadelphia, to attend to chartering the vessels With these arrangements, I left Washington on the 28th February.

* * * * * *

"I beg to hand herewith a statement, prepared by Capt. Hodges, of the vessels chartered, which exhibits the prices paid, and the parties from whom they were taken, viz:

"113 Steamers, at an average price per day $215 10
188 Schooners " " . . 24 45
88 Barges " " . 14 27

"In thirty-seven days from the time I received the order in Washington, (and most of it was accomplished in thirty days,) these vessels transported from Perryville, Alexandria, and Washington, to Fort Monroe—(the place of departure having been changed, which caused delay)—121,500 men, 14,592 animals; 1,150 wagons, 44 batteries; 74 ambulances; besides pontoon bridges, telegraph materials, and the enormous quantity of equipage, &c., required for an army of such magnitude. The only loss of which I have heard, is eight mules and nine barges, which latter went ashore in a gale within a few miles of Fort Monroe, the cargoes being saved With this trifling exception, not the slightest accident has occurred, to my knowledge.

"I respectfully, but confidently, submit that, for economy and celerity of movement, this expedition is without a parallel on record.

"JOHN TUCKER Ass't-Sec of War"

THE ENEMY'S BATTERIES ON THE POTOMAC

In the meantime the destruction of the batteries on the lower Potomac, by crossing our troops opposite them, was considered, and preparations were even made for throwing Hooker's division accross the river to carry them by assault. Finally, however, after an adverse report from Brig.-Gen. J. G. Barnard, chief engineer, given below, who made a reconnoissance of the positions; and in view of the fact that it was still out of the power of the navy department to furnish suitable vessels to co-operate with the land troops, this plan was abandoned as impracticable A close examination of the enemy's works and their approaches, made after they were evacuated, showed that the decision was a wise one The only means, therefore, of accomplishing the capture of these works, so much desired by the President, was by a movement by land, from the left of our lines, on the right, bank of the Potomac, a movement obviously unwise.

The attention of the Navy Department, as early as Aug 12, 1861, had been called to the necessity of maintaining a strong force of efficient war vessels on the Potomac.

Headq's, Div'n. Potomac, Wash., Aug. 12, 1861.
Hon GID WELLES, Sec U S Navy.

SIR,—I have, to-day, received additional information which convinces me that it is more than probable that the enemy will, within a very short time, attempt to throw a respectable force from the mouth of Acquia Creek into Maryland. This attempt will probably be preceded by the erection of batteries at Mathias and White House Points. Such a movement on the part of the enemy, in connection with others probably designed, would place Washington in great jeopardy. I most earnestly urge that the strongest possible naval force be at once concentrated near the mouth of Acquia Creek, and that the most vigilant watch be maintained day and night, so as to render such passage of the river, absolutely impossible.

I recommend that the Minnesota, and any other vessels available from Hampton Roads, be at once ordered up there, and that a great quantity of coal be sent to that vicinity, sufficient for several weeks' supply. At least one strong war vessel should be kept at Alexandria, and I again urge the concentration of a strong naval force in the Potomac without delay

If the naval department will render it absolutely impossible for the enemy to cross the river below Washington, the security of the capital will be greatly increased.

I cannot too earnestly urge an immediate compliance with these requests

I am, sir, very respectfully, your ob't serv't,
G B McCLELLAN, M.-G Com'g

It was on the 27th Sept't, 1861, that Gen. Barnard, chief engineer, in company with Capt. Wyman, of the Potomac Flotilla, had been instructed to make a reconnoissance of the enemy's batteries as far as Mathias Point In his report of his observations, he says:—"Batteries at High Point and Cockpit Point, and thence down to Chopawampsic, *cannot* be prevented We may, indeed, prevent their construction on *certain* points, but along here, somewhere, the enemy can establish, in spite of us, as many batteries as he chooses What is the remedy? Favorable circumstances, not to be anticipated nor made the basis of any calculations, might justify and render successful the attack of a peculiar battery. To suppose that we can capture *all*, and by mere attacks of this kind prevent the navigation being molested, is very much the same as to suppose that the hostile army in our own front can prevent us building and maintaining field-works to protect Arlington and Alexandria, by capturing them one and all as fast as they are built."

In another communication upon the subject of crossing troops for the purpose of destroying the batteries on the Virginia side of the Potomac, Gen Barnard says:

"The operation involves the forcing of a very strong line of defence of the enemy, and all that we would have to do, if we were really opening a campaign against them there.

"It is true we hope to force this line by turning it, by landing on Freestone Point.

"With reason to believe that this may be successful, it cannot be denied that it involves a risk of failure

"Should we then, considering all the consequences which may be involved, enter into the operation merely to capture the Potomac batteries? I think not

"Will not the Ericsson, assisted by one other gun-boat, capable of keeping along side these batteries, so far control their fire as to keep the navigation sufficiently free as long as we require it? Capt Wyman says yes"

It was the opinion of competent naval officers, and I concur with them, that had an adequate force of strong and well armed vessels been acting upon the Potomac from the beginning of August, it would have been next to impossible for the rebels to have constructed or maintained batteries upon the banks of the river. The enemy never occupied Mathias Point, nor any other point on the river, which was out of supporting distance from their main army

When the enemy commenced the construction of these batteries, the army of the Potomac was not in condition to prevent it; then destruction by our army would have afforded but a temporary relief, unless we had been strong enough to hold the entire line of the Potomac. This could be done either by driving the enemy from Manassas and Aquia Creek by main force, or by manoeuvring to compel them to evacuate their positions The latter course was finally pursued and with success

THE BALTIMORE AND OHIO RAILROAD.

About the 20th of Feb, 1862, additional measures were taken to secure the re-opening of the Baltimore and Ohio Railroad The preliminary operations of Gen. Lander for this object are elsewhere described

I had often observed to the President, and to members of the Cabinet, that the reconstruction of this railway could not be undertaken, until we were in a condition to fight a battle to secure it I regarded the possession of Winchester and Strasburg as necessary to cover the railway in rear, and it was not until the month of February that I felt prepared to accomplish this very desirable, but not vital purpose

The whole of Bank's division, and two brigades of Sedgwick's division, were thrown across the river at Harper's Ferry, leaving one brigade of Sedgwick's division to observe and guard the Potomac from Great Falls to the mouth of the Monocacy. A sufficient number of troops of all arms, were held in readiness in the vicinity of Washington, either to march via Leesburg, or to move by rail to Harper's Ferry, should this become necessary in carrying out the objects in view The subjoined notes from a communication subsequently addressed to the War Department, will sufficiently explain the conduct of these operations.

NOTES:— 'When I started for Harper's Ferry, I plainly stated to the President and Secretary of War, that the chief object of the operation would be to open the Baltimore and Ohio Railroad, by crossing the river in force at Harper's Ferry; that I had collected the material for making a permanent bridge by means of canal-boats; that from the nature of the river, it was doubtful whether such a bridge could be constructed; that if it could not, I would at least occupy the ground in front of Harper's Ferry, in order to cover the rebuilding of the railroad bridge, and finally, when the communications were perfectly secure, move on Winchester.

When I arrived at the place, I found the batteau bridge nearly completed; the holding ground proved better than had been anticipated, the weather was favorable, there being no wind I at once crossed over the two brigades which had arrived, and took steps to hurry up the other two belonging respectively to Bank's and Sedgwick's divisions The difficulty of crossing supplies had not then become apparent. That night I telegraphed for a regiment of regular cavalry and four batteries of heavy artillery, to come up the next day (Thursday) besides directing Keyes's division of infantry to be moved up on Friday

Next morning the attempt was made to pass the canal-boats through the lift lock, in order to commence at once the construction of a permanent bridge; it was then found for the first time that the lock was too small to permit the passage of the boats, it having been built for a class of boats running on the Shenandoah Canal, and too narrow by some four or six inches for the canal-boats. The lift locks above and below are all large enough for the ordinary boats I had seen them at Edward's Ferry thus used. it had always been represented to the engineers by the military railroad employees and others, that the lock was large enough, and the difference being too small to be detected by the eye, no one had thought of measuring it, or suspected any difficulty I thus suddenly found myself unable to build the permanent bridge A violent gale had arisen, which threatened the safety of our only means of communication, the narrow approach to the bridge was so crowded and clogged with wagons, that it was very clear that under existing circumstances nothing more could be done than to cross over the baggage and supplies of the two brigades of these instead of being able to cross both during the morning, the last arrived only in time to go over just before dark. It was evident that the troops under orders, would only be in the way, should they arrive and that it would not be possible to subsist them for a rapid march for Winchester. It was therefore deemed necessary to countermand the order, content ourselves with covering the reopening of the railroad for the present, and in the mean time use every exertion to establish, as promptly as possible, depots of forage and subsistence on the Virginia side, to supply the troops and enable them to move on Winchester, independently of the bridge. The next day (Friday) I sent a strong reconnoissance to Charleston, and under its protection went there myself. I then determined to hold that place, and to move the troops composing Lander's and Williams' commands at once on Martinsburg and Bunker Hill, thus effectually covering the reconstruction of the railroad.

"Having done this, and taken all the steps in my power to ensure the rapid transmission of supplies over the river, I returned to this city, well satisfied with what had been accomplished. While up the river I learned that the President was dissatisfied with the state of affairs—but on my return here, understood from the Sec. of War, that, upon learning the whole state of the case, the President was fully satisfied. I contented myself, therefore, with giving to the Secretary a brief statement about as I have written it here.'

The design aimed at was entirely compassed, and before the first of April, the date of my departure for the Peninsula, the railroad was in running order. As a demonstration upon the left flank of the enemy, this movement no doubt assisted in determining the evacuation of his lines on the eighth and ninth of March.

PREPARATIONS TO MOVE FROM WASHINGTON.

Upon my return from Harper's Ferry, on the 28th of Feb, the preparations necessary to carry out the wishes of the President and Sec. of War in regard to destroying the batteries on the lower Potomac, were at once undertaken. Mature reflection convinced me that this operation would require the movement of the entire army, for I felt sure that the enemy would resist it with his whole strength. I undertook it with great reluctance, both on account of the extremely unfavorable condition of the roads, and my firm conviction that the proposed movement to the lower Chesapeake would necessarily, as it subsequently did, force the enemy to abandon all his positions in front of Washington. Besides, it did not forward my plan of campaign to precipitate this evacuation by any direct attack, nor to subject the army to needless loss of life and material, by a battle near Washington, which could produce no decisive results. The preparations for a movement towards the Occoquan, to carry the batteries, were, however, advanced as rapidly as the season permitted, and I had invited the commanders of divisions to meet at headquarters on the 8th of March, for the purpose of giving them their instructions, and receiving their advice and opinions in regard to their commands, when an interview with the President indicated to me the possibility of a change in my orders.

His Excellency sent for me at a very early hour on the morning of the 8th, and renewed his expressions of dissatisfaction with the affairs at Harper's Ferry, and with my plans for the new movement down the Chesapeake. Another recital of the same facts which had before given satisfaction to his Excellency, again produced, as I supposed, the same result. The views which I expressed to the President were reinforced by the results of a meeting of my general officers at headquarters. At that meeting, my plans were laid before the division commanders, and were approved by a majority of those present. Nevertheless, on the same day, two important orders were issued by the President, without consultation with me. The first of these was the General War Order No 2, directing the formation of army corps, and assigning their commanders.

I had always been in favor of the principle of an organization into army corps, but preferred deterring its practical execution, until some little experience in campaign, and on the field of battle, should show what general officers were most competent to exercise these high commands; for it must be remembered, that we then had no officers whose experience in war, on a large scale, was sufficient to prove that they possessed the necessary qualifications. An incompetent commander of an army corps, might cause irreparable damage, while it was not probable that an incompetent division commander could cause any very serious mischief. These views had frequently been expressed by me to the President and members of the Cabinet; it was, therefore, with as much regret as surprise, that I learned the existence of this order.

The first order has been given above, the second order was as follows:

Executive Mansion, Washington, March 8, '62. President's General War Order, No 3

Ordered. That no change of the base of operations of the army of the Potomac, shall be made without leaving in and about Washington such a force as, in the opinion of the General-in-Chief, and the commanders of army corps, shall leave said city entirely secure.

That no more than two army corps (about fifty thousand troops) of said army of the Potomac, shall be moved en route for a new base of operations, until the navigation of the Potomac, from Washington to the Chesapeake Bay, shall be freed from enemy's batteries, and other obstructions or until the President shall hereafter give express permission.

That any movement, as aforesaid, en route for a new base of operations, which may be ordered by the General-in-Chief, and which may be intended to move upon the Chesapeake Bay, shall begin to move upon the bay as early as the 18th of March last, and the Gen-in-Chief shall be responsible that it so moves as early as that day

Ordered · That the army and navy co-operate in an immediate effort to capture the enemy's batteries upon the Potomac between Washington and the Chesapeake Bay

L Thomas, Adj't Gen   Ab. Lincoln

After what has been said already in regard to the effect of a movement to the lower Chesapeake, it is unnecessary for me to comment upon this document, further than to say, that the time of beginning the movement, depended upon the state of readiness of the transports, the entire control of which had been placed, by the Secretary of War, in the hands of one of the assistant secretaries and not under the Quartermaster General, so that, even if the movement were not impeded by the condition imposed in regard to the batteries on the Potomac, it could not have been in my power to begin it before the 18th of March, unless the Ass't Sec'y of War had completed his arrangements by that time.

Meanwhile important events were occurring, which materially modified the designs for the subsequent campaign. The appearance of the Merrimac off Old Point Comfort, and the encounter with the U.S Squadron on the 8th of March, threatened serious derangement of the plan for the Peninsular movement But the engagement between the Monitor and the Merrimac on the 9th of March, demonstrated so satisfactorily the power of the former, and the other naval preparations were so extensive and formidable, that the security of Fort Monroe, as a base of operations, was placed beyond a doubt, and, although the James River was closed to us, the York River, with its tributaries, was still open as a line of water communication with the Fortress The general plan, therefore, remained undisturbed, although less promising in its details than when the James River was in our control.

On Sunday, the 9th of March, information from various sources made it apparent that the enemy was evacuating his positions at Centreville and Manassas, as well as on the upper and lower Potomac. The President and Secretary of War were present when the most positive information reached me, and I expressed to them my intention to cross the river immediately, and there gain the most authentic information, prior to determining what course to pursue

The retirement of the enemy towards Richmond had been expected, as the natural consequence of the movement to the Peninsula, but their adoption of this course, immediately on ascertaining that such a movement was intended, while it relieved me from the results of the undue anxiety of my superiors, and attested the character of the design, was unfortunate in that the then almost impassable roads between our positions and theirs, deprived us of the opportunity for inflicting damage, usually afforced by the withdrawal of a large army in the face of a powerful adversary

The retirement of the enemy, and the occupation of the abandoned positions, which necessarily followed presented an opportunity for the troops to gain some experience on the march and bivouac, preparatory to the campaign, and to get rid of the superfluous baggage and other "impediments," which accumulate so easily around an army encamped for a long time in one locality

A march to Manassas and back could produce no delay in embarking for the lower Chesapeake, as the transports could not be ready for some time, and it afforded a good intermediate step between the quiet and comparative comfort of the camps around Washington, and the rigors of active operations, besides accomplishing the important object of determining the positions and perhaps the future designs of the enemy, with the possibility of being able to harrass their rear

I therefore issued orders during the night of the 9th of March for a general movement of the army the next morning towards Centreville and Manassas, sending in advance two regiments of cavalry under Col Averil, with orders to reach Manassas if possible, ascertain the exact condition of affairs, and do whatever he could to retard and annoy the enemy, if really in retreat. At the same time, I telegraphed to the Secretary of War, that it would be necessary to defer the organization of army corps until the completion of the projected advance upon Manassas, as the divisions could not be brought together in time The Secretary replied, requiring immediate compliance with the President's order, but on my again representing that this would compel the abandonment or postponement of the movement to Manassas, he finally consented to its postponement. At noon, on the 10th of March, the cavalry advance, reached the enemy's lines at Centreville, passing through his recently occupied camps and works, and finding still burning heaps of military stores and much valuable property

SECRET SERVICE

Immediately after being assigned to the command of the troops around Washington, I organized a secret service force under Mr Allen Pinkerton, whose assumed name was E J Allen, a very experienced and efficient person. This force, up to the time I was relieved from command, was continually occupied in procuring, from all possible sources, information regarding the strength, positions and movements of the enemy All spies, "contrabands," deserters, refugees, and many prisoners of war, coming into our lines from the front, were carefully examined—first, by the outpost and division commanders, and then by my chief-of-staff and the provost-marshal-general. Their statements, taken in writing, and in many cases under oath, from day to day, for a long period previous to the evacuation of Manassas, comprised a mass of evidence which, by careful digests and collations, enabled me to estimate with considerable accuracy the strength of the enemy before us. Summaries, showing the character and results of the labors of the secret service force, accompany this report, and I refer to them for the facts they contain, and as a measure of the ignorance which led some journals at that time, and persons in high office, unwittingly to trifle with the reputation of an army, and to delude the country with Quaker-gun stories of the defenses, and gross understatements of the numbers, of the enemy.

The following orders were issued for the examination of persons coming from the direction of the enemy:

Headquarters, Army of the Potomac, Washington, Dec 16, 1861.—*Circular*. The Major-General commanding directs, That all deserters, prisoners, spies, "contrabands," and all other persons whatever, coming or brought within our lines from Virginia, shall be taken immediately to the quarters of the commander of the division within whose lines they may come or be brought, without previous examination by any one, except so far as may be necessary for the officer commanding the advanced guard, to elicit information regarding his particular post; That the division commander examine all such persons himself, or delegate such duty to a proper officer of his staff, and allow no other persons to hold any communication with them That he then immediately send them, with a sufficient guard, to the provost marshal in this city for further examination and safe keeping, and that stringent orders be given to all guards having such persons in charge not to hold any communication with them whatever; and further, that the information elicited from such persons shall be immediately communicated to the major-general commanding or to the chief-of-staff, and to no other person whatever.

The major-general commanding further directs that a sufficient guard be placed around every telegraph station pertaining to this army, and that such guards be instructed not to allow any person, except the regular telegraph corps, general officers, and such staff officers as may be authorized by their chief, to enter or loiter around said stations within hearing of the sound of the telegraphic instruments.

By command of Maj.-Gen McClellan, S. Williams, Asst.-Adj.-Gen

Headquarters, Army of the Potomac, Washington, Feb 26, 1862

GENERAL ORDERS, No 27.

* * * *

All deserters from the enemy, prisoners, and other persons coming within our lines will be taken at once to the provost marshal of the nearest division, who will examine them in presence of the division commander, or an officer of his staff designated for the purpose. This examination will only refer to such information as may affect the division and those near it, especially those remote from general headquarters. As soon as this examination is completed, and it must be made as rapidly as possible, the person will be sent under proper guard to the provost-marshal-general with a statement of his replies to the questions asked. Upon receiving him the provost-marshal-general will at once send him with this statement to the chief-of-staff of the Army of the Potomac, who will cause the necessary examination to be made The provost-marshal-general will have the custody of all such persons. Division commanders will at once communicate to other division commanders all information thus obtained which affects them . . .

By command of Maj.-Gen McClellan, S Williams, Asst.-Adj.-Gen

In addition to the foregoing orders, the division commanders were instructed whenever they desired to send out scouts towards the enemy, to make known the object at headquarters, in order that I might determine whether we had the information it was proposed to obtain, and that I might give the necessary orders to other commanders so that the scouts should not be molested by the guards.

It will be seen from the report of the chief of the secret service corps, dated March 8th, that the forces of the rebel army of the Potomac at that date were as follows

At Manassas, Centreville, Bull Run, Upper Occoquan, and vicinity, 80,000 men; at Brooks's Station, Dumfries, Lower Occoquan and vicinity, 18,000 men; at Leesburg and vicinity, 4,500 men; in the Shenandoah Valley, 13,000 men; Total number, 115,500.

About three hundred field-guns, and from twenty-six to thirty siege-guns were with the rebel army in front of Washington

The report made on the 17th of March, after the evacuation of Manassas and Centreville corroborates the statements contained in the report of the 8th, and is fortified by the affidavits of several railroad engineers, conductors, baggage-masters, &c , whose opportunities for forming correct estimates were unusually good These affidavits will be found in the accompanying reports of the chief of the secret service corps

ENEMY'S WORKS AT AND NEAR MANASSAS—A reconnoissance of the works at Centreville made by Lieut McAlester, U.S Engineers, on March 14th, 1862, and a survey of those at Manassas made by a party of the U S Coast Survey in April, 1862, confirmed also my conclusions as to the strength of the enemy's defenses

Those at Centreville consisted of two lines, one facing east, and the other north. The former consisted of seven works, viz.: one bastion-fort, two redoubts, two lunettes, and two batteries, all containing embrasures for forty guns, and connected by infantry parapets and double caponnieres. It extended along the crest of the ridge about one mile and three-quarters from its junction with the northern front, to ground thickly wooded, and impassable to an attacking column. The northern front extended about one mile and a quarter to Great Rocky Run, and thence three-quarters of a mile further, to thickly wooded impassable ground in the valley of Cub Run. It consisted of six lunettes and batteries, with embrasures for thirty-one guns, connected by an infantry parapet in the form of a cremaillere line with redans.

At the town of Centreville, on a high hill commanding the rear of all the works within range, was a large hexagonal redoubt with ten embrasures.

Manassas Station was defended in all directions by a system of detached works, with platforms for heavy guns arranged for marine carriages, and connected by infantry parapets. This system was rendered complete by a very large work with sixteen embrasures, which commanded the highest of the other works by about fifty feet.

Sketches of the reconnoissances above referred to will be found among the maps appended to this report.

From this it will be seen that the positions selected by the enemy at Centreville and Manassas were naturally very strong, with impassable streams and broken ground, affording ample protection to their flanks, and that strong lines of intrenchments swept all the available approaches.

Although the history of every former war has conclusively shown the great advantages which are possessed by an enemy acting on the defensive and occupying strong positions defended by heavy earthworks, yet, at the commencement of this war but few civilians in our country, and indeed, not all military men of rank, had a just appreciation of the fact.

New levies that have never been in battle, cannot be expected to advance without cover under the murderous fire from such defenses, and carry them by assault. This is work in which veteran troops frequently falter, and are repulsed with loss. That an assault of the enemy's positions, in front of Washington, with the new troops composing the army of the Potomac, during the winter of 1861-2, would have resulted in defeat and demoralization, was too probable. The same army, though enured to war in many battles hardly fought and bravely won, has thrice under other generals, suffered such disasters as it was no excess of prudence then to avoid.

My letter to the Secretary of War, dated February 3d, 1862, and given above, expressed the opinion that the movement to the Peninsula, would compel the enemy to retire from his position at Manassas, and free Washington from danger.

When the enemy first learned of that plan, they did thus evacuate Manassas. During the Peninsula campaign, as at no former period, northern Virginia was completely in our possession, and the vicinity of Washington free from the presence of the enemy. The ground so gained was not lost, nor Washington again put in danger, until the enemy learned of the orders for an evacuation of the Peninsula, sent to me at Harrison's Bar, and were again left free to advance northward, and menace the national capital. Perhaps no one now doubts that the best defense of Washington, is a Peninsula attack on Richmond.

THE PRESIDENT'S ORDER RELIEVING GEN'L McCLELLAN OF THE COMMAND-IN-CHIEF.—My order for the organization of the army corps, was issued on the 13th of March. It has been given above.

While at Fairfax Court House, on March 12th, I was informed through the telegraph by a member of my staff, that the following document had appeared in the "National Intelligencer," of that morning.

Exec Mansion, Washington, March 11, 1862.
President's War Order, No. 3.

Maj.-Gen. McClellan, having personally taken the field at the head of the army of the Potomac, until otherwise ordered, he is relieved from the command of the other military departments, he retaining command of the department of the Potomac.

Ordered further, That the departments now under the respective commands of Generals Halleck and Hunter, together with so much of that under Gen. Buell as lies west of a north and south line indefinitely drawn through Koxville, Tennessee, be consolidated and designated the Department of the Mississippi, and that, until otherwise ordered, Major-Gen Halleck have command of said department.

Ordered also, That the country west of the Department of the Potomac, and east of the Department of the Mississippi, be a military department, to be called the Mountain Department, and that the same be commanded by Maj.-Gen Fremont.

That all the commanders of departments, after the receipt of this order by them, respectively report, severally and directly, to the Secretary of War, and that prompt, full, and frequent reports, will be expected of all and each of them.   A. B. LINCOLN.

Though unaware of the President's intention to remove me from the position of general-in-chief, I cheerfully acceded to the disposition he saw fit to make of my services, and so informed him in a note, on the 12th of March, in which occur these words:

"I believe I said to you some weeks since, in connection with some Western matters, that no feeling of self-interest or ambition, should ever prevent me from devoting myself to the service. I am glad to have the opportunity to prove it, and you will find that, under present circumstances, I shall work just as cheerfully as before, and that no consideration of self will, in any manner, interfere with the discharge of my public duties. Again thanking you for official and personal kindness you have so often evinced towards me, I am, &c."

A RECONNOISSANCE.

On the 14th of March, a reconnoissance of a large body of cavalry, with some infantry, under command of Gen. Stoneman, was sent along the Orange and Alexandria railroad, to determine the position of the enemy, and, if possible, force his rear across the Rappahannock; but the roads were in such condition, that, finding it impossible to subsist his men, Gen Stoneman was forced to return, after reaching Cedar Run. The following dispatch from him recites the result of this expedition.

Headqrs, Union Mills, March 16, 1862

Col Colburn:—We arrived here last evening about dark; we got corn for horses; no provisions for men; Bull Run too high to cross, had we stayed an hour longer, we should not have got here to-day, owing to the high water in the streams, felt the enemy cautiously, and found him in force at Warrenton Junction, saw two regiments of cavalry, and three bodies of infantry, on the other side of Cedar Run, had we crossed, should not have been able to get back for high water, had three men of 5th Cavalry hit driving in enemy's pickets; one slightly wounded in the head.

Enemy acted confidently, and followed us some way back on the road, but did not molest us in any way. Enemy's force consisted of Stewart's and Ewell's cavalry, a battery of artillery, and some infantry; railroad bridges all burnt down up to Warrenton Junction, still entire beyond, but all in readiness to burn at a moment's warning, having dry wood piled upon them; heard cars running during the night before last, probably bringing up troops from Rappahannock; heard of two regiments of infantry at Warrenton, engaged in impressing the militia and securing forage; heard of a large force of infantry this side of Rappahannock River having come up to Warrenton Junction from Acquia Creek day before yesterday, bridges all destroyed this side of Broad Run. The aids who take this will give you further particulars. Very respectfully, &c

Geo Stoneman, Brig -Gen. Com'g

DEFENSE OF WASHINGTON.

The main body of the army was, on the 11th of March, moved back to the vicinity of Alexandria to be embarked, leaving a part of Gen. Sumner's corps at Manassas, until other troops could be sent to relieve it.

Before it was withdrawn, a strong reconnoissance under Gen Howard was sent towards the Rappahannock, the result of which appears in the following dispatch.

Warrenton Junction, March 29, 1862.

Gen S Williams:—Express just received from Gen Howard. He drove the enemy across the Rappahannock bridge, and is now in camp on this bank of and near the Rappahannock River. The enemy blew up the bridge in his retreat. There was skirmishing during the march, and a few shots exchanged by the artillery, without any loss on our part. Their loss, if any, is not known. Gen Howard will return to this camp to-morrow morning.

E V Sumner, Brig -Gen

The line of the Rappahannock and the Manassas Gap railroad was thus reasonably secure from menace by any considerable body of the enemy.

On the 13th of March, a council of war was assembled at the Fairfax Court House, to discuss the military status. The President's Order No 3, of March 8th, was considered. The following is a memorandum of the proceedings of the council.

Headquarters, Army of the Potomac, Fairfax Court House, March 13, 1862

A council of the Generals commanding army corps at the headquarters of the army of the Potomac, were of the opinion.

1. That the enemy having retreated from Manassas to Gordonsville, behind the Rappahannock and Rapidan, it is the opinion of generals commanding army corps that the operations to be carried on will be best undertaken from Old Point Comfort, between the York and James Rivers

Provided—

1st. That the enemy's vessel, Merrimac, can be neutralized.

2d That the means of transportation sufficient for an immediate transfer of the force to its new base can be ready at Washington and Alexandria, to move down the Potomac, and,

3d That a' naval auxiliary force can be had to silence or aid in silencing the enemy's batteries on the York River

4th The force to be left to cover Washington shall be such as to give an entire feeling of security for its safety from menace.—(Unanimous)

II If the foregoing cannot be, the army should then be moved against the enemy, behind the Rappahannock, at the earliest possible moment, and the means of reconstructing bridges, repairing railroads, and stocking them with material sufficient for supplying the army, should at once be collected for both the Orange and Alexandria and Acquia and Richmond railroads.—(Unanimous)

N. B That, with the forts on the right bank of the Potomac fully garrisoned, and those on the left bank occupied, a covering force in front of the Virginia line of 25 000 men would suffice —(Keyes, Heintzelman and McDowell)

A total of 40,000 men for the defense of the city would suffice —(Sumner.)

This was assented to by myself, and immediately communicated to the War Department. The following reply was received the same day:

War Department, March 13, 1862.
To Maj.-Gen. Geo. B. McClellan,—

The President, having considered the plan of operations agreed upon by yourself and the army corps, makes no objection to the same, but gives the following directions as to its execution:

1st. Leave such force at Manassas Junction as shall make it entirely certain that the enemy shall not repossess himself of that position and line of communication.

2d. Leave Washington entirely secure.

3d. Move the remainder of the force down the Potomac—choosing a new base at Fortress Monroe or anywhere between here and there, or, at all events, move such remainder of the army at once in pursuit of the enemy by some route.

Edwin M. Stanton, Sec. of War.

My preparations were at once begun in accordance with these directions, and on the 16th of March the following instructions were sent to Generals Banks and Wadsworth:

Headq's, Army of the Potomac, March 16 '62.
Sir,—You will post your command in the vicinity of Manassas, intrench yourself strongly, and throw cavalry pickets well out to the front.

Your first care will be the rebuilding of the railway from Washington to Manassas and to Strasburg, in order to open your communications with the Valley of the Shenandoah. As soon as Manassas Gap Railway is in running order intrench a brigade of infantry, &c., four regiments, with two batteries, at or near the point where the railway crosses the Shenandoah. Something like two regiments of cavalry should be left in that vicinity to occupy Winchester, and thoroughly scour the country south of the railway and up the Shenandoah Valley as well as through Chester Gap, which might perhaps, be advantageously occupied by a detachment of infantry well intrenched. Block houses should be built at all the railway bridges. Occupy by grand guards Warrenton Junction or Warrenton itself, and also some little more advanced point on the Orange and Alexandria Railway, as soon as the railway bridge is repaired.

Great activity should be observed by the cavalry. Besides the two regiments at Manassas another regiment of cavalry will be at your disposal, to scout towards the Occoquan, and probably a fourth towards Leesburg.

To recapitulate: The most important points which should engage your attention are as follows:

1st. A strong force, well intrenched, in the vicinity of Manassas, perhaps even Centerville, and another force, (a brigade), also well intrenched, near Strasburg.

2d. Block houses at the Railway bridges.

3d. Constant employment of the cavalry well to the front.

4th. Grand Guards at Warrenton Junction and in advance as far as the Rappahannock, if possible.

5th. Great care to be exercised to obtain full and early information as to the enemy.

6th. The general object is to cover the line of the Potomac and Washington.

The foregoing is communicated by command of Maj.-Gen. McClellan.

S. Williams, Assistant-Adjt.-Gen.
To Maj.-Gen. N. P. Banks,
Com'd'g 5th Corps Army of the Potomac.

Headq's, Army of the Potomac, March 16, '62.
Sir,—The command to which you have been assigned by instructions of the President, as Military Governor of the District of Columbia, embraces the geographical limits of the district, and will also include the city of Alexandria, the defensive works south of the Potomac from the Occoquan to Difficult Creek, and the post of Fort Washington.

I enclose a list of the troops, and of the defenses embraced in these limits.

General Banks will command at Manassas Junction, with the divisions of Williams and Shields, composing the 5th Corps, but you should, nevertheless, exercise vigilance in your front—carefully guard the approaches in that quarter, and maintain the duties of advanced guards. You will use the same precautions on either flank.

All troops not actually needed for the police of Washington and Georgetown, for the garrisons north of the Potomac, and for other indicated special duties, should be moved to the south side of the river.

In the centre of your front you should post the main body of your troops, and proper proportions at suitable distances towards your right and left flanks. Careful patrols will be made, in order thoroughly to scour the country in front from right to left.

It is specially enjoined upon you to maintain the forts and their armaments in the best possible order, to look carefully to the instruction and discipline of their garrisons, as well as all other troops under your command, and by frequent and rigid inspections to insure the attainment of these ends.

The care of the railways, canals, depots, bridges and ferries, within the above-named limits, will devolve upon you, and you are to insure their security and provide for their protection by every means in your power. You will also protect the depots of the public stores, and transmit the stores to troops in active service.

By means of patrols you will thoroughly scour the neighboring country, south of the eastern branch, and also on your right, and you will use every possible precaution to intercept mails, goods, and persons passing unauthorized to the enemy's lines. The necessity of maintaining good order within your limits, and especially in the capital of the nation, cannot be too strongly enforced.

You will forward and facilitate the movement of all troops destined for the active part of the army of the Potomac, and especially the transit of detachments to their proper regiments and corps

The charge of the new troops arriving in Washington, and all troops temporarily there, will devolve upon you. You will form them into provisional brigades, promote their instruction and discipline, and facilitate their equipment.

Report all arrivals of troops—their strength, composition and equipment—by every opportunity.

Besides the regular reports and returns, which you will be required to render to the adjutant-general of the army, you will make to these headquarters a consolidated report of your command every Sunday morning, and monthly returns on the last day of each month.

The foregoing instructions are communicated by command of Maj.-Gen. McClellan

S. WILLIAMS, Assistant Adgt.-Gen.
To Brig.-Gen J. S. Wadsworth,
Military Gov. of the District of Columbia

THE PLAN OF CAMPAIGN ON THE PENINSULA

Headquarters, Army of the Potomac,
Theological Seminary, Va, March 19, 1862.
Hon. E. M. Stanton, Secretary of War:

SIR,—I have the honor to submit the following notes on the proposed operations of the active portion of the army of the Potomac.

The proposed plan of campaign is to assume Fort Monroe as the first base of operations, taking the line by Yorktown and West Point upon Richmond as the line of operations, Richmond being the objective point. It is assumed that the fall of Richmond involves that of Norfolk and the whole of Virginia, also that we shall fight a decisive battle between West Point and Richmond, to give which battle the rebels will concentrate all their available forces, understanding, as they will, that it involves the fate of their cause. It therefore follows:

1st. That we should collect all our available forces and operate upon adjacent lines, maintaining perfect communication between our lines.

2d. That no time should be lost in reaching the field of battle.

The advantages of the Peninsula between the York and James Rivers are too obvious to need explanation. It is also clear that West Point should as soon as possible be reached and be our main depot, that we may have the shortest line of land transportation for our supplies and the use of the York River.

There are two methods of reaching this point.

1st. By moving directly from Fort Monroe as a base, and trusting to the roads for our supplies, at the same time landing a strong corps as near Yorktown as possible, in order to turn the rebel lines of defense south of Yorktown, then to reduce Yorktown and Gloucester, by a siege in all probability, involving a delay of weeks perhaps.

2d. To make a combined naval and land attack upon Yorktown, the first object of the campaign. This leads to the most rapid and decisive results. To accomplish this the navy should at once concentrate upon the York River all their available and most powerful batteries. Its reduction should not, in that case, require many hours. A strong corps would be pushed up the York, under cover of the navy, directly upon West Point, immediately upon the fall of Yorktown and we could at once establish our new base of operations at a distance of some twenty-five miles from Richmond, with every facility for developing and bringing into play the whole of our available force on either or both banks of the James.

It is impossible to urge too strongly the absolute necessity of the co-operation of the navy, as a part of this programme; without it the operations may be prolonged for many weeks, and we may be forced to carry in front several strong positions, which, by their aid, could be turned without serious loss of either time or men.

It is also of first importance to bear in mind the fact already alluded to, that the capture of Richmond necessarily involves the prompt fall of Norfolk, while an operation against Norfolk, if successful, as the beginning of the campaign, facilitates the reduction of Richmond merely by the demoralization of the rebel troops involved, and that after the fall of Norfolk we should be obliged to undertake the capture of Richmond by the same means which would have accomplished it in the beginning, having meanwhile afforded the rebels ample time to perfect their defensive arrangements, for they could well know from the moment the army of the Potomac changed its base to Fort Monroe that Richmond must be its ultimate object.

It may be summed up in few words that, for the prompt success of this campaign, it is absolutely necessary that the navy should at once throw its whole available force, its most powerful vessels, against Yorktown. There is the most important point—there the knot to be cut. An immediate decison upon the subject matter of this communication is highly desirable, and seems called for by the exigencies of the occasion.

I am, sir, very respectfully, your ob't serv't.
GEO. B. McCLELLAN, Major General.

A REDUCTION OF FORCE

In the meantime the troops destined to form the active army were collected in camps convenient to the points of embarkation, and every preparation made to embark them as rapidly as possible, when the transports were ready.

A few days before sailing for Fort Monroe, while still encamped near Alexandria, I met the President by appointment, on a steamer. He then informed me that he had been strongly pressed to take General Blenker's division from my command and give it to General Fremont. His Excellency was good enough to suggest several reasons for not taking Blenker's division from me. I assented to the force of his suggestions, and was extremely gratified by his decision to allow the division to remain with the army of the Potomac. It was, therefore, with surprise that I received on the 31st the following note,

Exec. Mansion, Washington, March 31, '62
Maj.-Gen. McClellan,

MY DEAR SIR.—This morning I felt constrained to order Blenker's division to Fremont, and I will write this to assure you that I did so with great pain, understanding that you would wish it otherwise. If you could know the full pressure of the case, I am confident you would justify it, even beyond a mere acknowledgement, that the commander-in-chief may order what he pleases.

Yours very truly, A. LINCOLN

To this, I replied in substance, that I regretted the order, and could ill-afford to lose 10,000 troops which had been counted upon in forming my plan of campaign, but as there was no remedy I would yield and do the best I could without them. In a conversation with the President a few hours afterwards, I repeated verbally the same thing, and expressed my regret that Blenker's division had been given to Fremont, from any "pressure" other than the requirements of the national exigency. I was partially relieved, however, by the President's positive and emphatic assurance that I might have confident that no more troops beyond these 10,000 should, in any event, be taken from me, or in any way detached from my command.

OPERATIONS IN THE SHENANDOAH VALLEY.

At the time of the evacuation of Manassas by the enemy, Jackson was at Winchester, our forces occupying Charlestown, and Shield's reaching Bunker Hill on the 11th. On the morning of the 12th, a brigade of Gen. Bank's troops, under Gen. Hamilton, entered Winchester, the enemy having left at 5 o'clock the evening before, his rear guard of cavalry leaving an hour before our advance entered the place. The enemy having made his preparations for evacuation some days before, it was not possible to intercept his retreat. On the 13th, the mass of Banks' corps was concentrated in the immediate vicinity of Winchester, the enemy being in the rear of Strasburg. On the 19th Gen. Shields occupied Strasburg, driving the enemy twenty miles south, to Mount Jackson.

On the 20th the first division of Banks' corps, commenced its movement towards Manassas, in compliance with my letter of instructions of the 16th.

Jackson probably received information of this movement, and supposed that no force of any consequence was left in the vicinity of Winchester, and upon the falling back of Shields to that place on the 20th, for the purpose of enticing Jackson in pursuit, the latter promptly followed, whereupon ensued a skirmish on the 22d, in which Gen. Shields was wounded, and an affair at Winchester on the 23d, resulting in the defeat of Jackson, who was pursued as rapidly as the exhaustion of our troops, and the difficulty of obtaining supplies, permitted. It is presumed that the full reports of the battle of Winchester, were forwarded direct to the War Department by Gen. Banks.

It being now clear that the enemy had no intention of returning by the Manassas route, the following letter of April 1st, was written to Gen. Banks.

Head-Quarters, Army of the Potomac, on Board the Commodore, April 1, 1862
Maj.-Gen. N. P. Banks, Com'ng Fifth Corps,—

GENERAL.—The change in affairs in the valley of the Shenandoah, has rendered necessary a corresponding departure, temporarily at least, from the plan we some days since agreed upon.

In my arrangements, I assume you have with you a force amply sufficient to drive Jackson before you, provided he is not reinforced largely. I also assume that you may find it impossible to detach anything towards Manassas for some days, probably not until the operations of the main army have drawn all the rebel force toward Richmond.

You are aware that General Sumner has for some days been at Manassas Junction, with two divisions of infantry, six batteries, and two regiments of cavalry, and that a reconnoissance to the Rappahannock, forced the enemy to destroy the railroad bridge at Rappahannock Station, on the Orange and Alexandria Railroad. Since that time our cavalry have found nothing on this side of the Rappahannock in that direction, and it seems clear that we have no reason to fear any return of the rebels in that quarter. Their movements near Fredericksburg, also indicate a final abandonment of that neighborhood. I doubt whether Johnson will now reinforce Jackson, with a view of offensive operations. The time is probably passed when he could have gained anything by doing so. I have ordered in one of Sumner's divisions (that of Richardson, late Sumner's) to Alexandria for embarkation, Blenker's has been detached from the Army of the Potomac, and ordered to report to General Fremont.

Abercrombie is probably at Warrenton Junction to-day; Geary is at White Plains.

Two regiments of cavalry have been ordered out, and are now on their way to relieve the two regiments of Sumner.

Four thousand infantry, and one battery leave Washington at once for Manassas. Some 3,000 more will move in one or two days, and soon after some 3,000 additional.

I will order Blenker to march on Strasburg, and to report to you for temporary duty, so that, should you find a large force in your front, you can avail yourself of his aid. As soon as possible, please direct him on Winchester, thence to report to the adjutant-general of the army for orders, but keep him until you are sure what you have in front.

In regard to your own movements, the most important thing at present is to throw Jackson well back, and then to assume such a position as to enable you to prevent his return. As soon as the railway communications are re-established, it will be, probably, important and advisable to move on Staunton, but this would require secure communications, and a force of from 25,000 to 30,000 for active operations. It should also be nearly coincident with my own move on Richmond; at all events, not so long before it as to enable the rebels to concentrate on you, and then return on me. I fear that you cannot be ready in time, although it may come in very well with a force less than that I have mentioned, after the main battle near Richmond. When General Sumner leaves Warrenton Junction, General Abercrombie will be placed in immediate command of Manassas and Warrenton Junction, under your general orders. Please inform me frequently, by telegraph, and otherwise, as to the state of things in your front.

I am very truly yours,
GEO. B. MCCLELLAN, Maj.-Gen Com'g

P.S.—From what I have just learned it would seem that the two regiments of cavalry intended for Warrenton Junction have gone to Harper's Ferry. Of the four additional regiments placed under your orders, two should, as promptly as possible, move by the shortest route on Warrenton Junction. I am, sir, very respectfully, Your obedient servant,
GEO. B. MCCLELLAN, Maj.-Gen Com'g

This letter needs no further explanation than to say that it was my intention, had the operations in that quarter remained under my charge, either to have resumed the defensive positions marked out in the letter of March 16, or to have advanced General Banks upon Staunton, as might in the progress of events seem advisable. It is to be remembered that when I wrote the preceding and following letters of April 1, I had no expectation of being relieved from the charge of the operations in the Shenandoah Valley and in front of Washington, the President's War Order No. 3 giving no intimation of such an intention; and that, so far as reference was made to final operations after driving Jackson back and taking such a position as to prevent his return, no positive orders were given in the letter—the matter being left for future consideration, when the proper time arrived for a decision.

TROOPS LEFT IN AND NEAR WASHINGTON.

From the following letter to the adjutant-general, dated April 1, 1862, it will be seen that I left for the defense of the national capital and its approaches, when I sailed for the Peninsula, 73,456 men, with 109 pieces of light artillery, including the 32 pieces in Washington alluded to, but not enumerated in my letter to the adjutant-general. It will also be seen that I recommended other available troops in New York (more than 4,000) to be at once ordered forward to reinforce them.

Headquarters, Army of the Potomac,
Steamer Commodore, April 1, 1862.
Brig.-Gen L Thomas, Adjutant-General U S A.

GENERAL—I have to request that you will lay the following communication before the Hon Secretary of War.

The approximate numbers and positions of the troops left near and in rear of the Potomac is as follows:—

Gen. Dix has, after guarding the railroads under his charge, sufficient to give him 5,000 for the defense of Baltimore, and 1,988 available for the eastern shore, Annapolis, &c. Fort Delaware is very well garrisoned by about 400 men.

The garrisons of the forts around Washington amount to 10,600 men, other disposable troops now with Gen Wadsworth being about 11,400 men.

The troops employed in guarding the various railways in Maryland amount to some 3,359 men. These it is designed to relieve, being old regiments, by dismounted cavalry, and to send forward to Manassas.

Gen. Abercrombie occupies Warrenton with a force which including Col. Geary at White Plains and the cavalry to be at his disposal, will amount to some 7,780 men, with 12 pieces of artillery.

I have the honor to request that all the troops organized for service in Pennsylvania and New York, and in any of the Eastern States, may be ordered to Washington. I learn from Gov. Curtin that there are some 3,500 men now ready in Pennsylvania. This force I should be glad to have sent to Manassas. Four thousand men from Gen. Wadsworth I desire to be ordered to Manassas. These troops, with the railroad guards above alluded to, will make up a force under the command of Gen Abercrombie of something like 18,639 men.

It is my design to push Gen. Blenker's division from Warrenton upon Strasburg. He should remain at Strasburg long enough to allow matters to assume a definite form in that region, before proceeding to his ultimate destination.

The troops in the valley of the Shenandoah will thus be, including Blenker's division, 10,028 strong, with 24 pieces of artillery, Banks' 5th Corps, which embraces the command of Gen. Shields, 19,687 strong, with 41 guns—some 3,652 disposable cavalry and the railroad guards, about 2,100 men—amount to about 35,467 men.

It is designed to relieve Gen Hooker by one regiment, say 850 men, being, with some 500 cavalry, 1,350 men on the lower Potomac. To recapitulate:—

At Warrenton there is to be,	7,780 men
At Manassas, say	10,859 "
In the valley of the Shenandoah,	35,167 "
On the lower Potomac,	1,450 "
In all,	55,456 "

There would thus be left for the garrisons and the front of Washington under Gen Wadsworth some 18,000 men, inclusive of the batteries under instruction

The troops organizing or ready for service in New York I learn will probably number more than four thousand These should be assembled at Washington, subject to disposition where their services may be most required I am, very respectfully, your obedient servant, Geo B McClellan, Maj-Gen Com'g.

The following letter from Gen Barry shows that thirty-two (32) field-guns with men, horses and components, were also left in Washington City when the army sailed These were the batteries under instruction referred to above

Headquarters, Inspector of Artillery,
Washington, Dec 16, 1862

Maj-Gen McClellan, U S A

General —It having been stated in various public prints, and in a speech of Senator Chandler, of Michigan, in his place in the U S Senate, quoting what he stated to be a portion of the testimony of Brig-Gen Wadsworth, military governor of Washington, before the Joint Senate and House Committee, on the subject of the war, that Maj-Gen McClellan had left an insufficient force for the defence of Washington, and "*not a gun on wheels*"

I have to contradict this charge as follows:

From official reports made at the time to me (the chief of artillery of the army of the Potomac) and now in my possession, by the commanding officer of the light artillery troops left in camp in the city of Washington by your order, it appears that the following named field-officers were left,

Battery "C" 1st N.Y. Artillery, Capt Barnes, 2 guns; battery "K" 1st N Y Artillery, Capt Crounse, 6 guns; battery "L" 2d N Y Artillery, Capt Robinson, 6 guns; 9th N Y independant battery, Capt Morozowi, 6 guns; 16th N Y independent battery, Capt Locke; battery "A" 2d battery N Y. Artillery, Capt Hogan, 6 guns; battery "B" 2d battery, N Y Artillery, Capt McMahon, 6 guns, total of batteries, 32 guns

With the exception of a few horses, which could have been obtained from the quartermaster's department in a few hours, the batteries were all fit for immediate service, excepting the 16th N. Y. battery, which, having been previously ordered on Gen. Wadsworth's application, to report to him for special service, was unequipped with either guns or horses

I am gen , very respectfully, your ob't sev't,
Wm F Barry, B-G Inspec of Art, U S Army

It is true that Blenker's division, which is included in the forces enumerated by me, was under orders to reinforce Gen Fremont, but the following dispatch from the Secretary of War, dated March 31, 1862, will show that I was authorized to detain him at Strasburg until matters assumed a definite form in that region before proceeding to his ultimate destination, in other words until Jackson was disposed of, and had he been detained there, instead of moving on to Harper's Ferry and Franklin, with other orders, it is probable that Gen Banks would have defeated Jackson, instead of being himself obliged subsequently to retreat to Williamsport

War Dept., Washington, D C, March 31, '62.
Maj-Gen McClellan.

The order in respect to Blenker is not designed to hinder or delay the movement of Richardson or any other force He can remain wherever you desire him so long as required for your movements, and in any position you desire The order is simply to place him in position for reinforcing Fremont, as soon as your dispositions will permit, and he may go to Harper's Ferry, by such route and at such time, as you shall direct—state your own wishes as to the movement—when and how it shall be made

Edwin M Stanton, Secretary of War

Without including Gen Blenker's division, there were left 67,428 men, and 85 pieces of light artillery, which, under existing circumstances, I deemed more than adequate to insure the perfect security of Washington against any force the enemy could bring against it, for the following reasons:

The light troops I had thrown forward under Gen. Stoneman, in pursuit of the rebel army, after the evacuation of Manassas and Centreville, had driven their rear guard across Cedar Run, and subsequent expeditions from Sumner's corps had forced them beyond the Rappahannock; they had destroyed all the railway bridges behind them, thereby indicating that they did not intend to return over that route. Indeed, if they had attempted such a movement, their progress must have been slow and difficult, as it would have involved the reconstruction of the bridges, and if my orders for keeping numerous cavalry patrols well out to the front, to give timely notice of any approach of the enemy, had been strictly enforced, (and I left seven regiments of cavalry for this express purpose,) they could not, by any possibility have reached Washington before there would have been ample time to concentrate the entire forces left for its defense, as well as those at Baltimore, at any necessary point

It was clear to my mind, as I reiterated to the authorities, that the movement of the army to the Peninsula, would have the effect to draw off the rebel army from Manassas to the defense of their capital, and thus free Washington from menace This opinion was confirmed the moment the movement commenced or rather as soon as the enemy became aware of our intentions, for, with the exception of Jackson's force of some 15,000, which his instructions show to have been intended to operate in such way as to prevent McDowell's corps from being sent to reinforce me, no rebel force of any magnitude made its appearance in front of Washington during the progress of our operations on the Peninsula, nor until the order was given for my return from Harrison's Landing was Washington again threatened.

Surrounded as Washington was with numerous and strong fortifications well garrisoned, it was manifest that the enemy could not afford to detach from his main army a force sufficient to assail them.

It is proper to remark, that just previous to my departure for Fort Monroe, I sent my chief-of-staff to Gen Hitchcock, who at that time held staff relations with his excellency the President and the Secretary of War, to submit to him a list of the troops I proposed to leave for the defense of Washington, and the positions in which I designed posting them. Gen Hitchcock, after glancing his eye over the list, observed that he was not the judge of what was required for defending the capital, that Gen McClellan's position was such as to enable him to understand the subject much better than he did, and he presumed that if the force designated was in his judgment sufficient, nothing more would be required. He was then told by the chief-of-staff that I would be glad to have his opinion, as an old and experienced officer. To this he replied, that as I had the entire control of the defenses for a long time, I was the best judge of what was needed, and he declined to give any other expression of opinion at that time.

On the 2d of April, the day following my departure for Fort Monroe, Generals Hitchcock and Thomas were directed by the Secretary of War to examine and report whether the President's instructions to me of March 8th and 13th had been complied with. On the same day their report was submitted and their decision was,

"That the requirements of the President, that this city (Washington) shall be left entirely secure, has not been fully complied with."

The President, in his letter to me on the 6th of April, says:

"And now allow me to ask, do you really think I should permit the line from Richmond, via Manassas Junction, to this city to be entirely open, except what resistance could be presented by less than 20,000 unorganized troops?"

In the report of Generals Hitchcock and Thomas, alluded to, it is acknowledged that there was no danger of an attack from the direction of Manassas in these words.

"In regard to occupying Manassas Junction, as the enemy have destroyed the railroads leading to it, it may be fair to assume that they have no intention of returning for the re-occupation of their late position, and therefore no large force would be necessary to hold that position."

That as remarked before, was precisely the view I took of it, and this was enforced by the subsequent movements of the enemy.

In another paragraph of the report, it is stated that 55,000 men was the number considered adequate for the defense of the capital. That Gen. McClellan, in his enumeration of the forces left, had included Banks' army corps, operating in the Shenandoah Valley, but whether this corps should be regarded as available for the protection of Washington, they decline to express an opinion.

At the time this report was made, the only enemy on any approach to Washington, was Jackson's force, in front of Banks in the Shenandoah Valley, with the Manassas Gap Railroad leading from this valley to Washington, and it will be admitted, I presume, that Banks occupying the Shenandoah Valley, was in the best position to defend, not only that approach to Washington, but the roads to Harper's Ferry and above. The numbers of troops left by me for the defenses of Washington, as given in my letter to the adjutant-general, were taken from the latest official returns of that date, and these, of course, constitute the most trustworthy and authentic source, from which such information could be obtained.

Another statement made by General Hitchcock, before the "Committee on the Conduct of the War," in reference to this same order, should be noticed. He was asked the following question

"Do you understand now that the movement made by Gen McClellan to Fort Monroe, and up the York River, was in compliance with the recommendation of the council of generals commanding corps, and held at Fairfax Court House, on the 13th of March last, or in violation of it?"

To which he replied as follows:

"I have considered, and do now consider that, it was in violation of the recommendation of that council, in two important particulars, one particular, being that portion of this report which represents the council as agreeing to the expedition by way of the Peninsula, *provided*, the rebel steamer Merrimac could first be neutralized. That important provision Gen McClellan disregarded."

* * * * *

The second particular alluded to by General Hitchcock, was in reference to the troops left for the defense of Washington, which has been disposed of above.

In regard to the steamer Merrimac I have also stated, that so far as our operations on York River were concerned, the power of this vessel was neutralized. I now proceed to give some of the evidence which influenced me in coming to that conclusion.

Previous to our departure for the Peninsula, Mr. Watson, Assistant Secretary of War, was sent by the President to Fort Monroe, to consult with Flag Officer Goldsborough upon this subject. The result of that consultation is contained in the following extract from the evidence of Admiral Goldsborough before the "Committee on the Conduct of the War" viz "I told Mr.

Watson, Assistant-Secretary of War, that the President might make his mind perfectly easy about the Merrimac going up York River, that she could never get there, for I had ample means to prevent that."

Captain G. V. Fox, Assistant-Secretary of the Navy, testifies before the Committee as follows:

"Gen. McClellan expected the Navy to neutralize the Merrimac, and I promised that it should be done."

Gen. Keyes, commanding 4th Army Corps, testifies as follows before the Committee:

"During the time that the subject of the change of base was discussed, I had refused to consent to the Peninsula line of operations, until I had sent word to the Navy Department and asked two questions. 1st. Whether the Merrimac was certainly neutralized or not? 2d. Whether the navy was in a condition to co-operate efficiently with the army, to break through between Yorktown and Gloucester Point? To both of these questions answers were returned in the affirmative, that is, the Merrimac was neutralized, and the navy was in a condition to cooperate efficiently to break through between Yorktown and Gloucester Point."

ORDERS FOR THE FORTIFICATION OF MANASSAS JUNCTION

Before starting for the Peninsula, I instructed Lieut.-Col. B. S. Alexander, of the U. S. corps of engineers, to visit Manassas Junction and its vicinity for the purpose of determining upon the defensive works necessary to enable us to hold that place with a small force. The accompanying letters from Col. Alexander will show what steps were taken by him to carry into effect this important order.

I regret to say that those who succeeded me in command of the region in front of Washington, whatever were the fears for its safety, did not deem it necessary to carry out my plans and instructions to him.

Had Manassas been placed in condition for a strong defense and its communications secured as recommended by Col. Alexander, the result of Gen. Pope's campaign would probably have been different.

Washington, D. C., April 2, 1862.

Sir,—You will proceed to Manassas at as early a moment as practicable and mark on the ground the works for the defense of that place, on the positions which I indicated to you yesterday. You will find two carpenters experienced in this kind of work ready to accompany you, by calling on Mr. Dougherty, the master carpenter of the treasury Extension.

The general idea of the defense of this position is to occupy the fringe of elevations, which lies about half way between Manassas depot and the junction of the railroad, with a series of works, open to the rear so that they may be commanded by the work hereafter to be described.

There will be at least four of these works, three of them being on the left of the railroad leading from Alexandria, at the positions occupied by the enemy's works. The other on the right of this road on the position we examined yesterday. The works of the enemy to the north of this latter position, numbered Nos. 1 and 2 on Lieut. Comstock's sketch, may also form part of the front line of our defenses; but the sides of these works, looking towards Manassas station should be leveled, so that the interior of the works may be seen from the latter position.

Embrasures should be arranged in all these works for *field* artillery. The approaches should be such, that a battery can drive into the works. The number of embrasures in each battery will depend upon its size and the ground to be commanded. It is supposed that there will be from four to eight embrasures in each battery.

The other works of the enemy looking towards the east and south, may be strengthened so as to afford sufficient defense in these directions. The work, No. 3, on Lieut. Comstock's sketch may be also strengthened and arranged for field artillery when time will permit. This work is in a good position to cover a retreat, which would be made down the valley in which the railroad runs towards Bull Run.

At Manassas station there should be a fort constructed. The railroad will pass through this fort, and the depot, if one should be built, should be placed in its rear. This latter work should be regarded as the key of the position. It should be as large as the nature of the ground will permit.

By going down the slopes, which are not steep, it may be made large enough to accommodate 2,000 or 3,000 men. The top of the position need not be cut away, it will be better to throw up the earth into a large traverse which may also be a bomb proof. Its profile should be strong, and its ditches should be flanked. It should receive a heavy armament of 24 or 32 pounders, with some rifled (Parrot) 20 or 30 pounders. Its guns should command all the exterior works, so that these works could be of no use to the enemy, should he take them. In accommodating the fort to the ground, this consideration should not be lost sight of.

After tracing these works on the ground, you will make a sketch embracing the whole of them, showing their relative positions and size. This sketch should embrace the junction of the railroads and the ground for some distance around the mainwork. It need not be made with extreme accuracy. The distances may be paced or measured with a tape-line. The bearings may be taken by compass.

Having located the works and prepared your sketch, you will report to Capt. Frederick E. Prime of the corps of engineers, who will furnish you the means of construction.

Very respectfully, your obedient servant,

B. S. ALEXANDER Lt.-Col. A. D. C.

To Capt. Fred. R. Munther *Present*

Washington, D. C., April 6, 1862.

Brig-Gen J. G. Barnard,

Chief Engineer army of the Potomac

Sir,—I enclose you herewith a copy of the

instructions which I gave to Capt. Munther, in reference to the defenses of Manassas.

As there has been a new department created (that of the Rappahannock) it is possible that you and I, as well as Gen McClellan, are relieved from the further consideration of this subject at the present time.

I will, however, state for your information, should the subject ever come before you again, that in my opinion the communication with Manassas by land should be secured.

To effect this in the best manner, so far as my observations extended, I think the bridge over Bull Run, near Union Mills and just above the railroad bridge, should be rebuilt or thoroughly repaired, and that a small work, or perhaps two or three open batteries, should be erected on the adjacent heights, to protect it as well as the railroad bridge

The communication by land would then be through or near Centreville, over the road used by the enemy.

I write this for fear something should detain me here, but I hope to leave here to join you to-morrow. My health is much improved

Very respectfully, your obedient servant,
B S ALEXANDER, Lt.-Col, A D C

I may be permitted also to mention that the plans also (unexecuted by my successor) indicated by my letter of instructions to General Banks dated March 16, 1862, for intrenching Chester Gap and the point where the Manassas Gap Railroad crosses the Shenandoah, were for the purpose of preventing even the attempt at such a raid as that of Jackson in the month of May following.

MILITARY INCIDENTS OF THE FIRST PERIOD

Before taking up the history of the embarkation and the Peninsular campaign, I should remark that during the fall and winter of 1861-2, while the army of the Potomac was in position in front of Washington, reconnoissances were made from time to time, and skirmishes frequently occurred, which were of great importance in the education of the troops, accustoming them to the presence of the enemy, and giving them confidence under fire. There were many instances of individual gallantry displayed in these affairs; the reports of most of them will be found among the documents which accompany this report.

One of the most brilliant of these affairs was that which took place at Dramsville on Dec 20, 1861, when the 3d brigade of McCall's Division, under Brig.-Gen. E O. C Ord, with Easton's Battery, routed and pursued four regiments of infantry, and a battery of six pieces.

The operations of Brig.-Gen. F. W. Lander on the Upper Potomac during the months of January and February, 1862, illustrated the attempts of General Jackson against the Ohio Railroad Cumberland, &c., and obliged him to fall back to Winchester His constitution was impaired by the hardships he had experienced, and on the 2d of March the fearless General Lander expired, a victim to the excessive fatigues of the campaign.

SECOND PERIOD
PART I
THE MOVEMENT TO THE PENINSULA.

The council, composed of four corps commanders, organized by the President of the United States, at its meeting on the 13th of March, adopted Fort Monroe as the base of operations for the movement of the army of the Potomac upon Richmond.

For the prompt and successful execution of the projected operation, it was regarded by all as necessary that the whole of the four corps should be employed, with at least the addition of ten thousand men drawn from the forces in the vicinity of Fortress Monroe; that position and its dependencies being regarded as amply protected by the naval force in its neighborhood, and the advance of the main army up the Peninsula, so that it could be safely left with a small garrison.

In addition to the land forces, the co-operation of the navy was desired in the projected attack upon the batteries at Yorktown and Gloucester, as well as in controlling the York and James Rivers for the protection of our flanks, and the use of transports, bringing supplies to the army. With these expectations, and for reasons stated elsewhere in this report, my original plan of moving by Urbana and West Point was abandoned, and the line with Fortress Monroe as a base adopted In the arrangements for the transportation of the army to the Peninsula by water, the vessels were originally ordered to rendezvous mainly at Annapolis, but upon the evacuation of Manassas and the batteries of the lower Potomac by the enemy, it became more convenient to embark the troops and material at Alexandria, and orders to that effect were at once given.

In making the preliminary arrangements for the movement, it was determined that the First Corps (Gen McDowell's) should move as a unit, first, and effect a landing either at the *Sand-Box*, some four miles south of Yorktown in order to turn all the enemy's defenses at Ship Point, Howard's Bridge, Big Bethel, etc, or else, should existing circumstances render it preferable, land on the Gloucester side of York River, and move on West Point.

The transports, however, arrived slowly and few at a time. In order, therefore, to expedite matters, I decided to embark the army by divisions as transports arrived, keeping army corps together as much as possible, and to collect the troops at Fortress Monroe In determining the order of embarkation, convenience and expedition were especially consulted, except that the First Corps was to be embarked last, as I intended to move it in mass to its point of disembarkation, and to land it on either bank of the York, as might then be determined

On the 17th of March, Hamilton's division, the 3d corps embarked at Alexandria, and proceeded to Fort Monroe, with the following orders.

Washington, D C., March 17, 1862.
Gen C S. Hamilton, Com'dg Division:

You will, on your arrival at Fort Monroe, report to Gen Wool, and request him to assign you ground for encamping your division. You will remain at Fort Monroe until further orders from Gen McClellan. Should Gen Wool require the services of your division in repelling an attack you will please obey his orders, and use every effort to carry out his views.

R. B. MARCY, Chief of-Staff

On the 22d of March, as soon as transportation was ready, Gen Fitz John Porter's division of the same corps embarked. Gen. Heintzelman was ordered to accompany it, under the following instructions.

Headquarters, Army of the Potomac,
Summary, March 22, 1862
Brig-Gen S P Heintzelman, Com'g 3d Corps:

GENERAL.—Upon the disembarkation of Porter's division at Fort Monroe, I have to request that you will move your two divisions (Porter's and Hamilton's) some three or four miles out from the fort to find good camping places where wood and water can be readily obtained, and where your position will be good in a defensive point of view. You may find it advisable to place one division on or near the road leading to Yorktown from Newport News, the other upon that leading to Yorktown direct from Fort Monroe.

If you find that the nature of the country will permit easy communication and mutual support between the two divisions, it will be best to place one on each road. It will be best to remain pretty near the fort for the present, in order to give the impression that our object is to attack Norfolk rather than Yorktown. You will do well, however, to push strong reconnoissances well to the front, to ascertain the position of the enemy and his pickets. I will, as soon as possible, reinforce you by the 3d division of your corps, and it is probable that a part or the whole of the 4th corps will also move from Fort Monroe; this will probably be determined before your disembarkation is completed, and you will be informed accordingly.

My desire would be to make no important move in advance until you are fully prepared to follow it up, and give the enemy no time to recover.

The quartermasters of your corps will receive detailed instructions, in regard to land transportation, from Gen Van Vliet.

It will be advisable to mobilize your corps with the least possible delay and have it prepared for an advance. I have directed extra clothing, ammunition, etc. to be sent to Fort Monroe, so that all deficiencies may be supplied without delay.

Please report to me frequently and fully the condition of things on the new field of operations and whatever intelligence you gain as to the enemy.

Engage guides in sufficient numbers at once, and endeavor to send out spies. I am very truly yours, GEO B McCLELLAN, Maj.-Gen Com'g

The remaining divisions embarked as rapidly as transports could be supplied.

On the 1st of April I embarked, with the headquarters on the steamer Commodore, and reached Fort Monroe on the afternoon of the 2d.

In consequence of the delay in the arrival of the horse transports at Alexandria, but a small portion of the cavalry had arrived, and the artillery reserve had not yet completed its disembarkation.

I found there the 3d Pennsylvania Cavalry, and the 5th Regular Cavalry; the 2d Regular Cavalry and a portion of the 1st had arrived, but not disembarked. So few wagons had arrived that it was not possible to move Casey's division at all for several days, while the other divisions were obliged to move with scant supplies.

As to the force and position of the enemy, the information then in our possession was vague and untrustworthy. Much of it was obtained from the staff officers of General Wool, and was simply to the effect that Yorktown was surrounded by a continuous line of earthworks, with strong water batteries on the York River, and garrisoned by not less than 15,000 troops, under the command of Gen J. B Magruder. Maps which had been prepared by the Topographical Engineers under Gen Wool's command were furnished me, in which, the Warwick River was represented as flowing parallel to, but not crossing the road from Newport News to Williamsburg, making the so-called Mulberry Island a real island, and we had no information as to the true course of the Warwick *across* the Peninsula, nor of the formidable line of works which it covered.

Information which I had collected during the winter placed Gen Magruder's command at from 15,000 to 20,000 men, independently of General Huger's force at Norfolk estimated at about 15,000. It was also known that there were strong defensive works at or near Williamsburg.

Knowing that Gen Huger could easily spare some troops to reinforce Yorktown, that he had indeed done so, and that Johnston's army of Manassas could be brought rapidly by the James and York rivers to the same point, I proceeded to invest that town without delay.

The accompanying map of Colonel Cram, United States Topographical Engineers attached to Gen Wool's staff given to me as the result of several months' labors, indicated the feasibility of the design. It was also an object of primary importance to reach the vicinity of Yorktown before the enemy was reinforced sufficiently to enable him to hold in force his works at Big Bethel, Howard's Bridge, Ship Point, etc., on the road from Newport News. This was the more urgent as it was now evident that some days must elapse before the 1st corps could arrive.

Everything possible was done to hasten the disembarkation of the cavalry, artillery and wagons in the harbor, and on the 3d the orders of march were given for the following day.

There were at Fort Monroe and its vicinity on the 3d, ready to move, two divisions of the 3d corps, two divisions of the 4th corps, one division of the 2d corps, and Syke's brigade of regular infantry, together with Hunt's artillery reserve, and the regiments of cavalry before named, in all about 58,000 men and 100 guns. Richardson's and Hooker's divisions of the 2d and 3d corps had not yet arrived, and Casey's division of the 4th corps was unable to move for want of wagons.

ANOTHER REDUCTION OF FORCE

Before I left Washington an order had been issued by the War Department, placing Fort Monroe and its dependencies under my control, and authorizing me to draw from the troops under General Wool, a division of about 10,000 men, which was to be assigned to the 1st corps. During the night of the 3d I received a telegram from the adjutant-general of the army, stating that, by the President's order, I was deprived of all control over Gen. Wool and the troops under his command, and forbidden to detach any of his troops without his sanction.

This order left me without any base of operations under my own control, and to this day I am ignorant of the causes which led to it.

CO-OPERATION OF THE NAVY

On my arrival at Fort Monroe the James River was declared, by the naval authorities, closed to the operations of their vessels, by the combined influence of the enemy's batteries on its banks and the confederate steamers Merrimac, Yorktown, Jamestown, and Teazer. Flag-officer Goldsborough, then in command of the United States squadron in Hampton Roads, regarded it (and, no doubt, justly) as his highest and most imperative duty to watch and neutralize the Merrimac, and as he designed using his most powerful vessels in a contest with her, he did not feel able to detach, for the assistance of the army, a suitable force to attack the water batteries at Yorktown and Gloucester. All this was contrary to what had been previously stated to me, and materially affected my plans. At no time during the operations against Yorktown was the navy prepared to lend us any material assistance in its reduction, until after our land batteries had partially silenced the works.

ADVANCE FROM FORT MONROE

I had hoped, let me say, by rapid movements, to drive before me or capture the enemy on the Peninsula, open the James River, and press on to Richmond before he should be materially reinforced from other portions of his territory. As the narrative proceeds, the causes will be developed which frustrated these apparently well-grounded expectations.

I determined, then, to move the two divisions of the 4th corps by the Newport News and Williamsburg road, to take up a position between Yorktown and Williamsburg, while the two divisions of the 3d corps moved direct from Fort Monroe upon Yorktown, the reserves moving so as to support either corps, as might prove necessary. I designed, should the works at Yorktown and Williamsburg offer a serious resistance, to land the 1st corps, reinforced, if necessary, on the left bank of the York, or on the Severn, to move it on Gloucester and West Point, in order to take in reverse whatever force the enemy might have on the Peninsula, and compel him to abandon his positions.

In the commencement of the movement from Fort Monroe, serious difficulties were encountered from the want of precise topographical information as to the country in advance.

Correct local maps were not to be found, and the country, though known in its general features, we found to be inaccurately described, in essential particulars, in the only maps and geographical memoirs or papers to which access could be had; erroneous courses to streams and roads were frequently given, and no dependence could be placed on the information thus derived. This difficulty has been found to exist with respect to most portions of the State of Virginia, through which my military operations have extended. Reconnoissances, frequently under fire, proved the only trustworthy sources of information. Negroes, however truthful their reports, possessed or were able to communicate, very little accurate and no comprehensive topographical information.

On the 3d the following orders were given for the movement of the 4th.

"Porter's and Hamilton's divisions, and Averill's cavalry of the 3d corps, and Sedgwick's division of the 2d corps, under Brig.-Gen. Heintzelman, commanding 3d corps, will move to-morrow in the following order: Porter's division, with Averill's cavalry at 6 A.M., over the New Market and New Bridges to Big Bethel and Howard's Bridge. The division will send forward to the batteries where the Ship Point road intersects the main Yorktown road, a sufficient force to hold that point, and cut off the garrison of the Ship Point batteries; the whole division may be used for this purpose, if necessary, and if possible the batteries should be occupied by our troops to-morrow. The portion of the division not necessary for this purpose will encamp at Howard's Bridge.

"Hamilton's division will march at 7 A.M., by the New Market Bridge, taking the direct road to Big Bethel, and will encamp on Howard's Creek.

"Sedgwick's division will march at 8 A.M., by the New Market Bridge, taking the direct road to Big Bethel, and will also encamp at Howard's Bridge.

"Brig.-Gen. Keyes, commanding 4th Corps, will move with Smith's and Couch's divisions at 6 A.M., (Smith's division in advance), by the James River road, the 5th Regular Cavalry, temporarily assigned to this corps, will move with Smith's division, which will encamp at Young's Mills, throwing forward at least one brigade to the road from Big Bethel to Warwick. Couch's division will encamp at Fisher's Creek.

"The reserve cavalry, artillery, and infantry will move at 8.30 A.M., by the New Market Bridge to Big Bethel, where it will encamp, on the march it will keep in the rear of Sedgwick's division."

The following is an extract from the orders issued on the 4th for the march of the 5th:

"The following movements of the army will be carried out to-morrow (5th)

"Gen Keyes will move forward Smith's division at 6 A M, via Warwick Court House, and the road leading near the Old Ship Yard, to the Half Way House on the Yorktown and Williamsburg road

Gen Couch's division will march at 6 A M, to close up on Gen Smith's division at the Half Way House

"Gen Keyes' command will occupy and hold the narrow dividing ridge near the Half Way House so as to prevent the escape of the garrison at Yorktown by land, and prevent reinforcements being thrown in

"Gen Heintzelman will move forward Gen. Porter's two brigades at 6 A M., upon the advanced guard when the entire division will advance to a point about two and three quarters miles from Yorktown, where the road turns abruptly to the north, and where a road comes in from Warwick Court House. Gen Hamilton's division will move at 6 A M and follow Gen Porter's division, camping as near it as possible. Gen Sedgwick's division will march at 5 A M, as far as the Warwick road which enters the main Yorktown road near Dr Power's house, and will await further orders

The reserves will march at 6 A.M, upon the main Yorktown road halting for further orders at Dr Power's house, the infantry leading, the artillery following next, and the cavalry in rear.

"Gen Sedgwick's division will, for the present, act with the reserve, and he will receive orders from head-quarters"

In giving these orders of march for the 4th and 5th, it was expected that there would be no serious opposition at Big Bethel, and that the advance of the 3d Corps beyond that point would force the enemy to evacuate the works at Young's Mills while our possession of the latter would make it necessary for him to abandon those at Howard's Bridge, and the advance thence on Yorktown would place Ship Point in our possession, together with its garrison, unless they abandoned it promptly. The result answered the expectation

During the afternoon of the 4th, Gen Keyes obtained information of the presence of some 5 000 to 8 000 of the enemy, in a strong position at Lee's Mills. the nature of that position in relation to the Warwick not being at that time understood, I instructed Gen. Keyes to attack and carry this position on coming in front of it.

Early in the afternoon of the 5th, the advance of each column was brought to a halt: that of Heintzelman (Porter's division) in front of Yorktown, after overcoming some resistance at Big Bethel and Howard's Bridge: that of Keyes (Smith's division) unexpectedly before the enemy's works at Lee's Mills, where the road from Newport News to Williamsburg crosses Warwick River. The progress of each column had been retarded by heavy rains on that day, which had made the roads almost impassable to the infantry of Keye's column and impracticable to all but a small portion of the artillery, while the ammunition provision, and forage could not be brought up at all.

When Gen Keyes's approached Lee's Mills his left flank was exposed to a sharp artillery fire from the further bank of the Warwick, and upon reaching the vicinity of the mill, he found it altogether stronger than was expected, unapproachable by reason of the Warwick River, and incapable of being carried by assault.

The troops composing the advance of each column were, during the afternoon under a warm artillery fire—the sharpshooters even of the right column being engaged, when covering reconnoissances

THE FIRST CORPS WITHDRAWN BY ORDER OF THE PRESIDENT

It was at this stage and moment of the campaign that the following telegram was sent to me:

Adjutant General's Office, April 4th, 1862.
GEN MCCLELLAN,—

By direction of the President Gen McDowell's army corps has been detached from the force under your immediate command; and the general is to report to the Secretary of War, letter by mail.

L THOMAS, Adjutant-General

The President having promised in our interview following his order of March 31st, withdrawing Blenker's division of 10,00 men from my command, that nothing of the sort should be repeated, that I might rest assured that the campaign should proceed with no further deductions from the force upon which its operations had been planned I may confess to having been shocked at this order, which, with that of the 31st ult., removed nearly 60,000 men from my command, and reduced my force by more than one-third after its task had been assigned, its operations planned, its fighting begun To me the blow was most discouraging It frustrated all my plans for impending operations It fell when I was too deeply committed to withdraw. It left me incapable of continuing operations which had been begun. It compelled the adoption of another, a different, and a less effective plan of campaign It made rapid and brilliant operations impossible. It was a fatal error

It was now, of course, out of my power to turn Yorktown by West Point; I had, therefore, no choice left, but to attack it directly in front, as I best could with the force at my command Reconnoissances made under me on that and the following day, determined that the sources of the Warwick River were near Yorktown, commanded by its guns, while that stream for some distance from its mouth on the James River was controlled by the confederate gun-boats; that the fords had been destroyed by dams, the approaches to which were generally through dense forests and deep swamps, and defended by extensive and formidable works, that timber felled for defensive purposes, and the flooding of the roads caused by the dams had made these works apparently inaccessible and impossible to turn; that Yorktown was strongly fortified, armed and garrisoned, and connected with the defenses of the Warwick by forts and intrenchments, the ground in front of which was swept by the guns of Yorktown. It was also ascertained that the garrisons had been and were daily being reinforced by troops from Norfolk, and the army under Gen J. E. Johnston

Heavy rains made the roads to Fort Monroe impassable and delayed the arrival of troops, ammunition and supplies, while storms prevented, for several days, the sailing of transports from Hampton Roads, and the establishment of depots on the creeks of York River near the army.

The ground bordering the Warwick River is covered by very dense and extensive forests, the clearings being small and few. This, with the comparative flatness of the country, and the alertness of the enemy everywhere in force, rendered thorough reconnoissances slow, dangerous and difficult; yet, it was impossible otherwise to determine whether any assault was anywhere practicable, or whether the more tedious, but sure operations of a siege must be resorted to

I made on the 6th and 7th, close personal reconnoissances of the right and left of the enemy's positions, which, with information acquired already, convinced me that it was best to prepare for an assault by a preliminary employment of heavy guns, and some siege operations. Instant assault would have been simple folly

On the 7th, I telegraphed to the President as follows

Head-quarters Army of Potomac, April 7th, 1862

To the President, Washington, D C,—

Your telegram of yesterday received In reply I have the honor to state that my entire force for duty amounts to only about (85,000) eighty-five thousand men. Gen. Wool's command, as you will observe from the accompanying order, has been taken out of my control, although he has most cheerfully co-operated with me The only use that can be made of his command, is to protect my communications in rear of this point. At this time only fifty-three thousand men have joined me, but they are coming up as rapidly as my means of transportation will permit

Please refer to my dispatch to the Secretary of War of to-night, for the details of our present situation

Geo B. McClellan, Maj-General

On the same day I sent the following.

Head-Quarters, Army of the Potomac, in front of Yorktown, April 7, 1862, 7 P M.

Hon. E M Stanton, Sec of War,—

Your telegram of yesterday, arrived here while I was absent examining the enemy's right, which I did pretty closely

The whole line of the Warwick, which really heads within a mile of Yorktown, is strongly defended by detached redoubts, and other fortifications, armed with heavy and light guns The approaches, except at Yorktown, are covered by the Warwick, over which there is but one, or at most, two passages, both of which are covered by strong batteries It will be necessary to resort to the use of heavy guns and some siege operations, before we can assault All the prisoners state that Gen J F Johnston arrived at Yorktown yesterday with strong reinforcements. It seems clear that I shall have the whole force of the enemy on my hands, probably not less than (100 000) one hundred thousand men and possibly more. In consequence of the loss of Blenker's division, and the 1st corps, my force is possibly less than that of the enemy, while they have all the advantage of positions

I am under great obligations to you for the offer that the whole force and material of the government, will be as fully and speedily under my command as heretofore, or as if the new departments had not been created

Since my arrangements were made for this campaign, at least (50,000) fifty thousand men have been taken from my command

Since my dispatch of the 5th instant, five divisions have been in close observation of the enemy, and frequently exchanging shots When my present command all joins, I shall have about (85,000) eighty-five thousand men for duty, from which a large force must be taken for guards, escorts, etc With this army I could assault the enemy's works, and perhaps carry them; but were I in possession of their intrenchments, and assailed by double my numbers, I should have no fears as to the result

Under the circumstances that have been developed since my arrival here, I feel fully impressed with the conviction, that here is to be fought the great battle that is to decide the existing contest. I shall of course, commence the attack as soon as I can get up my siege train, and shall do all in my power to carry the enemy's works, but to do this with a reasonable degree of certainty, requires, in my judgment, that I should, if possible, have at least, the whole of the 1st Corps to land upon the Severn River, and attack Gloucester in the rear My present strength will not admit of a detachment sufficient for this purpose, without materially impairing the efficiency of this column. Flag-officer Goldsborough, thinks the works too strong for his available vessels, unless I can turn Gloucester I send, by mail, copies of his letter, and one of the commander of the gunboats here

Geo B McClellan, Maj-Gen

THE SIEGE OF YORKTOWN

I had provided a small siege train, and moderate supplies of intrenching tools, for such a contingency as the present Immediate steps were taken to secure the necessary additions

While the engineer officers were engaged in ascertaining the character and strength of all the defenses, and the configuration of the ground in front of Yorktown, in order to determine the point of attack, and to develop the approaches, the troops were occupied in opening roads to the depots established at the nearest available points on branches of York River. Troops were brought to the front as rapidly as possible, and on the 10th of April the army was posted as follows: Heintzelman's corps, composed of Porter's, Hooker's and Hamilton's division, in front of York- town, extending in the order named from the mouth of Wormley's Creek to the Warwick road opposite Winn's Mills; Sumner's corps, Sedgwick's division only having arrived on the left of Hamilton, extending down the Warwick and opposite the Winn's Mills works; Keyes's corps, (Smith's, Couch's, and Casey's divisions,) on the left of Sedgwick facing the works at the one-gun battery, Lee's Mills, etc., on the west bank of the Warwick. Sumner, after the 6th of April, commanded the left wing, composed of his own and Keyes's corps.

Throughout the preparations for, and during the siege of Yorktown, I kept the corps under Gen. Keyes, and afterwards the left wing under Gen. Sumner engaged in ascertaining the character of the obstacles presented by the Warwick, and the enemy intrenched on the right bank, with the intention, if possible, of overcoming them and breaking that line of defense, so as to gain possession of the road to Williamsburg, and cut off Yorktown from its supports and supplies. The forces under Gen. Heintzelman were engaged in similar efforts upon the works between Winn's Mills and Yorktown. Gen. Keyes's report of the 16th of April, enclosing reports of brigade commanders engaged in reconnoissances up to that day, said, "that no part of his (the enemy's line opposite his) line, as far as discovered, can be taken by assault without an enormous waste of life." Reconnoissances on the right flank demonstrated the fact that the Warwick was not passable in that direction except over a narrow dam, the approaches to which were swept by several batteries and intrenchments, which could be filled quickly with supports sheltered by the timber immediately in rear.

Gen. Barnard, chief engineer of the Army of the Potomac, whose position entitled his opinions to the highest consideration, expressed the judgment that those formidable works could not, with any reasonable degree of certainty, be carried by assault. Gen. Keyes, commanding the 4th army corps, after the examination of the enemy's defenses on the left, before alluded to, addressed the following letter to the Hon. Ira Harris, U. S. Senate, and gave me a copy. Although not strictly official it describes the situation at that time in some respects so well that I have taken the liberty of introducing it here.

Headquarters 4th Corps,
Warwick Court House, Va., April 7, 1862.

MY DEAR SENATOR.—The plan of campaign on this line was made with the distinct understanding that *four* army corps should be employed, and that the navy should co-operate in the taking of Yorktown, and also (as I understood it) support us on our left by moving gunboats up James River.

To-day I have learned that the 1st corps, which, by the President's order, was to embrace four divisions, and one division (Blenker's) of the 2d corps, have been withdrawn altogether from this line of operations, and from the Army of the Potomac. At the same time, as I am informed, the navy has not the means to attack Yorktown, and is afraid to send gunboats up James River for fear of the Merrimac.

The above plan of campaign was adopted unanimously by Gen. McDowell and Brig.-Gen's Sumner, Heintzelman and Keyes, and was concurred in by Maj.-Gen. McClellan, who first proposed Urbana as our base.

This army being reduced by forty-five thousand troops, some of them the best in the service, and without the support of the navy, the plan to which we are reduced bears scarcely any resemblance to the one I voted for.

I command the James River column, and I left my camp, near Newport News, the morning of the 4th instant. I only succeeded in getting my artillery ashore the afternoon of the day before, and one of my divisions had not all arrived in camp the day I left, and, for the want of transportation, has not yet joined me. So you will observe that not a day was lost in the advance; and in fact we marched so quickly and so rapidly that many of our animals were twenty-four and forty-eight hours without a ration of forage. But, notwithstanding the rapidity of our advance, we are stopped by a line of defense nine or ten miles long, strongly fortified by breastworks, erected nearly the whole 'distance, behind a stream or succession of ponds no where fordable, one terminus being Yorktown and the other ending in the James River, which is commanded by the enemy's gunboats. Yorktown is fortified all around with bastioned works, and on the water side, it and Gloucester are so strong that the navy are afraid to attack either.

The approaches on our side are generally through low, swampy, or thickly-wooded ground over roads which we are obliged to repair or to make, before we can get forward our carriages. The enemy is in great force, and is constantly receiving reinforcements from the two rivers. The line in front of us is therefore one of the strongest ever opposed to an invading force in any country.

You will then ask, why I advocated such a line for our operations? My reasons are few, but, I think, good.

With proper assistance from the navy, we could take Yorktown, and then, with gunboats on both rivers, we could beat any force opposed to us on Warwick River, because the shot and shells from the gunboats would nearly overlap across the Peninsula, so that, if the enemy should retreat, and retreat he must, he would have a long way to go without rail or steam transportation and every soul of his army must fall into our hands or be destroyed.

Another reason for my supporting the new base and plan was, that this line, it was expected, would furnish water transportation nearly to Richmond.

Now, supposing we succeed in breaking through the line in front of us, what can we do next? The roads are very bad, and if the enemy retains command of James River, and we do not first reduce Yorktown, it would be impossible for us to subsist this army three marches beyond where it is now. As the roads are at present it is with the utmost difficulty that we can subsist in the position it now occupies.

You will see, therefore, by what I have said, that the force originally intended for the capture of Richmond should be all sent forward. If I thought the four army corps necessary when I supposed the navy would co-operate, and when I judged of the obstacles to be encountered by what I learned from maps and the opinions of officers stationed at Fort Monroe, and from all other sources, how much more should I think the full complement of troops requisite, now that the navy cannot co-operate, and now that the enemy's lines and the number of his guns and men prove to be immeasurably greater than I had been supposed to expect!

The line in front of us, in the opinion of all the military men here who are at all competent to judge, is one of the strongest in the world, and the force of the enemy capable of being increased beyond the numbers we now have to oppose to him. Independently of the strength of the lines in front of us, and of the force of the enemy behind them, we cannot advance until we get command of York River or James River. The efficient co-operation of the navy is, therefore, absolutely essential, and so I considered it when I voted to change our base from the Potomac to Fort Monroe.

An iron-clad boat must attack Yorktown, and if several strong gunboats could be sent up James River also, our success will be certain and complete, and the rebellion will soon be put down.

On the other hand, we must butt against the enemy's works with heavy artillery and a great waste of time, life and material.

If we break through and advance, both our flanks will be assailed from two great watercourses in the hands of the enemy; our supplies would give out, and the enemy, equal, if not superior, in numbers, would, with other advantages, beat and destroy this army.

The greatest master of the art of war has said that "if you would invade a country successfully, you must have *one* line of operations and one army, under one general." But what is our condition? The State of Virginia is made to constitute the command, in part or wholly, of some six generals, viz: Fremont, Banks, McDowell, Wool, Burnside, and McClellan, besides the scrap, over the Chesapeake, in the care of Dix.

The great battle of the war is to come off. If we win it, the rebellion will be crushed. If we lose it, the consequences will be more horrible than I care to foretell. The plan of campaign I voted for, if carried out with the means proposed, will certainly succeed. If any part of the means proposed are withheld or diverted, I deem it due to myself to say that our success will be uncertain.

It is no doubt agreeable to the commander of the 1st corps to have a separate department, and as this letter advocates his return to Gen McClellan's command, it is proper to state that I am not at all influenced by personal remark or dislike to any of my seniors in rank. If I were to credit all the opinions which have been poured into my ears, I must believe that, in regard to my present fine command, I owe much to Gen McDowell and nothing to Gen McClellan. But I have disregarded all such officiousness, and I have from last July to the present day, supported Gen McClellan and obeyed all his orders with as hearty a good will as though he had been my brother or the friend to whom I owed most. I shall continue to do so to the last, and so long as he is my commander, and I am not desirous to displace him and would not if I could. He left Washington with the understanding that he was to execute a definite plan of campaign with certain prescribed means. The plan was good and the means sufficient, and, without modification, the enterprise was certain of success. But, with the reduction of force and means, the plan is entirely changed, and is now a bad plan, with means insufficient for certain success.

Do not look upon this communication as the offspring of despondency. I never despond, and when you see me working the hardest, you may be sure that fortune is frowning upon me. I am working *now*, to my utmost.

Please show this letter to the President, and I should like also that Mr Stanton should know its contents. Do me the honor to write to me as soon as you can, and believe me, with perfect respect, Your obedient servant,

E D KEYES, Brig.-Gen Comd'g 4th Army Corps.
Hon. Ira Harris, U S Senate.

On the 7th of April and before the arrival of the divisions of Generals Hooker, Richardson and Casey, I received the following dispatches from the President and Secretary of War:

Washington, April 6, 1862   8 p.m.
Gen G B McClellan—Yours of 11 a m to-day received. Secretary of War informs me that the forwarding of transportation, ammunition, and Woodbury's Brigade, under your orders, is not and will not be interfered with. You have over one hundred thousand troops with you, independent of Gen Wool's command. I think you had better break the enemy's line from Yorktown to Warwick River at once. This will probably use time as advantageously as you can.
A. LINCOLN, President.

Washington, April 6, 1862   2 p.m.
Gen G. B. McClellan.—The President directs me to say that your dispatch to him has been received. General Sumner's corps is on the road to join you, and will go forward as fast as possible. Franklin's division is now on the advance towards Manassas. There is no means of transportation here to send it forward in time to be of service to you in your present operations. Telegraph frequently, and all in the power of the government shall be done to sustain you as occasion requires.
EDWIN M STANTON, Secretary of War.

By the 9th of April I had acquired a pretty

good knowledge of the enemy's works and the obstacles to be overcome.

On that day I received the following letter from the President.

Washington, April 9th, 1862.
Major General McClellan:—

My Dear Sir,—Your dispatches, complaining that you are not properly sustained, while they do not offend me, do pain me very much.

Blenker's division was withdrawn from you before you left here, and you know the pressure under which I did it, and, as I thought, acquiesced in it, certainly without reluctance.

After you left I ascertained that less than twenty thousand unorganized men, without a single battery, were all you designed to be left for the defense of Washington and Manassas Junction; and part of this even was to go to Gen. Hooker's old position. Gen. Banks' old corps, once designed for Manassas Junction, was diverted and tied up on the line of Winchester and Strasburg, and could not leave it without again exposing the upper Potomac, and the Baltimore and Ohio Railroad. This presented (or would present, when McDowell and Sumner should be gone) a great temptation to the enemy to turn back from the Rappahannock and sack Washington. My explicit order that Washington should, by the judgment of *all* the commanders of army corps, be left entirely secure, had been neglected. It was precisely this that drove me to detain McDowell.

I do not forget that I was satisfied with your arrangement to leave Banks at Manassas Junction; but when that arrangement was broken up and *nothing* was substituted for it, of course I was constrained to substitute something for it myself. And allow me to ask, "Do you really think I should permit the line from Richmond *via* Manassas Junction to this city to be entirely open, except what resistance could be presented by twenty thousand unorganized troops?" This is a question which the country will not allow me to evade.

There is a curious mystery about the *numbers* of the troops now with you. When I telegraphed you on the 6th, saying you had over a hundred thousand with you, I had just obtained from the Secretary of War a statement taken, as he said, from your own returns, making 108,000 then with you and *en route* to you. You now say you will have but 85,000 when all *en route* to you shall have reached you. How can the discrepancy of 23,000 be accounted for?

As to General Wool's command, I understand it is doing for you precisely what a like number of your own would have to do, if that command was away.

I suppose the whole force which has gone forward for you is with you by this time, and if so I think it is the precise time to strike a blow. By delay the enemy will relatively gain upon you —that is, he will gain faster, by *fortifications* and *reinforcements*, than you can by reinforcements alone.

And once more, let me tell you, it is indispensable to *you* that you strike a blow. I am powerless to help this. You will do me the justice to remember I always insisted that going down the bay in search of a field instead of fighting at or near Manassas, was only shifting and not surmounting a difficulty, that we would find the same enemy, and the same or equal intrenchments, at either place. The country will not fail to note—is now noting—that the present hesitation to move upon an intrenched enemy, is but the story of Manassas repeated.

I beg to assure you that I have never written you, or spoken to you, in greater kindness of feeling than now, nor with a fuller purpose to sustain you, so far as in my most anxious judgment I consistently can. But you must act.

Yours, very truly,   A. LINCOLN.

With great deference to the opinions and wishes of His Excellency the President, I most respectfully beg leave to refer to the facts which I have presented, and those contained in the accompanying letter of General Keyes, with the reports of General Barnard and other officers as furnishing a reply to the above letter. His Excellency could not judge of the formidable character of the works before us as well as if he had been upon the ground, and whatever might have been his desire for prompt action (certainly no greater than mine) I feel confident, if he could have made a personal inspection of the enemy's defenses, he would have forbidden me from risking the safety of the army and the possible successes of the campaign on a sanguinary assault of an advantageous and formidable position, which even if successful, could not have been followed up to any other or better result than would have been reached by the regular operations of a siege. Still less could I forego the conclusions of my most instructed judgment for the mere sake of avoiding the personal consequences intimated in the President's dispatch.

The following extracts from the report of the chief engineer—Brig.-Gen. J. G. Barnard,—embody the result of our reconnoissances and give with some degree of detail, the character and strength of the defenses of Yorktown and the Warwick, and some of the obstacles which the army contended against and overcame.

EXTRACTS FROM GEN. BARNARD'S REPORT.

"The accompanying drawing—Map No 2— gives with accuracy the outline and armament of the fortifications of Yorktown proper, with the detached works immediately connected with it.

"The three bastioned fronts looking towards our approaches appear to have been earliest built, and have about 15 feet thickness of parapet, and 8 feet to 10 feet depth of ditch, the width varying much, but never leaving less, at top of the scarp, than 15 feet: I think, generally, much more.

"The works extending around the town, from the western salient of fronts just mentioned, appear to have been finished during the last winter and spring. They have formidable profiles, 18 feet thickness of parapet, and generally, 10 feet depth of ditch.

"The water-batteries had, generally, 18 feet parapet, the guns in barbette

"They were—as well as the works mentioned—carefully constructed with well made sod-revetments

"There were numerous traverses between the guns, and ample magazines; how sufficient in bomb-proof qualities, I am unable to say

"The two first guns of the works on the heights, bear upon the water as well as the land, and were of heavy calibre

"The list herewith, gives all the guns in position, or for which there were emplacements The vacant emplacements were all occupied before the evacuation by siege-guns, rifled 1½ inch, 24-pounders and 18-pounders

"In Fort Magruder—the first exterior work—there were found 1 8-inch Columbiad, 1 42-pounder, and 1 8-inch siege-howitzer, the two former 'en barbettee' The sketch will show the emplacements for guns on field and siege-carriages, making, I think, with the foregoing, 22 Two of these were placed behind traverses with embrasures covered by bridges.

"The two external redoubts, with the connecting parapets, formed a re-entrant with the fronts of attack, and all the guns bore on our approaches

"It will be seen, therefore, that our approaches were swept by the fire of at least 49 guns, nearly all of which were heavy, and many of them the most formidable guns known, besides that two-thirds of the guns of the water-batteries, and all the guns of Gloucester, bore on our right batteries, though under disadvantageous circumstances.

"The ravine, behind which the left of the Yorktown fronts of attack was placed, was not very difficult, as the heads formed depressions in front of their left imperfectly seen by their fire, and from which access could be had to the ditches, but we could not be sure of this fact before the evacuation. The enemy held, by means of a slight breastwork, and rifle trenches, a position in advance of the heads of their ravines, as far forward as the Brunt House.

"The ravines, which head between the Yorktown fortifications and the exterior works, are deep and intricate. They were tolerably well seen, however, by the works which run westwardly from the Yorktown works, and which were too numerous and complicated to be traced on paper

"Fort Magruder, the first lunette on our left, appears to have been built at an early period.

"The external connection between this work, was first a rifle trench, probably afterwards enlarged into a parapet, with external ditch, and an emplacement for four guns in or near the small redan in the centre.

"Behind this they had constructed numerous epaulments with connecting boyans not fully arranged for infantry fires, and mainly intended, probably, to protect their camps and reserves against the destructive effects of our artillery.

"From the 'red redoubt,' these trenches and epaulments, ran to the woods and rivulet which forms a head of the Warwick, and continue almost without break to connect with the works at Winn's Mills This stream just mentioned, (whatever be its name, the term 'Warwick,' according to some, applying only to the tidal channel from the James River, up as high as Lee's Mill), was inundated by a number of dams, from near where its head is crossed by the epaulments mentioned, down to Lee's Mill.

"Below Lee's Mill, the Warwick follows a tortuous course through salt marshes of 200 or 300 yards in width, from which the land rises up boldly to a height of 40 or 50 feet

"The first group of works is at Winn's Mill, where there is a dam and bridge. The next is, to guard another dam between Winn's and Lee's Mills, (this is the point attacked by General Smith, on the 16th ultimo, and where Lieut. Merrill was wounded, the object of the attack was merely to prevent the further construction of works, and feel the strength of the position) A work, of what extent is not now known, was at the sharp angle of the stream, just above Lee's Mill, and a formidable group of works was at Lee's Mill, where there was also a dam and bridge.

"From Lee's Mill a line of works extends across Mulberry Island (or it is supposed to do so).

"At Southall's Landing is another formidable group of works, and from here, too, they extend apparently across the James

"These groups of field works were connected by rifle trenches or parapets, for nearly the whole distance.

"They are far more extensive than may be supposed, from the mention of them I make, and every kind of obstruction which the country affords, such as abattis, marsh, inundation, &c., was skillfully used. The line is certainly one of the most extensive known to modern times

"The country on both sides the Warwick, from near Yorktown down, is a dense forest, with few clearings. It was swampy, and the roads impassable during the heavy rains we have constantly had, except where our own labors have corduroyed them.

"If we could have broken the enemy's line across the isthmus, we could have invested Yorktown, and it must, with its garrison, have soon fallen into our hands.

"It was not deemed practicable, considering the strength of that line, and the difficulty of handling our forces (owing to the impracticable character of the country), to do so.

' If we could take Yorktown, or drive the enemy out of that place, the enemy's line was no longer tenable. This we could do by siege operations It was deemed too hazardous to attempt the reduction of the place by assault"

The plan of the approaches and their defenses, as determined upon and finally executed, is exhibited in the accompanying map. It was, in words, to open the first parallel as near as possible to the works of the enemy, and under its protection to establish, almost simultaneously, batteries along the whole front, extending from York River, on the right, to the Warwick, on the left—a chord of about one mile in length The principal approaches were directed against the east end of the main work (which was most heavily armed and bore both on the water and land), and lay between Wormley's Creek and York River. There, also, were placed the most of the batteries designed to act against the land front, to enfilade the water batteries and to act upon Gloucester. I designed at the earliest moment to open simultaneously with several batteries, and as soon as the enemy's guns, which swept the neck of land between Wormley's Creek and the Warwick, were crippled and then fire kept down, to push the trenches as far forward as necessary, and to assault Yorktown and the adjacent works.

The approaches to the batteries, the necessary bridges and the roads to the depots, had been vigorously pushed to completion, by the troops under Gens. Heintzelman and Sumner, and were available for infantry, and in some instances for artillery, on the 17th of April, when the batteries and their connections were commenced, and labor upon them kept up, night and day, until finished.

Some of the batteries on easy ground and concealed from the view of the enemy, were early completed and armed, and held ready for any emergency, but not permitted to open, as the return fire of the enemy would interfere too much with the labor on other and more important works. The completion of the more exposed and heaviest batteries was delayed by storms, preventing the landing of guns and ammunition. It having been discovered that the enemy were receiving artillery stores at the wharf in Yorktown, on May 1st, Battery No. 1 was opened with effect upon the wharf and town.

On the 22d of April, Gen. Franklin, with his division from Gen. McDowell's corps, had arrived and reported to me. The garrison of Gloucester Point had been reinforced and the works strengthened, but as this division was too small to detach to the Severn, and no more troops could be spared, I determined to act on Gloucester by disembarking it on the north bank of the York River, under the protection of the gunboats. The troops were mainly kept on board ship while the necessary preparations were made for landing them, and supporting them in case of necessity. For a full account of this labor, I refer to the report of Lieut.-Col. B. S. Alexander, of the Engineer Corps, detailed for this expedition.

While the siege works were being rapidly completed, the roads on the left wing necessary for communication and advance were opened and corduroyed over the marshes, batteries were erected to silence the enemy's guns and drive him from his works at Winn's and Lee's Mills, preparatory to the general attack, active reconnoissances were continually going on, and attempts in force made to drive the enemy from the banks.

The result of various reconnoissances made under the immediate direction of Gen. W. F. Smith, commanding 2d division, 4th corps, led to the belief that the weakest point of that part of the enemy's lines, was opposite a field, where it was ascertained that there was a dam covered by a battery known to contain at least one gun. It was determined to push a strong reconnoissance on this point, to silence the enemy's fire, and ascertain the actual strength of the position, being prepared to sustain the reconnoitering party by a real attack, if found expedient.

Gen. W. F. Smith was directed to undertake the operation on the 16th of April. He silenced the enemy's guns, discovered the existence of other works previously concealed and unknown, and sent a strong party across the stream, which was finally forced to retire with some loss; but Gen. Smith intrenched himself in a position immediately overlooking the dam and the enemy's works, so as to keep them under control, and prevent the enemy using the dam as a means of crossing the Warwick to annoy us.

Many times towards the end of the month, the enemy attempted to drive in our pickets and take our rifle-pits near Yorktown, but always without success. As the siege progressed it was with great difficulty that the rifle-pits on the right could be excavated and held, so little covering could be made against the hot fire of the enemy's artillery and infantry. Their guns continued up to a late hour of the night of the 3d of May.

Our batteries would have been ready to open on the morning of the 6th of May at latest, but on the morning of the 4th it was discovered that the enemy had already been compelled to evacuate his position during the night, leaving behind him all his heavy guns uninjured and a large amount of ammunition and supplies.

For the details of the labors of this siege, I refer to the accompanying reports and journals of Brig.-Gen. J. G. Barnard, chief engineer, charged with the selection and laying out, and completion of the approaches and batteries; of Brig. Gen. W. F. Barry, chief of artillery, charged with arming and supplying with ammunition all the siege and field batteries; and of Brig.-Gen. Fitz John Porter, director of the siege, to whom was assigned the guarding of the trenches, the assembling and distribution of the working parties, &c, &c.

THE PURSUIT TO WILLIAMSBURG.

Early in the morning of the 4th, upon the enemy's abandoning his lines at Yorktown I ordered all the available cavalry force, with four batteries of horse artillery, under Brig.-Gen. Stoneman, chief of cavalry, in immediate pursuit, by the Yorktown and Williamsburg road, with orders to harass the enemy's rear, and try to cut off such of his forces as had taken the Lee's Mill and Williamsburg road.

Gen. Heintzelman was directed to send Hooker's division forward on the Yorktown and Williamsburg road to support Gen. Stoneman; and Gen. Smith was ordered to proceed with his division on the Lee's Mill and Williamsburg road for the same purpose, afterwards the divisions of Gens. Kearney, Couch and Casey were put en route, the first on the Yorktown road, and the others on the Lee's Mill road. These roads unite about a quarter of a mile south of Fort Magruder and are connected by cross-roads at several points between Yorktown and Williamsburg. After these directions had been given, Gen. Sumner, (the officer second in rank in the Army of the Potomac) was ordered to proceed to the front and take immediate charge of operations until my arrival.

Gen. Stoneman moved forward promptly with his command (consisting of four batteries of horse-artillery under Lieut.-Col. Hays, the 1st and 6th U. S. cavalry, the 3d Pennsylvania, and 8th Illinois and Barker's squadron) meeting with but little opposition until he arrived in front of the enemy's works, about two miles east of Williamsburg. At a point about eight miles from Yorktown, in accordance with my instructions he detached Gen Emory with Benson's battery, the 3d Pennsylvania cavalry (Col. Averell) and Barker's squadron, to gain the Lee's Mill road and endeavor, with the assistance of Gen Smith, to cut off the portion of the enemy's rear-guard, which had taken that route. Gen Emory had some sharp skirmishes with a regiment of cavalry, and a battery under Gen Stuart, and drove them in the direction of Lee's Mill. Gen. Smith having met with obstructions in his front, had transferred his column by a cross-road to the Yorktown and Williamsburg road, so that Gen. Emory finding no force to co-operate with him was unable to cut off the rear-guard, and they succeeded in escaping by a circuitous route, along the bank of the James River.

The position in which Gen. Stoneman encountered the enemy is about four miles in extent, the right resting on College Creek, and the left on Queen's Creek, nearly three-fourths of its front being covered by tributaries of those two creeks, upon which there are ponds. The ground between the heads of the tributary streams is a cultivated plain, across which a line of detached works had been constructed, consisting of Fort Magruder, a large work in the centre with a bastion front, and twelve other redoubts and epaulements for field-guns.

The parapet of Fort Magruder is about six feet high and nine feet thick, the ditch nine feet wide and nine feet deep, filled with water. The length of the interior crest is about 600 yards. The redoubts have strong profiles, but are of small dimensions, having faces of about forty yards. The woods in front of the position were felled, and the open ground in front of the works was dotted with numerous rifle pits.

The roads leading from the lower part of the Peninsula towards Williamsburg, one along the York River—the Yorktown road—and the other along the James,—the Lee's Mill road—unite between the heads of the tributary streams a short distance in front of Fort Magruder, by which they are commanded, and debouch from the woods just before uniting. A branch from the James River road leaves it about one and three quarter miles below Fort Magruder, and unites with the road from Allen's Landing to Williamsburg, which crosses the tributary of College Creek over a dam at the outlet of a pond, and passes just in rear of the line of works, being commanded by the three redoubts on the right of the line.

At about the same distance from Fort Magruder a branch leaves the York River road, and crosses the tributary of Queen's Creek on a dam, and passing over the position and through the woods in its rear, finally enters Williamsburg. This road is commanded by redoubts on the left of the line of works.

Gen. Stoneman debouched from the woods with his advance guard—consisting of a part of the 1st U S. Cavalry and one section of Gibson's battery under the command of Gen Cook—and the enemy immediately opened on him with several field-pieces from Fort Magruder, having the correct range and doing some execution. Gibson's battery was brought into position as rapidly as the deep mud would permit, and returned the fire, while the 6th U S. Cavalry was sent to feel the enemy's left. This regiment passed one redoubt, which it found unoccupied, and appeared in the rear of a second, when a strong cavalry force, with infantry and artillery, came down upon it, whereupon the regiment was withdrawn. The rear squadron, under command of Captain Saunders, repelled a charge of the enemy's cavalry in the most gallant manner. In the meantime the enemy was being reinforced by infantry, and the artillery fire becoming very hot, Gen. Stoneman, having no infantry to carry the works, ordered the withdrawal of the battery. This was accomplished, with the exception of one piece which could not be extricated from the mud. The enemy attempted to prevent the movement, but their charges were met by the 1st U S. Cavalry, under command of Lieut.-Colonel Grier, and they were driven back, losing several officers and one stand of colors. Gen. Stoneman then took up a defensive position a short distance in the rear of the first, to await the arrival of the infantry. The advance of General Smith's column reached Skiff's Creek about 11½ o'clock, and found the bridge over the stream in flames, and the road impassable. A practicable route to the Yorktown road having been discovered, the division, by order of General Sumner, moved on by that road, and reached Gen Stoneman's position about 5½ o'clock. General Sumner arriving with it, assumed command.

Generals Heintzelman and Keyes also arrived during the afternoon near the Half-Way House. The head of General Hooker's column encountered Smith's division, filing into the road, and was obliged to halt between three and four hours, until it had passed. Gen Hooker then followed on, and at Checcecahe Church turned off, by Gen Heintzelman's direction, taking a cross-road, and moved out on the Lee's Mill road, thus changing places with Gen Smith. Marching part of the night, he came in sight of Fort Magruder early in the morning of the 5th.

General Smith's division, having been deployed General Sumner ordered an attack on the works in his front, but the lines having been thrown into confusion while moving through the dense forest, and darkness coming on, the attempt, for that night, was abandoned. The troops bivouacked in the woods, and a heavy rain began, which continued until the morning of the 6th, making the roads, already in a very bad condition, almost impassable.

THE BATTLE OF WILLIAMSBURG.

During the morning of the 5th, General Sumner reconnoitered the position in his front, and at 11 o'clock, ordered Hancock's brigade, of Smith's division, to take possession of a work on the enemy's left, which had been found to be unoccupied. The remainder of Smith's division occupied the woods in front, without being actually engaged. The divisions of Couch and Casey, had received orders during the night to march at daylight, but on account of the terrible condition of the roads, and other impediments, were not able to reach the field until after 1 o'clock, p m, at which time the first brigade of Couch's division arrived, and was posted in the centre, on Hooker's right. The other two brigades came up during the afternoon, followed by Casey's division. In the meantime, General Hooker having reconnoitered the enemy's position, began the attack at 7½ o'clock, a m, and for a while silenced the guns of Fort Magruder, and cleared the ground in his front. But the enemy being continually reinforced, until their strength greatly exceeded his, made attack after attack, endeavoring to turn his left. For several hours his division struggled gallantly against the superior numbers of the enemy. Five guns of Webber's battery were lost, and between 3 and 4 o'clock, his ammunition began to give out. The loss had been heavy and the exhaustion of the troops was very great. At this time the division of General Kearney came up, who, at 9 a m, had received orders to reinforce Hooker, and who had succeeded, by the greatest exertion, in passing Casey's troops and pushing on the front through the deep mud. General Kearney at once gallantly attacked, and thereby prevented the loss of another battery, and drove the enemy back at every point, enabling Gen Hooker to extricate himself from his position, and withdraw his wearied troops.

Peck's brigade, of Couch's division, as has been mentioned before, was immediately on its arrival, ordered by Gen Sumner to deploy on Hooker's right. This was promptly done, and the attacks of the enemy at that point were repulsed. Gen Peck, held his position until late in the afternoon, when he was relieved by the other two brigade's of Couch's division, and they were in quiet possession of the ground when night closed the contest.

The vigorous action of these troops relieved Gen Hooker considerably. Gen Emory, had been left with his command, on the night of the 4th, to guard the branch of the Lee's Mill road, which leads to Allen's Farm, and on the morning of the 5th it was ascertained that by this route the enemy's right could be turned. A request for infantry for this purpose, was made to Gen Heintzelman, who, late in the afternoon, sent four regiments and two batteries of Kearney's division, the first disposable troops he had, and directed Gen. Emory to make the attack. With these reinforcements, his force amounted to about 3,000 men, and 3 batteries. Gen Emory, on account of want of knowledge of the ground, and the lateness of the hour, did not succeed in this movement. It involved some risks, but if successful, might have produced important results. At 11 a m., as before mentioned, Gen Smith received orders from General Sumner, to send one brigade across a dam on our right, to occupy a redoubt on the left of the enemy's line; Hancock's brigade was selected for this purpose. He crossed the dam, took possession of the first redoubt, and afterwards finding the second one vacated, he occupied that also, and sent for reinforcements to enable him to advance further, and take the next redoubt, which commanded the plain between his position and Fort Magruder, and would have enabled him to take in reverse, and cut the communication of the troops engaged with Generals Hooker and Kearney. The enemy soon began to show himself in strength before him, and, as his rear and right flank were somewhat exposed, he repeated his request for reinforcements. Gen Smith was twice ordered to join him with the rest of his division, but each time the order was countermanded at the moment of execution; Gen. Sumner not being willing to weaken the centre. At length, in reply to Gen. Hancock's repeated messages for more troops, Gen. Sumner sent him an order to fall back to his first position; the execution of which, Gen. Hancock deferred as long as possible, being unwilling to give up the advantage already gained, and fearing to expose his command by such a movement.

During the progress of these events I had remained at Yorktown, to complete the preparations for the departure of Gen Franklin's and other troops to West Point by water, and to make the necessary arrangements with the naval commander, for his co-operation.

By pushing Gen Franklin, well supported, by water to the right bank of the Pamunkey opposite West Point, it was hoped to force the enemy to abandon whatever works he might have on the Peninsula below that point, or be cut off. It was of paramount importance that the arrangements to this end should be promptly made.

At an early hour of the morning, I had sent two of my aids (Lieut.-Col Sweitzer and Maj Hammerstein) to observe the operations in front, with instructions to report to me everything of importance that might occur. I received no information from them leading me to suppose that there was anything occurring of more importance than a simple affair of a rear guard, until about 1 o'clock, p m, when a dispatch arrived from one of them that everything was not progressing favorably; this was confirmed a few minutes later by the reports of Governor Sprague and Major Hammerstein, who came directly from the scene of action.

Completing the necessary arrangements, I returned to my camp without delay, rode rapidly to the front, a distance of some fourteen miles, through roads much obstructed by troops and wagons, and reached the field between 4 and 5 p m, in time to take a rapid survey of the ground. I soon learned that there was no direct communication between our centre and the left under Gen Heintzelman. The centre was chiefly in the nearer edge of the woods situated between us and the enemy. As heavy firing was heard in the direction of Gen. Hancock's command, I immediately ordered Gen Smith to proceed with his two remaining brigades to support that par of the line. Gen Naglee, with his brigade received similar orders I then directed our centre to advance to the further edge of the woods, mentioned above, which was done; and attempted to open direct communication with Gen Heintzelman, but was prevented by the marshy state of the ground in the direction in which the attempt was made Before Generals Smith and Naglee could reach the field of Gen Hancock's operations, although they moved with great rapidity, he had been confronted by a superior force Feigning to retreat slowly, he awaited their onset, and then turned upon them. after some terrific volleys of musketry he charged them with the bayonet, routing and dispersing their whole force, killing, wounding and capturing from 500 to 600 men, he, himself losing only thirty-one men

This was one of the most brilliant engagements of the war, and Gen. Hancock merits the highest praise for the soldierly qualities displayed, and his perfect appreciation of the vital importance of his position

Night put an end to all the operations here, and all the troops who had been engaged in this contest slept on the muddy field without shelter, and many without food

Notwithstanding the report I received from Gen Heintzelman during the night, that Gen Hooker's division had suffered so much that it could not be relied upon next day, and that Kearney's could not do more than hold its own, without reinforcements—being satisfied that the result of Hancock's engagement was to give us possession of the decisive point of the battlefield—during the night I countermanded the order for the advance of the divisions of Sedgwick and Richardson, and directed them to return to Yorktown, to proceed to West Point by water

Our loss during the day, the greater part of which was sustained by Hooker's division, was as follows: killed, 456, wounded, 1,400; missing, 372 Total, 2,228.

On the next morning we found the enemy's position abandoned, and occupied fort Magruder and the town of Williamsburg, which was filled with the enemy's wounded, to whose assistance eighteen of their surgeons were sent by Gen J E Johnston, the officer in command. Several guns and caissons which the enemy could not carry off on account of the mud were secured

Col Averill was sent forward at once with a strong cavalry force, to endeavor to overtake the enemy's rear guard He found several guns abandoned and picked up a large number of stragglers, but the conditions of the road and the state of his supplies forced him to return after advancing a few miles

It is my opinion that the enemy opposed us here with only a portion of his army When our cavalry first appeared, there was nothing but the enemy's rear guard in Williamsburg, although troops were brought back during the night and the next day, to hold the works as long as possible, in order to gain time for the trains, etc, already well on their way to Richmond, to make their escape.

Our troops were greatly exhausted by the laborious march through the mud from their positions in front of Yorktown, and by the protracted battle through which they had just passed, many of them were out of rations and ammunition, and one division in its anxiety to make a prompt movement had marched with empty haversacks. The supply trains had been forced out of the roads on the 4th and 5th, to allow the troops and artillery to pass to the front, and the roads were now in such a state, that it was almost impossible to pass even empty wagons over them. Gen Hooker's division had suffered so bad that it was in no condition to follow the enemy even if the roads had been good, under these circumstances, an immediate pursuit was impossible

Steps were at once taken to care for and remove the wounded, and to bring up provisions, ammunition and forage. The condition of the roads, as has been said, rendered it next to impossible to accomplish this by land from Yorktown: a temporary depot was therefore promptly established on Queen's Creek, and supplies drawn, and the wounded shipped from that point

ADVANCE TO THE CHICKAHOMINY.

The Divisions of Franklin, Sedgwick, Porter, and Richardson were sent from Yorktown by water to the right bank of the Pamunkey, in the vicinity of West Point. The remaining divisions, the train, and the reserve artillery moved subsequently by land

Early on the morning of the 7th, Gen Franklin had completed the disembarkation of his division, and had placed it in a good position to cover the landing place, both his flanks and a large portion of the front being protected by water

Dana's brigade of Sedgwick's division arrived during the morning

At about 9, a m, a large force of the enemy appeared, consisting of Whiting's division and other troops, and between 10 and 11, they attacked the part of the line held by Newton's brigade

The action continued until 3 p m, when the enemy retired, all his attacks having been repulsed This affair, the most important in which the division had been engaged, was highly creditable to Gen Franklin and his command. For the details I refer to this report, which is herewith submitted. Our loss was 40 killed, 104 wounded, and 41 missing Total 194, which includes a large proportion of officers.

Cavalry reconnoissances were sent out from Williamsburg on the 6th and 7th, and on the 8th Gen Stoneman moved, with an advance guard of cavalry, artillery, and infantry, to open communication with Gen Franklin

As soon as our supplies had been received, and the condition of the roads had become a little better, though still very bad, the advance of the remaining troops was begun, Smith's division moving on the 8th

On the 10th, headquarters were at Roper's Church, 19 miles from Williamsburg All the divisions which had moved by land (except Hooker's) being in the vicinity of that place. We we no in direct communication with the portion of the army which had gone by water, and we began to draw supplies from Eltham. On account of the small number and narrowness of the roads in this neighborhood, movements were difficult and slow.

On the 13th, headquarters, and the divisions of Franklin, Porter, Sykes and Smith, reached Cumberland, which was made a temporary depot Couch and Casey were then near New Kent Court House, Hooker and Kearney near Roper's Church, and Richardson and Sedgwick near Eltham

On the 14th and 15th much rain fell

On the 15th and 16th the divisions of Franklin, Smith and Porter were with great difficulty moved to White House, five miles in advance So bad was the road that the train of one of these divisions required thirty-six hours to pass over this short distance

G n. Stoneman had occupied this place some days before, after several successful skirmishes in which our cavalry proved superior to that of the enemy The reports of these affairs are appended

About this time, with the consent of the President, two additional corps were organized, viz the 5th Provisional Corps, consisting of the divisions of Porter and Sykes, and the Reserve Artillery under the command of F J Porter, and the 6th Provisional Corps, consisting of the divisions of Franklin and Smith, under the command of Gen W B Franklin

Headquarters reached White House on the 16th, and a permanent depot was at once organized there.

On the 19th, headquarters, and the corps of Porter and Franklin, moved to Tunstall's Station, five miles from White House.

On the 20th more rain fell

On the 21st the position of the troops was as follows

Stoneman's Advance Guard, one mile from New Bridge

Franklin's Corps, three miles from New Bridge, with

Porter's Corps, at supporting distance in its rear.

Sumner's Corps, on the railroad, about three miles from the Chickahominy, connecting the right with the left

Keyes's Corps, on New Kent Road, near Bottom's Bridge, with

Heintzelman's Corps, at supporting distance in its rear

The ford at Bottom's Bridge was in our possession, and the re-building of the bridge, which had been destroyed by the enemy, was commenced

On the 22d headquarters moved to Coal Harbor

On the 26th the railroad was in operation as far as the Chickahominy, and the railroad bridge across that stream nearly completed.

SECOND PERIOD.

PART II

OPERATIONS BEFORE RICHMOND.

When, on the 20th of May, our advanced light troops reached the banks of the Chickahominy River, at Bottom's Bridge, they found that this, as well as the railroad bridge, about a mile above, had been destroyed by the enemy.

The Chickahominy in this vicinity is about forty feet wide, fringed with a dense growth of heavy forest trees, and bordered by low, marshy bottom-lands, varying from half a mile to a mile in width

Our operations embraced that part of the river between Bottom's and Meadow Bridges, which covered the principal approaches to Richmond from the east

Within these limits the firm ground, lying above high-water mark, seldom approaches near the river on either bank, and no locality was found within this section, where the high ground came near the stream on both sides It was subject to frequent, sudden and great variations in the volume of water, and a rise of a few feet overflowed the bottom-lands on both sides.

At low water it could be forded at almost any point, but during high water it rose above a fording stage, and could then be crossed only at the few points where bridges had been constructed These bridges had all been destroyed by the enemy on our approach, and it was necessary not only to reconstruct these, but to build several others

The west bank of the river, opposite the New and Mechanicsville bridges, was bordered by elevated bluffs, which afforded the enemy commanding positions to fortify, establish his batteries, enfilading the approaches upon the two principal roads to Richmond, in one night, and resist the reconstruction of the important bridges. This obliged us to select other less exposed points for our crossings.

As the enemy was not in great force opposite Bottom's Bridge, on the arrival of our left at that point, and as it was important to secure a lodgment upon the right bank before he should have time to concentrate his forces and contest the passage, I forthwith ordered Casey's division to ford the river and occupy the opposite heights This was promptly done on the 20th, and reconnoissances were at once pushed out in advance

These troops were directed to throw up defenses in an advantageous position to secure our left flank Gen. Heintzelman's corps was thrown forward in support, and Bottom's Bridge immediately rebuilt

In the meantime our centre and right were advanced to the river above, and on the 24th we carried the village of Mechanicsville, driving the enemy out with our artillery, and forcing them across the bridge which they destroyed. Gen. Naglee on the same day dislodged a force of the enemy from the vicinity of the "Seven Pines" on the Bottom's Bridge road, and our advance on the left secured a strong position near that place.

All the information obtained from deserters, negroes and spies, indicated that the enemy occupied in force all the approaches to Richmond from the east, and that he intended to dispute every step of our advance beyond the Chickahominy, and the passage of the stream opposite our right That their army was superior to our in numbers did not admit of a doubt. Strong defenses had been constructed around Richmond.

Impressed by these facts with the necessity of strengthening the army for the struggle, I did not fail to urge repeatedly upon my superiors the importance of reinforcing the Army of the Potomac with every disposable man, in order to insure the success of an attack upon the rebel capital.

On the 10th of May I telegraphed as follows:—
Camp at Ewell's Farm, three miles beyond
Williamsburg, May 10, 1862, 5 A M.
Hon. Edwin M Stanton, Secretary of War.

From the information reaching me from every source, I regard it as certain that the enemy will meet us with all his force, on or near the Chickahominy. They can concentrate many more men than I have, and are collecting troops from all quarters, especially well-disciplined troops from the South. Casualties, sickness, garrisons and guards, have much reduced my numbers, and will continue to do so. I shall fight the rebel army with whatever force I may have; but duty requires me to urge that every effort be made to reinforce me without delay with all the disposable troops in Eastern Virginia, and that we concentrate all our forces, as far as possible, to fight the great battle now impending, and to make it decisive.

It is possible that the enemy may abandon Richmond without a serious struggle; but I do not believe he will—and it would be unwise to count on anything but a stubborn and desperate defense, a life and death contest. I see no other hope for him than to fight this battle, and we must win it. I shall fight them whatever their force may be; but I ask for every man that the Department can send me. No troops should now be left unemployed. Those who entertain the opinion that the rebels will abandon Richmond without a struggle, are in my judgment badly advised, and do not comprehend their situation, which is one requiring desperate measures.

I beg that the President and Secretary will maturely weigh what I say, and leave nothing undone to comply with my request. If I am not reinforced, it is probable that I will be obliged to fight nearly double my numbers, strongly intrenched. I do not think it will be at all possible for me to bring more than (70,000) seventy thousand men upon the field of battle.

Geo. B McClellan, Maj.-Gen Com'g

On the 14th of May I sent the following telegram to the President:
Camp at Cumberland, May 14, 1862
His Excellency, Abraham Lincoln, President of the U S:

I have more than twice telegraphed to the Secretary of War, stating, that in my opinion the enemy were concentrating all their available force to fight this army in front of Richmond, and that such ought to be their policy. I have received no reply whatever to any of these telegraphs.

I beg leave to repeat their substance to your Excellency, and to ask that kind consideration which you have ever accorded to my representations and views. All my information from every source accessible to me, establishes the fixed purpose of the rebels to defend Richmond against this army by offering us battle with all the troops they can collect from east, west, and south and my own opinion is confirmed by that of all my commanders whom I have been able to consult.

Casualties, sickness, garrisons, and guards have much weakened my force, and will continue to do so. I cannot bring into actual battle against the enemy more than eighty thousand men at the utmost, and with them I must attack in position, probably intrenched, a much larger force—perhaps double my numbers. It is possible that Richmond may be abandoned without a serious struggle, but the enemy are actually in great strength between here and there, and it would be unwise, and even insane for me to calculate upon anything but a stubborn and desperate resistance. If they should abandon Richmond, it may well be that it is done with the purpose of making the stand at some place in Virginia south or west of there, and and we should be in condition to press them without delay. The confederate leaders must employ their utmost efforts against this army in Virginia, and they will be supported by the whole body of their military officers among whom there may be said to be no Union feeling, as there is also very little among the higher class of citizens in the seceding States.

I have found no fighting men in this Peninsula—all are in the ranks of the opposing foe.

Even if more troops than I now have should prove unnecessary for purposes of military occupation, our greatest display of imposing force in the capital of the rebel government will have the best moral effect. I most respectfully and earnestly urge upon your Excellency that the opportunity has come for striking a fatal blow at the enemies of the Constitution, and I beg that you will cause this army to be reinforced without delay by all the disposable troops of the government. I ask for every man that the government can send me. Any commander of the reinforcements, whom your Excellency may designate, will be acceptable to me, whatever expression I may have heretofore addressed to you on that subject.

I will fight the enemy, whatever their force may be, and whatever force I may have, and I firmly believe that we shall beat them, but our triumph should be made decisive and complete. The soldiers of this army love their government, and will fight well in its support: you may rely upon them. They have confidence in me as their general, and in you as their President. Strong reinforcements will at least save the lives of many of them. The greater our force, the more perfect will be our combinations, and the less our loss.

For obvious reasons, I beg you to give immediate consideration to this communication, and to inform me fully at the earliest moment of your final determination.

Geo. B McClellan, Maj.-Gen. Com

To which, on the 8th of May, I received this reply:

Hd.-Qu'rs, Dep'r. Potomac, May 18th, 1862.
To Maj.-Gen Geo. B McClellan,

Comd'g Army of Potomac before Richmond

General,—Your despatch to the President, asking reinforcements, has been received and carefully considered

The President is not willing to uncover the capital entirely, and it is believed that even if this were prudent it would require more time to effect a junction between your army and that of the Rappahannock, by way of the Potomac and York River, than by a land march. In order therefore to increase the strength of the attack upon Richmond at the earliest moment, Gen McDowell has been ordered to march upon that city by the shortest route. He is ordered, keeping himself always in position to save the capital from all possible attack, so to operate as to put his left wing in communication with your right wing, and you are instructed to co-operate so as to establish this communication as soon as possible by extending your right wing to the north of Richmond

It is believed that this communication can be safely established either north or south of the Pamunkey River

In any event you will be able to prevent the enemy's forces from leaving Richmond, and falling in overwhelming force upon Gen McDowell. He will move with between thirty-five and forty thousand men

A copy of the instructions to Gen. McDowell is with this. The specific task assigned to his command, has been to provide against any danger to the capital of the nation.

At your earnest call for reinforcements, he is sent forward to co-operate in the reduction of Richmond, but charged, in attempting this, not to uncover the city of Washington, and you will give no order, either before or after your junction, which can put him out of position to cover this city. You and he will communicate with each other by telegraph or otherwise, as frequently as may be necessary for sufficient co-operation. When Gen McDowell is in position on your right, his supplies must be drawn from West Point and you will instruct your staff-officers to be prepared to supply him by that route.

The President desires that Gen McDowell retain the command of the Department of the Rappahannock, and of the forces with which he moves forward

By order of the President,

EDWIN M. STANTON, Secretary of War.

From Washington, May 18, 2 P M

It will be observed, this order rendered it impossible for me to use the James River as a line of operations, and forced me to establish our depots on the Pamunkey, and to approach Richmond from the north

I had advised, and preferred, that reinforcements should be sent by water, for the reasons that their arrival would be more safe and certain and that I would be left free to rest the army on the James River, whenever the navigation of that stream should be opened. The land movement obliged me to expose my right in order to secure the junction and as the order for Gen McDowell's march was soon countermanded, I incurred great risk, of which the enemy finally took advantage, and frustrated the plan of the campaign. Had Gen McDowell joined me by water, I could have approached Richmond by the James, and thus avoided the delays and losses incurred in bridging the Chickahominy, and would have had the army massed in one body instead of being necessarily divided by that stream.

The following is a copy of the instructions to Gen McDowell

War Dep't., Wash'n., D C, May 17, 1862.

To Gen McDowell,

Com'g Dep't. of Rappahannock,—

General.—Upon being joined by General Shield's division, you will move upon Richmond by the general route of the Richmond and Fredericksburg Railroad, co-operating with the forces under Gen McClellan, now threatening Richmond from the line of the Pamunkey and York Rivers

While seeking to establish, as soon as possible, a communication between your left wing, and the right wing of Gen. McClellan, you will hold yourself always in such a position, as to cover the capital of the nation against a sudden dash of the rebel forces

Gen. McClellan will be furnished with a copy of these instructions, and will be directed to hold himself in readiness, to establish communication with your left wing, and to prevent the main body of the enemy's army from leaving Richmond and throwing itself upon your column, before the junction of the two armies is effected.

A copy of his instructions in regard to the employment of your force is annexed.

By order of the President,

EDWIN M. STANTON, Secretary of War

Having some doubts from the wording of the foregoing orders, as to the extent of my authority over the troops of Gen. McDowell, and as to the time when I might anticipate his arrival, on the 21st of May I sent this despatch:

Headquarters, Army of the Potomac. Camp near Tunstall's Station, Va May 21, 1862, 11 P M

His Excellency Abraham Lincoln,

President of the United States,—

Your dispatch of yesterday respecting our situation and the batteries at Fort Darling, was received while I was absent with advance, where I have been all this day. I have communicated personally with Capt. Goldsborough, and by letter with Capt Smith. The vessels can do nothing without co-operation on land, which I will not be in a condition to afford, for several days, circumstances must determine the propriety of a land attack

It rained again last night and rain on this soil soon makes the roads incredibly bad for army transportation. I personally crossed the Chickahominy to-day, at Bottom's Bridge Ford, and went a mile beyond, the enemy being about half a mile in front. I have three regiments on the other bank, guarding the rebuilding of the bridge. Keyes's corps is on the New Kent Road, near Bottom's Bridge. Heintzelman is on the same road, within supporting distance. Sumner is on the railroad, connecting right with left. Stoneman, with advanced guard, is within one mile of New Bridge. Franklin, with two divisions, is about two miles this side of Stoneman. Porter's division, with the reserves of infantry and artillery, is within supporting distance. Headquarters will probably be at Coal Head tomorrow, one mile this side of Franklin. All the bridges over the Chickahominy are destroyed. The enemy are in force on every road leading to Richmond, within a mile or two west of the stream. Their main body is on the road from New Bridge, encamped along it for four or five miles, spreading over the open ground on both sides. Johnston's head-quarters are about two miles beyond the bridge.

All accounts report their numbers as greatly exceeding our own. The position of the rebel forces, the declaration of the rebel authorities, the resolutions of the Virginia legislature, the action of the city government, the conduct of the citizens, and all other sources of information accessible to me, give positive assurance that our approach to Richmond involves a desperate battle between the opposing armies.

All our divisions are moving towards the foe. I shall advance steadily and carefully, and attack them according to my best judgment, and in such manner as to employ my greatest force.

I regret the state of things as to Gen. McDowell's command. One division added to this army for that effort would do more to protect Washington than his whole force can possibly do anywhere else in the field. The rebels are concentrating from all points for the two battles at Richmond and Corinth. I would still most respectfully suggest the policy of your concentrating here by movements on water. I have heard nothing as to the probabilities of the contemplated junction of McDowell's force with mine. I have no idea when he can start, what are his means of transportation, or when he may be expected to reach this vicinity. I fear there is little hope that he can join me overland, in time for the coming battle; delays, on my part, will be dangerous. I fear sickness and demoralization. This region is unhealthy for northern men, and unless kept moving I fear that our soldiers may become discouraged. At present our numbers are weakening from disease, but our men remain in good heart.

I regret, also, the configuration of the Department of the Rappahannock. It includes a portion even of the city of Richmond. I think that my own department should embrace the entire field of military operations designed for the capture and occupation of that city.

Again I agree with your Excellency that one good general is better than two bad ones.

I am not sure that I fully comprehend your orders of the 17th inst., addressed to myself and Gen. McDowell. If a junction is effected before we occupy Richmond, it must necessarily be east of the railroad to Fredericksburg, and within my department. This fact, my superior rank, and the express language of the 62d article of war, will place his command under my orders, unless it is otherwise specially directed by your Excellency, and I consider that he will be under my command, except that I am not to detach any portion of his forces or give any orders which can put him out of position to cover Washington. If I err in my construction I desire to be at once set right. Frankness compels me to say —anxious as I am for an increase of force—that the march of McDowell's force upon Richmond, by the shortest route, will in my opinion, uncover Washington, as to any interposition by it, as completely as its movement by water. The enemy cannot advance by Fredericksburg on Washington.

Should they attempt a movement, which to me seems utterly improbable, their route would be by Gordonsville and Manassas. I desire that the extent of my authority over McDowell may be clearly defined, lest misunderstandings and conflicting views may produce some of those injurious results which a divided command has so often caused. I would respectfully suggest that this danger can only be surely guarded against by explicitly placing Gen McDowell under my orders in the ordinary way, and holding me strictly responsible for the closest observance of your instructions. I hope, Mr President, that it is not necessary for me to assure you that your instructions would be observed in the utmost good faith, and that I have no personal feelings which could influence me to disregard them in any particular.

I believe that there is a great struggle before this army, but I am neither dismayed nor discouraged. I wish to strengthen its force as much as I can, but in any event I shall fight it with all the skill, caution and determination that I possess, and I trust that the result may either obtain for me the permanent confidence of my government, or that it may close my career.

GEO. B. MCCLELLAN, Maj.-Gen. Comd'g.

On the 24th I received the following reply:

May 24, 1862. From Washington 24th.

Maj-Gen G. B. McClellan,—I left Gen McDowell's camp at dark last evening. Shields' command is there, but is so worn that he cannot move before Monday morning, the 26th. We have so thinned our line to get troops for other places, that it was broken yesterday at Front Royal, with a probable loss to us of one regiment infantry, two companies cavalry, putting General Banks in some peril.

The enemy's forces under Gen. Anderson, now opposing Gen. McDowell's advance, have as their line of supply and retreat the road to Richmond.

If, in conjunction with McDowell's movements against Anderson, you could send a force from your right to cut off the enemy's supplies from Richmond, preserve the railroad bridges across the two forks of the Pomunkey, and intercept the enemy's retreat, you will prevent the army now opposed to you from receiving an accession of numbers of nearly 15,000 men, and if you succeed in saving the bridges, you will secure a line of roalroad for supplies in addition to the one you now have. Can you not do this almost as well as not, while you are building the Chickahominy bridges? McDowell and Shields both say they can, and positively will, move Monday morning. I wish you to march cautiously and safely.

You will have command of McDowell after he joins you, precisely as you indicated in your long dispatch to us of the 21st

A. LINCOLN, President

The information that McDowell's corps would march for Fredericksburg on the following Monday (the 26th), and that he would be under my command as indicated in my telegram of the 21st, was cheering news, and I now felt confident that he would, on his arrival, be sufficiently strong to overpower the large army confronting us

At an hour later on the same day I received the following

May 24 1862. From Washington, 4 p m., '62
Maj-Gen G B McClellan,—

In consequence of Gen Banks' critical position, I have been compelled to suspend Gen McDowell's movements to join you. The enemy are making a desperate push upon Harper's Ferry, and we are trying to throw Gen Fremont's force and part of Gen McDowell's in their rear
A. LINCOLN, President.

From which it will be seen that I could not expect Gen McDowell to join me in time to participate in immediate operations in front of Richmond, and on the same evening I replied to the President that I would make my calculations accordingly

It then only remained for me to make the best use of the forces at my disposal, and to avail myself, of all artificial auxiliaries, to compensate as much as possible for the inadequacy of men I concurred fully with the President in the injunction contained in his telegram of the 24th, that it was necessary with my limited force to move "cautiously and safely." In view of the peculiar character of the Chickahominy and the liability of the bottom-lands to sudden inundation, it became necessary to construct between Bottom's Bridge and Mechanicsville eleven new bridges, all long and difficult, with extensive log-way approaches

The entire army could probably have been thrown across the Chickahominy immediately after our arrival, but this would have left no force on the left bank to guard our communications, or to protect our right and rear. If the communication with our supply depot had been cut by the enemy, with our army concentrated on the right bank of the Chickahominy, and the stage of water as it was for many days after our arrival, the bridges carried away, and our means of transportation not furnishing a single day's supplies in advance, the troops must have gone without rations, and the animals without forage; the army would have been paralyzed.

It is true, I might have abandoned my communications and pushed forward to Richmond, trusting to the speedy defeat of the enemy and the consequent fall of the city, for a renewal of supplies; but the approaches were fortified, and the town itself was surrounded with a strong line of intrenchments requiring a greater length of time to reduce than our troops could have dispensed with rations.

Under these circumstances, I decided to retain a portion of the army on the left bank of the river until our bridges were completed.

It will be remembered that the order for the co-operation of Gen. McDowell was simply suspended, not revoked, and therefore I was not at liberty to abandon the northern approach

A very dashing and successful reconnoissance was made near New Bridge on the 24th of May, by Lieut Bowen, Topographical Engineers escorted by the 4th Michigan Volunteers and a squadron of the 2d U. S. Cavalry, commanded respectively by Col. Woodbury and Capt. Gordon

Our troops encountered a Louisiana regiment, and, with little loss, drove it back upon its brigade, killing a large number and capturing several prisoners. Great credit is due to the staff officers, as well as to Col Woodbury, Capt Gordon, and their commands, for their conduct on this occasion

The work upon the bridges was commenced at once, and pushed forward with great vigor; but the rains which from day today continued to fall, flooded the valley, and raised the water to a greater height than had been known for twenty years. This demolished a great amount of our labor; and our first bridges with their approaches, which were not made with reference to such extreme high water, were carried off or rendered impassable. We were obliged, with immense labor, to construct others much longer, more elevated, and stable. Our men worked in the water, exposed to the enemy's fire from the opposite bank

On the 25th May I received the following telegram

Washington, May 23, 1862
Maj-Gen McClellan,—

Your dispatch received. General Banks was at Strasburg with about 6,000 men—Shields having been taken from him to swell a column for McDowell to aid you at Richmond, and the rest of his force scattered at various places On the 23d a rebel force of seven to ten thousand fell upon one regiment and two companies guarding the bridges at Front Royal, destroying it entirely—crossed the Shenandoah, and on the 24th, yesterday, pushed on to get north of Banks to Winchester. Gen. Banks ran a race with them, beating them into Winchester yesterday evening. This morning a battle ensued between the two forces, in which Gen Banks was beaten back in full retreat towards Martinsburg, and probably is broken up into a total rout Geary on the Manassas Gap railroad, just now reports that Jackson is now near Front Royal with 10,000 following up and supporting, as I understand, the force now pursuing Banks. Also that another force of 10,000 is near Orleans, following on in the same direction Stripped bare as we are here, I will do all that we can do to prevent them crossing the Potomac at Harper's Ferry or above. McDowell has about 20,000 of his forces moving back to the vicinity of Front Royal, and Fremont, who was at Franklin, is moving to Harrisonburg, both these movements intended to go in the enemy's rear

One more of McDowell's brigades is ordered through here to Harper's Ferry, the rest of his forces remain for the present at Fredericksburg

We are sending such regiments and dribs from here and Baltimore as we can spare to Harper's Ferry, supplying their places in some sort by calling in militia from adjacent States. We have also eighteen cannon on the road to Harper's Ferry, of which arm there is not a single one at that point.

This is now our situation. If McDowell's force was now beyond our reach we should be entirely helpless. Apprehensions of something like this, and no unwillingness to sustain you has always been my reason for withholding McDowell's forces from you.

Please understand this, and do the best you can with the forces you have.
A. LINCOLN, President.

On the 25th, the following was also received:
Washington, May 25, 1862, 2 P. M.
Maj.-Gen McClellan:

The enemy is moving north in sufficient force to drive Gen Banks before him, precisely in what force we cannot tell. He is also threatening Leesburg and Geary on the Manassas Gap Railroad from both north and south—in precisely what force we cannot tell. I think the movement is a general and a concerted one, such as could not be if he was acting upon the purpose of a very desperate defense of Richmond. I think the time is near when you must either attack Richmond or give up the job, and come back to the defense of Washington. Let me hear from you instantly.
A. LINCOLN, President.

To which I replied as follows:
Coal Harbor, May 25, 1862.

Telegram received. Independently of it, the time is very near when I shall attack Richmond. The object of the movement is probably to prevent reinforcements being sent to me. All the information obtained from balloons, deserters, prisoners, and contrabands, agrees in the statement that the mass of the rebel troops are still in the immediate vicinity of Richmond, ready to defend it.

I have no knowledge of Banks position and force, nor what there is at Manassas, therefore cannot form a definite opinion as to the force against him.

I have two corps across Chickahominy, within six miles of Richmond, the others on this side at other crossings, within same distance, and ready to cross when bridges are completed.
G B McCLELLAN, Maj Gen. Com'g.
His Excellency, A Lincoln, President.

On the 26th, I received the following:
Washington, May 26, 1862, 12.40 A M.
Maj.-Gen. McClellan.

We have Gen Banks' official report. He has saved his army and baggage, and has made a safe retreat to the river, and is probably safe at Williamsport. He reports the attacking force at fifteen thousand.
A. LINCOLN, President.

On the 26th, I received the following.
Washington, May 26, 1862.
Maj.-Gen. G B McClellan.

Can you not cut the Acquia Creek Railroad, also what impression have you as to intrenched works for you to contend with in front of Richmond. Can you get near enough to throw shells into the city?
A LINCOLN, President.

On the same day I sent the following:
Coal Harbor, May 26, 1862.

Have cut the Virginia Central road in three places between Hanover C H and the Chickahominy. Will try to cut the other. I do not think Richmond intrenchments formidable, but am not certain. Hope very soon to be within shelling distance. Have railroad in operation from White House to Chickahominy. Hope to have Chickahominy bridge repaired to-night. Nothing of interest to-day.
GEO B. McCLELLAN, Maj.-Gen Com'g
His Excellency A. LINCOLN, President.

The interruption of the railroad here referred to was effected by the command of Brig.-Gen. Stoneman, and was intended to prevent the enemy from drawing supplies by that route, or from sending reinforcements to Anderson or Jackson

At 10 A. M I also sent the following dispatch

"Telegrams of last night received. I am glad to know affairs are not so bad as might have been. I would earnestly call your attention to my instructions to Gen Banks, of March 16th, to Gen Wadsworth of same date, and to my letter of April 1st to the adjutant-general. I cannot but think that a prompt return to the principles there laid down would relieve all probability of danger. I will forward copies by mail. I beg to urge the importance of Manassas and Front Royal in contradistinction to Fredericksburg.
GEO B McCLELLAN, Maj.-Gen.
His Excellency. A. Lincoln, President

Late on the 20th I sent the following:
Camp near New Bridge,
May 26 1862 7 30 P. M.

Have arranged to carry out your last orders. We are quietly closing in upon the enemy preparatory to the last struggle. Situated as I am I feel forced to take every possible precaution against disaster, and to secure my flanks against the probably superior force in front of me. My arrangements for to-morrow are very important, and if successful, will leave me free to strike on the return of the force detached.
GEO B McCLELLAN, Maj.-Gen
His Excellency, A. Lincoln, President.

BATTLE OF HANOVER COURT HOUSE

On the same day I received intelligence that a very considerable force of the enemy was in the vicinity of Hanover Court House, to the right and rear of our army, thus threatening our communications, and in a position either to reinforce Jackson, or to impede McDowell's junction, should he finally move to unite with us

On the same day I also received information from Gen. McDowell, through the Secretary of War, that the enemy had fallen back from Fredericksburg towards Richmond, and that Gen McDowell's advance was eight miles south of the Rappahannock. It was thus imperative to dislodge or defeat this force, independently even of the wishes of the President, as expressed in his telegram of the 26th. I intrusted this task to Brig.-Gen Fitz John Porter, commanding the 5th corps, with orders to move at daybreak on the 27th.

Through a heavy rain and over bad roads, that officer moved his command as follows:

Brig.-Gen. W. H. Emory led the advance with

the 5th and 6th regiments U S cavalry and Benson's horse battery of the 2d U S artillery taking the road from New Bridge via Mechanicsville to Hanover Court House.

Gen Morell's division, composed of the brigades of Martindale, Butterfield, and McQuade, with Berdan's regiment of sharpshooters, and three batteries under Capt. Charles Griffin, 5th U S. Artillery, followed on the same road

Col G K Warren, commanding a provisional brigade composed of the 5th and 13th New York, the 1st Connecticut Artillery acting as infantry, the 5th Pennsylvania Cavalry and Weeden's Rhode Island battery moved from his station at Old Church, by a road running to Hanover Court House, parallel to the Pamunkey After a fatiguing march of fourteen miles through the mud and rain, Gen Emory at noon reached a point about two miles from Hanover Court House where the road forks to Ashland, and found a portion of the enemy formed in line across the Hanover Court House road

Gen Emory had before this been joined by the 25th New York (of Martindale's brigade) and Berdan's sharpshooters, these regiments were deployed with a section of Benson's battery, and advanced slowly towards the enemy until reinforced by Gen Butterfield with four regiments of his brigade, when the enemy was charged and quickly routed, one of his guns being captured by the 17th New York under Col Lansing, after having been disabled by the fire of Benson's battery The firing here lasted about an hour The cavalry and Benson's battery were immediately ordered in pursuit, followed by Morell's infantry, and artillery, with the exception of Martindale's brigade. Warren's brigade having been delayed by repairing bridges &c now arrived too late to participate in this affair; a portion of this command was sent to the Pamunkey to destroy bridges and captured quite a number of prisoners, the remainder followed Morell's division In the meantime, Gen Martindale, with the few remaining regiments of his brigade, and a section of artillery advanced on the Ashland road, and found a force of the enemy's infantry, cavalry, and artillery in position near Peake's Station on the Virginia Central Railroad. he soon forced them to retire towards Ashland

The 25th New York having been ordered to rejoin him, Gen Martindale was directed to form his brigade and move up the railroad to rejoin the rest of the command at Hanover Court House

He sent one regiment up the railroad, but remained with the 2d Maine, afterwards joined by the 25th New York, to guard the rear of the main column.

The enemy soon returned to attack Gen. Martindale, who at once formed the 2d Maine, 25th New York and a portion of of the 44th New Jersey, with one section of Martin's battery, on the New Bridge Road, facing his own position of the morning, and then held his ground for an hour against large odds until reinforced

General Porter was at Hanover Court House, near the head of his column, when he learned that the rear had been attacked by a large force, He at once faced the whole column about, recalled the cavalry sent in pursuit towards Ashland, moved the 13th and 14th New York and Griffin's battery direct to Martindale's assistance, pushed the 9th Massachusetts, and 52d Pennsylvania of McQuade's brigade through the woods on the right (our original left) and attacked the flank of the enemy, while Butterfield with the 83d Pennsylvania, and 16th Michigan, hastened towards the scene of action by the railroad and through the woods further to the right, and completed the rout of the enemy. During the remainder of this and the following day our cavalry was active in the pursuit, taking a number of prisoners Captain Harrison of the U S. Cavalry with a single company, brought in as prisoners two entire companies of infantry, with their arms and ammunition A part of Rush's Lancers also captured an entire company with their arms

The immediate results of these affairs were some two hundred of the enemy's dead, buried by our troops, seven hundred and thirty prisoners sent to the rear, one 12-pounder howitzer, one caisson, a large number of small arms, and two railroad trains captured

Our loss amounted to 53 killed, 344 wounded and missing.

The force encountered and defeated was Gen. Branch's division of North Carolina and Georgia troops, supposed to have been some 9,000 strong Their camp at Hanover Court House was taken and destroyed

Having reason to believe that Gen Anderson with a strong force, was still at Ashland, I ordered Gen Syke's division of regulars to move on the 28th, from New Bridge to Hanover Court House, and remained there until the evening of the 20th, when they returned to their original camp

On the 28th, Gen Stoneman's command of cavalry, horse artillery, and two regiments of infantry, were also placed under General Porter's orders

On the same day I visited Hanover Court House whence I sent the following dispatch

Hanover Court House, May 28 2 P M

Porter's action of yesterday was truly a glorious victory—too much credit cannot be given to his magnificent division and its accomplished leader The rout of the rebels was complete, not a defeat but a complete rout Prisoners are constantly coming in, two companies have this moment arrived, with excellent arms.

There is no doubt that the enemy are concentrating everything on Richmond I will do my best to cut off Jackson, but am doubtful whether I can.

It is the policy and duty of the government to send me by water all the well drilled troops available. I am confident that Washington is in no danger. Engines and cars in large numbers have been sent up to bring down Jackson's command.

I may not be able to cut them off, but will try; we have cut all but the F. & R. R. R. The real issue is in the battle about to be fought in front of Richmond All our available troops should be collected here, not raw regiments, but well drilled troops It cannot be ignored that a desperate battle is before us, if any regiment of good troops remain unemployed it will be an irreparable fault committed

G B McClellan, Major-General
Hon. E M. Stanton, Sec of War.

Having ascertained the state of affairs, instructions were given for the operations of the following day

On the 28th a party under Major Williams, 6th U S Cavalry, destroyed the common road bridges over the Pamunkey and the Virginia Central Railroad bridge over the South Anna

On the 29th, he destroyed the Fredericksburg and Richmond bridge over the South Anna, and the Turnpike bridge over the same stream

On the same day, and mainly to cover the movement of Maj Williams, Gen Emory moved a column of cavalry toward Ashland, from Hanover Court House, the advance or this column, under Capt Chambliss, 5th U S. Cavalry, entered Ashland, driving out a party of the enemy, destroyed the railroad bridge over Stoney Creek, and broke up the railroad bridge and telegraph

Another column, of all arms, under Col. Warren, was sent on the same day, in the direct road to Ashland, and entered it shortly after General Emory's column had retired, capturing a small party there

Gen Stoneman, on the same day, moved to Ashland by Leach's Station, covering well the movements of the other column.

The objects of the expedition having been accomplished, and it being certain that the 1st corps would not join us at once, General Porter withdrew his command to their camps with the main army, on the evening of the 29th

On the night of the 27th and 28th, I sent the following dispatch to the Secretary of War

Headquarters, Army of the Potomac
Camp near New Bridge, May 28, 1862 12 30 a m

Porter has gained two complete victories over superior forces, yet I feel obliged to move there in the morning with reinforcements, to secure the complete destruction of the rebels in that quarter In doing so, I run some risk here, but I cannot help it The enemy are even in greater force than I had supposed I will do all that quick movements can accomplish, but you must send me all the troops you can, and leave to me full latitude as to choice of commanders It is absolutely necessary to destroy the rebels near Hanover Court House before I can advance.

Geo B. McClellan, Major-General
Hon E. M Stanton Sec of War.

In reply to which, I received the following from the President:

Washington, May 28, 1862.
Major-General McClellan,—

I am very glad of Gen F J Porter's victory, still, if it was a total rout of the enemy, I am puzzled to know why the Richmond and Fredericksburg Railroad was not seized again, as you say you have all the railroads but the Richmond and Fredericksburg. I am puzzled to see how, lacking that, you can have any, except the scrap from Richmond to West Point, the scrap of the Virginia Central, from Richmond to Hanover without more, is simply nothing. That the whole of the enemy is concentrating on Richmond, I think cannot be certainly known to you or me Saxton, at Harper's Ferry, informs us that a large force, supposed to be Jackson's and McEwell's, forced his advance from Charlestown to-day. Gen King telegraphed us from Fredericksburg, that contrabands give certain information, that fifteen thousand left Hanover Junction Monday morning to reinforce Jackson I am painfully impressed with the importance of the struggle before you, and shall aid you all I can consistently with my view of due regard to all points.

A LINCOLN.

At 6 P.M of the 29th, I sent the Secretary of War the following dispatch

Headquarters, Army of the Potomac,
May 29, 1862, 6 P M

Gen. Porter has gained information, that Gen. Anderson left his position in the vicinity of Fredericksburg, at 4 A M, Sunday, with the following troops:—1st S C, Col Hamilton, 1 battalion S C. Rifles, 34th and 38th N C, 45th Georgia, 12th, 13th and 14th S C, 3d Louisiana, 2 batteries of 4 guns each, namely, Letcher's Va, and McIntosh's S C batteries General Anderson and his command, passed Ashland yesterday evening, en route for Richmond, leaving men behind to destroy bridges over the telegraph road, which they traveled This information is reliable. It is also positively certain, that Branch's command was from Gordonsville, bound for Richmond, whither they have now gone

It may be regarded as positive, I think, that there is no rebel force between Fredericksburg and Junction.

G B McCLELLAN Major-Gen.
Hon E M. Stanton, Secretary of War

The following was also sent on the same day:

Headquarters. Army of the Potomac,
May 29, 1862.
Hon E M Stanton, Secretary of War,

A detachment from Gen F J. Porter's command, under Major Williams, 6th Cavalry, destroyed the South Anna railroad bridge, at about 9 A M to-day A large quantity of confederate public property was also destroyed at Ashland this morning R. B MARCY Chief-of-Staff

In reply to which the following was received:

Washington, May 29, 1862.
Gen. R B Marcy:

Your dispatch, as to South Anna and Ashland being seized by our forces this morning, is received Understanding these points to be on the Richmond and Fredericksburg Railroad, I heartily congratulate the country, and thank Gen. McClellan and his army for the seizure.

A LINCOLN

On the 30th I sent the following:

Headquarters, Army of the Potomac,
May 30, 1862.

From tone of your dispatches and President's, I do not think that you at all appreciate the value and magnitude of Porter's victory It has entirely relieved my right flank, which was seriously threatened, routed and demoralized a considerable portion of the rebel forces taken over seven hundred and fifty prisoners, killed and wounded large numbers one gun, many small arms and much baggage taken It was one of the handsomest things in the war, both in itself and its results Porter has returned, and my army is again well in hand Another day will make the probable field of battle passable for artillery It is quite certain that there is nothing in front of McDowell—(Fredericksburg) I regard the burning of South Anna bridges as the least important result of Porter's movements

G B McClellan, Major-Gen

Hon E M Stanton, Secretary of War

The results of the brilliant operation of Gen. Porter were the dispersal of Gen Branch's division, and the clearing of our right flank and rear It was rendered impossible for the enemy to communicate by rail with Fredericksburg, or with Jackson via Gordonsville, except by the very circuitous route of Lynchburg, and the road was left entirely open for the advance of McDowell had he been permitted to join the army of the Potomac.

His withdrawal towards Front Royal was, in my judgment a serious and fatal error, he could do no good in that direction; while, had he been permitted to carry out the orders of May 17, the united forces would have driven the enemy within the immediate intrenchments of Richmond before Jackson could have returned to its succor, and probably would have gained possession of that place I respectfully refer to the reports of General Porter and his subordinate commanders, for the names of the officers who deserve especial mention for the parts they took in these affairs But I cannot omit here my testimony to the energy and ability displayed by Gen Porter on this occasion, since to him is mainly due the successes there gained

OPERATIONS BEFORE RICHMOND

On the 20th of May a reconnoissance was ordered on the south side of the Chickahominy, towards James River This is accomplished by Brig-Gen H M Naglee, who crossed his brigade near Bottom's Bridge, and pushed forward to within two miles of James River, without serious resistance, or finding the enemy in force

The rest of the 4th Corps, commanded by Gen E D Keyes, crossed the Chickahominy on the 23d of May

On the 24th, 25th and 26th, a very gallant reconnoissance was pushed by Gen. Naglee, with his brigade, beyond the Seven Pines, and on the 25th the 4th Corps was ordered to take up and fortify a position in the vicinity of the Seven Pines The order was at once obeyed, a strong line of rifle-pits opened, and an abattis constructed a little in the rear of the point where the Nine Mile road comes into the Williamsburgh road.

On the same day General Heintzelman was ordered to cross with his corps (the 3d), and take a position two miles in advance of Bottom's Bridge, watching the crossings of White Oak Swamp, and covering the left and the rear of the left wing of the army Being the senior officer on that side the river, he was placed in command of both corps and ordered to hold the Seven Pines at all hazards, but not to withdraw the troops from the crossings of White Oak Swamp, unless in an emergency.

On the 28th Gen Keyes was ordered to advance Casey's division to "Fair Oaks" on the Williamsburg road, some three-quarters of a mile in front of the Seven Pines, leaving Gen Couch's division at the line of rifle-pits A new line of rifle-pits and a small redoubt for six field guns were commenced, and considerable of the timber in front of the line was felled on the two days following The picket line was established, reaching from the Chickahominy to White Oak Swamp.

On the 30th Gen Heintzelman, representing that the advance had met with sharp opposition in taking up their position, and that he considered the point a critical one, requested and obtained authority to make such disposition of his troops as he saw fit to meet the emergency He immediately advanced two brigades of Kearney's division about three-fourths of a mile in front of Savage's Station, thus placing them within supporting distance of Casey's division, which held the advance of the 4th Corps

BATTLE OF FAIR OAKS.

On the 30th the troops on the south side of the Chickahominy were in position as follows;

Casey's division on the right of the Williamsburg road, at right angles to it, the centre at Fair Oaks, Couch's division at Seven Pines, Kearney's division on the railroad, from near Savage's Station towards the bridge · Hooker's division on the borders of White Oak Swamp Constant skirmishing had been kept up between our pickets and those of the enemy, while these lines were being taken up and strengthened. Large bodies of Confederate troops were seen immediately to the front and right of Casey's position.

During the day and night of the 30th of May a very violent storm occurred The rain, falling in torrents, rendered work on the rifle-pits and bridges impracticable, made the roads almost impassable and threatened the destruction of the bridges over the Chickahominy

The enemy, perceiving the unfavorable position in which we were placed, and the possibility of destroying that part of our army which was apparently cut off from the main body by the rapidly rising stream, threw an overwhelming force (grand divisions of Gens D H Hill, Huger, Longstreet and G. W. Smith) upon the position occupied by Casey's division.

It appears, from the official reports of Gen Keyes and his subordinate commanders, that, at 10 o'clock A M., on the 31st of May, an aide-de-camp of Gen J. E Johnston was captured by Gen. Naglee's pickets. But little information as to the movements of the enemy was obtained from him, but his presence so near our lines excited suspicion and caused increased vigilance, and the troops were ordered by Gen. Keyes to be under arms at 11 o'clock

Between 11 and 12 it was reported to Gen. Casey that the enemy were approaching in considerable force on the Williamsburg road At this time Casey's division was disposed of as follows

Naglee's brigade, extending from the Williamsburg road to the Garnett field, having one regiment across the railroad. Gen. Wessels's brigade in the rifle-pits, and Gen Palmer's in the rear of Gen. Wessels, one battery of artillery in advance, with Gen. Naglee, one battery in rear of rifle-pits, to the right of the redoubt, one battery in rear of the redoubt, and another battery unharnessed in the redoubt.

Gen Couch's division holding the second line, had Gen Abercrombie's brigade on the right, along the Nine Mile road, with two regiments and one battery across the railroad, near Fair Oaks Station; Gen. Peck's brigade on the right, and Gen Devin's in the centre.

On the approach of the enemy Gen Casey sent forward one of Gen Palmer's regiments to support the picket line, but this regiment gave way, without making much, if any, resistance

Heavy firing at once commenced, and the pickets were driven in Gen Keyes ordered Gen Couch to move Gen Peck's brigade to occupy the ground on the left of the Williamsburg road, which had not before been occupied by our forces, and thus to support Gen Casey's left, where the first attack was the most severe. The enemy now came on in heavy force, attacking Gen. Casey simultaneously in front and on both flanks.

Gen. Keyes sent to Gen Heintzelman for reinforcements, but the messenger was delayed, so that orders were not sent to Gens Kearney and Hooker until near 3 o'clock, and it was nearly 5 P M when Gen Jamison's and Barry's brigades, of Gen Kearney's division, arrived on the field Gen Birney was ordered up the railroad, but, by Gen Kearney's order, halted his brigade before arriving at the scene of action. Orders were also dispatched for Gen Hooker to move up from White Oak Swamp, and he arrived after dark at Savage's Station

As soon as the firing was heard at headquarters, orders were sent to Gen. Sumner to get his command under arms, and be ready to move at a moment's warning. His corps, consisting of Gens Richardson's and Sedgwick's divisions, was encamped on the north side of the Chickahominy, some six miles above Bottom's Bridge. Each division had thrown a bridge over the stream opposite to its own position.

At 1 o'clock Gen Sumner moved the two divisions to their respective bridges, with instructions to halt and await further orders.

At 2 o'clock orders were sent from headquarters to cross these divisions without delay, and push them rapidly to Gen. Heintzelman's support. This order was received and communicated at half-past two, and the passage was immediately commenced.

In the meantime Gen Naglee's brigade, with the batteries of Gen Casey's division, which Gen Naglee directed, struggled gallantly to maintain the redoubt and rifle-pits against the overwhelming masses of the enemy. They were reinforced by a regiment from Gen. Peck's brigade.

The artillery under the command of Col. G D Bailey, 1st New York Artillery, and afterwards under Gen Naglee, did good execution on the advancing columns. The left of this position was however, soon turned, and a sharp cross-fire opened upon the gunners and the men in the rifle-pits Col Bailey Maj Van Valkenburg, and Adj't Ramsey, of the same regiment, were killed. Some of the guns in the redoubt were taken and the whole line was driven back upon the position occupied by Gen. Couch The brigades of Gens. Wessels and Palmer, with the reinforcements which had been sent them from Gen Couch, had also been driven from the field with heavy loss and the whole position occupied by Gen Casey's division was taken by the enemy

Previous to this time, Gen Keyes ordered Gen Couch to advance two regiments to relieve the pressure upon Gen. Casey's right flank. In making this movement Gen Couch discovered large masses of the enemy pushing towards our right and crossing the railroad, as well as a heavy column which had been held in reserve, and which was now making its way towards Fair Oaks Station Gen Couch at once engaged this column with these two regiments. but, though reinforced by two additional regiments, he was overpowered, and the enemy pushed between him and the main body of his division With these four regiments and one battery Gen Couch fell back about half a mile towards the Grape-Vine Bridge, where, hearing that Gen Sumner had crossed he formed line of battle facing Fair Oaks Station, and prepared to hold the position.

Gens Berry's and Jamison's brigades had by this time arrived in front of the Seven Pines Gen Berry was ordered to take possession of the woods on the left, and push forward so as to have a flank fire on the enemy's lines. This movement was executed brilliantly, Gen Berry pushing his regiment forward through the woods, until their rifles commanded the left of the camp and works occupied by Gen Casey's division in the morning Their fire on the pursuing columns of the enemy was very destructive, and assisted materially in checking the pursuit in that part of the field He held his position in these woods against several attacks of superior numbers, and after dark, being cut off by the enemy from the main body, he fell back towards White Oak Swamp, and, by a circuit, brought his men into our lines in good order.

Gen. Jamison, with two regiments—the other two of his brigade having been detached, one to Gen Peck and one to Gen. Birney—moved rapidly to the front on the left of the Williamsburg road, and succeeded for a time in keeping the abattis clear of the enemy. but large numbers of the enemy pressing past the right of his line, he too was forced to retreat through the woods towards White Oak Swamp, and in that way gained camp under cover of night.

Brig.-Gen Devins, who had held the centre of Gen Couch's division, had made repeated and gallant efforts to regain portions of the ground lost in front, but each time was driven back, and finally withdrew behind the rifle pits near Seven Pines.

Meantime, Gen Sumner had arrived with the advance of his corps, Gen. Sedgwick's division.

at the point held by Gen. Couch with four regiments and one battery. The roads leading from the bridge, were so miry, that it was only by the greatest exertion, Gen. Sedgwick had been able to get one of his batteries to the front.

The leading regiment (1st Minnesota, Col. Sully) was immediately deployed to the right of Couch to protect the flank, and the rest of the division formed in line of battle. Kirby's battery near the centre in an angle of the woods. One of Gen. Couch's regiments was sent to open communication with Gen. Heintzelman. No sooner were these dispositions made, than the enemy came in strong force, and opened a heavy fire along the line. He made several charges, but was repulsed with great loss, by the steady fire of the infantry, and the splendid practice of the battery. After sustaining the enemy's fire for a considerable time, Gen. Sumner ordered five regiments (the 34th New York, Col. Smith, 82d New York, Lieut.-Col. Hudson, 15th Mass., Lieut.-Col. Kimball, 20th Mass., Col. Lee, 7th Michigan, Maj. Richardson, the three former, of Gen. Gorman's brigade, the two latter, of Gen. Dana's brigade) to advance and charge with bayonet. This charge was executed in the most brilliant manner. Our troops, springing over two fences which were between them and the enemy, rushed upon his lines and drove him in confusion from that part of the field. Darkness now ended the battle for that day.

During the night, dispositions were made for its early renewal. Gen. Couch's division, and so much of Gen. Casey's as could be collected together, with Gen. Kearney's, occupied the rifle-pits near Seven Pines. Gen. Peck in falling back on the left, had succeeded, late in the afternoon, in rallying a considerable number of stragglers, and was taking them once more into the action, when he was ordered back into the intrenched camp by Gen. Kearney. Gen. Hooker brought up his division about dark, having been delayed by the heaviness of the roads, and the throng of fugitives from the field, through whom, the Colonel of the leading regiment (Starr) reports, he "was obliged to force his way with the bayonet." This division bivouacked for the night, in rear of the right of the rifle-pits, on the other side of the railroad. Gen. Richardson's division also came upon the field about sunset. He had attempted the passage of the Chickahominy by the bridge opposite his own camp, but it was so far destroyed, that he was forced to move Gen. Howard's and Meagher's brigades, with all his artillery, around by Gen. Sedgwick's bridge, while Gen. French's brigade, with the utmost difficulty, crossed by the other. Gen. Sedgwick's division, with the regiments under Gen. Couch, held about the same position as when the fight ceased; and Gen. Richardson, on his arrival, was ordered to place his division on the left, to connect with Gen. Kearney. Gen. French's brigade was posted along the railroad, and Gens. Howard's and Meagher's brigades, in second and third lines. All his artillery had been left behind, it being impossible to move it forward through the deep mud, as rapidly as the infantry pushed toward the field, but during the night, the three batteries of the division were brought to the front.

About five o'clock in the morning of the 1st of June, skirmishers, and some cavalry of the enemy, were discovered in front of Gen. Richardson's division. Capt. Pettit's battery (B, 1st N. Y.) having come upon the ground, threw a few shells among them, when they dispersed. There was a wide interval between Gen. Richardson and Gen Kearney. To close this, Gen. Richardson's line was extended to the left, and his first line moved over the railroad. Scarcely had they gained this position, when the enemy appearing in large force, from the woods in front, opened a heavy fire of musketry at short range, along the whole line. He approached very rapidly with columns of attack, formed on two roads which crossed the railroad. These columns were supported by infantry in line of battle on each side, cutting Gen French's line. He threw out no skirmishers, but appeared determined to carry all before him by one crushing blow. For nearly an hour the first line of Gen Richardson's division, stood and returned the fire, the lines of the enemy being reinforced and relieved, time after time, until finally Gen. Howard was ordered, with his brigade, to go to Gen French's assistance. He led his men gallantly to the front, and in a few minutes the fire of the enemy ceased, and his whole line fell back on that part of the field.

On the opening of the firing in the morning Gen Hooker pushed forward on the railroad with two regiments (5th and 6th New Jersey), followed by Gen. Sickles' brigade. It was found impossible to move the artillery of this division from its position, on account of the mud. On coming near the woods, which were held by the enemy in force, Gen Hooker found Gen. Birney's brigade, Col J. Hobart Ward in command, in line of battle. He sent back to hasten Gen. Sickles' brigade, but ascertained that it had been turned off to the left by Gen. Heintzelman to meet a column advancing in that direction. He at once made the attack with the two New Jersey regiments, calling upon Col. Ward to support him with Gen. Birney's brigade. This was well done, our troops advancing into the woods under a heavy fire, and pushing the enemy before them for more than an hour of hard fighting. A charge with the bayonet was then ordered by Gen. Hooker, with the 5th and 6th New Jersey, 3d Maine, and 38th and 40th New York, and the enemy fled in confusion, throwing down arms and even clothing in his flight. Gen. Sickles having been ordered to the right, formed line of battle on both sides of the Williamsburg road, and advanced under a sharp fire from the enemy deployed in the woods in front of him. After a brisk interchange of musketry fire while crossing the open ground, the Excelsior brigade dashed into the timber with the bayonet and put the enemy to flight.

On the right the enemy opened fire after half an hour's cessation, which was promptly responded to by Gen Richardson's division. Again the most vigorous efforts were made to break our line, and again they were frustrated by the steady courage of our troops. In about an hour Gen. Richardson's whole line advanced, pouring in their fire at close range, which threw the line of the enemy back in some confusion. This was followed up by a bayonet charge, led by Gen French in person, with the 57th and 66th New York, supported by two regiments sent by Gen. Heintzelman, the 71st and 73d New York, which turned the confusion of the enemy into precipitate flight. One gun captured the previous day was retaken.

Our troops pushed forward as far as the lines held by them on the 31st, before the attack. On the battle field there were found many of our own and the Confederate wounded, arms, caissons, wagons, subsistence stores, and forage, abandoned by the enemy in his rout. The state of the roads, and the impossibility of his manœuvring artillery, prevented further pursuit.

On the next morning a reconnoissance was sent forward, which pressed back the pickets of the enemy to within five miles of Richmond, but again the impossibility of forcing even a few batteries forward, precluded our holding permanently this position. The lines held previous to the battle were therefore resumed.

Gen J. E. Johnston reports loss of the enemy in Longstreet's and G. W. Smith's divisions at 4,283
Gen D. H. Hill, who had taken the advance in the attack, estimates his loss at 2,500

Which would give enemy's loss . 6,783
Our loss in Gen Sumner's corps 1,223
" Gen. Heintzelman's corps 1,394
" Gen Keyes' corps 3,120

Total . . . 5,737

Previous to the arrival of Gen Sumner upon the field of battle on the 31st of May, Gen Heintzelman, the senior corps commander present, was in the immediate command of the forces engaged. The first information I received that the battle was in progress, was a dispatch from him stating that Casey's division had given way. During the night of the 31st I received a dispatch from him dated 8.45 P M, in which he says. "I am just in—when I got to the front, the most of Gen Casey's division had dispersed" * * * "The rout of Gen. Casey's men had a most dispiriting effect on the troops as they came up. I saw no reason why we should have been driven back."

This official statement, together with other accounts, received previous to my arrival upon the battle-field, to the effect that Casey's division had given way without making a proper resistance, caused me to state in a telegram to the Secretary of War on the 1st, that this division "gave way unaccountably and discreditably.' Subsequent investigations, however, greatly modified the impressions first received, and I accordingly advised the Secretary of War of this in a dispatch on the 5th of June.

The official reports of Generals Keyes, Casey and Naglee, show that a very considerable portion of this division fought well, and that the brigade of Gen Naglee is entitled to credit for its gallantry. This division, among the regiments of which were eight of comparatively new troops, was attacked by superior numbers, yet, according to the reports alluded to, it "stood to attack for three hours before it was reinforced." A portion of the division was thrown into great confusion by the first onslaught of the enemy, but the personal efforts of General Naglee Colonel Bailey and others, who boldly went to the front and encouraged the men by their presence and example at this critical juncture, rallied a great part of the division, and thereby enabled it to act a prominent part in this severely contested battle. It therefore affords me great satisfaction to withdraw the expression contained in my first dispatch, and I cordially give my indorsement to the conclusion of the division commander, "that those parts of his command which behaved discreditably were exceptional cases."

On the 31st, when the battle of Fair Oaks commenced, we had two of our bridges nearly completed, but the rising waters floated the log-way approaches and made them almost impassable, so that it was only by the greatest efforts that Gen. Sumner crossed his corps and participated in that hard-fought engagement. The bridges became totally useless after this corps had passed, and others on a more permanent plan were commenced.

On my way to head-quarters, after the battle of Fair Oaks, I attempted to cross the bridge where Gen. Sumner had taken over his corps on the day previous. At the time Gen Sumner crossed, this was the only available bridge above Bottom's Bridge. I found the approach from the right bank for some 400 yards submerged to the depth of several feet, and on reaching the place where the bridge had been, I found a great part of it carried away, so that I could not get my horse over, and was obliged to send him to Bottom's Bridge, six miles below, as the only practicable crossing.

The approaches to New and Mechanicsville bridges were also overflowed, and both of them were enfiladed by the enemy's batteries, established upon commanding heights on the opposite side. These batteries were supported by strong forces of the enemy, having numerous rifle-pits in their front, which would have made it necessary, even had the approaches been in the best possible condition, to have fought a sanguinary battle, with but little prospect of success, before a passage could have been secured.

The only available means, therefore, of uniting our forces at Fair Oaks for an advance on Richmond soon after the battle, was to march the troops from Mechanicsville and other points on the left bank of the Chickahominy down to Bottom's Bridge, and thence over the Williamsburg road to the position near Fair Oaks, a distance of about twenty-three miles. In the condition of the roads at that time, this march could not have been made with artillery in less than two days, by which time the enemy would have been secure within his entrenchments around Richmond. In short, the idea of uniting the two wings of the army in time to make a vigorous pursuit of the enemy, with the prospect of overtaking him before he reached Richmond, only five miles distant from the field of battle, is simply absurd, and was, I presume, never for a moment seriously entertained by any one connected with the Army of the Potomac. An advance involving the separation of the two wings by the impassable Chickahominy would have exposed each to defeat in detail. Therefore I held the position already gained, and completed our crossings as rapidly as possible.

In the meantime the troops at Fair Oaks were directed to strengthen their positions by a strong line of intrenchments, which protected them while the bridges were being built, gave security to the trains, liberated a large fighting force, and offered a safe retreat in the event of disaster.

On the second of June I sent the following dispatch:—

Headquarters Army of the Potomac,
New Bridge, June 2d 1862, 10 30 A M.

Our left is everywhere advanced considerably beyond the positions it occupied before the battle.

I am in strong hopes that the Chickahominy will fall sufficiently to enable me to cross the right. We have had a terrible time with our communications, bridges and causeways built with great care, having been washed away with the freshet, leaving us almost cut off from communication. All that human labor can do is being done to accomplish our purpose.

Please regard the portion of this relating to condition of Chickahominy as confidential, as it would be serious if the enemy were aware of it. I do not yet know our loss, it has been very heavy on both sides, as the fighting was desperate, our victory complete. I expect still more fighting before we reach Richmond.

G. B. McCLELLAN Major-Gen.

Hon L M Stanton, Secretary of War.

On the same day I received the following from the Secretary of War:—

Washington, June 3, 1862.

Maj.-Gen. McC.—Your telegram has been received, and we are greatly rejoiced at your success not only in itself, but because of the dauntless spirit of the troops. You have received, of course, the order made yesterday in respect to Fortress Monroe. The object was to place at your command the disposable force of that department. The indications are that Fremont or McDowell will fight Jackson to-day, and as soon as he is disposed of another large body of troops will be at your service. The intelligence from Halleck shows that the rebels are fleeing, and pursued in force from Corinth. All interest now centres in your operations, and full confidence is entertained of your brilliant and glorious success.

E M S, Sec. of War.

OPERATIONS BEFORE RICHMOND.

On the 3rd I received the following from the President:—

Washington, June 3, 1862.

Maj.-Gen. McC.—With these continuous rains, I am very anxious about the Chickahominy, so close in your rear and crossing your line of communication. Please look well to it.

A L, President.

To which I replied as follows:—

Headquarters, Army of the Potomac New Bridge, June 3d 1862. Your dispatch of 5 p m just received. As the Chickahominy has been almost the only obstacle in my way for several days, your Excellency may be assured that it has been made, and will continue to be, to protect the communications across it. Nothing of importance, except that it is again raining.

G B McC, Maj.-Gen. Com'g.

A L, President, Washington.

My views of the condition of our army on the 4th are explained in the following dispatch to the President:—

Headquarters, Army of the Potomac, New Bridge, June 4th, 1862.—Terrible rain storm during the night and morning, not yet cleared off, Chickahominy flooded, bridges in bad condition, and still hard at work at them. I have taken every possible step to insure the security of the corps on the right bank, but I cannot reinforce them from here until my bridges are all safe, as my force is too small to insure my right and rear should the enemy attack in that direction, as they may probably attempt. I have to be very cautious now. Our loss in the late battle will probably exceed 5,000. I have not yet full returns. On account of the effect it might have on our own men and the enemy, I request that you will regard this information as confidential for a few days. I am satisfied that the loss of the enemy was very considerably greater, they were terribly punished. I mention these facts now merely to show you that the army of the Potomac has had serious work, and that no child's play is before it.

You must make your calculations on the supposition that I have been correct from the beginning, in asserting that the serious opposition was to be made here.

Geo B McC, Maj.-Gen Comd'g

A. L, President, Washington.

And in the following to the Secretary of War on the same day :

Headquarters, Army of the Potomac, New Bridge, June 4th, 1862.—Please inform me at once what reinforcements, if any, I can count upon having at Fortress Monroe or White House within the next three days, and when each regiment may be expected to arrive. It is of the utmost importance that I should know this immediately. The losses in the battle of the 31st and 1st will amount to 7,000. Regard this as confidential for the present.

If I can have five new regiments for Fort Monroe and its dependencies, I can draw three more old regiments from there safely. I can well dispose of four more raw regiments on my communications. I can well dispose of from fifteen to twenty well-drilled regiments among the old brigades, in bringing them up to their original effective strength. Recruits are especially necessary for the regular and volunteer batteries of artillery, as well as for the regular and volunteer regiments of infantry. After the losses in our last battle, I trust that I will be no longer regarded as an alarmist. I believe we have at least one more desperate battle to fight.

Geo B McC Maj.-Gen.

Hon. E M S., Sec of War

Also my dispatch to the Secretary of War of the 5th:

Headquarters, Army of the Potomac, New

Bridge June 5, 1862.—Rained most of the night—has now ceased, but it is not clear. The river still very high and troublesome. Enemy opened with several batteries on our brigades near here this morning; our batteries seem to have pretty much silenced them, though some firing still kept up. The rain forces us to remain in statu quo. With great difficulty a division of infantry has been crossed this morning to support the troops on the other side should the enemy renew the attack. I felt obliged to do this, although it leaves us rather weak here.

G. B. McC., Maj.-Gen. Comd'g.

Hon. E. M. S., Sec. of War.

On the 5th the Secretary telegraphed me as follows:—

Washington, June 5, 1862, 8.30 p.m.

Maj.-Gen. McC.,—I will send you five new regiments as fast as transportation can take them; the first to start to-morrow from Baltimore. I intend sending you part of McDowell's force as soon as it can return from its trip to Front Royal, probably as many as you want. The order to ship the new regiments to Fort Monroe has already been given. I suppose that they may be sent directly to the Fort. Please advise me of this as usual. E. M. S., Sec. of War.

On the 7th of June I telegraphed as follows:

Headquarters, Army of the Potomac,
June, 7, 1862, 4.40 p.m.

Hon. E. M. S.,—In reply to your dispatch of 2 p.m., to-day, I have the honor to state that the Chickahominy River has risen so as to flood the entire bottom to the depth of three and four feet. I am pushing forward the bridges in spite of this, and the men are working night and day, up to their waists in water, to complete them.

The whole face of the country is a perfect bog, entirely impassable for artillery or even cavalry, except directly in the narrow roads which renders any general movement either of this or the rebel army much out of the question, until we have more favorable weather.

I am glad to learn that you are pressing forward reinforcements so vigorously. I shall be in perfect readiness to move forward and take Richmond the moment McCall reaches here, and the ground will admit the passage of artillery. I have advanced my pickets about a mile to-day, driving off the rebel pickets, and securing a very advantageous position.

The rebels have several batteries established, commanding the debouches from two of our bridges, and fire upon our working parties continually, but as yet they have killed but very few of our men. G. B. McC., Maj.-General.

As I did not think it probable that any more reinforcements would be sent to me in time for the advance on Richmond, I stated in the foregoing dispatch that I should be ready to move when Gen. McCall's Division joined me; but I did not intend to be understood by this, that no more reinforcements were wanted, as will be seen from the following dispatch:

June 10, 1862, 3.30 p.m.—I have again information that Beauregard has arrived, and that some of his troops are to follow him. No great reliance, perhaps none whatever, can be attached to this, but it is possible, and ought to be their policy.

I am completely checked by the weather. The roads and fields are literally impassable for artillery, almost so for infantry. The Chickahominy is in a dreadful state, we have another rain storm on our hands.

I shall attack as soon as the weather and ground will permit, but there will be a delay, the extent of which no one can forsee, for the season is altogether abnormal.

In view of these circumstances, I present for your consideration the propriety of detaching largely from Halleck's army to strengthen this, for it would seem that Halleck has now no large organized force in front of him, while we have.

If this cannot be done, or even in connection with it, allow me to suggest the movement of a heavy column from Dalton upon Atlanta. If but the one can be done, it would better conform to military principles to strengthen this army, and even although the reinforcements might not arrive in season to take part in the attack upon Richmond, the moral effect would be great, and they would furnish valuable assistance in ulterior movements.

I wish to be distinctly understood that whenever the weather permits, I will attack with whatever force I may have, although a larger force would enable me to gain much more decisive results.

I would be glad to have McCall's infantry sent forward by water at once, without waiting for his artillery and cavalry.

If Gen. Prim returns via Washington, please converse with him as to the condition of affairs here. G. B. McC., Major-Gen.

Hon. E. M. S., Sec.-of-War.

Our work upon the bridges continued to be pushed forward vigorously until the 20th, during which time it rained almost every day, and the exposure of the men caused much sickness.

On the 11th the following was received from the Secretary of War.

Washington, June 11, 1862.

Maj.-Gen. G. B. McC.—Your dispatch of three thirty (3.30) yesterday has been received. I am fully impressed with the difficulties mentioned and which no art nor skill can avoid, but only endure, and am striving to the uttermost to render you every aid in the power of the Government.

Your suggestions will be immediately communicated to Gen. Halleck, with a request that he shall conform to them. At last advice he contemplated sending a column to operate with Mitchell against Chattanooga, and thence upon East Tennessee. Buell reports Kentucky and Tennessee to be in a critical condition demanding immediate attention. Halleck says the main body of Beauregard's force is with him at Okalona. McCall's force was reported yesterday as having embarked on its way to join you. It is intended to send the residue of McDowell's force also to join you as speedily as possible. Fremont had a hard fight day before yesterday, with Jackson's force at Union Church, eight miles from Harrisonburg. He claims the victory, but was pretty badly handled; it is clear that a strong force is operating with Jackson, for the purpose of detaining the forces here from you I am urging as fast as possible the new levies

Be assured general, that there never has been a moment when my desire has been otherwise than to aid you with my whole heart mind and strength since the hour we first met, and whatever others may say for their own purposes, you have never had and never can have any one more truly your friend, or more anxious to support, or more joyful than I shall be at the success, which I have no doubt, will soon be achieved by your arms E M S, Sec of War

On the 12th and 13th Gen McCall's division arrived

On the 13th of June two squadrons of the 5 h U S Cavalry, under the command of Capt. Royal, stationed near Hanover Old Church, were attacked and overpowered by a force of the enemy's cavalry numbering about 15,000 men, with four guns. They pushed on towards our depots, but at som distance from our main body and, though pursued, very cleverly made the circuit of the army repassing the Chickahominy at Long Bridge

The burning of two schooners laden with forage and fourteen government wagons, the destruction of some sutlers' stores, the killing of several of the guard and teamsters at Garlick's Landing, some little damage done at Tunstall's Station, and a little evil, were the precise results of this expedition

On the 14th I sent the following to the Sec'y of War —Head'qs., Army of the Potomac, Camp Lincoln June 14, 1862, midnight·

All quiet in every direction The stampede of last night has passed away Weather now very favorable I hope two days more will make the ground practicable I shall advance as soon as the bridges are completed, and the ground fit for artillery to move, at the same time I would be glad to have whatever troops can be sent to me I can use several new regiments to advantage It ought to be distinctly understood that McDowell and his troops are completely under my control

I received a telegram from him requesting that McCall's division might be placed so as to join him immediately on his arrival

That request does not breathe the proper spirit; whatever troops come to me must be disposed of so as to do the most good I do not feel that in such circumstances as those in which I am now placed, Gen McD should wish the general interests to be sacrificed for the purpose of increasing his command.

If I cannot fully control all his troops, I want none of them, but would prefer to fight the battle with what I have, and let others be responsible or the results

The department lines should not be allowed to interfere with me, but Gen McD and all his troops sent to me, should be placed completely at my disposal, to do with them as I think best In no other way can they be of assistance to me. I therefore request that I may have entire and full control The stake at issue is too great to allow personal considerations to be entertained. You know that I have none. The indications are, from our balloon reconnoissances and from all other sources, that the enemy are intrenching, daily increasing in numbers, and determined to fight desperately. G B McC Maj.-Gen. Com'g
Hon E M S, Sec'y of War

On the 20th the following was communicated to the President —Hdq's Army of the Potomac, Camp Lincoln, June 20, 1862 2 P M:

Your Excellency's dispatch of (11) A. M. received, also that of Gen Sigel

I have no doubt that Jackson has been reinforced from here. There is reason to believe that Gen R S Ripley has recently joined Lee's army, with a brigade or division from Charleston Troops have arrived recently from Goldsboro There is not the slightest reason to suppose that the enemy intends evacuating Richmond; he is daily increasing his defenses I find him every where in force, and every reconnoissance cost many valuable lives Yet I am obliged to feel my way foot by foot, at whatever cost, so great are the difficulties of the country By to-morrow night the defensive works covering our position on this side of the Chickahominy should be completed. I am forced to this by my inferiority of numbers, so that I may bring the greatest possible numbers into action, and secure the army against the consequences of unforeseen disaster I would be glad to have permission to lay before your Excellency by letter or telegraph my views as to the present state of military affairs throughout the whole country. In the meantime I would be pleased to learn the disposition, as to numbers and position, of the troops not under my command, in Virginia and elsewhere

His Ev'y. A. L., Pres't.   G. B. McC., M-G Com'g

To which I received this reply.

Washington, June 21, 1862, 6 P M.

Maj.-Gen. G. B. McC.—Your dispatch of yesterday, two P. M, was received this morning If it would not divert too much of your time and attention from the army under your immediate command, I would be glad to have your views as to the present state of military affairs throughout the whole country, as you say you would be glad to give them I would rather it should be by letter than by telegraph, because of the better chance of secresy As to the numbers and positions of the troops not under your command in Virginia and elsewhere, even if I could do it with accuracy, which I cannot, I would rather not transmit either by telegraph or letter, because of the chances of its reaching the enemy. I would be very glad to talk with you, but you cannot leave your camp, and I cannot well leave here.

A. L., President.

To which I sent the following reply·

Camp Lincoln, June 22, 1 P M—I have the honor to acknowledge the receipt of your telegram of 8 P. M, yesterday.

Under the circumstances as stated in your dispatch, I perceive that it will be better, at least, to defer, for the present, the communication I desired to make G B McC, Maj.-Gen Com'g.
His Excellency, the President

All the information I could obtain, previous to the 24th of June, regarding the movements of Gen. Jackson, led to the belief that he was at

Gordonsville, where he was receiving reinforcements from Richmond via Lynchburg and Staunton; but what his purposes were did not appear until the date specified, when a young man, very intelligent, but of suspicious appearance was brought in by our scouts from the direction of Hanover Court House. He at first stated that he was an escaped prisoner from Col. Kenly's Maryland regiment, captured at Front Royal, but finally confessed himself to be a deserter from Jackson's command, which he left near Gordonsville on the 21st. Jackson's troops were then, as he said, moving to Fredericshall, along the Virginia Central Railroad, for the purpose of attacking my rear on the 28th. I immediately dispatched two trusty negroes to proceed along the railroad, and ascertain the truth of the statement. They were unable, however, to get beyond Hanover Court House, where they encountered the enemy's pickets and were forced to turn back without obtaining the desired information. On that day I sent the following dispatch.

Headquarters Army of the Potomac, June 24 12 P. M. 1862.—A very peculiar case of desertion has just occurred from the enemy. The party states he left Jackson, Whiting and Ewell, fifteen brigades, at Gordonsville, on the 21st, that they were moving to Fredericshall, and that it was intended to attack my rear on the 28th. I would be glad to learn, at your earliest convenience, the most exact information you have as to the position and movements of Jackson, as well as the sources from which your information is derived, that I may the better compare it with what I have

G. B. McC. Maj.-Gen.

Hon. E. M. S. Secretary of War.

The following is his reply:

Washington, June 25, 2 35.

Maj.-Gen. McC.—We have no definite information as to the numbers or position of Jackson's force. Gen King yesterday reported a deserter's statement that Jackson's force was nine days ago, forty thousand men. Some reports place ten thousand rebels under Jackson at Gordonsville, others that his force is at Port Republic, Harrisonburg and Luray. Fremont yesterday reported rumors that Western Virginia was threatened and G. Kelly that Ewell was advancing to New Creek, where Fremont had his depots. The last telegram from Fremont contradicts this rumor. The last telegram from Banks says the enemy's pickets are strong in advance at Luray. The people decline to give any information of his whereabouts. Within the last two days, the evidence is strong that for some purpose the enemy is circulating rumors of Jackson's advance in various directions, with a view to conceal the real point of attack. Neither McDowell who is at Manassas, nor Banks and Fremont who are at Middletown appear to have any accurate knowledge of the subject. A letter transmitted to the department yesterday purporting to be dated Gordonsville on the 14th inst., stated that the actual attack was designed for Washington and Baltimore, as soon as you attacked Richmond, but that the report was to be circulated that Jackson had gone to Richmond in order to mislead. This letter looked very much like a blind, and induces me to suspect that Jackson's real movement now is toward Richmond. It came from Alexandria, and is certainly designed, like the numerous rumors put afloat, to mislead. I think, therefore that while the warning of the deserter to you may also be a blind, that it could not safely be disregarded. I will transmit to you any further information on this subject that may be received here. E. M. S. Sec. of War.

On the 25th our bridges and intrenchments being at last completed, an advance of our picket line on the left was ordered, preparatory to a general forward movement.

Immediately in front of the most advanced redoubt on the Williamsburg road was a large open field, beyond that a swampy belt of timber five hundred yards wide, which had been disputed ground for many days. Further in advance was an open field crossed by the Williamsburg road and the railroad, and commanded by a redoubt and rifle-pits of the enemy. It was decided to push our lines to the other side of these woods, in order to enable us to ascertain the nature of the ground, and to place Generals Heintzelman and Sumner in position to support the attack intended to be made on the old Tavern on the 26th or 27th by Gen Franklin, by assaulting that position in the rear.

Between 8 and 9 o'clock on the morning of the 25th the advance was begun by Gen Heintzelman's corps. The enemy were found to be in strong force along the line, and contested the advance stubbornly, but by sunset our object was accomplished. The troops engaged in this affair were the whole of Heintzelman's corps, Palmer's brigade of Couch's division of Keyes's corps and a part of Richardson's division of Sumner's corps. For the details I refer to the report of Gen Heintzelman.

The casualties, (not including those in Palmer's brigade, which have not been reported) were as follows—Officers killed 1, wounded 14 missing 1. Enlisted men killed 50 wounded 387, missing 63. Total 516.

The following telegrams were sent to the Secretary of War during the day from the field of operations:

Redoubt, No 3, June 25, 1862. 1 30 p m.

Hon E M S,—We have advanced our pickets on the left considerably, under sharp resistance. Our men behaved very handsomely. Some firing still continues. G B McC, Maj-Gen Comd'g

Redoubt No 3, June 25, 1862 3 15 p m.

Hon E M S Sec of War,—The enemy are making a desperate resistance to the advance of our picket lines. Kearney's and one half of Hooker's are where I want them.

I have this moment re-inforced Hooker's right with a brigade and a couple of guns, and hope in a few minutes to finish the work intended for the day. Our men are behaving splendidly. The enemy are fighting well also.

This is not a battle, merely an affair of Heintzelman's corps, supported by Keyes's, and thus far all goes well. We hold every foot we have gained. If we succeed in what we have undertaken it will be a very important advantage gained. Loss not large thus far. The fighting up to this time has been done by Gen Hooker's division, which has behaved as usual, that is most splendidly.

On our right, Porter has silenced the enemy's batteries in his front.

G. B. McC., Maj.-Gen. Com'd'g.

Redoubt No 3, June 25, 1862 5 p.m.

Hon E. M S. Sec of War,—The affair is over, and we have gained our point fully, and with but little loss, notwithstanding the strong opposition. Our men have done all that could be desired The affair was partly decided by two guns that Capt De Russy brought gallantly into action under very difficult circumstances The enemy was driven from the camp in front of this place, and is now quiet   G B McC, Maj Gen Com'g.

Also on the same day, the following:

Headquarters, Army of the Potomac, Camp Lincoln June 25, 1862, 6.15 p.m.—I have just returned from the field, and found your dispatch in regard to Jackson

Several contrabands just in, give information confirming supposition that Jackson's advance is at or near Hanover Court House, and that Beauregard arrived, with strong reinforcements, in Richmond yesterday.

I incline to think that Jackson will attack my right and rear. The rebel force is stated at 200-000, including Jackson and Beauregard. I shall have to contend against vastly superior odds if these reports be true. But this army will do all in the power of men, to hold their position and repulse any attack

I regret my great inferiority in numbers but feel that I am in no way responsible for it, as I have not failed to represent, repeatedly, the necessity of reinforcements, that this was the decisive point, and that all the available means of the government, should be concentrated here I will do all that a General can do, with the splendid army that I have the honor to command, and if it is destroyed by overwhelming numbers, can at least die with it, and share its fate.

But if the result of the action, which will probably occur to-morrow, or within a short time, is a disaster the responsibility can not be thrown on my shoulders, it must rest where it belongs Since I commenced this, I have received additional intelligence confirming the supposition in regard to Jackson's movements and Beauregard's arrival I shall probably be attacked to-morrow and now go on the other side of the Chickahominy, to arrange for the defence of that side   I fee' that there is no use in my again asking for reinforcements.   G B McC., Maj.-General.

E M S Sec of war.

NUMBERS OF THE ENEMY.

The report of the Chief of the "Secret Service Corps," herewith forwarded, and dated 26th June, shows the estimated strength of the enemy at the time of the evacuation of Yorktown to have been from 100 000 to 120,000. The same report puts his numbers on the 26th of June, at about 180,000, and the specific information obtained regarding their organization, warrants the belief, that this estimate did not exceed his actual strength

It will be observed that the evidence contained in the report, shows the following organizations, viz.:—two hundred regiments of infantry and cavalry, including the forces of Jackson and Ewell, just arrived; eight battalions of independent troops; five battalions of artillery; twelve companies o infantry and independent cavalry, besides forty-six companies of artillery; amounting in all to from forty to fifty brigades. There were, undoubtedly, many others whose designations we did not learn. The report also shows that numerous and heavy earth-works had been completed for the defence of Richmond, and, that in thirty-six of these, were mounted some two hundred guns.

THE SEVEN DAYS.

On the 26th the day upon which I had decided as the time for our final advance, the enemy attacked our right in strong force, and turned my attention to the protection of our communications and depots of supply.

The event was a bitter confirmation of the military judgment, which had been reiterated to my superiors from the inception, and through the progress of the Peninsular campaign

I notified the Secretary of war in the folllowing dispatch:

Headquarters, Army of the Potomac, Camp Lincoln, June 26, 1862, 12 m.—I have just heard that our cavalry pickets, on the left Bank of the Chickahominy, are being driven in; it is, probably, Jackson's advanced guard. I thus be true, you may not hear from me for some days, as my communications will probably be cut off. The case is, perhaps, a difficult one, but I shall resort to desperate measures, and will do my best to out-manœuvre, outwit, and out-fight the enemy. Do not believe reports of disaster, and do not be discouraged, if you learn that my communications are cut off, and even Yorktown in possession of the enemy. Hope for the best, and I will not deceive the hopes you formerly placed in me.

G. B. McC., Maj.-General

E M S, Secretary of War.

Headquarters, Army of the Potomac, Camp Lincoln, June 26, 1862 2.30 p m.—Your dispatch and that of President received. Jackson is driving in my pickets, &c., on other side of the Chickahominy It is impossible to tell where reinforcements ought to go, as I am yet unable to predict result of approaching battle. It will probably be better that they should go to Fort Monroe, and thence according to state of affairs when they arrive.

It is not probable that I can maintain telegraphic communication more than an hour or two longer.   G. B. McC, Major-General.

Hon. E. M. S., Sec of War.

On the same day I received the following dispatch from the Secretary of War:

Washington, June 25, 1862, 11 20 P M.

Maj.-Gen. G. B. McC.—Your telegram of 6.15 has just been received. The circumstances that have hitherto rendered it impossible for the government to send you any more reinforcements than has been done, have been so distinctly stated to you by the President, that it is needless for me to repeat them

Every effort has been made by the President

and myself to strengthen you. King's division has reached Falmouth. Shield's division and Rickett's division are at Manassas. The President designs to send a part of that force to aid you as speedily as it can be done.

E. M. S., Sec'y. of War.

Washington, June 26, 1862, 6 p. m.

Maj.-Gen. G. B McC.:—Arrangements are being made rapidly as possible to send 5,000 men, as fast as they can be brought from Manassas to Alexandria, and embarked, which can be done sooner than to wait for transportation at Fredericksburg. They will be followed by more, if needed. McDowell, Banks, and Fremont's force will be consolidated as the army of Virginia, and will operate promptly in your aid by land. Nothing will be spared to sustain you, and I have undoubting faith in your success. Keep me advised fully of your condition.

E. M. S., Sec'y of War.

But 5,000 of the reinforcements spoken of in these communications came to the army of the Potomac, and these reached us at Harrison's Bar after the seven days. In anticipation of a speedy advance on Richmond, to provide for the contingency of our communications with the depot at the White House being severed by the enemy, and at the same time to be prepared for a change of the base of our operations to James River, if circumstances should render it advisable, I had made arrangements more than a week previous (on the 18th) to have transports with supplies of provisions and forage, under a convoy of gunboats, sent up James River. They reached Harrison's Landing in time to be available for the army on its arrival at this point. Events soon proved this change of base to be, though most hazardous and difficult, the only prudent course.

In order to relieve the troops of the 6th corps on the 19th of June, Gen Reynolds and Gen Seymour's brigades, of Gen McCall's division (Pennsylvania Reserves), were moved from Gaines's Farm to a position on the Beaver Dam Creek; Gen Meade being held in reserve in front of Gaines's Farm. One regiment and a battery were thrown forward to the heights overlooking Mechanicsville, a line of pickets extended along the Chickahominy River, between the Mechanicsville and Meadow Bridges.

As has already been stated, I received, while engaged on the 25th, in directing the operations of Heintzelman's corps, information which strengthened my suspicions that Jackson was advancing with a large force upon our right and rear. On this day, Gen Casey, at the White House, was instructed to prepare for a vigorous resistance, and defensive works were ordered at Tunstall's Station. Early on the 25th, Gen. Porter was instructed to send out reconnoitering parties towards Hanover Court House to discover the position and force of the enemy, and to destroy the bridges on the Tolopotamy as far as possible

Up to the 26th of June, the operations against Richmond had been conducted along the roads leading to it from the east and north-east. The reasons which compelled the choice of this line of approach and our continuance upon it have been alluded to above.

The superiority of the James River route, as a line of attack and supply, is too obvious to need exposition. My own opinion on that subject had been early given, and need not be repeated here. The dissipation of all hope of co-operation by land of Gen. McDowell's forces, deemed to be occupied in the defense of Washington, their inability to hold or defeat Jackson, disclosed an opportunity to the enemy, and a new danger to my right, and to the long line of supplies from the White House to the Chickahominy, and forced an immediate change of base across the Peninsula. To that end, from the evening of the 26th, every energy of the army was bent. Such a base, in the presence of a powerful enemy, is one of the most difficult undertakings in war, but I was confident in the valor and discipline of my brave army, and knew that it could be trusted equally to retreat or advance, and to fight the series of battles now inevitable, whether retreating from victories, or marching through defeats, and, in short I had no doubt whatever of its ability, even against superior numbers, to fight its way through to the James, and get a position whence a successful advance upon Richmond would be again possible. Their superb conduct through the next seven days justified my faith.

On the same day (26th), Gen Van. Vliet chief quartermaster of the army of the Potomac, by my orders telegraphed to Col Ingalls quartermaster at the White House, as follows "Run the cars to the last moment, and load them with provisions and ammunition. Load every wagon you have with subsistence, and send them to Savage Station by way of Bottom's Bridge. If you are obliged to abandon White House, burn everything that you cannot get off. You must throw all our supplies up the James River as soon as possible, and accompany them yourself with all your force. It will be of vast importance to establish our depots on James River without delay, if we abandon White House. I will keep you advised of every movement so long as the wires work; after that, you must exercise your own judgment"

All these commands were obeyed. So excellent were the dispositions of the different officers in command of the troops, depots and gun-boats, and so timely the warning of the approach of the enemy, that almost everything was saved, and but a small amount of stores destroyed, to prevent their falling into the hands of the enemy.

Gen. Stoneman's communications with the main army being cut off, he fell back upon the White House, and thence to Yorktown when the White House was evacuated.

On the 26th orders were sent to all the corps commanders on the right bank of the Chickahominy to be prepared to send as many troops as they could spare on the following day to the left bank of the river, as will be seen from the appended telegrams. Gen Franklin received instructions to hold Gen Slocum's division in readiness by daybreak of the 27th and if heavy firing should at that time be heard in the direction of Gen. Porter, to move it at once to his assistance without further orders.

BEAVER DAM CREEK

At noon, on the 26th the approach of the enemy, who had crossed above Meadow Bridge, was discovered by the advanced pickets at that point, and at 12·30 P. M. they were attacked and driven in. All the pickets were now called in, and the regiment and battery at Mechanicsville withdrawn.

Meade's brigade was ordered up as a reserve in rear of the line, and shortly after Martindale's and Griffin's brigades of Morell's division, were moved forward and deployed on the right of McCall's division, towards Shady Grove Church, to cover that flank. Neither of these three brigades however, were warmly engaged, though two of Griffin's regiments relieved a portion of Reynolds's line just at the close of the action.

The position of our troops was a strong one, extending along the left bank of Beaver Dam Creek, the left resting on the Chickahominy, and the right in thick woods beyond the upper road from Mechanicsville to Coal Harbor. The lower or river road crossed the creek at Ellison's Mills Seymour's brigade held the left of the line, from the Chickahominy to beyond the mill, partly in woods and partly in cleared ground and Reynolds the right, principally in the woods and covering the upper road. The artillery occupied positions commanding the roads and the open ground across the creek

Timber had been felled, rifle-pits dug, and the position generally prepared with a care that greatly contributed to the success of the day. The passage of the creek was difficult along our whole front, and impracticable for artillery, except by the two roads, where the main efforts of the enemy were directed

At 3 P. M. he formed his line of battle, rapidly advanced his skirmishers, and soon attacked our whole line, making at the same time a determined attempt to force the passage of the upper road, which was successfully resisted by Gen Reynolds. After a severe struggle he was forced to retire, with very heavy loss

A rapid artillery fire, with desultory skirmishing, was maintained along the whole front, while the enemy massed his troops for another effort at the lower road, about two hours later, which was likewise repulsed by Gen. Seymour, with heavy slaughter The firing ceased and the enemy retired about 9 P M, the action having lasted six hours, with entire success to our arms. But few, if any, of Jackson's troops were engaged on this day, the portion of the enemy encountered were chiefly from the troops on the right bank of the river, who crossed near Meadow Bridge and at Mechanicsville. The information in my possession soon after the close of this action convinced me that Jackson was really approaching in large force. The position on Beaver Dam Creek, although so successfully defended, had its right flank too much in the air, and was too far from the main body to make it advisable to retain it longer. I therefore determined to send the heavy guns at Hogan's and Gaines's houses over the Chickahominy during the night, with as many of the wagons of the 5th Corps as possible, and to withdraw the corps itself to a position stretching around the bridges, where its flanks would be reasonably secure, and it would be within supporting distance of the main army. General Porter carried out my orders to that effect. It was not advisable at that time, even had it been practicable, to withdraw the 5th Corps to the right bank of the Chickahominy. Such a movement would have exposed the rear of the army, placed us between two fires, and enabled Jackson's fresh troops to interrupt the movement to James River by crossing the Chickahominy in the vicinity of Jones Bridge before we could reach Malvern Hill with our trains I determined, then to resist Jackson with the 5th Corps, reinforced by all our disposable troops, in the new position near the brigade heads, in order to cover the withdrawal of the trains and heavy guns, and to give time for the arrangements to secure the adoption of the James River, as our line of supplies in lieu of the Pamunkey. The greater part of the heavy guns and wagons having been removed to the right bank of the Chickahominy, the delicate operation of withdrawing the troops from Beaver Dam Creek was commenced shortly before daylight, and successfully executed

Meade's and Griffin's brigades were the first to leave the ground. Seymour's brigade covered the rear with the horse batteries of Captains Robertson and Tidball; but the withdrawal was so skillful and so gradual, and the repulse of the preceding day so complete, that although the enemy followed the retreat closely, and some skirmishing occurred, he did not appear in front of the new line in force till about noon of the 27th, when we were prepared to receive him.

About this time Gen Porter, believing that Gen. Stoneman would be cut off from him, sent him orders to fall back on the White House, and afterwards rejoin the army as best he could.

GAINES'S MILL

On the morning of the 27th of June, during the withdrawal of his troops to Mechanicsville to the selected position already mentioned, Gen Porter telegraphed as follows;

"I hope to do without aid, though I request that Franklin or some other command be held ready to reinforce me The enemy are so close that I expect to be hard pressed in front. I hope to have a position in position to cover the retreat, This is a delicate movement, but relying on the good qualities of the commanders of divisions and brigades, I expect to get back and hold the new line

This shows how closely Porter's retreat was followed.

Notwithstanding all the efforts used during the entire night to remove the heavy guns and wagons, some of the siege guns were still in position at Gaines's House after sunrise, and were finally hauled off by hand. The new position of the 5th Corps was about an arc of a circle, covering the approaches to the bridges which connected our right wing with the troops on the opposite side of the river.

Morell's division held the left line, in a strip of woods on the left bank of the Gaines's Mill stream, resting its left flank on the descent to the Chickahominy, which was swept by our artillery on both sides of the river, and extending into open ground on the right towards New Coal

Harbor. In this line Gen. Butterfield's brigade held the extreme left, Gen. Martindale's joined his right, and Gen. Griffin still further to the right, joined the left of Gen. Sykes' division, which, partly in woods and partly in open ground, extended in rear of Coal Harbor.

Each brigade had in reserve two of its own regiments; McCall's division, having been engaged on the day before, was formed in a second line in rear of the first; Meade's brigade on the left, near the Chickahominy; Reynolds' brigade on the right, covering the approaches from Coal Harbor and Dispatch Station to Sumner's Bridge, and Seymour's in reserve to the second line still further in rear. Gen P. St. G. Cooke, with five companies of the 5th Regular Cavalry, two squadrons of the 1st Regular Cavalry, and three squadrons of the 1st Pennsylvania Cavalry (lancers), were posted behind a hill in rear of the position, and near the Chickahominy, to aid in watching the left flank and defending the slope to the river.

The troops were all in position by noon, with the artillery on the commanding ground, and in the intervals between the divisions and brigades Besides the division batteries, there were Robertson's and Tidball's horse batteries from the artillery reserve, the latter posted on the right of Sykes' division, and the former on the extreme left of the line, in the valley of the Chickahominy.

Shortly after noon the enemy were discovered approaching in force, and it soon became evident that the entire position was to be attacked. His skirmishers advanced rapidly, and soon the fire became heavy along our whole front. At 2 p.m. Gen Porter asked for reinforcements. Slocum's division of the 6th corps was ordered to cross to the left bank of the river by Alexander's Bridge, and proceed to his support.

General Porter's first call for reinforcements, through Gen. Barnard, did not reach me, nor his demand for more axes through the same officer. By 3 p.m. the engagement had become so severe, and the enemy were so greatly superior in numbers, that the entire second line and reserves had been moved forward to sustain the first line against repeated and desperate assaults along the whole front. At 3 30 Slocum's division reached the field, and was immediately brought into action at the weak points of our line. On the left the contest was for the strip of woods running almost at right angles to the Chickahominy in front of Adam's House, or between that and Gaines's House. The enemy several times charged up to this wood, but were each time driven back with heavy loss. The regulars of Sykes' division on the right also repulsed several strong attacks. But our own loss, under the tremendous fire of such greatly superior numbers, was very severe, and the troops, most of whom had been under arms more than two days, were rapidly becoming exhausted by the masses of fresh men constantly brought against them. When Gen. Slocum's division arrived on the ground, it increased Gen. Porter's force to some 35,000, who were, probably, contending against about 70,000 of the enemy The line was severely pressed in several points, and, as its being pierced at any one would have been fatal, it was unavoidable for Gen. Porter, who was required to hold his position until night, to divide Slocum's division, and send parts of it, even single regiments, to the points most threatened. About 5 p.m. Gen Porter having reported his position as critical, French's and Meagher's brigades, of Richardson's division (2d corps), were ordered to cross to his support. The enemy attacked again, in great force, at 6 p.m., but failed to break our lines, though our loss was very heavy. About 7 p.m. they threw fresh troops against Gen Porter with still greater fury, and finally gained the woods held by our left This reverse, aided by the confusion that followed an unsuccessful charge by five companies of the 5th Cavalry, and followed, as it was, by more determined assaults on the remainder of our lines, now outflanked, caused a general retreat from our position, to the hill in rear, overlooking the bridge. French's and Meagher's brigades now appeared, driving before them the stragglers, who were thronging toward the bridge. These brigades advanced boldly to the front, and by their example, as well as by the steadiness of their bearing, reanimated our own troops, and warned the enemy that reinforcements had arrived. It was now dusk. The enemy already repulsed several times, with terrible slaughter, and hearing the shouts of the fresh troops, failed to follow up their advantage. This gave an opportunity to rally our men behind the brigades of Gen French and Meagher, and they again marched up the hill, ready to repulse another attack. During the night our thinned and exhausted regiments were all withdrawn in safety, and by the following morning all had reached the other side of the stream. The regular infantry formed the rear guard, and about 6 o'clock, on the morning of the 28th, crossed the river, destroying the bridge behind them.

Our loss in this battle, in killed, wounded and missing, was very heavy, especially in officers, many of whom were killed, wounded, or taken prisoners, while gallantly leading on their men, or rallying them to renewed exertions. It is impossible to arrive at the exact numbers lost in this desperate engagement, owing to the series of battles which followed each other in quick succession, and in which the whole army was engaged. No general returns were made, until after we had arrived at Harrison's Landing, when the losses for the whole seven days were estimated together.

Although we were finally forced from our first line, after the enemy had been repeatedly driven back, yet the objects sought for had been attained. The enemy was held at bay, our siege-guns and material were saved, and the right wing had now joined the main body of the army.

The number of guns captured by the enemy at this battle was 22 Three of which were lost by being run off the bridge during the final withdrawal.

Great credit is due for the efficiency and bravery with which this arm of the service (the artillery) was fought, and it was not until the last successful charge of the enemy, that the cannoneers were driven from their pieces, or struck down, and the guns captured. Deidrich's, Knieriem's, and Grimm's batteries, took position during the engagement in the front of General Smith's line on the right bank of the stream, and with a battery of siege-guns, served by the First Connecticut Artillery, helped to drive back the enemy in front of Gen Porter.

So threatening were the movements of the enemy, on both banks of the Chickahominy, that it was impossible to decide, until the afternoon, where the real attack would be made. Large forces of infantry were seen during the day, near the Old Tavern, on Franklin's right and threatening demonstrations were frequently made along the entire line, on this side of the river, which rendered it necessary to hold a considerable force in position to meet them.

On the 26th a circular was sent to the corps commanders on the right bank of the river, asking them how many of their troops could be spared to reinforce Gen Porter, after retaining sufficient to hold their positions for twenty-four hours.

To this the following replies were received:

Head'q's 3d Corps, June 26, 4 P M

Gen R B Marcy :— I think I can hold the intrenchments with four brigades for twenty-four hours. That would leave two brigades disposable for service on the other side of the river; but the men are so tired and worn out, that I fear they would not be in a condition to fight after making a march of any distance . . .

S. P. HEINTZELMAN, Brig.-Gen

Telegrams from Gen Heintzelman on the 25th and 26th had indicated that the enemy was in large force in front of Gen's Hooker and Kearney, and on the Charles City road, (Longstreet Hill and Huger), and Gen Heintzelman expressed the opinion on the night of the 25th that he could not hold his advanced position without reinforcements.

Gen Keyes telegraphed :

"As to how many men will be able to hold this position for 24 hours, I must answer, all I have, if the enemy is as strong as ever in front, it having at all times appeared to me that our forces on this flank are small enough."

On the morning of the 27th, the following dispatch was sent to Gen Sumner:

Head'q's Army of the Potomac, June 27, 8 15 A M

Gen E V Sumner :— Gen Smith just reports that "six or eight regiments have moved down to the woods in front of Gen Sumner."

R B MARCY, Chief-of-Staff

At 11 o'clock A M, Gen Sumner telegraphed as follows : — "The enemy threatens an attack on my right near Smith." At 12 30 P M he telegraphed "Sharp shelling on both sides." At 2 45 P M "Sharp musketry firing in front of Burns. We are replying with artillery and infantry. The man on the look-out reports some troops drawn up in line of battle about opposite my right and Smith's left, the number cannot be made out."

In accordance with orders given on the night of the 26th, Gen Slocum's division commenced crossing the river to support Gen Porter, soon after daybreak on the morning of the 27th, but, as the firing in front of Gen Porter ceased, the movement was suspended. At 2 P M Gen Porter called for reinforcements. I ordered them at once and at 3 25 P M sent him the following:

"Slocum is now crossing at Alexander's Bridge with his whole command. Enemy has commenced an infantry attack on Smith's left. I have ordered down Sumner's and Heintzelman's reserves, and you can count on the whole of Slocum's. Go on as you have begun."

During the day the following dispatches were received, which will show the condition of affairs on the right bank of the Chickahominy :

June 27, 1862.

To Col A V Colburn, Ass't-Adj-Gen :

Gen Smith thinks the enemy are massing heavy columns to the right of James Garnett's House, and on the other side of the river opposite it. Three regiments are reported to be moving from Sumner's to Smith's front. The arrangements are very good—made by Smith.

W. B. FRANKLIN, Brig.-Gen

Afterwards he telegraphed "The enemy has begun an attack on Smith's left with infantry. I know no details."

Afterwards the following : "The enemy has opened on Smith from a battery of three pieces, to the right of the White House. Our shells are bursting well, and Smith thinks Sumner will soon have a cross fire upon them that will silence them."

Afterwards, at 5 50 P M, the following was sent to Gen Keyes "Please send one brigade of Couch's division to these headquarters without a moment's delay. A staff officer will be here to direct the brigade where to go."

Subsequently the following was sent to Gens. Sumner and Franklin:

"Is there any sign of the enemy being in force in your front? Can you spare any more force to be sent to Gen Porter? Answer at once."

At 5.15 P M the following was received from Gen Franklin:

"I do not think it prudent to take any more troops from here at present."

Gen Sumner replied as follows :

"If the general desires to trust the defense of my position to the front line alone, I can send French with three regiments, and Meagher with his brigade to the right, everything is so uncertain that I think it would be hazardous to do it."

These two brigades were sent to reinforce Gen Porter, as has been observed.

At 5 25 I sent the following to Gen Franklin:

"Porter is hard pressed, it is not a question of prudence, but of possibilities. Can you possibly maintain your position until dark with two brigades? I have ordered eight regiments of Sumner's to support Porter, one brigade of Couch to this place, Heintzelman's brigade to go in rear of Sumner. If possible send a brigade to support Porter, it should follow the regiments ordered from Sumner."

"If it is possible send another brigade to reinforce Gen Smith. It is said three heavy columns of infantry are moving on him."

From the foregoing dispatches it will be seen that all disposable troops were sent from the right bank of the river to reinforce Gen Porter, and that the corps commanders were left with smaller forces to hold their positions than they deemed adequate.

To have done more, even though Porter's reverse had been prevented, would have had the still more disastrous result of imperilling the whole movement across the Peninsula

CHANGE OF BASE

The operations of this day proved the numerical superiority of the enemy, and made it evident that while he had a large army on the left bank of the Chickahominy, which had already turned our right, and was in position to intercept the communications with our depots at the White House; he was also in large force between our army and Richmond. I therefore effected a junction of our forces.

This might probably have been executed on either side of the Chickahominy, and if the concentration had been effected on the left bank, it is possible we might, with our entire force have defeated the enemy there; but at that time they held the roads leading to the White House, so that it would have been impossible to have sent forward supply trains in advance of the army in that direction, and the guarding of these trains would have seriously embarrassed our operations in the battle. We would have been compelled to fight if concentrated on that bank of the river. Moreover, we would at once have been followed by the enemy's forces upon the Richmond side of the river operating upon our rear, and it in the chances of war, we had been ourselves defeated in the effort we would have been forced to fall back to the White House, and probably to Fort Monroe, and as both our flanks and rear would then have been entirely exposed, our entire supply train, if not the greater part of the army itself might have been lost

The movements of the enemy showed that they expected this, and as they themselves acknowledged they were prepared to cut off our retreat in that direction. I therefore concentrated all our forces on the right bank of the river during the night of the 26th and the morning of the 27th, all our wagons, heavy guns, &c., were gathered there

I may be asked why, after the concentration of our forces on the right bank of the Chickahominy, with a large part of the enemy drawn away from Richmond, upon the opposite side, I did not, instead of striking for James River, fifteen miles below that place, at once march directly on Richmond

It will be remembered, that at this juncture the enemy was on our rear, and there was every reason to believe that he would sever our communications with our supply depot at the White House

We had on hand a limited supply of rations, and if we had advanced directly on Richmond it would have required considerable time to carry the strong works around that place, during which our men would have been destitute of food; and even if Richmond had fallen before our arms, the enemy could still have occupied our supply communications between that place and the gunboats, and turned their disaster into victory. If on the other hand, the enemy had concentrated all his forces at Richmond during the progress of our attack, and we had been defeated, we must in all probability have lost our trains before reaching the flotilla

The battles which continued day after day, in the progress of our flank movement to the James, with the exception of the one at Gaines's Mill, were successes to our arms, and the closing engagement at Malvern Hill was the most decisive of all.

On the evening of the 27th of June, I assembled the corps commanders at my headquarters, and informed them of the plan, its reasons, and my choice of route and method of execution

Gen Keyes was directed to move his corps, with its artillery and baggage across the White Oak Swamp bridge, and to seize strong positions on the opposite side of the swamp, to cover the passage of the other troops and trains

This order was executed on the 28th by noon. Before daybreak on the 28th I went to Savage's Station, and remained there during the day and night, directing the withdrawal of the trains and supplies of the army.

Orders were given to the different commanders to load their wagons with ammunition and provisions and the necessary baggage of the officers and men, and to destroy all property which could not be transported with the army. Orders were also given to leave with those of the sick and wounded who could not be transported, a proper complement of surgeons and attendants, with a bountiful supply of rations and medical stores

The large herd of 2,500 beef cattle was, by the chief commissary, Col. Clarke, transferred to the James River without loss

On the morning of the 28th, while Gen. Franklin was withdrawing his command from Golding Farm, the enemy opened upon Gen Smith's division, from Garnett's Hill, from the valley above, and from Gaines's Hill on the opposite side of the Chickahominy, and shortly afterwards two Georgia regiments attempted to carry the works about to be evacuated, but this work was repulsed by the 23d New York, and the 49th Pennsylvania Volunteers on picket, and a section of Mott's battery

Porter's corps was moved across White Oak Swamp during the day and night, and took up positions covering the roads leading from Richmond towards White Oak Swamp and Long Bridge. McCall's division was ordered on the night of the 28th, to move across the Swamp and take a proper position to assist in covering the remaining troops and trains. During the same night the corps of Sumner, Heintzelman, and the division of Smith, were ordered to an interior line, the left resting on Keyes's old intrenchments, and curving to the right so as to cover Savage's Station. Gen Slocum's division, of Franklin's corps, was ordered to Savage's Station in reserve. They were ordered to hold this position until dark of the 29th, in order to cover the withdrawal of the trains, and then to fall back across the Swamp and unite with the remainder of the army.

On the 28th I sent the following to the Secretary of War:

Headquarters Army of the Potomac Savage's Station, June 28, 1862 12.20 A M

I now know the whole history of the day. On

this side of the river, the right bank, we repulsed several strong attacks; on the left bank our men did all that men could do—all that soldiers could accomplish, but they were overwhelmed by vastly superior numbers soon after I had brought my last reserves into action. The loss on both sides is terrible. I believe it will prove to be the most desperate battle of the war. The sad remnants of my men behave as men—those battalions who fought most bravely, and suffered most, are still in the best order. My regulars were superb, and I count upon what are left to turn another battle in company with their gallant comrades of the volunteers. Had I twenty thousand, or even ten thousand fresh troops to use to-morrow I could take Richmond, but I have not a man in reserve, and shall be glad to cover my retreat, and save the material and personnel of the army.

If we have lost the day we have yet preserved our honor and no one need blush for the army of the Potomac. I have lost this battle, because my force was too small.

I again repeat that I am not responsible for this, and I say it with the earnestness of a general, who feels in his heart the loss of every brave man who has been needlessly sacrificed to-day I still hope to retrieve our fortunes, but to do this, the government must view the matter in the same earnest light that I do. You must send me very large reinforcements, and send them at once.

I shall draw back to this side of the Chickahominy and think I can withdraw all our material. Please understand that in this battle we have lost nothing but men, and those the best we have.

In addition to what I have already said, I only wish to say to the President that I think he is wrong in regarding me as ungenerous, when I said that my force was too weak. I merely reiterated a truth, which to-day has been too plainly proved. If at this instant I could dispose of ten thousand fresh men I could gain the victory to-morrow

I know that a few thousand more men, would have changed this battle from a defeat to a victory; as it is, the government must not, and cannot, hold me responsible for the result

I feel too earnestly to-night, I have seen too many dead and wounded comrades, to feel otherwise than that the government has not sustained this army. If you do not do so now, the game is lost. If I save this army now, I tell you plainly that I owe no thanks to you, or to any other persons in Washington.

You have done your best to sacrifice this army

G B McC, Maj.-Gen, to Hon E M Stanton, Sec of War

The headquarter's camp at Savage's Station, was broken up early on the morning of the 29th, and moved across White Oak Swamp

As the essential part of this day's operations was the passage of the trains across the Swamp, their protection against attack from the direction of New Market and Richmond, as well as the immediate and secure establishment of our communications with the gun-boats, I passed the day in examining the ground, directing the posting of the troops, and assuring the uninterrupted movement of the trains

In the afternoon I instructed Gen. Keyes to move during the night to James River, and occupy a defensive position near Malvern Hill, to secure our extreme left flank

Gen F J Porter was ordered to follow him and prolong the line towards the right. The trains were to be pushed on towards James River in rear of these corps and placed under the protection of the gun-boats as they arrived

A sharp skirmish with the enemy's cavalry, early this day on the Quaker Road, showed that his efforts were about to be directed towards impeding our progress to the river, and rendered my presence in that quarter necessary

ALLENS' FIELD

Gen Sumner vacated his works at Fair Oaks on June 29th, at day-light, and marched his command to Orchard Station, halting at Allen's Field, between Orchard and Savage's Stations.

The division of Richardson and Sedgwick, were formed on the right of the railroad, facing towards Richmond, Richardson holding the right, and Sedgwick joining the right of Heintzelman's corps

The first line of Richardson's division was held by Gen. French, Gen Caldwell supporting in the second. A log building in front of Richardson's division, was held by Col. Brooks with one regiment, (53d Pennsylvania Volunteers,) with Hazzard's battery on an elevated piece of ground, a little in rear of Col Brook's command

At 9 A M, the enemy commenced a furious attack on the right of Gen Sedgwick, but were repulsed. The left of Gen Richardson was next attacked, the enemy attempting in vain to carry the position of Col Brooks. Capt. Hazzard's battery, and Capt Pettit's battery, which afterwards replaced it, were served with great effect, while the 53d Pennsylvania kept up a steady fire on the advancing enemy, compelling them at last to retire in disorder. The enemy renewed the attack three times, but were as often repulsed

SAVAGE'S STATION

Gen Slocum arrived at Savage's Station at an early hour on the 29th, and was ordered to cross White Oak Swamp and relieve Gen Keyes' corps. As soon as Gen. Keyes was thus relieved, he moved towards James River, which he reached in safety, with all his artillery and baggage early on the morning of the 30th, and took up a position below Turkey Creek Bridge.

During the morning Gen. Franklin heard that the enemy, after having repaired the bridges, was crossing the Chickahominy in large force, and advancing toward Savage's Station. He communicated this information to Gen Sumner at Allen's Farm, and moved Smith's division to Savage's Station.

A little after noon Gen Sumner united his forces with those of Gen Franklin, and assumed command

I had ordered Gen Heintzelman, with his corps, to hold the Williamsburg road until dark at a point where were several field works, and a skirt of timber between these works and the railroad, but he fell back before night, and crossed White Oak Swamp at Brackett's Ford

Gen. Sumner in his report of the battle of Savage's Station says: "When the enemy appeared on the Williamsburg road, I could not imagine why Gen Heintzelman did not attack him, and not till some time afterwards did I learn, to my utter amazement that Gen Heintzelman had left the field and retreated with his whole corps (about 15,000 men) before the action commenced. This defection might have been attended with the most disastrous consequences, and although we beat the enemy signally and drove him from the field, we should certainly have given him a more crushing blow if Gen Heintzelman had been there with his corps."

Gen Heintzelman, in the report of the operations of his corps, says:

"On the night of the 28th of June I received orders to withdraw the troops of my corps from the advanced position they had taken on the 25th of June, and to occupy the intrenched lines about 1 mile in rear. A map was sent me showing me the positions Gen Sumner's and Gen Franklin's corps would occupy. About sunrise the next day our troops slowly fell back to the new position cautiously followed by the enemy taking possession of our camps as soon as we left them. From some misapprehension, Gen Sumner held a more advanced position than was indicated on the map furnished me, thus leaving a space of about three-fourths of a mile between the right of his corps and Gen Smith's division of Gen Franklin's corps. . . .

At 11 A M, on the 29th, the enemy commenced an attack on Gen Sumner's troops, a few shells falling within my lines. Late in the afternoon reports reached me that the rebels were in possession of Dr Trent's house, only a mile and a half from Savage's Station I sent several cavalry reconnoissances, and finally was satisfied of the fact Gen Franklin came to my headquarters, when I learned of the interval between his left and Gen Sumner's right, in which space Dr Trent's house is. Also that the rebels had repaired one of the bridges across the Chickahominy and were advancing

"I rode forward to see Gen Sumner, and met his troops falling back on the Williamsburg road, through my lines. Gen Sumner informed me that he intended to make a stand at Savage's Station, and for me to join him to determine upon the position This movement of Gen Sumner's uncovering my right flank it became necessary for me at once to withdraw my troops.

"I rode back to find Gen Sumner, after some delay from the mass of troops in the field, I found him and learned that the course of action had been determined on, so returned to my command and to give the necessary orders for the destruction of the railroad cars, ammunition and provisions still remaining on the ground

"The whole open space near Savage's Station was crowded with troops, more than I supposed could be brought into action judiciously. An aide from the commanding general had in the morning reported to me, to point out a road across the White Oak Swamp, starting from the left of Gen Kearney's position, and leading by Brackett's Ford. The advance of the column reached the Charles City Road at 6 1-2 P. M, and the rear at 10 P. M without accident.

The orders given by me to Generals Sumner, Heintzelman, and Franklin, were to hold the positions assigned them until dark. As stated by Gen Heintzelman, Gen Sumner did not occupy the designated position, but as he was the senior officer present on that side of the White Oak Swamp, he may have thought that the movements of the enemy justified a deviation from the letter of the orders It appears from his report that he assumed command of all the troops near Savage's Station, and determined to resist the enemy there, and that he gave Gen. Heintzelman orders to hold the same position as I had assigned him.

The aide sent by me to Gen Heintzelman, to point out the road across the swamp, was to guide him in retiring after dark

On reaching Savage's Station Sumner's and Franklin's commands were drawn up in line of battle in the large open field to the left of the railroad, the left resting on the edge of the woods, and the right extending down to the railroad.

Gen. Brooks, with his brigade, held the wood to the left of the field, where he did excellent service, receiving a wound, but retaining his command

Gen Hancock's brigade was thrown into the woods on the right and front

At 4 P. M. the enemy commenced his attack in large force by the Williamsburg road It was gallantly met by Gen Burns' brigade, supported and reinforced by two lines in reserve, and finally by the New York 69th Hazzard's and Pettit's batteries again doing good service Osborne's and Bramhall's batteries also took part effectively in this action, which was continued with great obstinacy until between 8 and 9 P M, when the enemy were driven from the field

MOVEMENTS TOWARDS JAMES RIVER.

Immediately after the battle the orders were repeated for all the troops to fall back and cross White Oak Swamp, which was accomplished during the night, in good order.

By midnight all the troops were on the road to White Oak Swamp Bridge, Gen French, with his brigade, acting as rear guard, and at 5 A M. on the 30th all had crossed, and the bridge was destroyed.

On the afternoon and night of the 29th, I gave the corps commanders their instructions for the operations of the following day As stated before, Porter's corps was to move forward to James River, and with the corps of Gen Keyes, to occupy a position at or near Turkey Bend, on a line perpendicular to the river, thus covering the Charles City road to Richmond, opening communication with the gun-boats, and covering the passage of the supply trains, which were pushed forward as rapidly as possible upon Haxall's plantation. The remaining corps were pressed onward, and posted so as to guard the approaches from Richmond as well as the crossing of the White Oak Swamp, over which the army had passed

Gen. Franklin was ordered to hold the passage of White-Oak Swamp Bridge, and cover the withdrawal of the trains from that point. His command consisted of his own corps, with Gen.

Richardson's division and Gen Naglee's brigade placed under his orders for the occasion.

Gen Slocum's division was on the right of the Charles City road.

On the morning of the 30th I again gave to the corps commanders within reach instructions for posting their troops. I found that, notwithstanding all the efforts of my personal staff and other officers, the roads were blocked by wagons, and there was great difficulty in keeping the trains in motion.

The engineer officers whom I had sent forward on the 28th to reconnoitre the roads, had neither returned nor sent me any reports or guides.

Gens Keyes and Porter had been delayed, one by losing the road, and the other in repairing an old road and had not been able to send me any information. We then knew of but one road for the movement of troops and our immense trains.

It was therefore necessary to post the troops in advance of this road, as well as our limited knowledge of the ground permitted, so as to cover the movements of the trains in rear.

I then examined the whole line from the swamp to the left, giving final instructions for the posting of the troops and the obstruction of the roads towards Richmond, and all corps commanders were directed to hold their positions until the trains had passed, after which a more concentrated position was to be taken up near James River.

Our force was too small to occupy and hold the entire line from the White-Oak Swamp to the river, exposed as it was to be taken in reverse by a movement across the lower part of the swamp, or across the Chickahominy below the swamp. Moreover the troops were then greatly exhausted, and required rest in a more secure position.

I extended my examinations of the country as far as Haxall's, looking at all the approaches to Malvern, which position I perceived to be the key to our operations in this quarter, and was thus enabled to expedite very considerably the passage of the trains, and to rectify the positions of the troops.

Everything being then quiet I sent aids to the different corps commanders to inform them what I had done on the left, and to bring me information of the condition of affairs on the right. I returned from Malvern to Haxall's, and, having made arrangements for instant communication from Malvern by signals, went on board of Capt Rodgers's gun-boat, lying near, to confer with him in reference to the condition of our supply vessels, and the state of things on the river.

It was his opinion that it would be necessary for the army to fall back to a position below City Point, as the channel there was so near the southern shore that it would not be possible to bring up the transports should the enemy occupy it. Harrison's Landing was, in his opinion, the nearest suitable point. Upon the termination of this interview, I returned to Malvern Hill, and remained there until shortly before daylight.

On the morning of the 30th Gen. Sumner was ordered to march with Sedgwick's division to Glendale ("Nelson's Farm").

Gen McCall's division (Pennsylvania Reserves) was halted during the morning on the New Market road, just in advance of the point where a road turns off to Quaker Church. His line was formed perpendicularly to the New Market road, with Meade's brigade on the right, Seymour's on the left, and Reynold's brigade, commanded by Col S G Simmons, of the 5th Pennsylvania, in reserve. Randall's regular battery on the right, Kern's and Cooper's batteries opposite the sentre, and Deitrich's and Kanerhem's batteries, of the artillery reserve, on the left—all in front of the artillery line. The country in Gen McCall's front was open, intersected toward the right by the New Market road, and a small strip of timber parallel to it. The open front was about 800 yards, its depth about 1,000 yards.

On the morning of the 30th Gen Heintzelman ordered the bridge at Brackett's Ford to be destroyed, and trees to be felled across that road and the Charles City road.

Gen Slocum's division was to extend to the Charles City road.

Gen Kearney's right to connect with Gen. Slocum's left.

Gen McCall's position was to the left of the Long Bridge road, in connection with Gen Kearney's left. Gen. Hooker was on the left of Gen. McCall.

WHITE-OAK SWAMP BRIDGE

Between 12 and 1 o'clk the enemy opened a cannonade upon the divisions of Smith and Richardson and Naglee's brigade at White-Oak Swamp Bridge. This artillery fire was continued by the enemy through the day, and he crossed some infantry below our position. Richardson's division suffered severely. Captain Ayres directed our artillery with great effect. Capt Hazzard's battery, after losing many cannoneers, and Capt Hazzard being mortally wounded, was compelled to retire. It was replaced by Pettit's battery, which partially silenced the enemy's guns.

Gen Franklin held his position until after dark, repeatedly driving back the enemy in their attempts to cross the White-Oak Swamp.

CHARLES CITY CROSS-ROADS, &c.

At 2 o'clock in the day the enemy were reported advancing in force by the Charles City road, and at half-past 2 o'clock the attack was made down the road on Gen Slocum's left, but was checked by his artillery. After this the enemy, in large force, comprising the divisions of Longstreet and A P Hill, attacked Gen. McCall whose division after severe fighting, was compelled to retire.

General McCall, in his report says

"About half-past two my pickets were driven in by strong advance, after some skirmishing without loss on our part. At 3 o'clock the enemy sent forward a regiment on the left centre and another on the right centre, to feel for a weak point. They were under cover of a shower of shells, and boldly advanced but were both driven back, on the left by the 12th regiment, and on the right by the 7th regiment . . . . For near two hours the battle raged hotly here . . . .

"At last the enemy was compelled to retire before the well-directed musketry fire of the reserves. The German batteries were driven to the rear,

but I rode up and sent them back. It was, however, of little avail, and they were soon after abandoned by the cannoneers. * * *
The batteries in front of the centre were boldly charged upon, but the enemy was speedily forced back. * * *

"Soon after this a most determined charge was made on Randall's battery by a full brigade advancing in wedge-shape, without order, but in perfect recklessness.

"Somewhat similar charges had, I have stated, been previously made on Cooper's and Kern's batteries by single regiments without success, they having recoiled before the storm of canister hurled against them.

"A like result was anticipated by Randall's battery, and the 4th regiment was requested not to fire until the battery had done with them. Its gallant commander did not doubt his ability to repel the attack, and his guns did indeed mow down the advancing host, but still the gaps were closed, and the enemy came in upon a run to the very muzzle of his guns.

"It was a perfect torrent of men, and they were in his battery before the guns could be removed. Two guns that were indeed successfully limbered and their horses killed and wounded, and were overturned on the spot, and the enemy dashing past drove the greater part of the 4th regiment before them. The left company (B) nevertheless stood its ground, with its captain, Fred A Conrad as did likewise certain men of other companies. I had ridden into the regiment and endeavored to check them, but with only partial success.

There was no running; but my division reduced by the previous battles to less than 6,000, had to contend with the divisions of Longstreet and A P Hill, considered two of the strongest and best among many of the Confederate army, numbering that day 18,000 or 20,000 men, and it was reluctantly compelled to give way before heavier force accumulated upon them."

Gen Heintzelman states, that about 5 P M Gen McCall's division was attacked in large force, evidently the principal attack; that in less than an hour the division gave way, and adds.

"Gen Hooker, being on his left, by moving to the right, repulsed the rebels in the handsomest manner, with great slaughter. Gen. Sumner, who was with Gen Sedgwick in McCall's rear, also greatly aided with his artillery and infantry in driving back the enemy. They now renewed their attack with vigor on Gen Kearney's left, and were again repulsed with heavy loss.

"This attack commenced about 4 P M, and was pushed by heavy masses with the utmost determination and vigor. Capt Thompson's battery, directed with great precision, firing double charges, swept them back. The whole open space 200 paces wide, was filled with the enemy, each repulse brought fresh troops. The third attack was only repulsed by the rapid volleys and determined charge of the 63d Pennsylvania, Col Hays, and half of the 37th New York Volunteers."

Gen McCall's troops soon began to emerge from the woods into the open field. Several batteries were in position and began to fire into the woods over the heads of our men in front. Captain De Russy's battery was placed on the right of Gen Sumner's artillery, with orders to shell the woods. Gen Burns's brigade was then advanced to meet the enemy, and soon drove him back. Other troops began to return from the White Oak Swamp.

Later in the day, at the call of Gen Kearney, Gen Taylor's 1st New Jersey brigade, Slocum's division, was sent to occupy a portion of Gen. McCall's deserted position, a battery accompanying the brigade. They soon drove back the enemy, who shortly after gave up the attack, contenting themselves with keeping up a desultory firing till late at night. Between 12 and 1 o'clock at night Gen. Heintzelman commenced to withdraw his corps, and soon after daylight both of his divisions, with Gen. Slocum's division and a portion of Gen Sumner's command, reached Malvern Hill.

On the morning of the 30th Gen Sumner, in obedience to orders, had moved promptly to Glendale, and upon a call from Gen Franklin for reinforcements, sent him two brigades which returned in time to participate and render good service in the battle near Glendale. Gen Sumner says of this battle:

"The battle of Glendale was the most severe action since the battle of Fair Oaks. About 3 o'clock P M. the action commenced, and after a furious contest, lasting till after dark, the enemy was routed at all points and driven from the field."

The rear of the supply trains and the reserve artillery of the army reached Malvern Hill about 4 P M. At about this time the enemy began to appear in Gen. Porter's front, and at 5 o'clock advanced in large force against his left flank, posting artillery under cover of a skirt of timber, with a view to engage our force on Malvern Hill, while with his infantry and some artillery he attacked Colonel Warren's brigade. A concentrated fire of about thirty guns were brought to bear on the enemy, which, with the infantry fire of Colonel Warren's command, compelled him to retreat, leaving two guns in the hands of Col Warren.

The gunboats rendered most efficient aid at this time, and helped to drive back the enemy. It was very late at night before my aides returned to give me the result of the day's fighting along the whole line, and the true position of affairs. While waiting to hear from Gen Franklin before sending orders to Gens. Sumner and Heintzelman, I received a message from the latter that Gen. Franklin was falling back, whereupon I sent Col. Coburn of my staff with orders to verify this, and if it were true, to order in Gens Sumner and Heintzelman at once. He had not gone far when he met two officers from Gen Franklin's headquarters with the information that he was falling back. Orders were then sent to Gens Sumner and Heintzelman to fall back also, and definite instructions were given as to the movement, which was to commence on the right. The orders met these troops already en route to Malvern. Instructions were also sent to Gen. Franklin as to the route he was to follow.

General Barnard then received full instructions

for posting the troops as she arrived. I then returned to Haxall's and again left for Malvern soon after daybreak, accompanied by several general officers. I once more made the entire circuit of the position, and then returned to Haxall's and rode down with Captain Rodgers to select the final location for the army and its depots. I returned to Malvern before the serious fighting commenced, and after riding along the lines and seeing most cause to feel anxious about the right, remained in that vicinity.

MALVERN HILL

The position selected for resisting the further advance of the enemy on the 1st of July, was with the left and centre of our lines resting on "Malvern Hill," while the right curved backwards through a wooded country toward a point below Haxall's on James River. Malvern Hill is an elevated plateau about a mile and a half by three-fourths of a mile net, well cleared of timber, and with several converging roads running over it. In front are numerous defensible ravines, and the ground slopes gradually toward the north and east to the woodland, giving clear ranges for artillery in those directions. Toward the northwest the plateau falls off more abruptly into a ravine which extends to James River. From the position of the enemy his most obvious lines of attack would come from the directions of Richmond and White Oak Swamp, and would almost of necessity strike us upon our left wing. Here, therefore, the lines were strengthened by massing the troops, and collecting the principal part of the artillery. Porter's corps held the left of the line (Sykes' division on the left, Morell's on the right), with the artillery of his two divisions advantageously posted, and the artillery of the reserve so disposed on the high ground that a concentrated fire of some sixty guns could be brought to bear on any point in his front or left. Colonel Tyler also had, with great exertion succeeded in getting ten of his siege guns in position on the highest point of the hill.

Couch's division was placed on the right of Porter; next came Kearney and Hooker, next Sedgwick and Richardson, next Smith and Slocum, then the remainder of Keyes' corps, extending by a backward curve nearly to the river. The Pennsylvania Reserve Corps was held in reserve and stationed behind Porter's and Couch's position. One brigade of Porter's was thrown to the left on the low ground, to protect the flank from any movement direct from the Richmond road. The line was very strong along the whole front of the open plateau; but from thence to the extreme right, the troops were more deployed. This formation was imperative, as an attack would probably be made on our left.

The right was rendered as secure as possible by slashing the timber and by barricading the roads. Commodore Rodgers, commanding the flotilla on James River, placed his gun-boats so as to protect our flanks, and to command the approaches from Richmond.

Between 9 and 10 A. M. the enemy commenced feeling along our whole left wing with his artillery and skirmishers, as far to the right as Hooker's division.

About two o'clock a column of the enemy was observed moving towards our right within the skirt of woods in front of Heintzelman's corps, but beyond the range of our artillery. Arrangements were at once made to meet the anticipated attack in that quarter; but though the column was long occupying more than two hours in passing, it disappeared, and was not again heard of. The presumption is, that it retired by the rear, and participated in the attack afterwards made on our left.

About 3 P. M. a heavy fire of artillery opened on Kearney's left and Couch's division, speedily followed up by a brisk attack of infantry on Couch's front. The artillery was replied to with good effect by our own, and the infantry of Couch's division remained lying on the ground until the advancing column was within short musketry range, when they sprang to their feet, and poured in a deadly volley, which entirely broke the attacking force, and drove them in disorder back over their own ground. This advantage was followed up until we had advanced the right of our line some seven or eight hundred yards and rested upon a thick clump of trees, giving us a stronger position, and a better fire.

Shortly after four o'clock the firing ceased along the whole front, but no disposition was evinced on the part of the enemy to withdraw from the field.

Caldwell's brigade, having been detached from Richardson's division, was stationed upon Couch's right, by Gen. Porter, to whom he had been ordered to report. The whole line was surveyed by the generals, and everything held in readiness to meet the coming attack. At 6 o'clock the enemy suddenly opened upon Couch and Porter with the whole strength of his artillery, and at once began pushing forward his columns of attack to carry the hill. Brigade after brigade, formed under cover of the woods, started at a run to cross the open space, and charge our batteries, but the heavy fire of our guns, with the cool and steady volleys of our infantry, in every case, sent them reeling back to shelter, and covered the ground with their dead and wounded. In several instances our infantry withheld their fire until the attacking columns, which rushed through the storm of canister and shell from our artillery, had reached within a few yards of our lines. They then poured in a single volley, and dashed forward with the bayonet, capturing prisoners and colors, and driving the routed columns in confusion from the field.

About seven o'clock, as fresh troops were accumulating in front of Porter and Couch, Meagher and Sickles were sent with their brigades as soon as it was considered prudent to withdraw any portion of Sumner's and Heintzelman's troops to reinforce that part of the line, and hold the position. These brigades relieved such regiments of Porter's corps and Couch's division, as had expended their ammunition, and batteries from the reserve were pushed forward to replace those whose boxes were empty. Until dark the enemy persisted in his efforts to take position so tenaciously defended; but despite his vastly superior numbers his repeated and desperate attacks were repulsed with fearful loss, and darkness ended the battle of Malvern Hill, though it was not until after 9 o'clock that the artillery ceased its fire

During the whole battle Com Rodgers added greatly to the discomfiture of the enemy, by throwing shells among his reserves and advancing columns

As the army in its movement from the Chickahominy to Harrison's Landing, was continually occupied in marching by night and fighting by day, its commanders found no time or opportunity for collecting data, which would enable them to give exact return of casualties in each engagement The aggregate of our entire losses, from the 26th of June to the first of July, inclusive, was ascertained after arriving at Harrison's Landing to be as follows —

List of the killed, wounded and missing, in the army of the Potomac, from the 26th June, 1862 to the 1st of July, 1862, inclusive

CORPS	Killed	Wound	Missg	Aggr
1st —McCall's Penn Reserves	253	1,240	1,581	3,074
2d —Sumner's	187	1,076	848	2,111
3d —Heintzelman's	189	1,051	833	2,073
4th —Keyes's	69	507	201	777
5th —Porter's	620	2,460	1,198	4,278
6th —Franklin's	245	1,313	1,179	2,737
Engineers		2	21	23
Cavalry	19	60	97	17
Total	1,582	7,709	5,958	15,249

MOVEMENT TO HARRISON'S LANDING

Although the result of the battle of Malvern was a complete victory, it was nevertheless necessary to fall back still further, in order to reach a point where our supplies could be brought to us with certainty As before stated, in the opinion of Capt Rodgers, commanding the gunboat flotilla, this could only be done below City Point Concurring in his opinion, I selected Harrison's Bar as the new position of our supplies of food, forage, and ammunition, made it imperative to reach the transports immediately

The greater portion of the transportation of the army having been started for Harrison's Landing during the night of the 30th of June and 1st of July, the order for the movement of the troops was at once issued upon the final repulse of the enemy at Malvern Hill.

The order prescribed a movement by the left and rear—Gen Keyes' corps to cover the manœuvre It was not carried out in detail as regards the divisions on the left, the roads being somewhat blocked by the rear of our trains. Porter and Couch were not able to move out as early as had been anticipated, and Porter found it necessary to place a rear-guard between his command and the enemy Col. Averill, of the 3d Pennsylvania Cavalry, was entrusted with this delicate duty He had under his command his own regiment and Lieut.-Col. Buchanan's brigade of regular infantry, and one battery. By a judicious use of the resources at his command, he deceived the enemy so as to cover the withdrawal of the left wing without being attacked, remaining himself on the previous day's battle-field until about 7 o'clock of the 2d July Meantime, Gen Keyes having received his orders, commenced vigorous preparations for covering the movement of the entire army, and protecting the trains It being evident that the immense number of wagons and artillery carriages pertaining to the army could not move with celerity along a single road, Gen Keyes took advantage of every accident of the ground to open new avenues, and to facilitate the movement. He made preparations for obstructing the roads after the army had passed so as to prevent any rapid pursuit, destroying effectually Turkey Bridge, on the main road, and rendering other roads and approaches temporarily impassable by felling trees across them. He kept the trains well closed up and directed the march so that the troops could march on each side of the roads not obstructing the passage, but being in good position to repel an attack from any quarter His dispositions were so successful that, to use his own words "I do not think more vehicles or more public property were abandoned on the march from Turkey Bridge than would have been left, in the same state of the roads, if the army had been moving toward the enemy, instead of away from him, and when it is understood that the carriages and teams belonging to this army, stretched out in one line, would extend not far from forty miles, the energy and caution necessary for their safe withdrawal from the presence of an enemy vastly superior in numbers, will be appreciated'

The last of the wagons did not reach the site selected at Harrison's Bar, until after dark on the 3d of July, and the rear guard did not move into their camp until everything was secure The enemy followed up with a small force, and on the 3d threw a few shells at the rear guard, but were quickly dispersed by our batteries, and the fire of the gun-boats

Great credit must be awarded to Gen Keyes, for the skill and energy which characterized his performance of the important and delicate duties entrusted to his charge

High praise is also due to the officers and men of the 1st Connecticut Artillery, Col Tyler, for the manner in which they withdrew all the heavy guns during the seven days, and from Malvern Hill Owing to the crowded state of the roads the teams could not be brought within a couple of miles of the position, but these energetic soldiers removed the guns by hand for that distance, leaving nothing behind

THIRD PERIOD

CLOSE OF THE PENINSULAR CAMPAIGN.

On the 1st of July, I received the following from the President:

Washington, July 1, 1862 3 30 P. M. Maj-Gen Geo B McClellan,—

It is impossible to reinforce you for your present emergency If we had a million of men, we could not get them to give you in time. We have not the men to send If you are not strong enough to face the enemy, you must find a place of security and wait, rest and repair

Maintain your ground if you can, but save the army at all events, even if you fall back to Fort Monroe We still have strength enough in the country, and will bring it out. A. LINCOLN

In a dispatch from the President to me on the 2d of July, he says

"If you think you are not strong enough

take Richmond just now I do not ask you to Try just now to save the army material and personnel and I will strengthen it for the offensive again as fast as I can.

The governors of eighteen states offer me a new levy of three hundred thousand, which I accept"

On the 3d of July, the following kind despatch was received from the President.

(*Extract*)

Washington, July 3, 1862. 3 P. M.

Maj.-Gen G B McC—Yours of 5 30 yesterday is just received I am satisfied that yourself, officers and men have done the best you could All accounts say better fighting was never done Ten thousand thanks for it   A LINCOLN
To G B McC

On the 4th, I sent the following to the President:

Headquarters Army of the Potomac, Harrison's Bar, James River July 4 1862

To the President,—I have the honor to acknowledge the receipt of your despatch of the 2d instant

I shall make a stand at this place, and endeavor to give my men the repose they so much require

After sending my communication on Tuesday the enemy attacked the left of our lines, and a fierce battle ensued, lasting until night; they were repulsed with great slaughter. Had their attack succeeded, the consequences would have been disastrous in the extreme This closed the hard fighting which had continued from the afternoon of the 26th ult. in a daily series of engagements, wholly unparalleled on this continent for determination and slaughter on both sides

The mutual loss in killed and wounded, is enormous That of the enemy certainly greatest On Tuesday evening the 1st. our army commenced its movement from Haxall's to this point. Our line of defence there, being too extended to be maintained by our weakened forces. Our train was immense, and about 4 A. M. on the 2d, a heavy storm of rain began, which continued during the entire day, and until the forenoon of yesterday

The road became horrible Troops, artillery, and wagons moved on steadily and our whole army men and material, was finally brought safe into this camp The last of the wagons reached here at noon yesterday. The exhaustion was very great, but the army preserved its morale, and would have repelled any attack which the enemy was in condition to make

We now occupy a line of heights about two miles from the James, a plain extending from there to the river. Our front is about three miles long These heights command our whole position, and must be maintained The gunboats can render valuable support on both flanks. If the enemy attack us in front, we must hold our ground as best we may, and at whatever cost.

Our positions can be carried only by overwhelming numbers The spirit of the army is excellent Stragglers are finding their regiments, and the soldiery exhibit the best results of discipline Our position is by no means impregnable, especially as a morass extends on this side of the high ground from our centre to the James on our right The enemy may attack in vast numbers, and if so our front will be the scene of a desperate battle which it lost, will be decisive. Our army is fearfully weakened by killed wounded and prisoners I cannot now approximate to any statement of our losses, but we are not beaten in any conflict The enemy were unable by their utmost efforts to drive us from any field. Never did such a change of base, involving a retrograde movement, and under incessant attacks from a most determined and vastly more numerous foe, partake so little of disorder We have lost no guns except 25 on the field of battle, 21 of which were lost by the giving way of McCall's division under the onset of superior numbers.

Our communications by the James River are not secure There are points where the enemy can establish themselves with cannon or musketry and command the river, and where it is not certain that our gunboats can drive them out. In case of this, or in case our front is broken, I will still make every effort to preserve at least the personnel of the army, and the events of the last few days leave no question that the troops will do all that their country can ask Send such reinforcements as you can. I will do what I can We are shipping our wounded and sick, and landing supplies The navy department should cooperate with us to the extent of its resources Captain Rodgers is doing all in his power, in the kindest and most efficient manner

When all the circumstances of the case are known, it will be acknowledged by all competent judges that the movement just completed by this army is unparalleled in the annals of war Under the most difficult circumstances, we have preserved our trains, our guns, our material, and, above all, our honor. G. B. McC, Maj.-Gen.

To which I received the following reply:

Washington, July 5, 1862   9 A. M.

Maj.-Gen. G. B McC, Commanding army of the Potomac

A thousand thanks for the relief your two despatches of 12 and 1 P M yesterday, gave me Be assured, the heroism and skill of yourself, officers, and men, is and forever will be appreciated

If you can hold your present position, we shall have the enemy yet   A LINCOLN

The following letters were received from his Excellency the President.

War Department, Washington City, D C. July 4th, 1862.

Maj.-Gen McC.—I understand your position as stated in your letter, and by Gen Marcy. To reinforce you so as to enable you to resume the offensive within a month, or even six weeks, is impossible. In addition to that arrived and now arriving from the Potomac (about ten thousand, I suppose), and about ten thousand I hope you will have from Burnside very soon, and about five thousand from Hunter a little later, I do not see how I can send you another man within a month. Under these circumstances, the defensive, for the present, must be your only care Save the army first, where you are, if you can, and secondly, by removal, if you must. You, on the ground, must be the judge as to which you w

attempt, and of the means for effecting it. I but give it as my opinion, that with the aid of the gunboats and the reinforcements mentioned above you can hold your present position, provided, and so long as, you can keep the James River open below you. If you are not tolerably confident you can keep the James River open, you had better remove as soon as possible. I do not remember that you have expressed any apprehension as to the danger of having your communication cut on the river below you, yet I do not suppose it can have escaped your attention,
Yours very truly, A. L.
P. S.—If at any time you feel able to take the offensive, you are not restrained from doing so.
A. L.

The following telegram was sent on the 7th:
Headquarters, Army of the Potomac, Berkeley July 7, 1862, 8.30 P. M.—As boat is starting I have only time to acknowledge receipt of dispatch by Gen. Marcy. Enemy have not attacked. My position is very strong, and daily becoming more so. If not attacked to-day, I shall laugh at them. I have been anxious about my communications. Had long consultation about it with Flag-officer Goldsborough last night; he is confident he can keep river open. He should have all gun-boats possible. Will see him again this morning. My men in splendid spirits, and anxious to try it again.

Alarm yourself as little as possible about me and don't lose confidence in this army.
A. L., President. G. B. McC.

While General-in-Chief, and directing the operations of all our armies in the field, I had become deeply impressed with the importance of adopting and carrying out certain views regarding the conduct of the war, which, in my judgment, were essential to its objects and its success. During an active campaign of three months in the enemy's country these were so fully confirmed that I conceived it a duty, in the critical position we then occupied, not to withhold a candid expression of the more important of these views from the commander-in-chief whom the constitution places at the head of the armies and navies, as well as of the government of the nation. The following is a copy of my letter to Mr. Lincoln:

Headquarters, Army of the Potomac Camp near Harrison's Landing, Va., July 7, 1862.
Mr. President,—You have been fully informed that the rebel army is in our front, with the purpose of overwhelming us by attacking our positions or reducing us by blocking our river communications. I can not but regard our condition as critical, and I earnestly desire, in view of possible contingencies, to lay before your Excellency, for your private consideration, my general views concerning the existing state of the rebellion, although they do not strictly relate to the situation of this army, or strictly come within scope of my official duties. These views amount to convictions, and are deeply impressed upon my mind and heart. Our cause must never be abandoned, it is the cause of free institutions and self government. The Constitution and the Union must be preserved, whatever may be the cost in time, treasure or blood. If secession is successful, other dissolutions are clearly to be seen in the future. Let neither military disaster, political faction, or foreign war, shake your settled purpose to enforce the equal operation of the laws of the United States upon the people of every State.

The time has come when the government must determine upon a civil and military policy covering the whole ground of our national trouble. The responsibility of determining, declaring, and supporting such civil and military policy, and of directing the whole course of national affairs in regard to the rebellion must now be assumed and exercised by you, or our cause will be lost. The constitution gives you power sufficient even for the present terrible exigency.

This rebellion has assumed the character of war, as such it should be regarded, and it should be conducted upon the highest principles known to Christian civilization. It should not be a war looking to the subjugation of the people of any State in any event. It should not be at all a war upon population, but against armed forces and political organizations. Neither confiscation of property, political executions of persons, territorial organization of States, or forcible abolition of slavery should be contemplated for a moment. In prosecuting the war, all private property and unarmed persons should be strictly protected, subject only to the necessity of military operations. All private property taken for military use should be paid or receipted for, pillage and waste should be treated as high crimes; all unnecessary trespass sternly prohibited, and offensive demeanor by the military towards citizens promptly rebuked. Military arrests should not be tolerated, except in places where active hostilities exist, and oaths not required by enactments constitutionally made should be neither demanded nor received. Military government should be confined to the preservation of public order and the protection of political rights. Military power should not be allowed to interfere with the relations of servitude, either by supporting or impairing the authority of the master, except for suppressing disorder, as in other cases. Slaves contraband under the act of Congress, seeking military protection, should receive it. The right of the government to appropriate permanently to its own service, claims to slave labor, should be asserted, and the right of the owner to compensation therefor should be recognized.

This principle might be extended, upon grounds of military necessity and security, to all the slaves within a particular State, thus working manumission in such State, and in Missouri, perhaps in Western Virginia also, and possibly even in Maryland, the expediency of such a measure is only a question of time.

A system of policy thus constitutional and conservative, and pervaded by the influences of Christianity and freedom, would receive the support of almost all truly loyal men, would deeply impress the rebel masses and all foreign nations, and it might be humbly hoped that it would commend itself to the favor of the Almighty.

Unless the principles governing the future corduct of our struggle shall be made known and approved, the effort to obtain requisite forces will be almost hopeless. A declaration of radical views, especially upon slavery, will rapidly disintegrate our present armies.

The policy of the government must be supported by concentrations of military power. The national forces should not be dispersed in expeditions, posts of occupation, and numerous armies, but should be mainly collected into masses, and brought to bear upon the armies of the confederate States. These armies thoroughly defeated, the political structure which they support would soon cease to exist.

In carrying out any system of policy which you may form, you will require a commander-in-chief of the army; one who possesses your confidence, understands your views, and who is competent to execute your orders by directing the military forces of the nation to the accomplishment of the objects by you proposed. I do not ask that place for myself. I am willing to serve you in such position as you may assign me, and I will do so as faithfully as ever subordinate served superior.

I may be on the brink of eternity, and as I hope for forgiveness from my Maker, I have written this letter with sincerity towards you, and from love of my country. Very respectfully, your obedient servant, G. B. McC., Maj.-Gen. Comd'g.

His Excellency A. L., President.

I telegraphed the President on the 11th as follows:

Headquarters, Army of the Potomac, Berkeley, July 11, 1862. 3 P.M.

We are very strong here now so far as defensive is concerned. Hope you will soon make us strong enough to advance and try it again. All in fine spirits. G B McC, Maj.-Gen Comd'g.

A. L., President.

These telegrams were sent on the 12th, 17th and 18th, to his Excellency the President.

Headquarters, Army of the Potomac, Berkeley, July 12, 1862, 7.15 P.M—Hill and Longstreet crossed into New Kent County via Long Bridge. I am still ignorant what road they afterwards took, but will know shortly.

Nothing else of interest since last dispatch, rain ceased and everything quiet. Men resting well but beginning to be impatient for another fight.

I am more and more convinced that this army ought not to be withdrawn from here, but promptly reinforced and thrown again upon Richmond. If we have a little more than half a chance we can take it. I dread the effects of any retreat upon the morale of the men.

G. B. McC. to A L, President

Headquarters, Army of the Potomac, Berkeley, July 17, 1862, 8 A.M—I have consulted fully with Gen Burnside and would commend to your favorable consideration the general's plan for bringing seven additional regiments from North Carolina, by leaving Newbern to the care of the gunboats. It appears manifestly to be our policy to concentrate here everything we can possibly spare from less important points to make sure of crushing the enemy at Richmond, which seems clearly to be the most important point in rebeldom. Nothing should be left to chance here. I would recommend that Gen. Burnside, with all his troops, be ordered to this army, to enable it to assume the offensive as soon as possible.

G B McC. to A. L.

Headquarters, Army of the Potomac, Berkeley, July 18, 1862, 8 A.M.—No change worth reporting in the state of affairs. Some twenty to twenty-five thousand of enemy at Petersburg, and others thence to Richmond. Those at Petersburg say they are part of Beauregard's army. New troops arriving via Petersburg. Am anxious to have determination of government, that no time may be lost in preparing for it. Hours are very precious now, and perfect unity of action necessary.

G B McC. to A. L.

The following was telegraphed to Gen. Halleck on the 28th:

Headquarters, Army of the Potomac, Berkeley, July 28, 1862. 8 A M.—Nothing especially new except corroboration of reports that reinforcements reaching Richmond from South. It is not confirmed that any of Bragg's troops are yet here. My opinion is more and more firm, that here is the defense of Washington, and that I should be at once reinforced by all available troops, to enable me to advance. Retreat would be disastrous to the army and the cause. I am confident of that.

G. B. McC. to Maj.-Gen. H. W. H., Comd'g. U. S Army.

On the 30th I sent the following to the general-in-chief:

Headquarters Army of the Potomac, Berkeley, July 30, 1862.

I hope that it may soon be decided what is to be done by his army; and that the decision may be to reinforce it at once. We are losing much valuable time, and that at a moment when energy and decision are sadly needed.

G B McC. to M.-Gen. H W. H Com U S A.

About half an hour after midnight, on the morning of August 1st, the enemy brought some light batteries to Coggin's Point and the Coles House on the right bank of James River, directly opposite Harrison's Landing, and opened a heavy fire upon our shipping and encampments. It was continued rapidly for about thirty minutes, when they were driven back by the fire of our guns. This affair was reported in the following dispatch: Headq's. Army of the Potomac, Berkeley, Aug 2. 1862, 8 A.M.

Firing of night before last killed some 10 men, and wounded about 15. No harm of the slightest consequence done to the shipping, although several struck. Sent party across river yesterday to the Coles House; destroyed it and cut down the timber, will complete work to-day; and also send party to Coggin's Point, which I will probably occupy. I will attend to your telegraph about pressing, at once, will send Hooker out. Give me Burnside, and I will stir these people up. I need more cavalry, have only 3,700 for duty in cavalry division.

Adj.-General's office forgot to send Sykes's commission, as maj.-gen. with those of other commanders. Do me the favor to hurry it on.

G. B. McC. to M.-Gen. H. W. H.

To prevent another demonstration of this character, and to secure a debouche on the south side of the James, it became necessary to occupy Coggin's Point, which was done on the 3d, and the enemy, as will be seen from the following dispatch, driven back towards Petersburg:

Headq's., Army of the Potomac, Berkeley, Aug. 3, 1862, 10 P. M.

Coggin's Point was occupied to-day, and timber felled so as to make it quite defensible. I went over the ground myself, and found that Duane had, as usual, selected an admirable position, which can be intrenched with a small amount of labor, so as to make it a formidable tete-de-pont, covering the landing of a large force. I shall begin intrenching it by the labor of contrabands to-morrow. The position covers the Coles House, which is directly in front of Westover. We have now a safe debouche on the south bank, and are secure against midnight cannonading. A few thousands more men would place us in condition at least to annoy and disconcert the enemy very much.

I sent Col. Averell this morning with 300 cavalry, to examine the country south side of the James, and try to catch some cavalry at Sycamore Church, which is on the main road from Petersburg to Suffolk, and some five miles from Coles House.

He found a cavalry force of 550 men, attacked them at once, drove in their advanced guard to their camp, where he had a sharp skirmish, and drove them off in disorder.

He burned their entire camp, with their commissary and quarter-master's stores, and then returned and recrossed the river. He took but two prisoners, had one man wounded by a ball, and one by a sabre cut. Capt. McIntosh made a handsome charge. The troops engaged were of the 5th regulars, and the Third Pennsylvania cavalry.

Col. Averell conducted this affair, as he does everything he undertakes, to my entire satisfaction.

G. B. McC. to Maj.-Gen. H. W. H., Com'g. U. S. A.

On the 1st of August, I received the following dispatches:

Washington, July 30, 1862. 8 P.M.

Maj.-Gen. G. B. McC.—A dispatch just received from Gen. Pope, says that deserters report that the enemy is moving south of James River, and that the force in Richmond is very small. I suggest that he be pressed in that direction, so as to ascertain the facts of the case.

H. W. H., Maj.-Gen.

Washington, July 30, 1862. 8 P.M.—Maj.-Gen. G. B. McC.—In order to enable you to move in any direction, it is necessary to relieve you of your sick. The surgeon-general has therefore been directed to make arrangements for them at other places, and the quarter-master-general to provide transportation. I hope you will send them away as quickly as possible, and advise me of their removal. H. W. H., Maj.-Gen.

It is clear that the general-in-chief attached some weight to the report received from Gen. Pope, and I was justified in supposing that the order in regard to removing the sick, contemplated an offensive movement, rather than a retreat, as I had no other data than the telegrams just given, from which to form an opinion as to the intentions of the government. The following telegram strengthened me in that belief.

Washington, July 31, 162   10 A M

Maj.-Gen. G. B. McC.—General Pope again telegraphs that the enemy is reported to be evacuating Richmond, and falling back on Danville and Lynchburg.   H. W. H., Maj.-Gen

In occupying Coggin's Point, as already described, I was influenced by the necessity of possessing a secure debouche on the south of the James, in order to enable me to move on the communications of Richmond in that direction, as well as to prevent a repetition of midnight cannonades.

To carry out Gen. Halleck's first order of July 30th, it was necessary first to gain possession of Malvern Hill, which was occupied by the enemy, apparently in some little force, and controlled the direct approach to Richmond. Its temporary occupation, at least, was equally necessary in the event of a movement upon Petersburg, or even the abandonment of the Peninsula. Gen. Hooker, with his own division and Pleasonton's cavalry, was therefore directed to gain possession of Malvern Hill on the night of the 2d August. He failed to do so, as the following dispatch recites:

Headquarters, Army of the Potomac, Berkeley, August 9, 1862   10 20 P M

The movement undertaken up the river last night failed, on account of the incompetency of guides. The proper steps have been taken to-day to remedy this evil, and I hope to be ready to-morrow night to carry out your suggestions as to pressing, at least, to accomplish the first indispensable step. G. B McC, Maj.-Gen Comd'g.

Maj.-Gen Halleck, Comd'g U. S. Army.

On the 4th Gen. Hooker was reinforced by Gen. Sedgwick's division, and, having obtained a knowledge of the roads, he succeeded in turning Malvern Hill, and driving the enemy back towards Richmond. The following is my report of this affair at the time:

Malvern Hill, August 5, 1862   1 P M

Maj.-Gen. H. W. Halleck, Comd'g U. S Army General Hooker, at 5 30 this morning, attacked a very considerable force of infantry and artillery stationed at this place, and carried it handsomely driving the enemy towards New Market, which is four miles distant, and where it is said they have a large force. We have captured 100 prisoners, killed and wounded several, with a loss on our part of only three killed and eleven wounded—among the latter two officers.

I shall probably remain here to-night, ready to act as circumstances may require, after the return of my cavalry reconnoissances.

The mass of the enemy escaped under the cover of a dense fog, but our cavalry are still in pursuit, and I trust may succeed in capturing many more.

This is a very advantageous position to cover an advance on Richmond, and only 14¾ miles distant, and I feel confident that, with reinforcements, I could march this army there in five days.

... instant learn that several brigades of the ... are four miles from here, on the Quaker ..., and I have taken steps to prepare to meet them.

Gen Hooker's dispositions were admirable, and his officers and men displayed their usual gallantry. G B McC, Major-Gen

On the same day the following telegram was sent:

Malvern Hill, Aug 5, 1862, 8 P M

Maj-Gen H. W. H., Commanding U S Army—Since my last dispatch Colonel Averell has returned from a reconnoissance in the direction of Savage's Station, towards Richmond. He encountered the 10th Virginia cavalry near White Oak Swamp Bridge, charged and drove them some distance towards Richmond, capturing 28 men and horses, and killing and wounding several.

Our troops have advanced twelve miles in one direction, and seventeen in another, towards Richmond, to-day.

We have secured a strong position on Coggin's Point, opposite our quartermaster's depot, which will effectually prevent the rebels from using artillery hereafter against our camps.

I learn this evening that there is a force of 20,000 men about six miles back from this point, on the south bank of the river, what their object is I do not know, but will keep a sharp look out on their movements.

I am sending off sick as rapidly as our transports will take them. I am also doing everything in my power to carry out your orders, to push reconnoissances towards the rebel capital, and hope soon to find out whether the reports regarding the abandonment of that place are true.
G B McC, Major-Gen

To the dispatch of 1 P M, August 5, the following answer was received:

Washington, August 6, 1862, 3 A M.

Maj-Gen G B McC—I have no reinforcements to send you. H. W. H. Maj-Gen

And soon after the following:

Washington, August 6, 1862

Maj-Gen G. B. McC—You will immediately send a regiment of cavalry and several batteries of artillery to Burnside's command at Acquia Creek. It is reported that Jackson is moving north with a very large force.
H W H, Major-General

On the 4th I had received Gen. Halleck's order of the 3d (which appears below), directing me to withdraw the army to Acquia, and on the same day sent an earnest protest against it.

A few hours before this, Gen. Hooker had informed me that his cavalry pickets reported large bodies of the enemy advancing and driving them in, and that he would probably be attacked at daybreak. Under these circumstances I had determined to support him, but as I could not get the whole army in position until the next afternoon, I concluded, upon the receipt of the above telegram from the general-in-chief, to withdraw Gen Hooker, that there might be the least possible delay in conforming to Gen Halleck's orders. I therefore sent to Gen. Hooker the following letter:

Headquarters, Army of the Potomac,
Berkeley, August 6, 1862 10 P M.

My dear General.—I find it will not be possible to get the whole army in position before some time to-morrow afternoon, which will be too late to support you and hold the entire position, should the enemy attack in large force at daybreak, which there is strong reason to suppose he intends doing.

Should we fight a general battle at Malvern, it will be necessary to abandon the whole of our works here, and run the risk of getting back here.

Under advices I have received from Washington, I think it necessary for you to abandon the position to-night, getting everything away before daylight.

Please leave cavalry pickets at Malvern, with orders to destroy the Turkey Creek Bridge when they are forced back.

The roads leading into Haxalls from the right should be strongly watched, and Haxalls at least held by strong cavalry force and some light batteries, as long as possible.

I leave the manner of the withdrawal entirely to your discretion.

Please signal to the fleet when the withdrawal is about completed.

Report frequently to these headquarters. Gen. Sumner was ordered up to support you, but will halt where this passes him, and will inform you where he is. G B McC, Maj-Gen Comd'g.

Gen. J. H., Comd'g at Malvern Hill.

And the following reply was sent to Gen. Halleck:

Headquarters, Army of the Potomac,
Berkeley, Aug. 6, 1862, 11 30 P M

Dispatch of to-day received. I have not quite four thousand cavalry for duty in cavalry division, so that I cannot possibly spare any more. I really need many more than I now have, to carry out your instructions.

The enemy are moving a large force upon Malvern Hill. In view of your dispatches, and the fact that I can not place the whole army in position before daybreak, I have ordered Hooker to withdraw during the night, if it is possible. If he can not do so, I must support him. Until this matter is developed, I can not send any batteries. I hope I can do so to-morrow, if transportation is on hand.

I will obey the order as soon as circumstances will admit. My artillery is none too numerous now. I have only been able to send off some twelve hundred sick, no transportation. There shall be no delay that I can avoid. G. B. McC., Maj-Gen. Comd'g.

Maj-Gen H W. H, Comd'g U. S Army.

Five batteries, with their horses and equipments complete, were embarked on the 7th and 8th. Simultaneously with Gen Hooker's operations upon Malvern, I despatched a cavalry force under Col. Averell towards Savage's Station, to ascertain if the enemy were making any movements towards our left flank. He found a rebel cavalry regiment near the White-Oak Swamp Bridge, and completely routed it, pursuing well towards Savage's Station.

These important preliminary operations assisted my preparations for the removal of the army to Acquia Creek, and the sending off our sick and supplies was pushed both day and night as rapidly as the means of transportation permitted.

On the subject of the withdrawal of the army from Harrison's Landing, the following correspondence passed between the General-in-chief and myself while the reconnoissances towards Richmond were in progress.

On the 2d of August I received the following:
Washington, Aug. 1, 1862, 3 45 P M.

Maj-Gen G B McC.—You have not answered my telegram [of July 30, 8 P.M.] about the removal of your sick. Remove them as rapidly as possible, and telegraph me when they will be out of your way. The President wishes an answer as early as possible.

To which this reply was sent: Headq's, Army of the Potomac, Berkeley, Aug 3, 1862, 11 P M.

Your telegram of 2d is received. The answer [to dispatch of July 30] was sent this morning. We have about 12,500 sick, of whom perhaps 4,000 might make easy marches. We have here the means to transport 1,200, and will embark tomorrow that number of the worst cases. With all the means at the disposal of the medical director, the remainder could be shipped in from 7 to 10 days. It is impossible for me to decide what cases to send off, unless I know what is to be done with this army.

Were the disastrous measures of a retreat adopted, all the sick who can not march and fight should be despatched by water. Should the army advance, many of the sick could be of service at the depots. If it is to remain here any length of time, the question assumes still a different phase.

Until I am informed what is to be done, I cannot act understandingly, or for the good of the service. If I am kept longer in ignorance of what is to be effected, I cannot be expected to accomplish the object in view. In the meantime I will do all in my power to carry out what I conceive to be your wishes.

G B McC. to M-Gen H W H, Com. U S A

The moment I received the instructions for removing the sick, I at once gave the necessary directions for carrying them out. With the small amount of transportation at hand, the removal of the severe cases alone would necessarily take several days, and in the meantime I desired information to determine what I should do with others.

The order required me to send them away "as quickly as possible, and to notify the Gen.-in-Chief *when they were removed.*"

Previous to the receipt of the dispatch of the 2d of August, not having been advised of what the army under my command was expected to do, or which way it was to move, if it moved at all, I sent the following dispatch:

Headq's, Army of the Potomac, Berkeley, Aug 3, 1862

I hear of sea steamers at Fort Monroe, are they for removing my sick? If so, to what extent am I required to go in sending them off?

There are not many who need go.

As I am not in any way informed of the intentions of the government in regard to this army, I am unable to judge what proportion of the sick should leave here, and must ask for specific orders.

G B McC to Maj-Gen. H W H

If the army was to retreat to Fort Monroe, it was important that it should be unincumbered with any sick, wounded, or other men who might at all interfere with its mobility, but if the object was to operate directly on Richmond from the position we then occupied, there were many cases of slight sickness which would speedily be cured, and the patients returned to duty. As the service of every man would be important in the event of a forward offensive movement, I conceived it to be of the utmost consequence that I should know what was to be done. It was to ascertain this that I sent the dispatch of 11 P M of the 3d, before receiving the following telegram.

Washington, Aug 3, 1862 7 45 P M

Maj-Gen Geo B McC—I have waited most anxiously to learn the result of your forced reconnoissance towards Richmond, and also whether all your sick have been sent away, and I can get no answer to my telegram. It is determined to withdraw your army from the Peninsula to Acquia Creek. You will take immediate measures to effect this, covering the movement the best you can. Its real object and withdrawal should be concealed even from your own officers. Your material and transportation should be removed first. You will assume control of all the means of transportation within your reach, and apply to the naval forces for all the assistance they can render you. You will consult freely with the commander of these forces. The entire execution of the movement is left to your discretion and judgment. You will leave such forces as you may deem proper at Fort Monroe, Norfolk, and other places which we must occupy.

H W H, Maj-Gen Comd'g U S A

I proceeded to obey this order with all possible rapidity, firmly impressed, however, with the conviction that the withdrawal of the army of the Potomac from Harrison's Landing, where its communications had, by the co-operation of the gun-boats, been rendered perfectly secure, would at the time have the most disastrous effect upon our cause. I did not, as the commander of that army, allow the occasion to pass without distinctly setting forth my views upon the subject to the authorities, as in the following telegram.

Headquarters, Army of the Potomac, Berkely, Aug 4, 1862 12 M

Your telegram of last evening is received. I must confess that it has caused me the greatest pain I ever experienced for I am convinced that the order to withdraw this army to Acquia Creek will prove disastrous to our cause.

I fear it will be a fatal blow.

Several days are necessary to complete the preparations for so important a movement as this, and while they are in progress, I beg that careful consideration may be given to my statements.

This army is now in excellent discipline and condition. We hold debouche on both banks of the James River, so that we are free to act in any direction and with the assistance of the gun-boats I consider our communications as now secure. We are twenty-five miles from Richmond, and are not likely to meet the enemy in force sufficient to fight a battle, until we have marched fifteen to eighteen miles, which brings us practically within ten miles of Richmond. Our longest line of land transportation would be from this point twenty-five miles; but with the aid of the gun-boats we can supply the army by water during its advance, certainly to within twelve miles of Richmond.

At Acquia Creek we would be seventy-five miles from Richmond, with land transportation all the way.

From here to Fort Monroe, is a march of about seventy miles, for I regard it as impracticable to withdraw this army and its material, except by land.

The result of the movement would thus be a march of one hundred and forty-five miles to reach a point now only twenty-five miles distant, and to deprive ourselves entirely of the powerful aid of the gun-boats and water transportation. Add to this the certain demoralization of this army, which would ensue, the terribly depressing effect upon the people of the North, and the strong probability that it would influence foreign powers to recognize our adversaries, and there appear to me sufficient reasons to make it my imperative duty to urge, in the strongest terms afforded by our language, that this order may be rescinded, and that, far from recalling this army it be promptly reinforced to enable it to resume the offensive.

It may be said that there are no reinforcements available. I point to Burnside's force, to that of Pope, not necessary to maintain a strict defensive in front of Washington and Harper's Ferry, to those portions of the army of the west not required for a strict defensive there. Here directly in front of this army, is the heart of the rebellion; it is here that all our resources should be collected to strike the blow which will determine the fate of the nation. All points of secondary importance elsewhere should be abandoned, and every available man brought here—a decided victory here, and the military strength of the rebellion is crushed—it matters not what partial reverses we may meet with elsewhere. Here is the true defense of Washington; it is here on the banks of the James that the fate of the Union should be decided.

Clear in my convictions of right, strong in the consciousness that I have ever been, and still am actuated solely by love of my country, knowing that no ambitious or selfish motives have influenced me from the commencement of this war, I do now, what I never did in my life before, I entreat that this order may be rescinded.

If my counsel does not prevail, I will with a sad heart obey your orders to the utmost of my power, directing to the movement which I clearly foresee will be one of the utmost delicacy and difficulty, whatever skill I may possess.

Whatever the result may be, and God grant that I am mistaken in my forebodings, I shall at least have the internal satisfaction that I have written and spoken frankly, and have sought to do the best in my power to avert disaster from my country. G. B. McC., Maj.-Gen. Comd'g.

Maj.-Gen. H. W. H., Comd'g U. S. A.

Soon after sending this telegram, I received the following in reply to mine of 11 P. M. of the 3d:

Washington, Aug. 4, 1862, 12 45 P. M.

Maj.-Gen. G. B. McC.:—My telegram to you yesterday will satisfy you in regard to future operations. It was expected that you would have sent off your sick as directed, without waiting to know what were or would be the intentions of the government respecting future movements. The President expects that the instructions which were sent to you yesterday, with his approval, will be carried out with all possible dispatch and caution. The quarter-master-general is sending to Fort Monroe all the transportation he can collect. H. W. H., Maj.-Gen.

To which the following is my reply:

Headquarters, Army of the Potomac,
Berkeley, August 5, 1862, 7 A. M.

Your telegram of yesterday received, and is being carried out as promptly as possible. With the means at my command, no human power could have moved the sick in the time you say you expected them to be moved. G. B. McC, Maj.-Gen.

Maj.-Gen. W. H. H., Comd'g U. S. A.

My efforts for bringing about a change of policy were unsuccessful, as will be seen from the following telegram and letter received by me in reply to mine of 12 M. of the 4th.

Washington, August 5, 1862, 12 M.

Maj.-Gen. G. B. McC.:—You cannot regret the order of withdrawal more than I did the necessity of giving it. It will not be rescinded, and you will be expected to execute it with all possible promptness. It is believed that it can be done now without serious danger. This may not be so if there should be any delay.

I will write you my views more fully by mail. H. W. H., Maj.-Gen. Comd'g U. S. A.

The letter was as follows:

Headquarters of the Army,
Washington, Aug. 6, 1862

Maj.-Gen. McC., Comd'g. &c., Berkeley, Va.

General,—Your telegram of yesterday was received this morning, and I immediately telegraphed a brief reply, promising to write you more fully by mail.

You, General, certainly could not have been more pained at receiving my order, than I was at the necessity of issuing it. I was advised by high officers, in whose judgment I had great confidence, to make the order immediately on my arrival here, but I determined not to do so until I could learn your wishes from a personal interview: and even after that interview I tried every means in my power to avoid withdrawing your army, and delayed my decision as long as I dared to delay it.

I assure you, General, it was not a hasty and unconsidered act, but one that caused me more anxious thought than any other of my life. But after full and mature consideration of all the *pros and cons*, I was reluctantly forced to the conclusion that the order must be issued. There was, to my mind, no alternative.

Allow me to allude to a few of the facts in the

case You and your officers, at our interview, estimated the enemy's forces in and around Richmond at two hundred thousand men Since then, you and others report that they have received and are receiving large reinforcements from the South

Gen Pope's army, now covering Washington, is only about forty thousand Your effective force is only about ninety thousand You are about thirty miles from Richmond, and Gen Pope eighty or ninety, with the enemy directly between you, ready to fall with his superior numbers upon one or the other, as he may elect Neither can reinforce the other in case of such an attack If Gen Pope's army be diminished to reinforce you, Washington, Maryland, and Pennsylvania would be left uncovered and exposed. If your force be reduced to strengthen Pope you would be too weak to even hold the position you now occupy, should the enemy turn round and attack you in full force In other words the old army of the Potomac is split into two parts, with the entire force of the enemy directly between them They can not be united by land without exposing both to destruction, and yet they must be united. To send Pope's forces by water to the Peninsula is under present circumstances, a military impossibility The only alternative is to send the forces on the Peninsula to some point by water, say Fredericksburg, where the two armies can be united

Let me now allude to some of the objections which you have urged You say that the withdrawal from the present position will cause the certain demoralization of the army, "which is now in excellent discipline and condition" I can not understand why a simple change of position to a new and by no means distant base, will demoralize an army in excellent discipline, unless the officers themselves assist in that demoralization, which I am satisfied they will not. Your change of front from your extreme right at Hanover Court House to your present position was over thirty miles, but I have not heard that it demoralized your troops, notwithstanding the severe losses they sustained in effecting it.

A new base on the Rappahannock at Fredericksburg brings you within about sixty miles of Richmond, and secures a reinforcement of forty or fifty thousand fresh and disciplined troops Moreover, you yourself suggested that a junction might be effected at Yorktown; but that a flank march across the Isthmus would be more hazardous than to retire to Fort Monroe. You will remember that Yorktown is two or three miles further from Richmond than Fredericksburg is Besides the latter is between Richmond and Washington, and covers Washington from any attack by the enemy

The political effect of the withdrawal may at first be unfavorable; but I think the public are beginning to understand its necessity, and that they will have much more confidence in a united army, than in its separated fragments

But you will reply, why not reinforce me here, so that I can strike Richmond from my present position? To do this you said at our interview, that you required thirty thousand additional troops I told you that it was impossible to give you so many You finally thought you would have "some chance" of success with twenty thousand. But you afterwards telegraphed me that you would require thirty-five thousand, as the enemy was being largely reinforced If your estimate of the enemy's strength was correct, your requisition was perfectly reasonable, but it was utterly impossible to fill it until new troops could be enlisted and organized, which would require several weeks

To keep your army in its present position until it could be so reinforced, would almost destroy it in that climate The months of August and September are almost fatal to whites who live on that part of James River, and even after you receive the reinforcements asked for, you admitted that you must reduce Fort Darling and the river batteries, before you could advance on Richmond It is by no means certain that the reduction of these fortifications would not require considerable time, perhaps as much as those at Yorktown This delay might not only be fatal to the health of your army, but in the meantime Gen Pope's forces would be exposed to the heavy blows of the enemy without the slightest hope of assistance from you.

In regard to the demoralizing effect of a withdrawal from the Peninsula to the Rappahannock, I must remark that a large number of your highest officers, indeed, a majority of those whose opinions have been reported to me, are decidedly in favor of the movement Even several of those who originally advocated the line of the Peninsula, now advise its abandonment

I have not inquired, and do not wish to know by whose advice, or for what reasons the army of the Potomac was separated into two parts with the enemy between them I must take things as I find them. I find the forces divided, and I wish to unite them Only one feasible plan has been presented for doing this. If you or any one else had presented a better plan, I certainly should have adopted it. But all of your plans require reinforcements, which it is impossible to give you. It is very easy to *ask* for reinforcements, but it is not so easy to give them when you have no disposable troops at your command

I have written very plainly, as I understand the case, and I hope you will give me credit for having fully considered the matter, although I may have arrived at very different conclusions from your own.

Very respectfully, your obedient servant,
H. W H., Gen-in-Chief.

On the 7th I received the following telegram:
Washington, Aug 7, 1862 10 A.M.
Maj.-Gen. G B McC —You will immediately report the number of sick sent off since you received my order; the number still to be shipped, and the amount of transportation at your disposal, that is, the number of persons that can be carried on all the vessels which by my order you were authorized to control

H W H Maj-Gen.

To which I made this reply
Headq's, Army of the Pot'c, Aug 7, '62, 10 40 P.M.
Maj Gen. H W H, Com U S. A.—In reply to

your despatch of 10 A. M. to-day I report the number of sick sent off since I received your order as follows: 3,740, including some that are embarked to-night, and will leave to-morrow morning. The number still to be shipped, is, as nearly as can be ascertained, 5,700.

The embarkation of five batteries of artillery horses, wagons etc., required most of our available boats except the ferry-boats. All the transports that can ascend to this place, have been ordered up, they will be here to-morrow evening. Col. Ingalls reports to me that there are no transports now available for cavalry and will not be for two or three days. As soon as they can be obtained, I shall send off the 1st New York cavalry.

After the transports with sick and wounded have returned, including some heavy draft steamers at Fort Monroe, that cannot come to this point, we can transport 25,000 men at a time. We have some propellers here, but they are laden with commissary supplies, and are not available. The transports now employed in transporting sick and wounded, will carry 12,000 well infantry soldiers. Those at Fort Monroe, and of too heavy draft to come here, will carry 8,000 or 10,000 infantry. Several of the largest steamers have been used for transporting prisoners of war, and have only been available for the sick to-day.

G. B. McC., Maj.-Gen.

The report of my chief quartermaster upon the subject is as follows:

Headquarters Army of the Potomac, Office of Chief Quartermaster, Harrison's Landing, Aug. 7, 1862.

GENERAL.—I have the honor to return the papers herewith which you sent me, with the following remarks:

We are embarking five batteries of artillery with their horses, baggage, etc., which requires the detaining of most of our available boats, except the ferry-boats.

The medical department has 10 or 12 of our largest transport vessels which, if disposable, could carry 12,000 men. Besides, there are some heavy draft steamers at Fort Monroe, that cannot come to this point, but which can carry 8,000 or 10,000 infantry.

I have ordered all up here that can ascend to this depot. They will be here to-morrow evening. As it now is after the details already made, we cannot transport from this place more than 5,000 infantry.

There are no transports now available for cavalry. From and after to-morrow, if the vessels arrive, I could transport 10,000 infantry. In two or three days a regiment of cavalry can be sent if required.

If you want and ship from Yorktown or Fort Monroe, after the sick and wounded transports are at my disposal, we can transport 25,000 at a time. The number that can be transported, is contingent on circumstances referred to.

Most of the propellers here are laden with commissary or other supplies, and most of the tugs are necessary to tow off sail craft, also laden with supplies.

I am very respectfully, your most obedient servant, RUFUS INGALLS, Chief Quartermaster.
Gen. R. B. Marcy, Chief of Staff.

On the 9th I received this despatch:

Washington, Aug. 9, 1862. 12.45 P. M.

MAJ.-GEN. G. B. McC.—I am of opinion that the enemy is massing his forces in front of Generals Pope and Burnside, and that he expects to crush them, and move forward to the Potomac. You must send reinforcements instantly to Acquia Creek.

Considering the amount of transportation at your disposal, your delay is not satisfactory, you must move with all possible celerity.
H. W. H., Maj.-Gen.

To which I sent the following reply:

Headquarters, Army of the Potomac, Berkeley, Aug. 10, 1862. 8 A. M.

Telegram of yesterday received. The batteries sent to Burnside, took the last available transport yesterday morning. Enough have since arrived to ship one regiment of cavalry to-day.

The sick are being embarked as rapidly as possible. There has been no unnecessary delay as you assert, not an hour, but everything has been and is being pushed as rapidly as possible to carry out your orders.

G. B. McC. to Maj. Gen. H. W. H., Comd'g U. S. Army.

The following report, made on the same day by the officer then in charge of the transports exposes the injustice of the remark in the despatch of the general-in-chief, that, "considering the amount of transportation at your disposal, your delay is not satisfactory."

Assistant Quartermaster's office, Army of the Potomac, Harrison's Landing, Va., Aug. 10, 1862.

GEN. M. C. MEIGS Quartermaster General U. S. Army, Washington.—Col. Ingalls being himself ill has requested me to telegraph to you concerning the state and capacity of the transports now here.

On the night of the 8th I despatched eleven steamers, principally small ones, and six schooners, with five batteries of heavy horse artillery, none of which have yet returned.

Requisition is made this morning for transportation of one thousand cavalry to Acquia Creek. All the schooners that had been chartered for carrying horses, have been long since discharged or changed into freight vessels.

A large proportion of the steamers now here are still loaded with stores, or are in the floating hospital service, engaged in removing the sick. To transport the one thousand cavalry to-day will take all the available steamers now here not engaged in the service of the harbor. These steamers could take a large number of infantry, but are not well adapted to the carrying of horses, and much space is thus lost.

Several steamers are expected here to-day, and we are unloading schooners rapidly. Most of these are not chartered, but are being taken for the service required at same rates of pay as other chartered schooners.

If you could cause a more speedy return of the steamers sent away from here, it would facilitate matters. C. G. SAWTELLE, Capt. and A. Q. M. Comd'g Depot.

Our wharf facilities at Harrison's Landing were very limited, admitting but few vessels at one time. These were continually in use as long as there were disposable vessels, and the officers of the medical and quartermaster's departments, with all their available forces, were incessantly occupied, day and night in embarking and sending off the sick men, troops and material.

Notwithstanding the repeated representations I made to the general-in-chief that such were the facts, on the 10th I received the following:

Washington, Aug 10, 1862, 12 P M.

Maj-Gen G B McC.—The enemy is crossing the Rapidan in large force. They are fighting Gen Pope to-day; there must be no further delay in your movements. That which has already occurred was entirely unexpected, and must be satisfactorily explained. Let not a moment's time be lost, and telegraph me daily what progress you have made in executing the order to transfer your troops. H. W H, Maj-Gen.

To which I sent this reply:

Headquarters, Army of the Potomac,
Berkeley, Aug 10, 1862, 12 30 P M.

Your despatch of to-day is received. I assure you again that there has not been any unnecessary delay in carrying out your orders. You are probably laboring under some great mistake as to the amount of transportation available here. I have pushed matters to the utmost in getting off our sick, and the troops you ordered to Burnside.

Col Ingalls has more than once informed the Quartermaster General of the condition of our water transportation. From the fact that you directed me to keep the order secret, I took it for granted that you would take the steps necessary to provide the requisite transportation. A large number of transports for all arms of service, and for wagons should at once be sent to Yorktown and Fort Monroe. I shall be ready to move the whole army by land, the moment the sick are disposed of. You may be sure that not an hour's delay will occur that can be avoided. I fear you do not realize the difficulty of the operation proposed. The regiment of cavalry for Burnside has been in course of embarkation to-day and to-night. Ten steamers were required for the purpose. Twelve hundred and fifty-eight sick loaded to-day and to-night. Our means exhausted, except one vessel returning to Fort Monroe in the morning, which will take some five hundred cases of slight sickness.

The present moment is probably not the proper one for me to refer to the unnecessarily harsh and unjust tone of your telegrams of late. It will, however make no difference in my official action.

G B McC to Maj-Gen H W H Comd'g U S Army.

On the 11th this report was made:

Headquarters, Army of the Potomac, Berkely, Aug 11, 1862. 11 40 P M.

The embarkation of eight hundred and fifty cavalry and one brigade of infantry will be completed by two o'clock in the morning; five hundred sick were embarked to-day; another vessel arrived to-night and six hundred more sick are now being embarked. I still have some four thousand sick to dispose of. You have been grossly misled as to the amount of transportation at my disposal. Vessels loaded to their utmost capacity with stores and others indispensable for service here have been reported to you as available for carrying sick and well. I am sending off all that can be unloaded at Fort Monroe, to have them return here. I repeat that I have lost no time in carrying out your orders.

G B. McC, Maj-Gen Comd'g to Maj-Gen H W H Comd'g U S Army.

On the same day I received the following from the quartermaster in charge of the depot:

Assistant Quartermaster's Office, Army of the Potomac Harrison's Landing, Va Aug 11, 1862.

Colonel.—In reply to the communication from Gen Marcy, which was referred to me by you, I have to state that there are now in this harbor no disposable transports not already detailed either for the use of the hospital department, or the transportation of the N Y cavalry, or for the necessary service of the harbor. I think the steamers loading, and to be loaded with cavalry could take in addition, *three thousand infantry;* these boats are however directed to leave as fast as they are loaded; some have already started. The embarkation of this cavalry regiment is going on very slowly, and it is not in my power to hurry the matter, although I have had several agents of the department, and one commissioned officer at the wharf to render all the assistance possible. The entire army is this morning turning in to be stored on vessels knapsacks officer's baggage and other surplus property, and with our limited wharf facilities, it is impossible, unless the regular issues of forage, &c are suspended, to avoid great confusion and delay with what is already ordered to be done; of course, if any infantry is ordered to embark on these cavalry transports, the confusion and difficulties will be increased.

I know of no boats that may be expected here to-day, except the "South America" and "Fanny Cadwallader" (a propeller) which were ordered to be sent back from Fort Monroe.

The transports with the artillery left for Acquia Creek on the night of the 8th and the morning of the 9th. They were ordered to return immediately. I am, very respectfully, your obedient servant, C G SAWTELLE.

Capt and A Q M Comd'g Depot
Lieut-Col Rufus Ingalls A D C and chief Q M Army of the Potomac.

On the 12th I received the following:

Washington Aug 12 1862 12 M.

Maj-Gen G B McClellan.—The quartermaster general informs me that nearly every available steam vessel in the country is now under your control. To send more from Philadelphia, Baltimore, and New York, would interfere with the transportation of army supplies, and break up the channels of travel by which we are to bring forward the new troops. Burnside moved nearly thirteen thousand troops to Acquia Creek, in less than two days, and his transports were immediately sent back to you. All vessels in the James River and Chesapeake Bay were placed, at your disposal, and it was supposed that eight or ten thousand of your men could be transported daily. In addition to steamers there is a large fleet of sailing vessels which could be used as transports. The bulk of your material on shore, it was thought, could be sent to Fort Monroe covered by that part of the army which could not get water transportation. Such were the views of the government here; perhaps we were misinformed as to the facts; if so, the delay could be explained. Nothing in my telegram was intentionally harsh or unjust, but the delay was so unexpected that an explanation was required. There has been and is the most urgent necessity for dispatch and not a single moment must be lost in getting additional troops in front of Washington. H. W. H. Maj-Gen.

I telegraphed the following reply: Headq's, Army of the Pot'c, Berkeley, Aug 12, '62, 11 P M

Your dispatch of noon to-day received. It is positively the fact that no more men could have embarked hence than have gone, and that no unnecessary delay has occurred. Before your orders received Col Ingalls directed all available vessels to come from Monroe. Officers have been sent to take personal direction. Have heard nothing here of Burnside's fleet. There are some vessels at Monroe, such as Atlantic and Baltic, which draw too much to come here. Hospital accommodations exhausted this side New York. Propose filling Atlantic and Baltic with serious cases for New York, and to encamp slight cases for the present at Monroe. In this way can probably get off the 3,400 sick still on hand by day after to-morrow night. I am sure that you have been misinformed as to the availability of vessels on hand. We cannot use heavy loaded supply vessels for troops or animals, and such constitute the mass of those here, which have been represented to you as capable of transporting this army. I fear you will find very great delay in embarking troops and material at Yorktown and Monroe, both from want of vessels and of facilities for embarkation. At least two additional wharves should be built at each place. I ordered two at the latter some two weeks ago, but you countermanded the order.

I learn that wharf accommodations at Acquia are altogether inadequate for landing troops and supplies to any large extent. Not an hour should be lost in remedying this. Great delays will ensue there from shallow water. You will find a large deficiency in horse transports; we had nearly 200 when we came here. I learn of only 20 provided now, they carry about 50 horses each. More hospital accommodations should be provided. We are much impeded here because our wharves are used night and day to land current supplies. At Monroe a similar difficulty will occur. With all the facilities at Alexandria and Washington six weeks about were occupied in embarking this army and its material.

Burnside's troops are not a fair criterion for rate of embarkation. All his means were in hand —his outfit specially prepared for that purpose, and his men habituated to the movement.

There shall be no unnecessary delay, but I cannot manufacture vessels. I state these difficulties from experience, and because it appears to me that we have been lately working at cross purposes, because you have not been properly informed by those around you who ought to know the inherent difficulties of such an undertaking.

It is not possible for any one to place this army where you wish it, ready to move, in less than a month. If Washington is in danger now, this army can scarcely arrive in time to save it; it is in much better position to do so from here than from Acquia. Our material can only be saved by using the whole army to cover it if we are pressed. If sensibly weakened by detachments, the result might be the loss of much material and many men. I will be at the telegraph office tomorrow morning to talk with you.
G B McC to H W H, Washington, D C

To the reasons given in the foregoing dispatch, to show why Gen Burnside's movement from Fort Monroe was not a fair criterion for our operations the following may be added:

He was not encumbered by either sick or wounded men.

He had no cavalry, artillery, wagons or teams. His force consisted of infantry alone, with a few ambulances and officers' horses.

His baggage was already on the transports where it had remained since his arrival from North Carolina, and his men had only to resume their places on board.

The cavalry and artillery mentioned in my dispatches of the 7th, 10th and 11th were sent to supply his total deficiency in those arms.

I may also repeat that the vessels used by Gen Burnside had not returned from Acquia when the army left Harrison's Bar.

It will be seen from the concluding paragraph of the foregoing dispatch, that in order to have a more direct, speedy and full explanation of the condition of affairs in the army than I could by sending a single dispatch by steamer to the nearest telegraph office at Jamestown Island some seventy miles distant, and waiting ten hours for a reply, I proposed to go in person to the office. On my arrival at Jamestown Island there was an interruption in the electric current, which rendered it necessary for me to continue on to Fort Monroe, and cross the Chesapeake Bay to Cherry Stone Inlet on the "Eastern Shore," where I arrived late in the evening and immediately sent the annexed dispatches.

Cherry Stone, Aug. 13, 1862, 11 30 P M.—Please come to office: wish to talk to you. What news from Pope? G B McC, Maj-Gen
Maj-Gen H. W. H., Washington.

Cherry Stone Inlet, Aug 14, 1862 12 30 A M—Started to Jamestown Island to talk with you, found cable broken, and came here. Please read my long telegram [See above dispatch of Aug 12, 11 P M.] All quiet at camp. Enemy burned wharves at City Point yesterday. No rebel pickets within eight miles of Coggin's Point yesterday. Richmond prisoners state that large force, with guns, left Richmond, northward Sunday.
G. B. McC Maj.-Gen.   Maj-Gen H W H, Wash

To which the following reply was received:

Washington, August 14, 1862, 1 40 A M.—I have read your dispatch. There is no change of plans. You will send up your troops as rapidly as possible. There is no difficulty in landing them. According to your own accounts there is now no difficulty in withdrawing your forces. Do so with all possible rapidity.
Maj.-Gen. G. B. McC.   H. W. H., Maj.-Gen.

Before I had time to decipher and reply to this dispatch, the telegraph operator in Washington informed me that Gen Halleck had gone out of the office immediately after writing this dispatch, without leaving any intimation of the fact for me or waiting for any information as to the object of my journey across the bay. As there was no possibility of other communication with him at that time, I sent the following dispatch, and returned to Harrison's Landing

Cherry Stone Inlet, Aug 14, 1862, 1 40 A M
Your orders will be obeyed I return at once I had hoped to have had a longer and fuller conversation with you, after traveling so far for the purpose G B McC, Maj-Gen.
Maj-Gen W H H, Washington, D. C

On the 14th and 15th, and before we had been able to embark all our sick men, two army corps were put in motion towards Fort Monroe This was reported in the annexed despatch

Headquarters, Army of the Potomac,
Berkeley, Aug 16, 1862, 11 P M
Movement has commenced by land and water. All sick will be away to-morrow night Everything being done to carry out your orders I don't like Jackson's movements, he will suddenly appear where least expected Will telegraph fully and understandingly in the morning G B McC, Maj-Gen
Maj-Gen H, Washington, D. C

The phrase "movement has commenced," it need not be remarked, referred obviously to the movement of the main army, after completing the necessary preliminary movements of the sick, etc, etc.

The perversion of the term to which the general-in-chief saw fit to give currency in a letter to the Secretary of War, should have been here rendered impossible by the despatches which precede this of the 14th, which show that the movement really began immediately after the receipt of the order of August 4th

The progress made in the movement on the 15th was reported in the following dispatches:

Headquarters, Army of the Potomac,
August 15, 1862, 12 M
Maj-Gen H, W H, Comd'g U S A :—Col Ingalls this moment reports that after embarking the remaining brigade of McCall's division, with the sick which are constantly accumulating, the transports now disposable will be consumed.

Two of my army corps marched last night and this morning en route for Yorktown, one via Jones's Bridge, and the other via Barrett's Ferry, where we have a pontoon bridge. The other corps will be pushed forward as fast as the roads are clear, and I hope before to-morrow morning to have the entire army in motion

A report has just been received from my pickets that the enemy in force is advancing on us from the Chickahominy, but I do not credit it—shall know soon. Should any more transports arrive here before my departure, and the enemy do not show such a force in our front as to require all the troops I have remaining to insure the safety of the land movement with its immense train, I shall send every man by water that the transports will carry G B McC, Maj-Gen.

Headquarters, Army of the Potomac,
Berkeley, Aug 15, 1862, 1 30 P M
The advance corps and the trains are fairly started. I learn nothing more in relation to re-reported advance of rebels via Jones's Bridge. Shall push the movement as rapidly as possible. G B McC., Maj-Gen.
Maj-Gen. H. W. H., Washington, D C

Headquarters, Army of the Potomac, Berkeley, August 15, 1862 10 P M
Coggin's Point is abandoned The whole of McCall's division, with its artillery, is now en route for Burnside. We have not yet transportation sufficient for our sick I hope we will get it to-morrow Porter is across the Chickahominy, near its mouth, with his wagons and the reserve artillery.

Heintzelman at Jones's Bridge, with a portion of his corps. They will all be up by morning.

Averell's cavalry on the other side. All quiet thus far. I cannot get the last of the wagons as far as Charles City Court-house before some time to-morrow afternoon I am hurrying matters with the utmost rapidity possible Wagons will move all night G B McC, Maj-Gen Comd'g
Maj-Gen H W H., Washington, D C

After the commencement of the movement, it was continued with the utmost rapidity, until all the troops and material were en route, both by land and water, on the morning of the 16th

Late in the afternoon of that day, when the last man had disappeared from the deserted camps, I followed with my personal staff in the track of the grand army of the Potomac, bidding farewell to the scene still covered with the marks of its presence, and to be forever memorable in history as the vicinity of its most brilliant exploits.

THE RETURN TO THE POTOMAC

Previous to the departure of the troops, I had directed Capt Duane, of the Engineer Corps, to proceed to Barrett's Ferry, near the mouth of the Chickahominy, and throw across the river at that point a pontoon bridge This was executed promptly and satisfactorily, under the cover of gun-boats, and an excellent bridge of about two thousand feet in length was ready for the first arrival of troops. The greater part of the army with its artillery, wagon trains etc, crossed it rapidly, and in perfect order and safety, so that on the night of the 17th, everything was across the Chickahominy, except the rear-guard, which crossed early on the morning of the 18th, when the pontoon bridge was immediately removed

Gen Porter's corps, which was the first to march from Harrison's Landing, had been pushed forward rapidly, and on the 16th reached Williamsburg, where I had directed him to halt until the army was across the Chickahominy

On his arrival at Williamsburg, however, he received an intercepted letter, which led to the belief that Gen Pope would have to contend against a very heavy force then in his front Gen Porter therefore, very properly took the responsibility of continuing his march directly on to Newport News, which place he reached on the morning of the 18th of August, having marched his corps sixty miles in the short period of three days and one night, halting one day at the crossing of the Chickahominy

The embarkation of this corps commenced as soon as transports were ready, and on the 20th it had all sailed for Acquia Creek. I made the following report from Barrett's Ferry.

Headquarters Army of the Potomac,
Barrett's Ferry, Chickahominy,
August 17, 1862, 11 A. M.

Everything is removed from our camp at Harrison's Bar—no property nor men left behind. The Fifth Corps is at Williamsburg, with all its wagons and the reserve artillery. The Third Corps is on the march from Jones's Bridge to Williamsburg, via Diascund Bridge, and has probably passed the latter before this hour. Averell's cavalry watches everything in that direction.

The mass of the wagons have passed the pontoon bridge here, and are parked on the other side. Peck's wagons are now crossing, his division will soon be over. Headquarters wagons follow Peck's. I hope to have everything over to-night, and the bridge removed by daylight. May be delayed beyond that time. Came here to see Burnside, otherwise should have remained with the rear-guard. Thus far all is quiet, and not a shot fired that I know of since we began the march. I shall not feel entirely secure until I have the whole army beyond the Chickahominy. I will then begin to forward troops by water as fast as transportation permits. G. B. McC., Maj.-Gen. Comd'g.

Maj.-Gen. W. H. H., Comd'g U. S. A., Washington, D. C.

On the 18th and 19th our march was continued to Williamsburg and Yorktown, and on the 20th the remainder of the army was ready to embark at Yorktown, Fort Monroe, and Newport News. The movement of the main body of the army on this march was covered by Gen. Pleasonton, with his cavalry and horse-artillery. That officer remained at Haxall's until the army had passed Charles City Court House, when he gradually fell back, picking up the stragglers as he proceeded, and crossed the bridge over the Chickahominy after the main body had marched towards Williamsburg. His troops were the last to cross the bridge, and he deserves great credit for the manner in which he performed his duty. Gen. Averell did a similar service in the same satisfactory way, in covering the march of the 3d Corps.

As the campaign on the Peninsula terminated here, I cannot close this part of my report without giving an expression of my sincere thanks and gratitude to the officers and men I had the honor to command.

From the commencement to the termination of this most arduous campaign, the army of the Potomac always evinced the most perfect subordination, zeal and alacrity in the performance of all the duties required of it.

The amount of severe labor accomplished by this army in the construction of intrenchments, roads, bridges, &c, was enormous; yet all the work was performed with the most gratifying cheerfulness and devotion to the interests of the service.

During the campaign ten severely contested and sanguinary battles had been fought, besides numerous small engagements, in which the troops exhibited the most determined enthusiasm and bravery. They submitted to exposure, sickness, and even death without a murmur. Indeed they had become veterans in their country's cause, and richly deserved the warm commendation of the government.

It was in view of these facts that this seemed to me an appropriate occasion for the general-in-chief to give, in general orders, some appreciative expression of the services of the army while upon the Peninsula. Accordingly, on the 18th, I sent him the following dispatch:

Headquarters, Army of the Potomac, August 18, 1862, 11 P M.—Please say a kind word to the army, that I can repeat to them in general orders, in regard to their conduct at Yorktown, Williamsburg, West Point, Hanover Court House, and on the Chickahominy, as well as in regard to the seven days, and the recent retreat.

No one has ever said anything to cheer them but myself. Say nothing about me, merely give my men and officers credit for what they have done. It will do you much good, and strengthen you much with them if you issue a handsome order to them in regard to what they have accomplished. They deserve it.

G. B. McC., Major-Gen.
Major-Gen H., Comd'g. U. S Army,
Washington, D. C.

As no reply was received to this communication, and no order was issued by the general-in-chief, I conclude that my suggestion did not meet with his approbation.

All the personnel and material of the army had been transferred from Harrison's Landing to the different points of embarkation in the very brief period of five days, without the slightest loss or damage. Porter's Corps sailed from Newport News on the 19th and 20th, Heintzelman's corps sailed from Yorktown on the 21st. On that day I received the following telegram from the general-in-chief.

Washington, Aug. 21, 1862, 6 P. M.

Gen. McC.—Leave such garrisons in Fort Monroe, Yorktown, &c, as you may deem proper. They will be replaced by new troops as soon as possible. The forces of Burnside and Pope are hard pushed, and require aid as rapidly as you can send it. Come yourself as soon as you can. By all means see that the troops sent have plenty of ammunition. We have no time here to supply them. Moreover they may have to fight as soon as they land. H. W. H., M.-Gen Com.

To which the following are replies:

Headq's, Army of the Potomac, Fort Monroe,
August 21, 1862, 7.30 P M.

Your dispatch of 6 P M received. I have not lost an hour in sending troops, nor will I. Franklin is here, and I will try to get some of his troops on board to-night. I had already ordered all the ammunition forward. I will put headquarters on board ship early to-morrow morning, so that I can leave at a moment's notice. I hope that I can get off to-morrow. Shall I go in person to Acquia, or do you wish to see me first in Washington? If you wish it, I can probably ship quite an amount of ammunition for other troops than this army.

G. B. McC. to Maj.-Gen. H., Washington.

Headquarters, Army of the Potomac, Fort Monroe,
Aug. 21, 1862, 10.25 P M

I have ample supplies of ammunition for infantry and artillery, and will have it up in time I can supply any deficiencies that may exist in Ger Pope's army. Quite a number of rifled field-guns are on hand here. The forage is the only question for you to attend to. Please have that ready for me at Acquia. I want many more schooners for cavalry horses. They should have water on board when they come here.

If you have leisure, and there is no objection, please communicate to me fully the state of affairs and your plans. I will then be enabled to arrange details understandingly.

G. B. McC to Maj.-Gen H., Washington

Immediately on reaching Fort Monroe, I gave directions for strengthening the defenses of Yorktown, to resist an attack from the direction of Richmond, and left Gen Keyes, with his corps, to perform the work, and temporarily garrison the place.

I telegraphed as follows on the 22d:

Headq's, Army of the Potomac, Fort Monroe,
Aug. 22, 1862, 2 15 P M

Dispatch of to-day received. Franklin's corps is embarking as rapidly as possible. Sumner's corps is at Newport News ready to embark as fast as transportation arrives. Keyes is still at Yorktown putting it in a proper state of defense. I think that all of Franklin's corps will get off today and hope to commence with Sumner to-morrow. I shall then push off the cavalry and wagons.

G. B. McC to Maj.-Gen H W H, Wash'n

Headq's, Army of the Potomac, Fort Monroe,
Aug. 22, 1862, 3 40 P.M.

Two good ordnance sergeants are needed immediately at Yorktown and Gloucester. The new defenses are enlarged and commenced. I recommend that 5,000 new troops be sent immediately to garrison York and Gloucester. They should be commanded by an experienced general-officer, who can discipline and instruct them. About 900 should be artillery. I recommend that a new regiment whose colonel is an artillery officer, or graduate, be designated as heavy artillery, and sent there. A similar regiment is absolutely necessary here.

Maj.-Gen H W H, Com. U S A.

On the 23d Franklin's corps sailed. I reported this in the following despatch.

Headquarters, Army of the Potomac, Fort Monroe, Aug 23, 1862. 1 30 P. M

Franklin's corps has started. I shall start for Acquia in about half an hour. No transports yet for Sumner's corps.

G. B. McC. Maj-Gen   Maj-Gen H. W H, Com'd'g U S Army

THE CAMPAIGN OF GENERAL POPE

On that evening I sailed with my staff for Acquia Creek, where I arrived at daylight on the following morning, reporting as follows:

Headquarters, Army of the Potomac, Acquia Creek, Aug 24, 1861

I have reached here, and respectfully report for orders.

G. B. McC Maj-Gen   Maj-Gen H. Com'd'g U S Army

I also telegraphed as follows:

Headquarters, Army of the Potomac, Acquia Creek, August 24, 1862   2 P M

Your telegram received. Morell's scouts report Rappahannock Station burned and abandoned by Pope, without any notice to Morell or Sykes. This was telegraphed you some hours ago. Reynolds, Reno, and Stevens, are supposed to be with Pope, as nothing can be heard of them today. Morell and Sykes are near Morrisville Post Office, watching the lower fords of Rappahannock, with no troops between them and Rappahannock Station, which is reported abandoned by Pope. Please inform me immediately exactly where Pope is, and what doing; until I know that, I cannot regulate Porter's movements, he is much exposed now, and decided measures should be taken at once. Until I know what my command and position are to be, and whether you still intend to place me in the command indicated in your first letter to me, and orally through Gen, Burnside at the Chickahominy, I cannot decide where I can be of most use. If your determination is unchanged, I ought to go to Alexandria at once. Please define my position and duties.

G. B. McC. Maj-Gen to Maj-Gen H W H, com'd'g U. S Army

To which I received the following reply.

Washington, Aug 24, 1862

Maj-Gen McC—You ask me for information which I cannot give. I do not know either where General Pope is, or where the enemy in force is. These are matters which I have been all day most anxious to ascertain.

H W H, General-in-chief.

On the 26th, I received the following

Washington, Aug 26th, 1862   11 A M.

Maj-Gen G. B. McC.—There is reason to believe that the enemy is moving a large force into the Shenandoah Valley. Reconnoissances will soon determine. Gen Heintzelman's corps was ordered to report to Gen Pope, and Kearney's will probably be sent to-day against the enemy's flank. Don't draw any troops down the Rappahannock at present. We shall probably want them all in the direction of the Shenandoah. Perhaps you had better leave Gen Burnside in charge at Acquia Creek, and come to Alexandria, as very great irregularities are reported there. Gen Franklin's corps will march as soon as it receives transportation.

H W H, General-in-Chief

On receipt of this I immediately sailed for Alexandria, and reported as follows

Alexandria, August 27, 1862, 8 A M —I arrived here last night, and have taken measures to ascertain the state of affairs here, and that proper remedies may be applied. Just received a rumor that railway bridge over Bull Run was burnt last night.   G B McC Major-Gen

Major-Gen H Com'd'g U S A.

Alexandria, August 27 1862, 9 40 A M.—The town is quiet, although quite full of soldiers who are said to be chiefly convalescents. The affairs of the quartermaster's department are reported as going on well. It is said that the Bull Run bridge will be repaired by to-morrow. The disembarkation of Sumner's corps commenced at

Acquia yesterday afternoon. I found that he could reach Rappahannock Station earlier that way than from here. G. B. McC Maj.-Gen.
Major-Gen. H. W. H., Comd'g U. S. A.

On the same day I received the following:

Washington, August 27, 1862.

Major-Gen. McC.—Telegrams from General Porter to General Burnside just received, says that Banks is at Fayetteville. McDowell, Sigel and Ricketts near Warrenton, Reno on his right Porter is marching on Warrenton Junction to reinforce Pope Nothing said of Heintzelman Porter reports a general battle imminent Franklin's corps should move out by forced marches, carrying three or four days' provisions, and to be supplied as far as possible by railroad. Perhaps you may prefer some other road than to Centreville Colonel Haupt has just telegraphed about sending out troops, &c. Please see him and give him your directions. There has been some serious neglect to guard the railroad, which should be immediately remedied.

H W H, General-in-Chief

I replied as follows.

Alexandria, August 27, 1862, 10 20 A.M.—Telegram this moment received. I have sent orders to Franklin to prepare to march with his corps at once, and to repair here in person to inform me as to his means of transportation Kearney was yesterday at Rappahannock Station. Porter at Bealton, Kelly's Darnell's, &c Sumner will commence reaching Falmouth to day. Williams's Massachusetts Cavalry will be mostly at Falmouth to-day I loaned Burnside my personal escort, 1st squadron Fourth Regulars, to scout down Rappahannock I have sent for Couch's division to come at once As fast as I gain any information I will forward it, although you may already have it. G B McC, Major-Gen.

Major-Gen H W H, Washington, D. C

I also received the following telegrams.

Washington, August 27, 1862

Major-Gen. McC.—Direct General Casey to furnish you about five thousand of the new troops under his command Take entire direction of the sending out of the troops from Alexandria Determine questions of priority in transportation, and the places they shall occupy Pope's headquarters are near Warrenton Junction, but I can not ascertain the present position of his troops.

H W H., General-in-Chief

Washington, Aug 27, 1862.

Maj.-Gen. McC.:—I can get no satisfactory information from the front, either of the enemy or our troops There seems to have been great neglect and carelessness about Manassas. Franklin's corps should march in that direction as soon as possible. A competent officer should be sent out to take direction of affairs in that vicinity

H W H, Gen -in-Chief

Upon the receipt of these I immediately sent the following telegram to Generals Heintzelman and Porter

Alexandria, Aug. 27, 1862.

Where are you, and what is state of affairs? What troops in your front, right and left? Sumner is now landing at Acquia Where is Pope's left, and what of enemy? Enemy burned Bull Run bridge last night with cavalry force

G. B McC., Maj Gen

M.-G. Heintz'n, Warrenton, M.-G Porter, Bealton.

P. S. If these general officers are not at the places named, nearest operator will please have message forwarded.

I also telegraphed the General-in-Chief as follows:

Alexandria, Aug 27, '62, 10 50 P.M.

I have sent all the information I possess to Burnside, instructing him to look out well for his right flank between the Rappahannock and Potomac, and to send no trains to Porter without an escort I fear the cavalry who dashed at Bull Run last night may trouble Burnside a little I have sent to communicate with Porter and Heintzelman via Falmouth, and hope to give you some definite information in a few hours. I shall land the next cavalry I get hold of here, and send it out to keep open the communication between Pope and Porter, also to watch vicinity of Manassas. Please send me a number of copies of the best maps of present field of operations I can use 50 to advantage.

G. B. McC. to Maj.-Gen. H., Com'g

Alexandria, Aug 27, '62, 11.20 A M

In view of Burnside's dispatch, just received, would it not be advisable to throw the mass of Sumner's corps here, to move out with Franklin to Centreville or vicinity? If a decisive battle fought at Warrenton, a disaster would leave any troops on lower Rappahannock in a dangerous position. They would do better service in front of Washington

G. B McC to M-Gen H , Washington

Alexandria, Aug 27, '62, 12 5 P M

My aid has just returned from Gen Franklin's camp Reports that Gen's. Franklin, Smith, and Slocum are all in Washington He gave the order to next in rank to place the corps in readiness to move at once. I learn that heavy firing has been heard this morning at Centreville, and have sent to ascertain the truth. I can find no cavalry to send out on the roads Are the works garrisoned and ready for defense?

G B McC. to M-Gen H , Washington.

Alexandria, August 27, 1862, 12 20 P. M.

What bridges exist over Bull Run? Have steps been taken to construct bridges for the advance of troops to reinforce Pope, or to enable him to retreat if in trouble? There should be two gun-boats at Acquia Creek at once Shall I push the rest of Sumner's corps here or is Pope so strong as to be reasonably certain of success I have sent to inspect the works near here, and their garrisons As soon as I can find Gen Casey, or some other commanding officer, I will see to the railway, etc It would be well to have them report to me, as I do not know where they are. I am trying to find them and will lose no time in carrying out your orders. Would like to see Burnside G. B. McC., Maj -Gen.

Maj -Gen W. H , Washington

Alexandria, August 27 1862, 1 15 P. M

Franklin's artillery have no horses, except for four guns without caissons, I can pick up cavalry. In view of these facts, will it not be well to push Sumner's corps here by water as rapidly as possible, to make immediate arrangements for placing the works in front of Washington in an efficient condition of defense. I have no means of knowing the enemy's force between Pope and ourselves. Can Franklin, without his artillery or cavalry, effect any useful purpose in front? Should not Burnside at once take steps to evacuate Falmouth and Acquia, at the same time covering the retreat of any of Pope's troops who may fall back in that direction. I do not see that we have force enough in hand to form a connection with Pope, whose exact position we do not know. Are we safe in the direction of the valley? G. B. McC, Major-Gen

Maj-Gen H., Washington.

Alexandria, August 27, 1862, 1.35 p m

I learn that Taylor's brigade sent this morning to Bull Run bridge, is either cut to pieces or captured. That the force against them had many guns, and about five thousand infantry, receiving reinforcements every moment. Also, that Gainsville is in possession of the enemy. Please send some cavalry out towards Drainesville via Chain Bridge, to watch Lewinsville and Drainesville, and go as far as they can. If you will give me even one squadron of good cavalry here, I will ascertain the state of the case. I think our policy now is to make these works perfectly safe, and mobilize a couple of corps as soon as possible, but not to advance them until they can have them artillery and cavalry. I have sent for Col Tyler to place his artillerymen in the works. Is Fort Marcy securely held? McC

Gen. H

Alexandria, August 27, 1862, 2 30 p m

Maj-Gen H W. H, Comd'g U S Army—Sumner has been ordered to send here all of his corps that are within reach. Orders have been sent to Couch to come here from Yorktown with the least possible delay. But one squadron of my cavalry has arrived; that will be disembarked at once, and sent to the front. If there is any cavalry in Washington it should be ordered to report to me at once

I still think that we should first provide for the immediate defense of Washington on both sides of the Potomac. I am not responsible for the past, and can not be for the future, unless I receive authority to dispose of the available troops according to my judgment. Please inform me at once what my position is. I do not wish to act in the dark. G B McC, Maj-Gen

Alexandria, August 27, 1862, 2 30 p m

Maj-Gen H W. H, Comd'g U. S. A.—I have just received the copy of a dispatch from Gen Pope to you, dated 10 a m this morning, in which he says: "All forces now sent forward should be sent to my right at Gainsville"

I now have at my disposal here about ten thousand men of Franklin's corps, about twenty-eight hundred of Gen Tyler's brigade and Col Tyler's 1st Connecticut artillery, which I recommend should be held in hand for the defense of Washington. If you wish me to order any part of this force to the front, it is in readiness to march at a moment's notice to any point you may indicate.

In view of the existing state of things in our front, I have deemed it best to order Gen Casey to hold his men for Yorktown in readiness to move: but not to send them off till further orders G. B. McC, Maj-Gen.

On the 28th I telegraphed as follows :

Headquarters, Camp near Alexandria, Aug 28, 1862 410 p m

Gen. Franklin is with me here. I will know in a few minutes the condition of artillery and cavalry. We are not yet in condition to move, may be by to-morrow morning. Pope must cut through to-day, or adopt the plan I suggested. I have ordered troops to garrison the works at Upton's Hill. They must be held at any cost. As soon as I can see the way to spare them, I will send a corps of good troops there. It is the key to Washington, which cannot be seriously menaced as long as it is held.

G B McC to Maj-Gen. H, Washington, D C.

I received the following from the general-in chief

Washington, Aug 28, 1862

Maj-Gen McC—I think you had better place Sumner's corps, as it arrives, near the guns, and particularly at the Chain Bridge. The principal thing to be feared now is a cavalry raid into this city, especially in the night-time. Use Cox's and Tyler's brigade, and the new troops for the same object, if you need them. Porter writes to Burnside from Bristol, 9 30 a m, yesterday that Pope's forces were then moving on Manassas, and that Burnside would soon hear of them by way of Alexandria. Gen Cullum has gone to Harper's Ferry, and I have only a single regular officer for duty in the office. Please send some of your officers to-day to see that every precaution is taken at the forts against a raid; also at the bridge. Please answer. H. W H, General in Chief

On the 29th the following dispatch was telegraphed :

Camp near Alexandria, Aug. 29, 1862 10.20 a m—Franklin's corps is in motion. Started about 6 a m. I can give him but two squadrons of cavalry. I propose moving Gen Cox to Upton's Hill, to hold that important point, with its works, and to push cavalry scouts to Vienna via Freedom Hill and Hunter's Lane. Cox has two squadrons cavalry. Please answer at once whether this meets your approval. I have directed Woodbury, with the engineer brigade to hold Fort Lyon. Sumner detached last night two regiments to vicinity of Forts "Ethan Allen" and "Marcy." Meagher's brigade is still at Acquia. If he moves in support of Franklin, it leaves us without any reliable troops in and near Washington, yet Franklin is too weak alone. What shall be done? No more cavalry arrived. I have but three squadrons. Franklin has but forty rounds of ammunition, and no wagons to move more. I do not think Franklin is in condition to accomplish much if he meets with serious resistance

I should not have moved him but for your pressing order of last night. What have you from Vienna and Drainesville?

Geo B. McC to Maj-Gen H,. Washington.

To which the following is a reply:

Washington August 29, 1862, 12 M

Major-Gen McC—Upton's Hill arrangement is all right. We must send wagons and ammunition to Franklin as fast as they arrive. Meagher's brigade ordered up yesterday. Fitzhugh Lee was, it is said on good authority, in Alexandria on Sunday last for three hours. I have nothing from Drainesville.   H W H, Gen-in-Chief

On the same day the following was received from his Excellency the President:

Washington August 29, 1862, 2 30 P.M.

Maj-Gen McC—What news from direction of Manassas Junction? What, generally?   A L

To which I replied as follows:

Camp near Alexandria, August 29, 1862, 2 45 P.M.—The last news I received from the direction of Manassas, was from stragglers to the effect that the enemy were evacuating Centreville and retiring towards Thorofare Gap. This by no means reliable. I am clear that one of two courses should be adopted. 1st To concentrate all our available forces to open communication with Pope. 2d To leave Pope to get out of his scrape and at once use all our means to make the capital perfectly safe. No middle ground will now answer.

Tell me what you wish me to do and I will do all in my power to accomplish it. I wish to know what my orders and authority are. I ask for nothing, but will obey whatever orders you give. I only ask a prompt decision that I may at once give the necessary orders. It will not do to delay any longer.   G B McC Maj.-Gen.

A L President
and copy to Gen Halleck

To which the following is a reply

Washington August 29, 1862, 4 10 P M

Major-Gen McC—Yours of to-day just received. I think your first alternative, to wit, "To concentrate all our available forces to open communication with Pope" is the right one, but I wish not to control. That I now leave to Gen Halleck aided by your counsels.   A L

It had been officially reported to me from Washington, that the enemy in strong force was moving through Vienna, in the direction of the Chain Bridge and had a large force at Vienna. This report in connection with the dispatch of the general-in-chief on the 28th, before noted, induced me to direct Franklin to halt his command near Annandale, until it could be determined by reconnoissances to Vienna and towards Manassas, whether these reports were true. General Cox was ordered to send his small cavalry force from Upton's Hill towards Vienna and Dranesville in one direction and towards Fairfax Court House in the other, and Franklin to push his two squadrons towards Lewinsville, it would have been very injudicious to have pushed Franklin's small force beyond Annandale. It must be remembered that at this time we were cut off from direct communication with General Pope, that the enemy was by the last accounts at Manassas in strong force, and that Franklin had only from 10,000 to 11,000 men with an entirely insufficient force of cavalry and artillery.

In order to represent this condition of affairs in its proper light to the general-in-chief, and to obtain definite instructions from him, I telegraphed as follows:

Camp near Alexandria, August 29 1862, 12 M.—Have ordered most of the 12th Pennsylvania Cavalry to report to General Burnard for scouting duty towards Rockville, Poolesville, etc. If you apprehend a raid of cavalry on your side of the river, I had better send a brigade or two of Sumner's to near Tenallytown, where, with two or three old regiments in Forts Allen and Marcy, they can watch Chain Bridge and Tenallytown. Would it meet your views to post rest of Sumner's corps between Arlington and Fort Corcoran, whence they can either support Cox, Franklin, or Chain Bridge, and even Tenallytown? Franklin has only between 10,000 and 11,000 for duty. How far do you wish this force to advance?   G B McC.

Major-Gen H, Washington

Camp near Alexandria, Aug 29, 1862, 1 P M

I anxiously await reply to my last dispatch in regard to Sumner. Wish to give the order at once. Please authorize me to attach new regiments permanently to my old brigades. I can do much good to new and old troops in that way. I shall endeavor to hold a line in advance of Forts Allen and Marcy, at least with strong advanced guards. I wish to hold the line through Prospect Hill, Mackall's, Minor's, and Hall's Hills. This will give us timely warning. Shall I do as seems best to me with all the troops in the vicinity, including Franklin, who, I really think, ought not, under present circumstances, to advance beyond Annandale?   G B McC to Gen H.

On the same day I received a dispatch from the general-in-chief, in which he asks me why I halted Franklin at Annandale, to which I replied as follows:

Camp near Alexandria, Aug 29 1862, 8 P M

By referring to my telegrams of 10 30 A M 12 M and 1 P M, together with your reply of 2 40 P M, you will see why Franklin's corps halted at Annandale. His small cavalry force—all I had to give him—was ordered to push on as far as possible towards Manassas. It was not safe for Franklin to move beyond Annandale under the circumstances, until we knew what was at Vienna. Gen Franklin remained here until about 1 P M, endeavoring to arrange for supplies for his command. I am responsible for both these circumstances, and do not see that either was in disobedience to your orders. Please give distinct orders in reference to Franklin's movements to-morrow. I have sent to Col Haupt to push out construction and supply trains as soon as possible. General Tyler to furnish the necessary guards. I have directed Gen Banks's supply trains to start out to-night at least as far as Annandale, with an escort from Gen Tyler. In regard to to-morrow's movements, I desire definite instructions, as it is not agreeable to me to be accused of disobeying orders, when I have simply exercised the discretion you committed to me.

G B McC to M-Gen H., Wash'n, D C

On the same evening I sent the following dispatches:

Camp near Alexandria, Aug 29, '62, 10 P M

Not hearing from you, I have sent orders to

Gen Franklin to place himself in communication with Gen Pope as soon as possible, and at the same time cover the transit of Pope's supplies. Orders have been given for railway and wagon trains to move to Pope, with least possible delay. I am having inspections made of all the forts around city by members of my staff, with instructions to give all requisite orders. I inspected Worth and Ward myself this evening, found them in good order. Reports so far as heard from, are favorable as to condition of works.

G. B. McC. to Maj.-Gen. H., Washington.

Camp near Alexandria, Aug 29, 1862 10 P. M.

Maj.-Gen. H. W. H., General-in-Chief U. S. A. Washington, D. C.—Your dispatch received. Franklin's corps has been ordered to march at 6 o'clock to-morrow morning. Sumner has about fourteen thousand infantry, without cavalry or artillery, here. Cox's brigade of four regiments is here with two batteries of artillery. Men of two regiments, much fatigued, came in to-day. Tyler's brigade of three new regiments, but little drilled, is also here. All these troops will be ordered to hold themselves ready to march to-morrow morning, and all, except Franklin's, to await further orders. If you wish any of them to move towards Manassas please inform me.

Col. Wagner, 2d New York artillery, has just come in from the front. He reports strong infantry and cavalry force of rebels near Fairfax Court House, reports rumors from various sources, that Lee and Stuart, with large forces are at Manassas. That the enemy with one hundred and twenty thousand men, intend advancing on the forts near Arlington and Chain Bridge, with a view of attacking Washington and Baltimore. Gen Barnard telegraphs me to-night that the length of the line of fortifications on this side of the Potomac, requires two thousand additional artillery men, and additional troops to defend intervals, according to circumstances. At all events, he says in of 1 regiment should be added to the force at Chain Bridge, and a few regiments distributed along the lines, to give confidence to our new troops. I agree with him fully, and think our fortifications along the upper part of our line, on this side the river, very unsafe with their present garrisons, and the movements of the enemy seem to indicate attack upon those works.

G. B. McC., Maj.-Gen.

Camp near Alexandria, Aug 30, 1862, 11 30 A. M.

Maj.-Gen. H. W. H., General-in-Chief.—Your telegram of 9 A. M. received. Ever since Gen Franklin received notice that he was to march from Alexandria, he has been endeavoring to get transportation from the quartermaster at Alexandria, but he has uniformly been told that there was none disposable, and his command marched without wagons. After the departure of his corps, he procured twenty wagons to carry some extra ammunition, by unloading Banks's supply train. Gen. Sumner endeavored, by application upon the quartermaster's department, to get wagons to carry his reserve ammunition, but without success, and was obliged to march with what he could carry in his cartridge-boxes. I have this morning directed that all my headquarters wagons that are landed, be at once loaded with ammunition for Sumner and Franklin, but they will not go far towards supplying the deficiency.

Eighty-five wagons were got together by the quartermasters last night loaded with subsistence and sent forward at 1 a. m, with an escort, via Annandale. Every effort has been made to carry out your orders promptly. The great difficulty seems to consist in the fact, that the greater part of the transportation on hand at Alexandria and Washington has been needed for current supplies at the garrisons. Such is the state of the case, as represented to me by the quartermasters, and it appears to be true. I take it for granted that this has not been properly explained to you. G. B. McC., Maj.-Gen.

On the morning of the 30th, heavy artillery firing was heard in the direction of Fairfax Court House, which I reported to the general-in-chief. At 11 a. m. the following telegram was sent:

Camp near Alexandria, Aug 30, 1862, 11 A. M.

Have ordered Sumner to leave one brigade in vicinity of Chain Bridge, and to move the rest via Columbia pike on Annandale and Fairfax Court House. Is this the route you wish them to take? He and Franklin are both instructed to join Pope as promptly as possible. Shall Couch move out also when he arrives? G. B. Mc., Maj.-Gen.

Maj.-Gen. H. Washington.

On the same day I received the following:

Washington, Aug 30 1862 1 45 A. M.

Maj.-Gen McC,—Ammunition, and particularly for artillery must be immediately sent forward to Centreville for Gen Pope. It must be done with all possible dispatch,

H. W. H., General-in-Chief.

To which the following reply was made:

Camp near Alexandria, Aug 30, 1862 2 10 P. M.

I know nothing of the calibres of Pope's artillery. All I can do is to direct my ordnance officer, to load up all the wagons sent to him. I have already sent all my headquarters wagons. You will have to see that wagons are sent from Washington. I can do nothing more than give the order that every available wagon in Alexandria shall be loaded at once. The order to the brigade of Sumner that I directed to remain near Chain Bridge and Tenallytown should go from your headquarters, to save time. I understand you to intend it also to move. I have no sharpshooters except the guard around my camp. I have sent off every man but those, and will now send them with the train as you direct. I will also send my only remaining squadron of cavalry with Gen Sumner. I can do no more. You now have every man of the army of the Potomac who is within my reach.

G. B. McC. to Maj Gen H W. H.

At 10 30 P. M. the following telegram was sent:

Camp near Alexandria, Aug. 30, 1862 10 30 P. M.—I have sent to the front all my troops, with the exception of Couch's division, and have given the orders necessary to insure its being disposed of as you directed. I hourly expect the return of one of my aides, who will give authentic news from the field of battle.

I cannot express to you the pain and mortification I have experienced to-day in listening to the distant sound of the firing of my men. As I can be of no further use here, I respectfully ask that if there is a probability of the combat being renewed to-morrow, I may be permitted to go to the scene of battle with my staff merely to be with my own men; they will fight none the worse for my being with them. If it is not deemed best to intrust me with the command even of my own army, I simply ask to be permitted to share their fate on the field of battle. Please reply to this to-night.

I have been engaged for the last few hours in doing what I can to make arrangements for the wounded. I have started out all the ambulances now landed.

As I have sent my escort to the front, I would be glad to take some of Gregg's cavalry with me if allowed to go.

G. B. McC. to Maj-Gen. H. W. H., Com'd'g U. S. A., Washington, D. C.

To which on the following day I received this answer:

Washington, Aug. 31, 1862 — 9.18 A. M.

Maj-Gen. McC.—I have just seen your telegram of 11.5 last night. The substance was stated to me when received, but I did not know that you asked for a reply immediately. I cannot answer without seeing the President, as General Pope is in command, by his orders, of the department.

I think Couch's division should go forward as rapidly as possible, and find the battle-field.

H. W. H., General in Chief.

On the same day the following was received:

Washington, Aug. 31, 1862 — 12.15 P. M.

Maj-Gen. McC.—The subsistence department are making Fairfax Station their principal depot. It should be well guarded. The officer in charge should be directed to secure the depot by abattis against cavalry. As many as possible of the new regiments should be prepared to take the field. Perhaps some more should be sent in the vicinity of Chain Bridge.

H. W. H., General in Chief.

THE ARMY OF THE POTOMAC REMOVED FROM GEN. McCLELLAN'S COMMAND.

At 2.30 P. M. the following dispatch was telegraphed:

Camp near Alexandria, Aug. 31, 1862, 2.30 P. M. —Major Haller is at Fairfax Station, with my provost and headquarters guard and other troops. I have requested four more companies to be sent at once, and the precautions you direct to be taken.

I have no control over the new regiments, do not know where they are or anything about them, except those near here. Their commanding officers and those of the works are not under me. Where I have seen evils existing under my own eye I have corrected them. I think it is the business of General Casey to prepare the new regiments for the field, and a matter between him and General Barnard to order others to vicinity of Chain Bridge. Neither of them is under my command, and by the War Department order I have no right to give them orders.

Gen. H., Washington. G. B. McC.

To which the following is an answer:

Washington, August 31, 1862, 10.7 P. M.

Major-Gen. McC.—Since receiving your dispatch relating to command, I have not been able to answer any not of absolute necessity. I have not seen the order as published, but will write to you in the morning. You will retain the command of everything in this vicinity not temporarily to be Pope's army in the field.

I beg of you to assist me in this crisis with your ability and experience. I am entirely tired out. H. W. H., Gen.-in-Chief.

The order referred to in the preceding dispatches was as follows:

War Department, August 30, 1862.—The following are the commanders of the armies operating in Virginia:

General Burnside commands his own corps, except those that have been temporarily detached and assigned to General Pope.

General McClellan commands that portion of the Army of the Potomac that has not been sent forward to Gen. Pope's command.

General Pope commands the Army of Virginia and all the forces temporarily attached to it.

All the forces are under command of Major-Gen. Halleck, General-in-Chief.

E. D. Townsend, Assistant-Adj-Gen.

I was informed by Col. Townsend that the above was published by order of the Secretary of War.

At 11.30 P. M. I telegraphed the following:

Camp near Alexandria, Aug. 31, 1862, 11.30 P. M. — The squadron of the 2d Regular Cavalry that I sent with Gen. Sumner was captured to-day, about 2 P. M., some three miles from Fairfax Court House, beyond it on the Little River Pike, by Fitzhugh Lee, with 3,000 cavalry and three light batteries. I have conversed with the 1st sergeant, who says that when he last saw them they were within a mile of Fairfax. Pope had no troops on that road, this squadron getting there by mistake. There is nothing of ours on the right of Centreville but Sumner's corps. There was much artillery firing during the day. A rebel major told the sergeant that the rebels had driven in our entire left to-day. He says the road is filled with wagons and stragglers coming towards Alexandria. It is clear, from the sergeant's account, that we were badly beaten yesterday, and that Pope's right is entirely exposed.

I recommend that no more of Couch's division be sent to the front, that Burnside be brought here as soon as practicable, and that everything available this side of Fairfax be drawn in at once, including the mass of the troops on the railroad. I apprehend that the enemy will, or have by this time, occupied Fairfax Court-House, and cut off Pope entirely, unless he falls back to-night via Sangster's and Fairfax Station. I think these orders should be sent at once. I have no confidence in the dispositions made, as I gather them. To speak frankly, and the occasion requires it, there appears to be a total absence of brains, and I fear the total destruction of the army. I have some cavalry here that can carry out any orders you may have to send. The occasion is grave, and demands grave measures. The question is the salvation of the country. I learn that our loss yesterday amounted to 15,000. We cannot afford such losses without an object. It is my deliberate opinion that the interests of the nation demand that Pope should fall back to-night if possible, and not one moment is to be lost. I will use all the cavalry I have to watch our right. Please answer at once. I feel confident you can rely upon the information I give you. I shall be up all night and ready to obey any orders you give me.

G B McC, M.-G. to M.-Gen H., Washington.

To which this reply was received
Washington Sept. 1, '62, 1 30 p.m.
Maj. Gen McC.—Burnside was ordered up very early yesterday morning. Retain remainder of Couch's forces, and make arrangements to stop all retreating troops in line of works, or where you can best establish an outer line of defense. My news from Pope was up to 4 p.m., he was then all right. I must wait for more definite information before I can order a retreat as the falling back on the line of the works must necessarily be directed, in case of a serious disaster.

Give me all news that is reliable. I shall be up all night, and ready to act as circumstances may require. I am fully aware of the gravity of the crisis, and have been for weeks.

H W H, Gen.-in-Chief.

It will be seen from what has preceded that I lost no time that could be avoided in moving the army of the Potomac from the Peninsula to the support of the army of Virginia, that I spared no effort to hasten the embarkation of the troops at Fort Monroe, Newport News and Yorktown, remaining at Fort Monroe myself until the mass of the army had sailed, and that after my arrival at Alexandria I left nothing in my power undone to forward supplies and reinforcements to Gen Pope. I sent with the troops that moved all the cavalry I could get hold of, even my personal escort was sent out upon the line of the railway as a guard, with the provost and camp guard at headquarters, retaining less than 100 men, many of whom were orderlies, invalids, members of bands, etc., all the headquarter teams that I had were sent out with supplies and ammunition, none being retained even to move the headquarters camps. The squadron that habitually served as my personal escort was left at Falmouth with Gen Burnside, as he was deficient in cavalry.

FOURTH PERIOD.

On the 1st of September I went into Washington, where I had an interview with the general-in-chief, who instructed me verbally to take command of its defences, expressly limiting my jurisdiction to the works and their garrisons, and prohibiting me from exercising any control over the troops actively engaged in front under Gen Pope. During this interview, I suggested to the general-in-chief the necessity of his going in person, or sending one of his personal staff, to the army under Gen Pope, for the purpose of ascertaining the exact condition of affairs. He sent Col Kelton, his assistant adjutant-general.

During the afternoon of the same day I received a message from the general-in-chief, to the effect that he desired me to go at once to his house to see the President. The President informed me that he had reason to believe that the army of the Potomac was not cheerfully co-operating with and supporting Gen. Pope, that he had "always been a friend of mine," and now asked me, as a special favor, to use my influence in correcting this state of things. I replied, substantially, that I was confident that he was misinformed, that I was sure, whatever sentiment the army of the Potomac might entertain towards Gen. Pope, that they would obey his orders support him to the fullest extent, and do their whole duty. The President, who was much moved, again asked me to telegraph to "Fitz John Porter or some other of my friends," and try to do away with any feeling that might exist, adding that I could rectify the evil, and that no one else could. I thereupon told him that I would cheerfully telegraph to Gen Porter, or do anything else in my power, to gratify his wishes and relieve his anxiety, upon which he thanked me very warmly, assured me that he could never forget my action in the matter, etc., and left.

I then wrote the following telegram to Gen. Porter, which was sent to him by the general-in-chief.

Washington, Sept 1, 1862
Maj.-Gen Porter.—I ask of you for my sake, and that of the country, and the old army of the Potomac, that you and all my friends, will lend the fullest and most cordial co-operation to Gen Pope, in all the operations now going on. The destinies of our country, the honor of our army, are at stake, and all depends now upon the cheerful co-operation of all in the field. This week is the crisis of our fate. Say the same thing to my friends in the army of the Potomac, and that the last request I have to make of them is, that for their country's sake they will extend to Gen. Pope the same support they ever have to me. I am in charge of the defenses of Washington, and am doing all I can to render your retreat safe, should that become necessary. G B McC.

To which he sent the following reply
Fairfax Court House, 10 a m Sept 3, 1862
'You may rest assured that all your friends, as well as every lover of his country, will ever give, as they have given, to Gen Pope then cordial co-operation and constant support in the execution of all orders and plans. Our killed, wounded, and enfeebled troops attest our devoted duty." F. J Porter, Maj.-Gen Com'l'g

Gen G. B. McC., Washington

Neither at the time I wrote the telegram, nor at any other time, did I think for one moment that Gen Porter had been, or would be in any manner, derelict in the performance of his duty to the nation and its cause. Such an impression never entered my mind. The dispatch in question was written purely at the request of the President.

On the morning of the 2d, the President and Gen Halleck came to my house, when the President informed me that Colonel Kelton had returned from the front, that our affairs were in bad condition, that the army was in full retreat upon the defenses of Washington, the roads filled with stragglers, &c. He instructed me to take steps at once to stop and collect the stragglers, to place the works in a proper state of defense, and to go out to meet and take command of the army when it approached the vicinity of the works, then to put the troops in the best position for defense; committing everything to my hands.*

I immediately took steps to carry out these orders, and I sent an aide to General Pope with the following letter:

Headquarters, Washington, Sept 2, 1862
Maj.-Gen J Pope, Com'g. A V :

General,—Gen. Halleck instructed me to repeat to you the order he sent this morning to Washington without unnecessary delay. He feared that his messenger might miss you, and desired to take this double precaution.

In order to bring troops upon ground with which they are already familiar, it would be best to move Porter's corps upon Upton's Hill, that it may occupy Hall's Hill, etc.; McDowell's to Upton's Hill; Franklin's to the works in front of Alexandria; Heintzelman's to the same vicinity; Couch to Fort Corcoran, or, if practicable, to the Chain Bridge, Sumner either to Fort Albany or to Alexandria, as may be most convenient

In haste General, very truly yours,
G B. McC, Maj.-Gen U S A

In the afternoon I crossed the Potomac and rode to the front, and at Upton's Hill met the advance of McDowell's corps, and with it Generals Pope and McDowell After getting what information I could from them, I sent the few aids at my disposal to the left, to give instructions to the troops approaching in the direction of Alexandria, and hearing artillery firing in the direction of the Vienna and Langley road, by which the corps of Sumner, Porter and Sigel were returning, and learning from Gen Pope that Sumner was probably engaged, I went with a single aide and three orderlies by the shortest line to meet that column I reached the column after dark, and proceeded as far as Lewinsville, where I became satisfied that the rear corps (Sumner's) would be able to reach its intended position without any serious molestation I therefore indicated to Generals Porter and Sigel the positions they were to occupy, sent instructions to Gen Sumner, and at a late hour of the night returned to Washington

Next day I rode to the front of Alexandria, and was engaged in rectifying the positions of the troops, and giving orders necessary to secure the issuing of the necessary supplies, etc I felt sure on this day that we could repulse any attack made by the enemy on the south side of the Potomac.

THE MARYLAND CAMPAIGN.

On the 3d the enemy had disappeared from the front of Washington, and the information which received induced me to believe that he intended to cross the upper Potomac into Maryland This materially changed the aspect of affairs and enlarged the sphere of operations.

---

* The following, which was the only order sent on the subject was published on the 2d September It was accidentally omitted in preparing the report

WAR DEPARTMENT, ADJUTANT GENERAL'S OFFICE,
WASHINGTON, Sep 2 1862

Major General McClellan will have command of the fortifications of Washington, and of all the troops for the defense of the capital By order of
Maj Gen HALLECK,
E D. TOWNSEND, Ass't Adj t General.

---

a crossing in force, an active campaign would be necessary to cover Baltimore, prevent the invasion of Pennsylvania, and clear Maryland.

I therefore on the 3d ordered the 2d and 12th Corps to Tennallytown, and the 9th Corps to a point on the 7th Street Road near Washington, and sent such cavalry as was available to the fords near Poolesville, to watch and impede the enemy in any attempt to cross in that vicinity.

On the 5th the 2d and 12th Corps were moved to Rockville, and Couch's division (the only one of the 4th Corps that had been brought from the Peninsula) to Offut's Cross Roads.

On the 6th the 1st and 9th Corps were ordered to Leesboro, the 6th Corps and Syke's division of the 5th Corps to Tennallytown.

On the 7th the 6th Corps was advanced to Rockville, to which place my headquarters were moved on the same day.

All the necessary arrangements for the defence of the city, under the new condition of things, had been made, and General Banks was left in command, having received his instructions from me

I left Washington on the 7th of September At this time it was known that the mass of the rebel army had passed up to the south side of the Potomac in the direction of Leesburg, and and that a portion of that army had crossed into Maryland; but whether it was their intention to cross their whole force, with a view to turn Washington by a flank movement down the north bank of the Potomac, to move on Baltimore, or to invade Pennsylvania, were questions which at that time we had no means of determining. This uncertainty as to the intentions of the enemy obliged me, up to the 13th of September, to march cautiously, and to advance the army in such order as to continually keep Washington and Baltimore covered, and at the same time to hold the troops well in hand, so as to be able to concentrate and follow rapidly if the enemy took the direction of Pennsylvania, or to return to the defence of Washington, if, as was greatly feared by the authorities, the enemy should be merely making a feint with a small force to draw off our army, while with their main forces they stood ready to seize the first favorable opportunity to attack the capital.

In the meantime the process of reorganization rendered necessary after the demoralizing effects of the disastrous campaign upon the other side of the Potomac, was rapidly progressing, the troops were regaining confidence, and their former soldierly appearance and discipline was fast returning. My cavalry was pushed out continually in all directions, and all possible steps taken to learn the positions and movements of the enemy.

The following table shows the movements of the army from day to day, up to the 14th of September

[See next page]

The right wing, consisting of the 1st and 9th Corps, under the command of Major-General Burnside, moved on Frederick, the 1st Corps via Brookville, Cooksville and Ridgeville, and the 9th Corps via Damascus and New Market.

The 2d and 12th Corps, forming the centre,

under the command of General Sumner, moved on Frederick, the former via Clarksburg and Urbana, and the 12th Corps on a lateral road between Urbana and New Market, thus maintaining the communication with the right wing and covering the direct road from Frederick to Washington

The 6th Corps under the command of General Franklin, moved to Buckeystown via Darnestown, Dawsonville, and Barnville, covering the road from the mouth of the Monocacy to Rockville, and being in a position to connect with and support the centre should it have been necessary (as was supposed) to force the line of the Monocacy

Couch's division moved by the "River Road," covering that approach, watching the fords of the Potomac, and ultimately following and sup-supporting the 6th Corps.

The following extracts from telegrams received by me after my departure from Washington will show how little was known there about the enemy's movements, and the fears which were entertained for the safety of the capital.

On the 9th of September, General Halleck telegraphed me as follows:

"Until we can get better advices about the numbers of the enemy at Drainsville, I think we must be very cautious about stripping too much the forts on the Virginia side It may be the enemy's object to draw off the mass of our forces, and then attempt to attack from the Virginia side of the Potomac. Think of this."

Again on the 11th of Sept, Gen Halleck telegraphed me as follows:

"Why not order forward Keyes or Sigel? I think the main force of the enemy is in your front; more troops can be spared from here."

This dispatch, as published by the Committee on the Conduct of the War, and furnished by the general-in-chief, reads as follows. "Why not order forward Porter's or Sigel's? *If the main force of the enemy is in your front, more troops can be spared from here.*"

I remark that the original dispatch as received by me from the telegraph operator, is in the words quoted above. "*I think the main force of the enemy, &c.*"

In accordance with this suggestion, I asked, on the same day, that all the troops that could be spared should at once be sent to reinforce me, but none came

On the the 12th I received the following telegram from his Excellency the President:

"Governor Curtin telegraphs me. 'I have advices that Jackson is crossing the Potomac at Williamsport, and probably the whole rebel army will be drawn from Maryland.'" The President adds: "Receiving nothing from Harper's Ferry or Martinsburg to-day, and positive information from Wheeling, that the line is cut, corroborates the idea that the enemy is recrossing the Potomac. Please do not let him get off without being hurt."

On the 13th Gen. Halleck telegraphed as follows;

"Until you know more certainly the enemy's force south of the Potomac, you are wrong in thus uncovering the capital. I am of the opinion

		September	4th	6th	9th	10th	11th	12th	13th	14th
BURNSIDE	9th Corps, *Reno*		7th St Road	Leesboro	Brookeville		New Market	Frederick Ridgeville Newmarket and on the Monocacy	Middleton	South Mountain
SUMNER	1st Corps, *Hooker*		Upton's Hill	Leesboro	Brookville			Frederick	Frederick	South Mountain
	12th Corps, *Williams*		Tenallytown	Rockville	Middleburg	Damascus		Ijamsville Cross Roads Urbana	Frederick	South Mountain
	2d Corps, *Sumner*		Tenallytown	Rockville	Middleburg	Clarksburg	Clarksburg	Licksville Cross Roads	Frederick	South Mountain
FRANKLIN	6th Corps, *Franklin*		Alex. Semm's	Tenallytown	Darnestown	Barnsville	Poolesville	Licksville Cross Roads Barnville	Buckeystown	Burkettsville
	Couch's Division		Tennallytown	Offuts Cross Roads	Mouth of Seneca	Poolesville	Poolesville	Urbana	Licksville	Burkettsville
	Sykes's Division		Tenallytown	Rockville	Rockville	Rockville	Middleburg	Frederick	Middleton	Middleton

that the enemy will send a small column towards Pennsylvania to draw your forces in that direction, then suddenly move on Washington with the forces south of the Potomac, and those he may cross over."

Again, on the 11th, Gen Halleck telegraphed me that "scouts report a large force still on the Virginia side of the Potomac. If so, I fear you are exposing your left and rear."

Again, as late as the 16th, after we had the most positive evidence that Lee's army was in front of us I received the following:

War Department Sept. 16, 1862, 12.30 P. M.

Maj.-Gen. McC.—Yours of 7 a m is this moment received. As you give me no information in regard to the position of your forces, except those at Sharpsburg, of course I cannot advise. I think, however, you will find that the whole force of the enemy in your front has crossed the river. I fear now more than ever that they will recross at Harper's Ferry or below, and turn your left, thus cutting you off from Washington. This has appeared to me to be a part of their plan and hence my anxiety on the subject. A heavy rain might prevent it. H. W. H., General-in-Chief.

The importance of moving with all due caution, so as not to uncover the national capital, until the enemy's position and plans were developed, was, I believe, fully appreciated by me; and as my troops extended from the Baltimore and Ohio Railroad to the Potomac, with the extreme left flank moving along that stream and with strong pickets left in rear to watch and guard all the available fords, I did not regard my left or rear as in any degree exposed. But it appears from the foregoing telegrams that the general-in-chief was of a different opinion, and that my movements were, in his judgment, too precipitate, not only for the safety of Washington but also for the security of my left and rear.

The precise nature of these daily injunctions against a precipitate advance may now be perceived. The general-in-chief, in his testimony before the "Committee on the Conduct of the War," says "In respect to Gen. McClellan's going too fast, or too far from Washington, there can be found no such telegram from me to him; he has mistaken the meaning of the telegrams I sent him. I telegraphed him that he was going too far, not from Washington, but from the Potomac, leaving Gen Lee the opportunity to come down the Potomac and get between him and Washington. I thought Gen McClellan should keep more on the Potomac, and press forward his left rather than his right so as the more readily to relieve Harper's Ferry."

As I can find no telegram from the general-in-chief recommending me to keep my left flank nearer the Potomac, I am compelled to believe that when he gave this testimony he had forgotten the purport of the telegrams above quoted, and had also ceased to remember the fact, well known to him at the time, that my left, from the time I left Washington, always rested on the Potomac, and that my centre was continually in position to reinforce the left or right as occasion might require. Had I advanced my left flank along the Potomac more rapidly than the other columns marched upon the roads to the right, I should have thrown that flank out of supporting distance of the other troops, and greatly exposed it. And if I had marched the entire army in one column along the banks of the river instead of upon five different parallel roads, the column, with its trains, would have extended about fifty miles, and the enemy might have defeated the advance before the rear could have reached the scene of action. Moreover, such a movement would have uncovered the communications with Baltimore and Washington on our right, and exposed our left and rear.

I presume it will be admitted by every military man that it was necessary to move the army in such order that it could at any time be concentrated for battle, and I am of opinion that this object could not have been accomplished in any other way than the one employed. Any other disposition of our forces would have subjected them to defeat in detached fragments.

On the 10th of December, I received from my scouts information which rendered it quite probable that Gen. Lee's army was in the vicinity of Frederick, but whether his intention was to move towards Baltimore or Pennsylvania was not then known.

On the 11th I ordered Gen Burnside to push a strong reconnoissance across the National Road and the Baltimore and Ohio Railroad towards New Market, and if he learned that the enemy had moved towards Hagerstown, to press on rapidly to Frederick, keeping his troops constantly ready to meet the enemy in force. A corresponding movement of all the troops in the centre and on the left was ordered in the direction of Urbana and Poolesville.

On the 12th a portion of the right wing entered Frederick, after a brisk skirmish at the outskirts of the city and in the streets. On the 13th the main bodies of the right wing and centre passed through Frederick.

It was soon ascertained that the main body of the enemy's forces had marched out of the city on the two previous days, taking the roads to Boonsboro' and Harper's Ferry, thereby rendering it necessary to force the passes through the Catoctin and South Mountain ridges, and gain possession of Boonsboro' and Rohrersville before any relief could be extended to Col Miles at Harper's Ferry.

On the 13th an order fell into my hands issued by Gen Lee, which fully disclosed his plans, and I immediately gave orders for a rapid and vigorous forward movement.

The following is a copy of the order referred to:

Headq's, Army of North'n Virginia Sept 9, '62.
SPECIAL ORDERS, No 191

The army will resume its march to-morrow, taking the Hagerstown road. Gen Jackson's command will form the advance, and after passing Middletown, with such portions as he may select, will take the route towards Sharpsburg cross the Potomac at the most convenient point, and by Friday night take possession of the Baltimore and Ohio Railroad, capture such of the enemy as may be at Martinsburg, and intercept such as may attempt to escape from Harper's Ferry.

Gen Longstreet's command will pursue the same road as far as Boonsboro', where it will halt with the reserve, supply, and baggage trains of the army

Gen McLaws, with his own division and that of Gen R H Anderson, will follow Gen. Longstreet On reaching Middletown, he will take the route to Harper's Ferry, and by Friday morning possess himself of the Maryland Heights, and endeavor to capture the enemy at Harper's Ferry and vicinity

Gen Walker with his division, after accomplishing the object in which he is now engaged, will cross the Potomac at Cheek's Ford, ascend its right bank to Lovettsville, take possession of Loudon Heights if practicable, by Friday morning Keyes' ford on his left, and the road between the end of the mountain and the Potomac on his right He will, as far as practicable, co-operate with Gen McLaws and Gen Jackson, in intercepting the retreat of the enemy

Gen D H Hill's division will form the rear guard of the army pursuing the road taken by the main body The reserve artillery, ordnance, and supply trains &c, will precede Gen Hill

Gen Stuart will detach a squadron of cavalry to accompany the commands of Gen's Longstreet, Jackson and McLaws, and with the main body of the cavalry will cover the route of the army, and bring up all stragglers that may have been left behind

The commands of Gen Jackson, McLaws, and Walker, after accomplishing the objects for which they have been detached, will join the main body of the army at Boonsboro' or Hagerstown

Each regiment on the march, will habitually carry its axes in the regimental ordnance wagons, for use of the men at their encampments to procure wood, &c

By command of Gen R E LEE, R H CHILTON, A A G, to Maj-Gen D H HILL, C D

HARPER'S FERRY

In the report of a military commission, of which Maj-Gen. D Hunter was President, which convened at Washington, for the purpose of investigating the conduct of certain officers in connection with the surrender of Harper's Ferry, I find the following

"The commission has remarked freely on Col Miles, an old officer, who has been killed in the service of his country, and it can not, from any motives of delicacy, refrain from censuring those in high command, when it thinks such censure deserved.

"The general-in-chief has testified that Gen McC, after having received orders to repel the enemy invading the State of Maryland, marched only six miles per day, on an average, when pursuing this invading enemy

"The general-in-chief also testifies that, in his opinion, he could and should have relieved and protected Harper's Ferry, and in this opinion the commission fully concur"

I have been greatly surprised that this commission, in its investigations, never called upon me, nor upon any officer of my staff, nor, so far as I know, upon any officer of the army of the Potomac, able to give an intelligent statement of the movements of that army But another paragraph in the same report makes testimony from such sources quite superfluous. It is as follows

"By a reference to the evidence it will be seen that at the very moment Col Ford abandoned Maryland Heights, his little army was in reality relieved by Gen Franklin's and Sumner's corps at Crampton's Gap, within seven miles of his position"

The corps of Gens Franklin and Sumner were a part of the army which I at that time had the honor to command, and they were acting under my orders at Crampton's Gap, and elsewhere, and if, as the commission states Col Ford's "little army was in reality relieved" by those officers, it was relieved by me

I had, on the morning of the 10th, sent the following dispatch in relation to the command at Harper's Ferry:

Camp near Rockville, Sept 10, 1862, 9 P A M.

Maj-Gen. H W. H, Washington, D C —Col. Miles is at or near Harper's Ferry, as I understand, with nine thousand troops He can do nothing where he is, but could be of great service if ordered to join me I suggest that he be ordered to join me by the most practicable route. G B. McC, Maj.-Gen

To this I received the following reply

"There is no way for Col Miles to join you at present, his only chance is to defend his works till you can open communication with him H W H"

It seems necessary for a distinct understanding of this matter, to state that I was directed on the 12th to assume command of the garrison of Harper's Ferry, as soon as I should open communication with that place, and that when I received this order all communication from the direction in which I was approaching was cut off Up to that time, however, Col Miles could, in my judgment, have marched his command into Pennsylvania, by crossing the Potomac at Williamsport or above, and this opinion was confirmed by the fact that Col Davis marched the cavalry part of Col Miles' command from Harper's Ferry on the 14th, taking the main road to Hagerstown, and he encountered no enemy excepting a small picket near the mouth of the Antietam

Before I left Washington, and when there, there certainly could have been no enemy to prevent the withdrawal of the forces of Col. Miles I recommended to the proper authorities that the garrison of Harper's Ferry should be withdrawn via Hagerstown, to aid in covering the Cumberland Valley, or that, taking up the pontoon bridge and obstructing the railroad bridge, it should fall back to the Maryland Heights, and there hold out to the last In this position it ought to have maintained itself many days It was not deemed proper to adopt either of these suggestions, and when the matter was left to my discretion it was too late for me to do anything but endeavor to relieve the garrison I accordingly directed artillery to be fired by our advance, at frequent intervals, as a signal that relief was at hand. This was done, and as I afterwards learned, the reports of the cannon were distinctly heard at Harper's Ferry. It was confidently expected that Col. Miles would hold out until we had carried the mountain passes and were in condition to send a detachment to his relief. The left was therefore ordered to move through Crampton's Pass in front of Burkettsville, while the centre and right marched upon Turner's Pass in front of Middletown.

It may be asked by those who are not acquainted with the topography of the country in the vicinity of Harper's Ferry, why Franklin, instead of marching his column over the circuitous road from Jefferson via Burkettsville and Brownsville and thence up the river to Harper's Ferry. It was for the reason that I had received information that the enemy were anticipating our approach in that direction, and had established batteries on the south side of the Potomac which commanded all the approaches to Knoxville; moreover the road from that point winds directly along the river bank at the foot of a precipitous mountain where there was no opportunity of forming in line of battle, and where the enemy could have placed batteries on both sides of the river to enfilade our narrow approaching columns. The approach through Crampton's Pass, which debouches into Pleasant Valley in rear of Maryland Heights, was the only one which offered any reasonable prospect of carrying that formidable position. At the same time the troops upon that road were in better relation to the main body of our forces.

On the morning of the 14th a verbal message reached me from Col. Miles, which was the first authentic intelligence I had received as to the condition of things at Harper's Ferry. The messenger informed me that on the preceding afternoon Maryland Heights had been abandoned by our troops after repelling an attack of the rebels and that Col. Miles's entire force was concentrated at Harper's Ferry, the Maryland, Loudon and Bolivar Heights having been abandoned by him, and occupied by the enemy. The messenger also stated that there was no apparent reason for the abandonment of the Maryland Heights and that Col. Miles instructed him to say that he could hold out with certainty two days longer. I directed him to make his way back, if possible, with the information that I was approaching rapidly and felt confident I could relieve the place.

On the same afternoon I wrote the following letter to Col. Miles, and dispatched three copies by three different couriers, on different routes. I did not, however, learn that any of these men succeeded in reaching Harper's Ferry.

Middletown, Sept. 14, 1862.

Col. D. S. Miles:—Colonel: The army is being rapidly concentrated here. We are now attacking the pass on the Hagerstown road, over the Blue Ridge. A column is about attacking the Burkestsville and Boonsboro' Pass. You may count on our making every effort to relieve you; you may rely upon my speedily accomplishing that object. Hold out to the last extremity. If it is possible, reoccupy the Maryland Heights with your whole force. If you can do that, I will certainly be able to relieve you. As the Catoctin Valley is in our possession you can safely cross the river at Berlin or its vicinity, so far as opposition on this side of the river is concerned. Hold out to the last.

G. B. McC., Maj-Gen. Comd'g.

On the previous day I had sent Gen. Franklin the following instructions.

Headquarters, Army of the Potomac,
Camp near Frederick, Sept. 13, 1862. 6.20 P.M.
Major-Gen. W. B. Franklin Com'g 6th Corps

General,—I have now full information as to movements and intentions of the enemy. Jackson has crossed the Upper Potomac to capture the garrison at Martinsburg and cut off Miles's retreat toward the west. A division on the south side of the Potomac was to carry Loudon Heights, and cut off his retreat in that direction. McLaws, with his own command and the division of R. H. Anderson was to move by Boonsboro' and Rohrersville to carry the Maryland Heights. The signal officers inform me that he is now in Pleasant Valley. The firing shows that Miles still holds out. Longstreet was to move by Boonsboro', and there halt with the reserve trains; D. H. Hill to form the rear guard; Stuart's cavalry to bring up stragglers &c. We have cleared out all the cavalry this side the mountains, and north of us. The last I heard from Pleasonton he occupied Middletown after several sharp skirmishes. A division of Burnside's started several hours ago to support him. The whole of Burnside's command including Hooker's corps, march this evening and early to-morrow morning, followed by the corps of Sumner, and Banks's and Sykes's division upon Boonsboro', to carry that position. Couch has been ordered to concentrate his division and join you as rapidly as possible. Without waiting for the whole of that division to join you, you will move at day-break in the morning by Jefferson and Burkettsville upon the road to Rohrersville; I have reliable information that the mountain pass by this road is practicable for artillery and wagons. If this pass is not occupied by the enemy in force, seize it as soon as practicable, and debouch upon Rohrersville in order to cut off the retreat of or destroy McLaw's command. If you find this pass held by the enemy in large force, make all your dispositions for the attack, and commence it about half an hour after you hear severe firing at the pass on the Hagerstown pike, where the main body will attack. Having gained the pass, your duty will be first to cut off, destroy, or capture McLaws' command, and relieve Colonel Miles. If you effect this you will order him to join you at once with all his disposable troops, first destroying the bridges over the Potomac, if not already done, and leaving a sufficient garrison to prevent the enemy from passing the ford; you will then return by Rohrersville on the direct road to Boonsboro' if the main column has not succeeded in its attack. If it has succeeded, take the road from Rohrersville to Sharpsburg and Williamsport, in order either to cut off the retreat of Hill and Longstreet towards the Potomac, or to prevent the repassage of Jackson. My general idea is to cut the enemy in two, and beat him in detail I believe I have sufficiently explained my intentions. I ask of you at this important moment all your intellect, and the utmost activity that a general can exercise G. B. McC Maj.-Gen Com.

Again on the 14th I sent him the following:

Head-Quarters, Army of the Potomac,
Frederick, Sept 14, 1862 2 p. m.

Maj.-Gen Franklin.—Your dispatch of 12 30 just received. Send back to hurry up Couch Mass your troops and carry Burkettsville at any cost. We shall have strong opposition at both passes. As fast as the troops come up, I will hold a reserve in readiness to support you. If you find the enemy in very great force at the pass, let me know at once, and amuse them as best you can, so as to retain them there. In that event I will probably throw the mass of the army on the pass in front of here. If I carry that, it will clear the way for you, and you must then follow the enemy as rapidly as possible.

G B McC., Maj.-Gen Com.

SOUTH MOUNTAIN.

General Franklin pushed his corps rapidly forward towards Crampton's Pass and at about 12 o'clock on the 14th arrived at Burkettsville, immediately in rear of which he found the enemy's infantry posted in force on both sides of the road, with artillery in strong positions to defend the approaches to the pass.

Slocum's division was formed upon the right of the road leading through the gap, and Smith's upon the left. A line formed of Bartlett's and Torbet's brigades, supported by Newton, whose activity was conspicuous, advanced steadily upon the enemy at a charge on the right. The enemy were driven from their position at the base of the mountain, where they were protected by a stone wall, and steadily forced back up the slope until they reached the position of their battery on the road well up the mountain. Here they made a stand. They were, however, driven back, retiring their artillery in echelon, until, after an action of three hours, the crest was gained, and the enemy hastily fled down the mountain on the other side.

On the left of the road Brooks's and Irwin's brigades of Smith's division, formed for the protection of Slocum's flank, charged up the mountain in the same steady manner, driving the enemy before them until the crest was carried. 400 prisoners from seventeen different organizations, 700 stand of arms, one piece of artillery, and three colors, were captured by our troops in this brilliant action. It was conducted by Gen Franklin in all its details. These details are given in the report of Gen. Franklin, herewith submitted, and due credit awarded to the gallant officers and men engaged. The loss in Gen. Franklin's corps was 115 killed, 416 wounded, and 2 missing. The enemy's loss was about the same. The enemy's position was such that our artillery could not be used with any effect.

The close of the action found Gen Franklin's advance in Pleasant Valley on the night of the 14th, within three and a half miles of the point on Maryland Heights, (where he might on the same night, or on the morning of the 15th, have formed a junction with the garrison of Harper's Ferry had it not been previously withdrawn from Maryland Heights,) and within six miles of Harper's Ferry.

On the night of the 14th the following dispatch was sent to Gen Franklin:

Bolivar, Sept 15, 1 a.m.

General,— . . The commanding general directs that you occupy with your command the road from Rohrersville to Harper's Ferry, placing a sufficient force at Rohrersville to hold that position, in case it should be attacked by the enemy from Boonsboro'. Endeavor to open communication with Col Miles at Harper's Ferry, attacking and destroying such of the enemy as you may find in Pleasant Valley. Should you succeed in opening communication with Col Miles, direct him to join you with his whole command, with all the guns and public property he can carry with him. The remainder of the guns will be destroyed, the rest of the public property will also be destroyed. You will then proceed to Boonsboro', which place the commanding general intends to attack to-morrow, and join the main body of the army at that place. Should you find, however, that the enemy has retreated from Boonsboro' towards Sharpsburgh, you will endeavor to fall upon him and cut off his retreat.

By command of Maj.-Gen McClellan
G D R, Col & A D C to Gen F.

On the 15th the following were received from Gen Franklin.

At the foot of the Mountain in Pleasant Valley,
3 m's from Rohrersville, Sept 15, 8 50 a m.

General,—My command started at daylight this morning, and I am waiting to have it closed up here. Gen Couch arrived about 10 o'clock last night. I have ordered one of his brigades and one battery to Rohrersville, or to the strongest points in its vicinity. The enemy is drawn up in line of battle about two miles to our front, —one brigade in sight. As soon as I am sure that Rohrersville is occupied I shall move forward to attack the enemy. This may be two hours from now. If Harper's Ferry is fallen, and the cessation of firing makes me fear that it has, it is my opinion that I should be strongly reinforced. . . .

W. B F., M.-Gen Com. 6th C. to Gen G B McC.

Sept 15, 11 a m

General —I have received your dispatch by Capt. O'Keefe. The enemy is in large force in my front, in two lines of battle stretching across the valley, and a large column of artillery and infantry on the right of the valley, looking towards Harper's Ferry. They outnumber me two to one. It of course will not answer to pursue the enemy under these circumstances. I shall communicate with Burnside as soon as possible. In the meantime I shall wait here until I learn what is the prospect of reinforcement. I have not the force to justify an attack on the force I see in front. I have had a very close view of it, and its position is very strong. Respectfully, W. B Franklin, Maj.-Gen.

Maj.-Gen. G. B. McC, Comd'g

Col. Miles surrendered Harper's Ferry at 8 a. m on the 15th, as the cessation of the firing indicated, and Gen Franklin was ordered to remain where he was, to watch the large force in front of him, and protect our left and rear until the night of the 16th, when he was ordered to join the main body of the army at Keedysville, after sending Couch's division to Maryland Heights

While the events which have just been described were taking place at Crampton's Gap, the troops of the centre and right wing, which had united at Frederick on the 13th, were engaged in the contest for the possession of Turner's Gap.

On the morning of the 13th, Gen Pleasonton was ordered to send McReynolds's brigade and a section of artillery in the direction of Gettysburg, and Rush's regiment towards Jefferson, to communicate with Franklin, to whom the 6th U. S. Cavalry and a section of artillery had previously been sent, and to proceed with the remainder of the force in the direction of Middletown in pursuit of the enemy

After skirmishing with the enemy all the morning, and driving them from several strong positions, he reached Turner's Gap of the South Mountain in the afternoon, and found the enemy in force, and apparently determined to defend the pass. He sent back for infantry to General Burnside, who had been directed to support him, and proceeded to make reconnoissance of the position

The South Mountain is at this point about 1000 feet in height, and its general direction is from north-east to south-west. The National Road from Frederick to Hagerstown crosses it nearly at right angles from Turner's Gap, a depression which is some 400 feet in depth. The mountain on the north side of the turnpike is divided into two crests or ridges by a narrow valley, which, though deep at the pass, becomes a slight depression at about a mile to the north. There are two country roads, one to the right of the turnpike, and the other to the left, which give access to the crests overlooking the main road. The one to the left called the "old Sharpsburg road," is nearly parallel to, and about half a mile distant from the turnpike, until it reaches the crest of the mountain, when it bends off to the left

The other road, called the "old Hagerstown road" passes up a ravine in the mountain, about a mile from the turnpike, and, bending to the left over and along the first crest, enters the turnpike at the Mountain House, near the summit of the pass

On the night of the 13th the positions of the different corps were as follows

Reno's corps, at Middletown, except Rodman's division at Frederick

Hooker's corps, on the Monocacy, two miles from Frederick

Sumner's Corps near Frederick; Banks' Corps ditto; Sykes's Division, ditto; Franklin's Corps at Buckeystown; Couch's Division, at Licksville.

The orders from headquarters, for the march on the 14th were as follows

13th, 11 20 p m.—Hooker to march at daylight to Middletown

13th, 11 30 p m.—Sykes to move at 6 a. m., after Hooker, on the Middletown and Hagerstown road

14th, 1 a. m.—Artillery Reserve to follow Sykes closely.

13th, 6 45 p m.—Sumner to move at 7 a. m.

14th 9 a. m.—Sumner ordered to take the Shookstown road to Middletown

13th, 6 46 p m.—Couch ordered to move to Jefferson with his whole division

On the 14th, Gen Pleasonton continued his reconnoissance. Gibson's battery, and afterwards Benjamin's battery, (of Reno's corps), were placed on high ground to the left of the turnpike, and obtained a direct fire on the enemy's position in the gap

General Cox's division, which had been ordered up to support Gen Pleasonton, left its bivouac near Middletown, at 6 a. m. The first brigade reached the scene of action at 9 a. m., and was sent up the old Sharpsburg road by Gen Pleasonton, to feel the enemy and ascertain if he held the crest on that side in strong force. This was soon found to be the case, and Gen Cox having arrived with the other brigade, and information having been received from Gen. Reno that the column would be supported by the whole corps, the division was ordered to assault the position

Two 20-pound Parrotts of Simmons's battery and two sections of McMullin's battery were left in the rear, in position near the turnpike, where they did good service during the day against the enemy's batteries in the gap

Col Scammon's brigade was deployed, and, well covered by skirmishers, moved up the slope to the left of the road, with the object of turning the enemy's right, if possible. It succeeded in gaining the crest and establishing itself there in spite of the vigorous resistance of the enemy, who was posted behind stone walls and in the edges of timber, and the fire of a battery which poured in canister and case-shot on the regiment on the right of the brigade.

Col Crooke's brigade marched in column, at supporting distance. A section of McMullin's battery, under Lieutenant Croome (killed while serving one of his guns), was moved up with great difficulty, and opened with canister at very short range on the enemy's infantry, by whom (after having done considerable execution) it was soon silenced and forced to withdraw.

One regiment of Crooke's brigade was now deployed on Scammon's left, and the other two in his rear, and they several times entered the first line and relieved the regiment in front of them when hard pressed. A section of Simmon's battery was brought up and placed in an open space in the woods, where it did good service during the rest of the day. The enemy several times attempted to retake the crest, advancing with boldness, but were each time repulsed. They then withdrew their battery to a point more to the right, and formed columns on both our flanks.

It was now about noon, and a lull occurred in the contest, which lasted about two hours, during which the rest of the corps was coming up. Gen Wilcox's division was the first to arrive. When he reached the base of the mountain, Gen Cox advised him to consult Gen. Pleasonton as to a position. The latter indicated that on the right, afterwards taken up by Gen. Hooker. Gen Wilcox was in the act of moving to occupy this ground when he received an order from Gen Reno to move up the old Sharpsburg road, and take a position to its right, overlooking the turnpike. Two regiments were detached to support Gen Cox, at his request. One section of Cook's battery was placed in position near the turn of the road (on the crest), and opened fire on the enemy's batteries across the gap. The division was proceeding to deploy to the right of the road when the enemy suddenly opened (at 150 yards) with a battery which enfiladed the road at that point, drove off Cook's cannoneers with their limbers, and causing a temporary panic, in which the guns were nearly lost. But the 79th New York and 17th Michigan promptly rallied, changed front under a heavy fire, and moved out to protect the guns, with which Capt Cook had remained. Order was soon restored, and the division formed in line on the right of Cox, and was kept concealed as much as possible under the hill-side until the whole line advanced. It was exposed not only to the fire of the battery in front but also to that of the batteries on the other side of the turnpike, and lost heavily.

Shortly before this time Generals Burnside and Reno arrived at the base of the mountain, and the former directed the latter to move up the divisions of Generals Sturgis and Rodman to the crest held by Cox and Wilcox, and to move upon the enemy's position with his whole force as soon as he was informed that Gen Hooker (who had first been directed to attack on the right) was advanced up the mountain. Gen Reno then went to the front and assumed the direction of affairs the positions having been explained to him by Gen Pleasonton.

Shortly before this time I arrived at the point occupied by Gen. Burnside, and my headquarters were located there until the conclusion of the action.

Gen Sturgis had left his camp at 1 P.M., and reached the scene of action about half past three P.M. Clark's battery of his division was sent to assist Cox's left, by order of Gen Reno, and two regiments (2d Maryland and 6th New Hampshire) were detached by Gen Reno and sent forward a little distance on the left of the turnpike. His division was formed in rear of Wilcox's, and Rodman's division was divided, Col Fairchild's brigade being placed on the extreme left and Col Harland's under Gen Rodman's personal supervision on the right.

My order to move the whole line forward, and take or silence the enemy's batteries in front was executed with enthusiasm. The enemy made a desperate resistance, charging our advancing lines with fierceness, but they were everywhere routed, and fled. Our chief loss fell on Wilcox's division. The enemy's battery was found to be across a gorge and beyond the reach of our infantry, but its position was untenable and it was hastily removed and not again put in position near us. But the batteries across the gap still kept a fire of shot and shell.

Gen Wilcox praises very highly the conduct of the 17th Michigan in this advance—a regiment which had been organized scarcely a month, but which charged the advancing enemy in flank in a manner worthy of veteran troops, and also that of the 45th Pennsylvania, which bravely met them in front.

Cook's battery now reopened fire. Sturgis's division was moved to the flank of Wilcox's occupying the new ground gained on the further side of the slope, and his artillery opened on the batteries across the gap. The enemy made an effort to turn our left about dark, but were repulsed by Fairchild's brigade and Clark's battery.

At about 7 o'clock the enemy made another effort to regain the lost ground, attacking along Sturgis's front and part of Cox's. A lively fire was kept up until nearly nine o'clock, several charges being made by the enemy and repulsed with slaughter, and we finally occupied the highest part of the mountain. Gen Reno was killed just before sunset, while making a reconnoissance to the front, and the command of the corps devolved upon Gen Cox.

In Gen Reno the nation lost one of its best general officers. He was a skillful soldier, a brave and honest man.

There was no firing after ten o'clock, and the troops slept on their arms, ready to renew the fight at daylight; but the enemy quietly retired from the front during the night, abandoning their wounded and leaving their dead in large numbers scattered on the field.

While these operations were progressing on the left of the main column, the right, under Gen. Hooker, was actively engaged. His corps left the Monocacy early in the morning and its advance reached the Catoctin Creek about 1 P M. Gen Hooker then went forward to examine the ground.

At about 1 o'clock Gen. Meade's division was ordered to make a diversion in favor of Reno. The following is the order sent:

September 14. 1 P M

Maj.-Gen Hooker,

General,—General Reno requests that a division of yours may move up on the right (north) of the main road. General McClellan desires you to comply with this request, holding your whole corps in readiness to support the movement, and taking charge of it yourself. Sumner's and Banks's corps have commenced arriving. Let General McClellan be informed as soon as you commence your movement.

Geo. D Ruggles, Col, A.-A.-G & A.-D.-C.

Meade's division left Catoctin Creek about 2 o'clock, and turned off to the right from the main road on the old Hagerstown road to Mount Tabor Church, where Gen Hooker was, and deployed a short distance in advance, its right resting about one and a half miles from the turnpike. The enemy fired a few shots from a battery on the mountain side, but did no considerable damage. Cooper's Battery "B," 1st Pennsylvania Artillery, was placed in position on high ground at about half-past three o'clock, and fired at the enemy on the slope but soon ceased by order of Gen Hooker and the position of our lines prevented any further use of artillery by us on this part of the field. The 1st Massachusetts Cavalry was sent up the valley to the right to observe the movements if any, of the enemy in that direction, and one regiment of Meade's Division, posted to watch a road coming in in the same direction. The other divisions were deployed as they came up. General Hatch's on the left, and General Ricketts', which arrived about 5 P. M., in the rear.

General Gibbon's brigade was detached from Hatch's division by General Burnside for the purpose of making a demonstration on the enemy's centre up the main road, as soon as the movements on the right and left had sufficiently progressed.

The 1st Pennsylvania Rifles, of General Seymour's brigade, were sent forward as skirmishers to feel the enemy, and it was found that he was in force. Meade was then directed to advance his division to the right of the road, so as to outflank them if possible, and then to move forward and attack, while Hatch was directed to take with his division, the crest on the left of the old Hagerstown road, Rickett's division being held in reserve.

Seymour's brigade was sent up to the top of the slope on the right of the ravine, through which the road runs, and then move along the summit parallel to the road, while Col. Gallagher's and Col. Magilton's brigades moved in the same direction along the slope and in the ravine. The ground was of the most difficult character for the movements of troops, the hillside being very steep and rocky, and obstructed by stone walls, fences and timber. The enemy was soon encountered, and in a short time the action became general along the whole front of the division. The line advanced steadily up the mountain side where the enemy was posted behind trees and rocks, from which he was gradually dislodged. During this advance Col. Gallagher, commanding 3d brigade was severely wounded, and the command devolved upon Lieut.-Col. Robt. Anderson.

General Meade, having reason to believe that the enemy were attempting to outflank him on his right, applied to Gen. Hooker for reinforcements. General Duryea's brigade, of Rickett's division was ordered up, but it did not arrive until the close of the action. It was advanced on Seymour's left, but only one regiment could open fire before the enemy retired, and darkness intervened. General Meade speaks highly of General Seymour's skill in handling his brigade on the extreme right, securing by his manoeuvres the great object of the movement, the outflanking of the enemy.

While Gen. Meade was gallantly driving the enemy on the right General Hatch's division was engaged in a severe contest for the possession of the crest on the left of the ravine. It moved up the mountain in the following order: two regiments of General Patrick's brigade deployed as skirmishers, with the other two regiments of the same brigade supporting them. Col. Phelps's brigade in line of battalions in mass at deploying distance. General Doubleday's brigade, in the same order, bringing up the rear. The 21st New York having gone straight up the slope, instead of around to the right, as directed, the 2d United States Sharpshooters was sent out in its place.

Phelps's and Doubleday's brigades were deployed in turn as they reached the woods, which began about half way up the mountain. Gen. Patrick, with his skirmishers, soon drew the fire of the enemy, and found him strongly posted behind a fence which bounded the cleared space on the top of the ridge, having in his front the woods, through which our line was advancing, and in his rear a cornfield, full of rocky ledges, which afforded good cover to fall back if dislodged.

Phelps's brigade gallantly advanced under a hot fire, to close quarters, and after ten or fifteen minutes of heavy firing on both sides (in which Gen. Hatch was wounded while urging on his men), the fence was carried by a charge, and our line advanced a few yards beyond it, somewhat sheltered by the slope of the hill. Doubleday's brigade now under the command of Lieut-Col. Hoffman, (Col. Wainwright having been wounded) relieved Phelps's, and continued firing for an hour and-a-half, the enemy, behind ledges of rocks some thirty or forty paces in our front, making a stubborn resistance, and attempting to charge on the least cessation of our fire. About dusk Colonel Christian's brigade, of Rickett's division, came up and relieved Doubleday's brigade which fell back into line behind Phelps. Christian's brigade continued the action for thirty or forty minutes, when the enemy retired, after having made an attempt to flank us on the left, which was repulsed by the 76th New York, and 7th Indiana.

The remaining brigade of Rickett's division, (General Hartsuff's), was moved up in the centre, and connected Meade's left with Doubleday's right. We now had possession of the summit of the first ridge which commanded the turnpike on both sides of the mountain, and the troops were ordered to hold their positions until further orders and slept on their arms. Late in the afternoon General Gibbon, with his brigade, and one section of Gibbon's battery, (B, 4th U. S. Artillery), was ordered to move up the main road on the enemy's centre. He advanced a regiment on each side of the road, preceded by skirmishers, and followed by the other two regiments in double column, the artillery moving on the road until within range of the enemy's guns which were firing on the column from the gorge. The brigade advanced steadily, driving the enemy before it from his positions in the woods and behind stone walls, until it reached a point well up towards the top of the pass; when the enemy having been reinforced by three regiments, opened a heavy fire on the front, and on both flanks. The fight continued until 9 o'clock, the enemy being entirely repulsed, and the brigade, after having suffered severely, and having expended all its ammunition, including even the cartridges of the dead and wounded, continued to hold the ground it had so gallantly won until 12 o'clock when it was relieved by General Gorman's brigade of Sedgwick's division, Sumner's corps, (except the 6th Wisconsin, which remained on the field all night.) Gen. Gibbon, in his delicate movement, handled his brigade with as much precision and coolness, as if upon parade, and the bravery of his troops could not be excelled.

The 2d Corps, (Sumner's), and the 12th Corps,

(Williams), reached their final positions shortly after dark. General Richardson's division was placed near Mount Tabor Church, in a position to support our right if necessary; the 12th Corps, and Sedgwick's division, bivouacked near Bolivar, in a position to support our centre and left.

Gen. Sykes's division of regulars, and the artillery reserve halted for the night at Middletown, so that, on the night of the 14th, the whole army was massed in the vicinity of the field of battle, in readiness to renew the action the next day or to move in pursuit of the enemy. At daylight our skirmishers were advanced, and it was found that he had retreated during the night, leaving his dead on the field, and his wounded uncared for. About fifteen hundred prisoners were taken by us during the battle, and the loss to the enemy in killed, was much greater than our own, and probably also in wounded. It is believed that the force opposed to us at Turner's Gap consisted of D. H. Hill's corps, (15,500), and a part, if not the whole of Longstreet's and perhaps a portion of Jackson's, probably some 30,000 in all. We went into action with about 30,000 men, and our losses amounted to 1,568 aggregate, (312 killed, 1,234 wounded, 22 missing.)

On the next day I had the honor to receive the following very kind dispatch from his Excellency the President.

War Dep't, Washington Sept. 15, '62, 2 45 p.m.
Your dispatch of to-day received. God bless you, and all with you. Destroy the rebel army if possible. A. LINCOLN
To Maj.-Gen. McC.

ANTIETAM.

On the night of the battle of South Mountain, orders were given to the corps commanders to press forward their pickets at early dawn. This advance revealed the fact that the enemy had left his positions, and an immediate pursuit was ordered; the cavalry under Gen. Pleasonton, and the three corps under Gen's Sumner, Hooker and Mansfield, (the latter of whom had arrived that morning and assumed command of the 12th [Williams's] corps,) by the national turnpike and Boonsboro'; the corps of Gen's Burnside and Porter (the latter command at that time consisting of but one weak division, Sykes's) by the old Sharpsburg road; and Gen. Franklin to move into Pleasant Valley, occupy Rohrersville by a detachment, and endeavor to relieve Harper's Ferry.

Gen's Burnside and Porter, upon reaching the road from Boonsboro' to Rohrersville, were to reinforce Franklin or to move on Sharpsburg, according to circumstances.

Franklin moved towards Brownsville, and found there a force of the enemy much superior in numbers to his own, drawn up in a strong position to receive him.

At this time the cessation of firing at Harper's Ferry indicated the surrender of that place.

The cavalry overtook the enemy's cavalry in Boonsboro, made a dashing charge, killing and wounding a number, and capturing 250 prisoners and two guns.

Gen. Richardson's division, of the 2d Corps, pressing the rear guard of the enemy with vigor, passed Boonsboro and Keadysville and came up on the main body of the enemy occupying in large force a strong position a few miles beyond the latter place.

It had been hoped to engage the enemy on the 15th accordingly instructions were given that if the enemy were overtaken on the march, they should be attacked at once; if found in heavy force and in position, the corps in advance should be placed in position for attack, and await my arrival. On reaching the advance position of our troops, I found but two divisions, Richardson's and Sykes's, in position, the other troops were halted in the road, the head of the column some distance in rear of Richardson.

The enemy occupied a strong position on the heights, on the West side of Antietam Creek, displaying a large force of infantry and cavalry, with numerous batteries of artillery, which opened on our columns as they appeared in sight on the Keadysville and Sharpsburg turnpike, which fire was returned by Captain Tidball's light battery, 2d United States Artillery, and Pettit's battery, 1st New York Artillery.

The division of General Richardson, following close on the heels of the retreating foe, halted and deployed near Antietam River, on the right of the Sharpsburg road. Gen. Sykes, leading on the division of regulars on the old Sharpsburg road, came up and deployed to the left of Gen. Richardson, on the left of the road.

Antietam Creek, in this vicinity, is crossed by four stone bridges, the upper one on the Keadysville and Williamsport road, the 2d on the Keadysville and Sharpsburg turnpike, some two and a half miles below, the third about a mile below the second, on the Rohrersville and Sharpsburg road, and the fourth near the mouth of Antietam Creek, on the road leading from Harper's Ferry to Sharpsburg, some three miles below the third. The stream is sluggish, with few and difficult fords.

After a rapid examination of the position I found that it was too late to attack that day, and at once directed the placing of the batteries of position of the centre, and indicated the bivouacs for the different corps, massing them near and on both sides of the Sharpsburg turnpike. The corps were not all in their positions until the next morning after sunrise.

On the morning of the 16th it was discovered that the enemy had changed the position of his batteries. The masses of his troops were, however, still concealed behind the opposite heights. Their left and centre were upon and in front of the Sharpsburg and Hagerstown turnpike, hidden by woods and irregularities of the ground; their extreme left resting upon a wooded eminence near the cross roads to the north of J Miller's farm, then left resting upon the Potomac. Their line extended south, the right resting upon the hills to the south of Sharpsburg, near Snaveley's farm.

The bridge over the Antietam, described as No 3, near this point was strongly covered by riflemen protected by rifle-pits, stone fences, &c., and enfiladed by artillery. The ground in front of this line consisted of undulating hills, their crests in turn commanded by others in their rear. On all favorable points the enemy's artillery was posted, and their reserves hidden from view by the hills on which their line of battle was formed, could manœuvre unobserved by our army, and from the shortness of their line, could rapidly reinforce any point that attacked by our attack. Their position stretching across the angle formed by the Potomac and Antietam, their flanks and rear protected by these streams, was one of the strongest to be found in this region of country, which is well adapted to defensive warfare.

On the right near Keadysville, on both sides of the Sharpsburg turnpike were Sumner's and Hooker's corps. In advance, on the right of the turnpike and near the Antietam river, Gen. Richardson's division of Gen. Sumner's corps was posted. Gen. Sykes' division of Gen. Porter's corps was on the left of the turnpike, and in line with Gen. Richardson, protecting the bridge, No. 2, over the Antietam. The left of the line opposite to and some distance from bridge No. 3, was occupied by Gen. Burnside's corps. Before giving Gen. Hooker his orders to make the movement which will presently be described, I rode to the left of the line to satisfy myself that the troops were properly posted there to secure our left flank from any attack made along the left bank of the Antietam as well as to enable us to carry bridge No. 3.

I found it necessary to make considerable changes in the position of Gen. Burnside's corps, and directed him to advance to a strong position in the immediate vicinity of the bridge, and to reconnoitre the approaches to the bridge carefully.

In rear of Gen's Sumner's and Hooker's corps, near Keadysville, Gen. Mansfield's corps was massed, the cavalry on the turnpike in rear of Keadysville. On the ridge of the first line of hills overlooking the Antietam, and between the turnpike and Pry's house, on the right of the road, were placed Capts Taft's, Langner's, Von Kleiser's, and Lieut Weaver's batteries of 20-pounder Parrot guns. On the crest of the hill, in the rear and right of bridge No. 3, Capt. Weed's 3-inch and Lieutenant Benjamin's 20-pounder batteries. Gen. Franklin's corps, and Gen. Couch's division held a position in Pleasant Valley, in front of Brownsville with a strong force of the enemy in their front. Gen. Morell's division of Porter's corps was en route from Boonsboro' and Gen. Humphrey's division of new troops, en route from Frederick Md. About daylight on the 16th the enemy opened a heavy fire of artillery on our guns in position which was promptly returned. Their fire was silenced for the time but was frequently renewed during the day. In the heavy fire of the morning, Major Arndt, commanding 1st battalion 1st New York Artillery was mortally wounded, while directing the operations of his batteries.

It was afternoon before I could move the troops to their positions for attack, being compelled to spend the morning in reconnoitering the new position taken up by the enemy, examining the ground, finding fords and clearing their approaches, and hurrying up the ammunition and supply trains, which had been delayed by the rapid march of the troops over the few practicable approaches from Frederick. These had been crowded by the masses of infantry, cavalry and artillery, pressing on with the hope of overtaking the enemy before he could form to resist an attack, many of the troops were out of rations on the previous day, and a good deal of their ammunition had been expended in the severe action of the 14th.

My plan for the impending general engagement was to attack the enemy's left with the corps of Hooker and Mansfield, supported by Sumner's, and if necessary, Franklin's, and as soon as matters looked favorably there to move the corps of Gen. Burnside against the enemy's extreme right, upon the ridges running to the south and rear of Sharpsburg, and having carried their position to press along the crest towards our right, and whenever either of these flank movements should be successful to advance our centre with all their forces then disposable.

About 2 p.m. Gen. Hooker, with his corps consisting of Gen. Rickett's, Meade's and Doubleday's divisions, was ordered to cross the Antietam at a ford, and at bridge No. 1 a short distance above, to attack, and if possible turn the enemy's left. Gen. Sumner was ordered to cross the corps of Gen. Mansfield (the 12th) during the night, and hold his own (the 2d) corps ready to cross early the next morning. On reaching the vicinity of the enemy's left, a sharp contest commenced with the Pennsylvania Reserves, the advance of Gen. Hooker's corps, near the house of Dr. Miller. The enemy was driven from the strip of woods where he was first met, the firing lasted until after dark, when Gen. Hooker's corps rested on their arms on ground won from the enemy.

During the night Gen. Mansfield's corps, consisting of Gen's Williams's and Green's divisions, crossed the Antietam at the same ford and bridge that Gen. Hooker's corps had passed, and bivouacked on the farm of J. Poffenberger, about a mile in rear of Gen. Hooker's position. At daylight, on the 17th, the action was commenced by the skirmishers of the Pennsylvania Reserves. The whole of Gen. Hooker's corps was soon engaged, and drove the enemy from the open field in front of the first line of woods, into a second line of woods beyond, which runs to the eastward of and nearly parallel to the Sharpsburg and Hagerstown turnpike.

This contest was obstinate, and as the troops advanced the opposition became more determined and the numbers of the enemy greater. Gen. Hooker then ordered up the corps of Gen. Mansfield which moved promptly towards the scene of action. The 1st division, Gen. Williams, was deployed to the right on approaching the enemy, Gen. Crawford's brigade on the right, its right resting on the Hagerstown turnpike, on his left Gen. Gordon's brigade. The 2d division, Gen. Green's, joining the left of Gordon's, extended as far as the burnt buildings to the north and east of the white church on the turnpike. During the deployment that gallant veteran General Mansfield, fell mortally wounded while examining the ground in front of his troops. General Hartsuff, of Hooker's corps, was severely wounded while bravely pressing forward his troops, and was taken from the field.

The command of the 12th corps fell upon Gen. Williams Five regiments of the 1st division of this corps were new troops. One brigade of the 2d division was sent to support Gen Doubleday's The 124th Pennsylvania Volunteers were pushed across the turnpike into the woods beyond J Miller's house, with orders to hold the position as long as possible.

The line of battle of this corps was formed, and it became engaged at about 7 A M, the attack being opened by Knapp's Pennsylvania, Cothran's New York and Hampton's Pittsburg batteries To meet this attack the enemy had pushed a strong column of troops into the open fields in front of the turnpike, while he occupied the woods on the west of the turnpike in strong force. The woods (as was found by subsequent observation) were traversed by the out-cropping ledges of rock Several hundred yards to the right and rear was a line which commanded the debouche of the woods, and in the fields between was a long line of stone fences, continued by breastworks of rails which covered the enemy's infantry from our musketry The same woods formed a screen, behind which his movements were concealed, and his batteries on the hill and the rifle works covered from the fire of our artillery in front

For about two hours the battle raged with varied success, the enemy endeavoring to drive our troops into the second line of wood, and ours in turn to get possession of the line in front. Our troops ultimately succeeded in forcing the enemy back into the woods near the turnpike, Gen Green, with his two brigades, crossing into the woods to the left of the Dunker church During this conflict Gen Crawford, commanding 1st division after Gen Williams took command of the corps, was wounded, and left the field Gen Green, being much exposed and applying for reinforcements, the 13th New York and 27th Indiana, with the 3d Maryland, were sent to his support with a section of Knapp's battery.

At about 9 o'clock A M, Gen Sedgwick's division of Gen Sumner's corps arrived Crossing the ford previously mentioned, this division marched in three columns to the support of the attack on the enemy's left On nearing the scene of action the columns were halted, faced to the front, and established by Gen Sumner in three parallel lines by brigade, facing towards the south and west; Gen Gorman's brigade in front, Gen Dana's second, and Gen Howard's third, with a distance between the lines of some seventy paces.

The division was then put in motion, and moved upon the field of battle under fire from the enemy's concealed batteries on the hill beyond the woods, passing diagonally to the front across the open space and to the front of the 1st division of Gen Williams corps—this latter division withdrew

Entering the woods on the west of the turnpike, and driving the enemy before them the first line was met by a heavy fire of musketry and shell from the enemy's breastworks and the batteries on the hill commanding the exit from the woods Meantime a heavy column of the enemy had succeeded in crowding back the troops of Gen Green's division, and appeared in rear of the left of Sedgwick's division. By command of Gen. Sumner, Gen. Howard faced the third line to the rear, preparatory to a change of front, to meet the column advancing on the left, but this line now suffering from a destructive fire both in front and on its left, which it was unable to return, gave way towards the right and rear in considerable confusion, and was soon followed by the first and second lines

Gen Gorman's brigade, and one regiment of Gen Dana's, soon rallied and checked the advance of the enemy on the right. The second and third lines now formed on the left of Gen Gorman's brigade, and poured a destructive fire upon the enemy.

During Gen Sumner's attack he ordered Gen. Williams to support him Brig -Gen. Gordon, with a portion of his brigade, moved forward, but when he reached the woods the left of Gen Sedgwick's division had given way, and finding himself, as the smoke cleared up, opposed to the enemy in force, with his small command, he withdrew to the rear of the batteries at the second line of woods As Gen Gordon's troops unmasked our batteries on the left, they opened with canister, the batteries of Capt Cothran, 1st New York, and "I," 1st U. S. Artillery, commanded by Lieut Woodruff, doing good service. Unable to stand this deadly fire in front and the musketry fire from the right, the enemy again sought shelter in the woods and rocks beyond the turnpike

During this assault Gen's Sedgwick and Dana were seriously wounded and taken from the field. Gen Sedgwick, though twice wounded and faint from loss of blood, retained command of his division for more than an hour after his first wound, animating his command by his presence Gen Howard assumed command after Gen Sedgwick retired.

At the time of Gen Sedgwick's advance Gen Hooker, while urging on his command, was seriously wounded in the foot and taken from the field. The repulse of the enemy offered opportunity to re-arrange the lines and re-organize the commands on the right, now more or less in confusion. The batteries of the Pennsylvania Reserve, on high ground near I Poffenburger's house, opened fire and checked several attempts of the enemy to establish batteries in front of our right, to turn that flank and enfilade the lines.

While this conflict was so obstinately raging on the right, Gen French was pushing his division against the enemy still further to the left. This division crossed the Antietam at the same ford as Gen Sedgwick, and immediately in his rear Passing over the stream in three columns, the division marched about a mile from the ford, then facing to the left, moved in three lines towards the enemy. Gen Max Weber's brigade in front, Col Dwight Morris's brigade of raw troops, undrilled and moving for the first time under fire, in the second, and Gen Kimball's brigade in the third. The division was first assailed by a fire of artillery, but steadily advanced, driving the enemy's skirmishers, and encountered the infantry in some force at the group of houses on Roulette's farm. Gen Weber's brigade gallantly advanced with an unwavering front, and drove the enemy from their position about the houses.

While Gen Weber was hotly engaged with the first line of the enemy, Gen. French received orders from Gen Sumner, his corps commander, to push on with renewed vigor to make a diversion in favor of the attack on the right. Leaving the new troops who had been thrown into some confusion from their march through corn-fiels, over fences, &c to form as a reserve, he ordered the brigade of Gen Kimball to the front, passing to the left of Gen. Weber. The enemy was pressed back to near the crest of the hill, where he was encountered in greater strength, posted in a sunken road running in a north-westerly direction and forming a natural rifle-pit. In a corn-field in rear of this road were also strong bodies of the enemy. As the line reached the crest of the hill, a gallant fire was opened on it from the sunken road and corn-field. Here a terrific fire of musketry burst from both lines, and the battle raged along the whole line with great slaughter. The enemy attempted to turn the left of the line, but were met by the 7th Virginia and 132d Pennsylvania Volunteers, and repulsed.

Foiled in this, the enemy made a determined assault on the front, but was met by a charge from our lines, which drove him back with severe loss, leaving in our hands some 300 prisoners, and several stands of colors. The enemy having been repulsed by the terrible execution of the batteries and the musketry fire on the extreme right, now attempted to assist the attack on Gen French's division, by assaulting him on his right, and endeavoring to turn his flank, but this attack was met and checked by the 14th Indiana and 8th Ohio volunteers, and by canister from Capt Tomkins's battery, 1st Rhode Island artillery. Having been under an almost continuous fire for nearly four hours, and their ammunition being nearly exhausted, the division now took position immediately below the crest of the heights on which they had so gallantly fought, the enemy making no attempt to regain their lost ground.

On the left of Gen French, Gen Richardson's division was hotly engaged. Having crossed the Antietam about 9 30 A M, at the ford crossed by the other divisions of Sumner's corps, it moved on a line nearly parallel to the Antietam, and formed in a ravine behind the high grounds overlooking Roulette's house. The 3d (Irish) brigade, commanded by Gen Meagher, on the right, the 2d brigade, commanded by Gen Caldwell, on his left, and the brigade commanded by Col. Brooks, 53d Pennsylvania Volunteers, in support. As the division moved forward to take its position on the field the enemy directed a fire of artillery against it, but owing to the irregularities of the ground, did but little damage.

Meagher's brigade advancing steadily, soon became engaged with the enemy posted to the left and in front of Roulette's house. It continued to advance under a heavy fire nearly to the crest of the hill overlooking Piper's house, the enemy being posted in the continuation of the sunken road and corn-field, before retired to. Here the brave Irish brigade opened upon the enemy a terrific musketry fire. All of Gen Sumner's corps was now engaged, Gen. Sedgwick on the right, Gen French in the centre and Gen Richardson on the left. The Irish brigade sustained its well earned reputation. After suffering terribly in officers and men, and strewing the ground with their enemies as they drove them back, their ammunition nearly expended, and their commander, Gen. Meagher, disabled by the fall of his horse, shot under him, this brigade was ordered to give place to Gen Caldwell's brigade which advanced to a short distance in its rear. The lines were passed by the Irish brigade, breaking by company to the rear, and Gen Caldwell's by company to the front, as steadily as on drill. Colonel Brook's brigade now became the second line.

The ground over which Gen's Richardson's and French's divisions were fighting was very irregular, intersected by numerous ravines, hills covered with growing corn, enclosed by stone walls, behind which the enemy could advance unobserved upon any exposed point of our lines. Taking advantage of this, the enemy attempted to gain the right of Richardson's position in a corn-field, near Roulette's house, where the division had become separated from that of General French. A change of front by the 52d New York and 2d Delaware Volunteers, of Colonel Brook's brigade, under Colonel Frank, and the attack made by the 52d Pennsylvania Volunteers, sent further to right by Col Brooks to close this gap in the line, and the movement of the 152d Pennsylvania and 7th Virginia Volunteers, of Gen French's division, before referred to, drove the enemy from the corn-field, and restored the line.

The brigade of General Caldwell, with determined gallantry, pushed the enemy back opposite the left and centre of this division, but sheltered in the sunken road they still held our forces on the right of Caldwell in check. Col Barlow, commanding the 61st and 64th New York regiments, of Caldwell's brigade, seeing a favorable opportunity, advanced these regiments on the left, taking the line on the sunken road in flank, and compelled them to surrender, capturing over three hundred prisoners, and three stands of colors.

The whole of the brigade, with the 57th and 66th New York regiments of Col Brooks's brigade who had moved these regiments into the first line now advanced with gallantry, driving the enemy before them in confusion into the corn-field beyond the sunken road. The left of the division was now well advanced, when the enemy, concealed by an intervening ridge, endeavored to turn its left and rear. Col. Cross 5th N. H, by a change of front to the left and rear, brought his regiment facing the advancing line. Here a spirited contest arose to gain a commanding height—the two opposing forces, moving parallel to each other, giving and receiving fire. The 5th, gaining the advantage, faced to the right and delivered its volley. The enemy staggered, but rallied and advanced desperately at a charge. Being reinforced by the 81st Pennsylvania regiment, these regiments met the advance by a counter charge. The enemy fled, leaving many killed, wounded, and prisoners, and the colors of the 4th North Carolina in our hands.

Another column of the enemy, advancing under shelter of a stone wall and corn-field, pressed down on the right of the division, but Col. Barlow again advanced the 61st and 64th New York against these troops, and, with the attack of Kimball's brigade on the right, drove them from this position.

Our troops on the left of this part of the line, having driven the enemy far back, they, with reinforced numbers, made a determined attack directly in front. To meet this Col. Barlow brought his two regiments to their position in line, and drove the enemy through the cornfield into the orchard beyond, under a heavy fire of musketry, and a fire of canister from two pieces of artillery in the orchard and a battery further to the right, throwing shell and case-shot. This advance gave us possession of Piper's house; the strong point contended for by the enemy at this part of the line, it being a defensible building, several hundred yards in advance of the sunken road.

The musketry fire at this point of the line now ceased. Holding Piper's house, General Richardson withdrew the line a little way to the crest of a hill, a more advantageous position. Up to this time this division was without artillery, and in the new position suffered severely from artillery fire, which could not be replied to. A section of Robertson's horse battery, commanded by Lieut. Vincent, 2d U. S Artillery, now arrived on the ground, and did excellent service. Subsequently a battery of brass guns, commanded by Capt Graham, 1st U. S. Artillery, arrived, and was posted on the crest of the hill, and soon silenced the two guns in the orchard. A heavy fire soon ensued between the battery further to right and our own. Captain Graham's battery was bravely and skillfully served, but, unable to reach the enemy, who had rifled guns of greater range than our smooth bores, retired by order of Gen. Richardson, to save it from useless sacrifice of men and horses. The brave general was himself mortally wounded while personally directing its fire.

Gen Hancock was placed in command of the division after the fall of General Richardson. Gen. Meagher's brigade, now commanded by Col. Burke of the 63d New York, having refilled their cartridge boxes, was again ordered forward, and took position in the centre of the line. The division now occupied one line in close proximity to the enemy, who had taken up a position in the rear of Piper's house.

Col Dwight Morris, with the 14th Connecticut and a detachment of the 108th New York, of Gen French's division, was sent by Gen. French to the support of Richardson's division. This command was now placed in an interval in the line between Gen Caldwell's and the Irish Brigade. The requirements of the extended line of battle had so engaged the artillery that the application of General Hancock for artillery for his division could not be complied with immediately by the chief of artillery, or the corps commanders in his vicinity. Knowing the tried courage of the troops, Gen Hancock felt confident that he could hold his position, although suffering from the enemy's artillery, but was too weak to attack, as the great length of the line he was obliged to hold prevented him from forming more than one line of battle, and, from his advanced position, this line was already partly enfiladed by the batteries of the enemy on the right, which were protected from our batteries opposite them by the woods at the Dunker church.

Seeing a body of the enemy advancing on some of our troops to the left of his position, General Hancock obtained Hexamer's battery from Gen. Franklin's corps, which assisted materially in frustrating this attack. It also assisted the attack of the 7th Maine of Franklin's corps, which, without other aid, made an attack against the enemy's line and drove in skirmishers who were annoying our artillery and troops on the right. Lieut. Woodruff, with battery "I," 2d U S Artillery, relieved Capt Hexamer, whose ammunition was expended. The enemy seemed at one time to be about making an attack in force upon this part of the line, and advancing a long column of infantry towards this division, but, on nearing the position, Gen. Pleasonton opening on them with sixteen guns, they halted, gave a desultory fire, and retreated, closing the operations on this portion of the field.

To return to the incidents occurring still further to the right.

Between 12 and 1 P M, Gen. Franklin's corps arrived on the field of battle, having left their camp near Crampton's Pass at 6 A M., leaving Gen Couch with orders to move with his division to occupy Maryland heights.

Gen, Smith's division led the column, followed by General Slocum's.

It was first intended to keep this corps in reserve on the east side of the Antietam, to operate on either flank or on the centre, as circumstances might require. But, on nearing Keadysville, the strong opposition on the right, developed by the attacks of Hooker and Sumner, rendered it necessary to send this corps at once to the assistance of the right wing. On nearing the field, hearing that one of our batteries ("A," 4th U S Artillery), commanded by Lieut. Thomas, who occupied the same position as Lieut Woodruff's battery in the morning, was hotly engaged, without supports, Gen. Smith sent two regiments to its relief from Gen. Hancock's brigade. On inspecting the ground, General Smith ordered the other regiment of Hancock's brigade, with Frank's and Cowen's batteries, 1st New York Artillery, to the threatened position; Lieut Thomas and Capt. Cothran, commanding batteries, bravely held their positions against the advancing enemy, handling their batteries with skill.

Finding the enemy still advancing, the 3d brigade of Smith's division, commanded by Colonel Irwin, 49th Pennsylvania Volunteers, was ordered up, and, passing through Lieut Thomas's battery, charged upon the enemy and drove back the advance until abreast of the Dunker Church. As the right of the brigade came opposite the woods, it received a destructive fire which checked the advance and threw the brigade somewhat into confusion. It formed again behind a rise of ground in the open space in advance of the batteries. General French having reported to General Franklin that his ammunition was nearly expended, that officer ordered General Brooks, with his brigade, to reinforce him. Gen Brooks formed his brigade on the right of General French, where they remained during the remainder of the day and night, frequently under the fire of the enemy's artillery. It was soon after the brigade of Col Irwin had fallen behind the rise of ground that the 7th Maine, by order of Col. Irwin, made the gallant attack already referred to.

The advance of General Franklin's corps was opportune. The attack of the enemy on the position, but for the timely arrival of his corps, must have been disastrous, had it succeeded in piercing the line between Gen Sedgwick's and French's divisions.

Gen Franklin ordered two brigades of Gen. Slocum's division, Gen Newton's and Col Torbert's, to form in column to assault the woods that had been so hotly contested before, by Gen's Sumner and Hooker; Bartlett's brigade was ordered to form as a reserve; at this time Gen. Sumner having command on the right, directed further offensive operations to be postponed, as the repulse of this, the only remaining corps available for attack, would peril the safety of the whole army.

Gen Porter's corps, consisting of Gen Sykes's division of regulars and volunteers, occupied a position on the east side of Antietam Creek, upon the main turnpike leading to Sharpsburg, and directly opposite the centre of the enemy's line. This corps filled the interval between the right wing and Gen Burnside's command, and guarded the main approach from the enemy's position to our trains of supplies.

It was necessary to watch this part of our line with the utmost vigilance, lest the enemy should take advantage of the first exhibition of weakness here to push upon us a vigorous assault for the purpose of piercing our centre and turning our rear, as well as to capture or destroy our supply trains. Once having penetrated this line the enemy's passage to our rear could have met with but feeble resistance, as there were no reserves to reinforce or close up the gap.

Towards the middle of the afternoon, proceeding to the right, I found that Sumner's, Hooker's, and Mansfield's corps had met with serious losses. Several general officers had been carried from the field severely wounded, and the aspect of affairs was anything but promising. At the risk of greatly exposing our centre, I ordered two brigades from Porter's corps, the only available troops, to reinforce the right. Six battalions of Sykes's regulars had been thrown across the Antietam bridge on the main road, to attack and drive back the enemy's sharpshooters, who were annoying Pleasonton's horse batteries in advance of the bridge. Warren's brigade of Porter's corps was detached to hold a position on Burnside's right and rear, so that Porter was left at one time with only a portion of Sykes's division, and one small brigade of Morell's division (but little over three thousand men) to hold his important position.

Gen. Sumner expressed the most decided opinion against another attempt during that day to assault the enemy's position in front as portions of our troops were so much scattered and demoralized. In view of these circumstances, after making changes in the positions of some of the troops, I directed the different commanders to hold their positions, and, being satisfied that this could be done without the assistance of the two brigades from the centre, I countermanded the order which was in course of execution.

Gen. Slocum's division replaced a portion of Gen Sumner's troops, and positions were selected for batteries in front of the woods. The enemy opened several heavy fires of artillery on the position of our troops after this, but our batteries soon silenced them.

On the morning of the 17th Gen Pleasonton, with his cavalry division, and the horse batteries, under Captains Robertson, Tidball and Lieut Haines, of the 2d U S artillery, was ordered to advance on the turnpike towards Sharpsburg across bridge No 2, and support the left of Sumner's line. The bridge being covered by a fire of artillery and sharpshooters, cavalry skirmishers were thrown out, and Capt Tidball's battery advanced by piece, and drove off the sharpshooters with canister sufficiently to establish the batteries above mentioned, which opened on the enemy with effect. The firing was kept up for about two hours, when, the enemy's fire slackening, the batteries were relieved by Randall's and Van Reed's batteries, U S Artillery. About 3 o'clock Tidball, Robertson and Haines returned to their positions on the west of Antietam, Capt. Gibson having been placed in position on the east side to guard the approaches to the bridge. These batteries did good service, concentrating their fire on the column about to attack Gen Hancock's position, and compelling it to find shelter behind the hills in rear.

Gen Sykes's division had been in position since the 16th, exposed to the enemy's artillery and sharpshooters.

Gen Morell had come up on the 16th, and relieved Gen. Richardson on the right of Gen Sykes, and, continually under the vigilant watch of the enemy, this corps guarded a vital point.

The position of the batteries under Gen Pleasanton being one of great exposure, the battalion of the 2d and 10th United States Infantry, under Capt Dwyer, 4th U S Infantry were sent across to assist in driving off the sharpshooters of the enemy.

The battalion of the 2d and 10th U. S. Infantry advancing far beyond the batteries, compelled the cannoneers of a battery of the enemy to abandon their guns. Few in number and unsupported, they were unable to bring them off. The heavy loss of this small body of men attests their gallantry.

The troops of Gen Burnside held the left of the line opposite bridge No 3. The attack on the right was to have been supported by an attack on the left. Preparatory to this attack, on the evening of the 16th, Gen Burnside's corps was moved forward and to the left, and took up a position nearer the bridge.

I visited Gen. Burnside's position on the 16th, and after pointing out to him the proper dispositions to be made of his troops during the day and night, informed him that me would probably be required to attack the enemy's right on the following morning, and directed him to make careful reconnoissances.

Gen. Burnside's corps, consisting of the divisions of Gens. Cox, Wilcox, Rodman, and Sturgis, was posted as follows: Col. Brooks's brigade, Cox's division, on the right, Gen Sturgis's division immediately in rear. On the left was Gen Rodman's division, with Gen Scammon's brigade, Cox's division in support.

Gen. Wilcox's division was held in reserve.

The corps bivouacked in position on the right of the 16th.

Early on the morning of the 17th, I ordered Gen. Burnside to form his troops, and hold them in readiness to assault the bridge in his front, and to await further orders.

At eight o'clock an order was sent to him by Lieutenant Wilson, Topographical Eengineers to carry the bridge, then to gain possession of the heights beyond, and to advance along their crest upon Sharpsburg and its rear.

After some time had elapsed, not hearing from him, I despatched an aid to ascertain what had been done. The aid returned with the information that but little progress had been made. I then sent him back with an order to Gen Burnside, to assault the bridge at once, and carry it at all hazards. The aide returned to me a second time, with the report that the bridge was still in the possession of the enemy. Whereupon I directed Col. Sackett, Inspector General, to deliver to Gen Burnside my positive order to push forward his troops without a moment's delay, and, if necessary, to carry the bridge at the point of the bayonet, and I ordered Col. Sackett to remain with Gen. Burnside and see that the order was executed promptly.

After these three hours' delay, the bridge was carried at 1 o'clock by a brilliant charge of the 51st New York and 51st Pennsylvania Volunteers. Other troops were then thrown over and the opposite bank occupied, the enemy retreating to the heights beyond.

A halt was then made by Gen Burnside's advance until 3 P M, upon hearing which I directed one of my aides—Col. Key—to inform Gen. Burnside that I desired him to push forward his troops with the utmost vigor and carry the enemy's position on the heights; that the movement was vital to our success; that this was a time when we must not stop for loss of life if a great object could be thereby accomplished. That if, in his judgment, his attack would fail, to inform me so at once, that his troops might be withdrawn and used elsewhere on the field. He replied that he would soon advance, and would go up the hill as far as a battery of the enemy on the left would permit. Upon this report I again immediately sent Col. Key to Gen. Burnside, with orders to advance at once, if possible, to flank the battery or storm it and carry the heights, repeating that if he considered the movement impracticable to inform me so, that his troops might be recalled. The advance was then gallantly resumed, the enemy driven from their guns, the heights handsomely carried, and a portion of the troops even reached the outskirts of Sharpsburg. By this time it was nearly dark, and strong reinforcements just then reaching the enemy from Harper's Ferry attacked Gen Burnside's troops on their left flank and forced them to retire to a lower line of hills nearer the bridge.

If this important movement had been consummated two hours earlier, a position would have been secured upon the heights from which our batteries might have enfiladed the greater part of the enemy s line, and turned their right and rear. Our victory might have been much more decisive.

The following is the substance of Gen. Burnside's operations, as given in his report:

Col Crook's brigade was ordered to storm the bridge. This bridge, No 3, is a stone structure of three arches, with stone parapets. The banks of the stream on the opposite side are precipitous, and command the eastern approaches to the bridge. On the hill side immediately by the bridge was a stone fence running parallel to the stream, the turns of the roadway as it wound up the hill were covered by rifle pits and breastworks of rails, &c. These works and the woods that covered the slopes were filled with the enemy's riflemen, and batteries were in position to enfilade the bridge and its approaches.

Gen Rodman was ordered to cross the ford below the bridge. From Col. Crook's position it was found impossible to carry the bridge.

Gen Sturgis was ordered to make a detail from his division for that purpose. He sent forward the 2d Maryland and 6th New Hampshire. These regiments made several successive attacks in the most gallant style, but were driven back.

The artillery of the left were ordered to concentrate their fire on the woods above the bridge. Col Crook brought a section of Capt Simmon's battery to a position to command the bridge. The 51st New York, and 51st Pennsylvania, were then ordered to assault the bridge. Taking advantage of a small spur of the hills which ran parallel to the river, they moved towards the bridge. From the crest of this spur they rushed, with bayonet fixed, and cleared the bridge.

The division followed the storming party, also the brigade of Col Crook, as support. The enemy withdrew to still higher ground, some five or six hundred yards beyond, and opened a fire of artillery on the troops in the new positions on the crest of the hill above the bridge.

Gen. Rodman's division succeeded in crossing the ford, after a sharp fire of musketry and artillery, and joined on the left of Sturgis; Scammon's brigade crossing as support. Gen Wilcox's division was ordered across to take position on Gen. Sturgis's right.

These dispositions being completed about 3 o'clock, the command moved forward, except Sturgis's division left in reserve. Clark's and Darrell's batteries accompanied Rodman's division; Cook's battery with Wilcox's division, and a section of Simmons's battery with Crook's brigade. A section of Simmon's battery, and Mullenburgh's and McMullin's batteries were in position. The order for the advance was obeyed by the troops with alacrity. Gen Wilcox's division, with Crook in support, moved up on both sides of the turnpike leading from the bridge to Sharpsburg. Gen Rodman's division, supported by Scammon's brigade on the left of Gen Wilcox. The enemy retreated before the advance of the troops. The 9th New York, of Gen Rodman's division, captured one of the enemy's batteries, and held it for some time. As the command was driving the enemy to the main heights on the left of the town, the light division of Gen A P. Hill arrived upon the field of battle from Harper's Ferry, and with a heavy artillery fire made a strong attack on the extreme left. To meet this attack, the left division diverged from the line of march intended, and opened a gap between it and the right. To fill up this, it was necessary to order the troops from the second line. During these movements, Gen Rodman was mortally wounded. Col. Harland's brigade, of Gen Rodman's division, was driven back. Col Scammon's brigade, by a change of front to rear on his right flank, saved the left from being driven completely in. The fresh troops of the enemy pouring in, and the accumulation of artillery against this command, destroyed all hope of its being able to accomplish anything more.

It was now nearly dark. Gen Sturgis was ordered forward to support the left. Notwithstanding the hard work in the early part of the day, his division moved forward with spirit. With its assistance, the enemy were checked and held at bay.

The command was ordered to fall back by Gen Cox, who commanded, on the field, the troops engaged in this attack beyond the Antietam. The artillery had been well served during the day. Night closed the long and desperately contested battle of the 17th. Nearly 200,000 men, and 500 pieces of artillery, were for fourteen hours engaged in this memorable battle. We had attacked the enemy in a position selected by the experienced engineer then in person directing their operations. We had driven them from their line on one flank, and secured a footing within it on the other. The army of the Potomac, notwithstanding the moral effect incident to previous reverses, had achieved a victory over an adversary invested with the prestige of recent success. Our soldiers slept that night, conquerors, on a field won by their valor, and covered with the dead and wounded of the enemy.

CONDITION OF THE ARMY AFTER ANTIETAM.

The night, however, brought with it grave responsibilities. Whether to renew the attack on the 18th, or to defer it, even with the risk of the enemy's retirement, was the question before me. After a night of anxious deliberation, and a full and careful survey of the situation and condition of our army and the strength and position of the enemy, I concluded that the success of an attack on the 18th was not certain. I am aware of the fact, that under ordinary circumstances, a general is expected to risk a battle if he has a reasonable prospect of success; but at this critical juncture, I should have had a narrow view of the condition of the country, had I been willing to hazard another battle with less than an absolute assurance of success. At that moment—Virginia lost, Washington menaced, Maryland invaded—the national cause could afford no risks of defeat. One battle lost, and almost all would have been lost. Lee's army might then have marched as it pleased on Washington, Baltimore, Philadelphia, or New York. It could have levied its supplies from a fertile and undevastated country, extorted tribute from wealthy and populous cities, and nowhere east of the Alleghanies, was there an other organized force able to arrest its march.

The following are among the considerations which led me to doubt the certainty of success in attacking before the 19th.

The troops were greatly overcome by the fatigue and exhaustion attendant upon the long continued and severely contested battle of the 17th, together with the long day and night marches to which they had been subjected during the previous three days.

The supply trains were in the rear, and many of the troops had suffered from hunger. They required rest and refreshment.

One division of Sumner's, and all of Hooker's corps, on the right, had, after fighting most valiantly for several hours, been overpowered by numbers, driven back in great disorder, and much scattered; so that they were for the time somewhat demoralized.

In Hooker's corps, according to the return made by Gen Meade, commanding, there were but 6729 men present on the 18th, whereas, on the morning of the 22d, there were 13,093 men present for duty in the same corps, showing that previous to, and during the battle, 6364 men were separated from their command.

Gen Meade, in an official communication upon this subject, dated Sept 18, 1862, says: "I enclose a field return of the corps made this afternoon, which I desire you will lay before the commanding-general. I am satisfied the great reduction in the corps since the recent engagements, is not due solely to the casualties of battle, and that a considerable number of men are still in the rear, some having dropped out on the march, and many dispersing and leaving yesterday during the fight. I think the efficiency of the corps, so far as it goes good. To resist an attack in our present strong position, I think they may be depended on; and I hope they will perform duty in case we make an attack, though I do not think their morale is as good for an offensive as a defensive movement."

One division of Sumner's Corps had also been overpowered, and was a good deal scattered and demoralized. It was not deemed by its corps commander, in proper condition to attack the enemy vigorously the next day.

Some of the new troops on the left, although many of them fought well during a part of the battle, and are entitled to great credit, were, at the close of the action, driven back and then morale impaired

On the morning of the 18th, Gen Burnside requested me to send him another division to assist in holding his position on the other side of the Antietam, and to enable him to withdraw his corps if he should be attacked by a superior force He gave me the impression that if he were attacked again that morning, he would not be able to make a very vigorous resistance I visited his position early determined to send General Morell's division to his aid, and directed that it should be placed on this side of the Antietam, in order that it might cover the retreat of his own corps from the other side of the Antietam, should that become necessary, at the same time it was in position to reinforce our centre or right, if that were needed Late in the afternoon, I found that although he had not been attacked, General Burnside had withdrawn his own corps to this side of the Antietam and sent over Morell's division alone to hold the opposite side

A large number of our heaviest and most efficient batteries had consumed all their ammunition on the 16th and 17th, and it was impossible to supply them until late on the following day

Supplies of provision and forage had to be brought up and issued, and infantry ammunition distributed

Finally, reinforcements to the number of 14,000 men to say nothing of troops from Pennsylvania, had not arrived, but were expected during the day

The 18th was therefore spent in collecting the dispersed giving rest to the fatigued, removing the wounded, burying the dead, and the necessary preparations for a renewal of the battle

Of the reinforcements, Couch's division, marching with commendable rapidity, came up into position at a late hour in the morning. Humphrey's division of new troops, in their anxiety to participate in the battle, which was raging when they received the order to march from Frederick, at about half past 3 P M on the 17th, pressed forward during the entire night, and the mass of the division reached the army on the following morning. Having marched more than twenty-three miles after 4 1-2 o'clock on the preceding afternoon, they were of course greatly exhausted and needed rest and refreshment Large reinforcements expected from Pennsylvania never arrived

During the 18th, orders were given for a renewal of the attack at daylight on the 19th.

On the night of the 18th, the enemy after passing troops in the latter part of the day from the Virginia shore, to their position behind Sharpsburg, as seen by our officers, suddenly formed the design of abandoning their position and retreating across the river

As their line was but a short distance from the river, the evacuation presented but little difficulty, and was effected before daylight.

About 2,700 of the enemy's dead were, under the direction of Major Davis, assistant-inspector-general, counted and buried upon the battle-field of Antietam A portion of their dead had been previously buried by the enemy This is conclusive evidence that the enemy sustained much greater loss than we

Thirteen guns, thirty-nine colors, upwards of fifteen thousand stand of small arms, and more than six thousand prisoners, were the trophies which attest the success of our arms in the battles of South Mountain, Crampton's Gap, and Antietam.

Not a single gun or color was lost by our army during these battles

Tabular Report of Casualties in the Army of the Potomac in the Battle of Antietam, on the 16th and 17th of September, 1862.

	General Officers Killed	General Officers Wound'd	Other Officers Killed	Other Officers Wound'd	Enlisted Men Killed	Enlisted Men Wound'd	Enlisted Men Missing	Aggregate Killed	Aggregate Wound'd	Aggregate Missing	Grand Aggreg
1st Corps. MAJ-GEN HOOKER											
1st Division								98	669	95	862
2d Division								153	898	137	1188
3d Division								97	449	23	569
Total								348	2016	255	2619
2d Corps. MAJ GEN SUMNER											
1st Division	1		20	39	92	860	24	212	900	24	1136
2d Division	2				355	1577	321	355	1579	321	2255
3d Division	1		21	50	272	1271	203	293	1322	203	1818
Total	4		41	89	819	3708	548	860	3801	548	5209
5th Corps. MAJ-GEN. F. J. PORTER											
1st Division											
2d Division											
3d Division				2	13	92	1	13	94	1	108
Artillery Reserve			1		7	13	1	8	13	1	22
Total			1	2	20	105	2	21	107	2	130
5th Corps MAJ-GEN FRANKLIN											
1st Division								5	58	2	65
2d Division								65	277	31	373
Total								70	335	33	438
9th Corps MAJ-GEN. BURNSIDE											
1st Division			2	20	44	261	7	46	281	7	337
2d Division			7	29	121	493	20	128	522	20	670
3d Division			8	40	212	743	70	220	783	70	1073
4th Division			5	7	33	145	23	38	152	23	213
Total			22		410	1645	120	432	1741	120	2293
12th Corps (GEN BANKS') BRIG-GEN WILLIAMS, Com'g											
1st Division			9	35	151	827	54	160	862	54	1076
2d Division			6	26	107	481	30	113	507	30	650
Artillery					1	15	1	1	15	1	17
Total			15	61	259	1323	85	274	1384	85	1743
MAJ-GEN COUCH'S Division				1		8			9		9
BRIG-GEN PLEASONTON'S Cavalry Division								5	23		28
Grand Total								2010	9416	1043	12469

Head-Quarters Army of the Potomac,
Camp near Sharpsburg, Sept 29, 1862
Official   S W., Assistant Adj't Gen

An estimate of the forces under the confederate General Lee, made up by direction of Gen. Banks from information obtained by the examination of prisoners, deserters, spies, &c, previous to the battle of Antietam, is as follows

Gen. T. J. Jackson's Corps, -------- 24,778 Men
" James Longstreet's Corps, ---- 23,342 "
" D H Hill's 2 Divisions, ----- 15,525 "
" J. E. B Stuart's Cavalry, ----- 6,400 "
" Ransom's and Jenkins's Brigades, 3,000 "
Forty-six Reg'ts not includ'd in above, 18,400 "
Artillery, estimated at 400 guns, --- 6,000 "

        Total, -------- 97,445 "

These estimates give the actual numbers of men preset and fit for duty.

Our own forces at the battle of Antietam were as follows

1st Corps, ------------ 14,856 Men
2nd Corps, ------------ 18,813 "
5th Corps, (one division not ar'd,) 12,930 "
6th Corps, ------------ 12,300 "
9th Corps, ------------ 13,819 "
12th Corps, ----------- 10,126 "
Cavalry Division, ------- 4,320 "

    Total in action, ---- 87,164 "

OPERATIONS AFTER ANTIETAM

When our cavalry advance reached the river on the morning of the 19th, it was discovered that nearly all the enemy's forces had crossed into Virginia during the night, their rear escaping under the cover of eight batteries, placed in strong positions upon the elevated bluffs on the opposite bank

General Porter, commanding the 5th Corps, ordered a detachment from Griffin's and Barnes's brigades, under General Griffin, to cross the river at dark and carry the enemy's batteries This was gallantly done under the fire of the enemy. Several guns, caissons etc, were taken, and their supports driven back half a mile.

The information obtained during the progress of this affair, indicated that the mass of the enemy had retreated on the Charlestown and Martinsburg roads towards Winchester To verify this, and to ascertain how far the enemy had retreated, General Porter was authorized to detach from his corps on the morning of the 20th, a reconnoitering party in greater force This detachment crossed the river, and advanced about a mile, when it was attacked by a large body of the enemy lying in ambush in the woods, and driven back across the river with considerable loss. This reconnoisance showed that the enemy was still in force on the Virginia bank of the Potomac, prepared to resist our further advance

It was reported to me on the 19th that General Stuart had made his appearance at Williamsport with some four thousand cavalry and six pieces of artillery, and that ten thousand infantry were marching on the same point from the direction of Winchester. I ordered General Couch to march at once with his division, and a part of Pleasanton's cavalry with Franklin's corps within supporting distance, for the purpose of endeavoring to capture this force General Couch made a prompt and rapid march to Williamsport, and attacked the enemy vigorously, but they made their escape across the river

I dispatched the following telegraphic report to the general-in-chief.

Headq's, Army of the Potomac, Sharpsburg, Sept 19 1862

Maj.-Gen. H W Halleck, Comd'g. U S. Army,— I have the honor to report that Maryland is entirely freed from the presence of the enemy, who has been driven across the Potomac No fears need now be entertained for the safety of Pennsylvania. I shall at once occupy Harper's Ferry.

G B McClellan, Maj.-Gen Comd'g

On the following day I received this telegram:

Washington, Sept 20, 1862   2 P.M

Maj.-Gen G B McC,— We are still left entirely in the dark in regard to your own movements and those of the enemy. This should not be so You should keep me advised of both, so far as you know them   H W. Halleck Gen.-in-Chief

To which I answered as follows:

Headq's, Army of the Potomac, near Sharpsburg, Sept 20, 1862   8 1 M.

Maj.-Gen Halleck, Gen.-in-Chief, Washington Your telegram of to-day is received. I telegraphed you yesterday all I knew, and had nothing more to inform you of until this evening. Williams's corps (Banks's) occupied Maryland Heights at 1 P M to-day The rest of the army is near here, except Couch's division, which is at this moment engaged with the enemy in front of Williamsport The enemy is retiring via Charlestown and Martinsburg on Winchester He last night re-occupied Williamsport by a small force, but will be out of it by morning I think he has a force of infantry near Sharpstown.

I regret that you find it necessary to couch every dispatch I have the honor to receive from you, in a spirit of fault-finding, and that you have not yet found leisure to say one word in commendation of the recent achievements of this army, or even to allude to them

I have abstained from giving the number of guns, colors, small arms, prisoners, &c, captured, until I could do so with some accuracy. I hope by to-morrow evening to be able to give at least an approximate statement

G B McClellan Maj.-Gen Comd'g.

On the same day I telegraphed as follows

Headq's, Army of the Potomac Sept 20, 1862

Maj.-Gen. H W. Halleck, Comd'g U S Army As the rebel army, now on the Virginia side of the Potomac, must in a great measure be dependent for supplies of ammunition and provisions upon Richmond, I would respectfully suggest that General Banks be directed to send out a cavalry force to cut their supply communications opposite Washington This would seriously embarrass their operations and will aid this army materially

G B McClellan, Maj.-Gen Comd'g

Maryland Heights were occupied by Gen Williams's corps on this day, and on the 22d Gen. Sumner took possession of Harper's Ferry

It will be remembered that at the time I was assigned to the command of the forces for the defense of the national capital, on the 2d day of September, 1862, the greater part of all the available troops were suffering under the disheartening influences of the serious defeat they had encountered during the brief and unfortunate campaign of General Pope. Their numbers were greatly reduced by casualties—their confidence was much shaken and they had lost something of that *esprit-du-corps* which is indispensable to the efficiency of an army. Moreover they had left behind, lost, or worn out the greater part of their clothing and camp equipage, which required renewal before they could be in proper condition to take the field again.

The intelligence that the enemy was crossing the Potomac into Maryland, was received in Washington on the 4th of September, and the Army of the Potomac was again put in motion, under my direction, on the following day—so that but a very brief interval of time was allowed to reorganize, or procure supplies.

The sanguinary battles of South Mountain and Antietam, fought by this Army a few days afterwards, with the reconnoissances immediately following, resulted in a loss to us of ten general officers, many regimental and company officers, and a large number of enlisted men, amounting in the aggregate to 15,220. Two army corps had been badly cut up, scattered and somewhat demoralized in the action of the 17th.

In Gen Sumner's corps alone, 41 commissioned officers and 819 enlisted men had been killed. 4 general officers, 89 other commissioned officers, and 3,708 enlisted men had been wounded, besides 548 missing, making the aggregate loss of this splendid veteran corps, in this one battle, 5,209.

In Gen Hooker's corps the casualties of the same engagement amounted to 2619.

The entire army had been greatly exhausted by unavoidable overwork fatiguing marches, hunger, and want of sleep and rest, previous to the last battle.

When the enemy recrossed the Potomac into Virginia, the means of transportation at my disposal were inadequate to furnish a single day's supply of subsistence in advance.

Many of the troops were new levies, some of whom had fought like veterans, but the morale of others had been a good deal impaired in those severely contested actions, and they required time to recover, as well as to acquire the necessary drill and discipline.

Under these circumstances, I did not feel authorized to cross the river with the main army, over a very deep and difficult ford in pursuit of the retreating enemy, known to be in strong force on the south bank, and thereby place that stream, which was liable at any time to rise above a fording stage, between my army and its base of supply.

I telegraphed on the 22d to the General-in-chief as follows:

"As soon as the exigencies of the service will admit of it, this army should be reorganized. It is absolutely necessary to secure its efficiency, that the old skeleton regiments should be filled up at once, and officers appointed to supply the numerous existing vacancies. There are instances where captains are commanding regiments, and companies are without a single commissioned officer."

On the 23d, the following was telegraphed to the General-in-chief:

Headq's, Army of the Potomac, Near Shepherdstown, Sept 23, 1862 9.30 A M.

Maj.-Gen H W Halleck, Gen-in-Chief, Wash'n.

From several different sources, I learn that Gen. R E Lee is still opposite to my position at Leestown between Shepherdstown and Martinsburg, and that Gen Jackson is on the Opequan Creek, about three miles from its mouth, both with large force. There are also indications of heavy reinforcements moving towards them from Winchester and Charlestown. I have therefore ordered Gen Franklin to take position with his corps at the cross roads, about one mile northwest of Bakersville, on the Bakersville and Williamport road and Gen Couch to establish his division near Downsville, leaving sufficient force at Williamsport to watch and guard the ford at that place. The fact of the enemy remaining so long in our front, and the indications of an advance of reinforcements, seem to indicate that he will give us another battle with all his available force.

As I mentioned to you before, our army has been very much reduced by casualties in the recent battles, and in my judgment all the reinforcements of old troops that can possibly be dispensed with around Washington and other places, should be instantly pushed forward by rail to this army. A defeat at this juncture would be ruinous to our cause. I cannot think it possible that the enemy will bring any forces to bear upon Washington till after the question is decided here, but if they should, troops can soon be sent back from this army by rail to reinforce the garrison there.

The evidence that I have that reinforcements are coming to the rebel army, consists in the facts, that long columns of dust extending from Winchester to Charlestown, and from Charlestown in this direction, and also troops moving this way, were seen last evening. This is corroborated by citizens. Gen Sumner, with his corps and Williams's (Banks's), occupies Harper's Ferry, and the surrounding heights. I think he will be able to hold his position until reinforcements arrive.

G B McClellan, Maj-Gen

On the 27th I made the following report:

Headq's, Army of the Potomac, Sept 27, 1862. 10 A.M'

Maj.-Gen Halleck, Gen-in-Chief, Washington—

All the information in my possession, goes to prove that the main body of the enemy is concentrated not far from Martinsburg, with some troops at Charlestown, not many in Winchester. Their movements of late, have been an extension towards our right, and beyond it. They are receiving reinforcements in Winchester, mainly, I think, of conscripts, perhaps entirely so.

This army is not now in condition to undertake another campaign, nor to bring on another battle, unless great advantages are offered by some mistake of the enemy, or pressing military exigencies render it necessary. We are greatly deficient in officers. Many of the old regiments are reduced to mere skeletons, the new regiments need in struction. Not a day should be lost in filling the old regiments—our main dependence, and in supplying vacancies among the officers by promotion.

My present purpose is to hold the army about as it is now, rendering Harper's Ferry secure, and watching the river closely, intending to attack the enemy should he attempt to cross to this side

Our possession of Harper's Ferry gives us the great advantage of a secure debouche, but we cannot avail ourselves of it until the railroad bridge is finished, because we cannot otherwise supply a greater number of troops than we now have on the Virginia side at that point When the river rises so that the enemy cannot cross in force I purpose concentrating the army somewhere near Harper's Ferry and there acting according to circumstances, viz, moving on Winchester, if from the position and attitude of the enemy, we are likely to gain a great advantage by doing so, or else devoting a reasonable time to the organization of the army instruction of the new troops, preparatory to an advance on whatever line may be determined. In any event I regard it as absolutely necessary to send new regiments at once to the old corps, for purposes of instruction, and that the old regiments be filled at once. I have no fears as to an attack on Washington by the line of Manassas. Holding Harper's Ferry as I do, they will not run the risk of an attack on their flank and rear, while they have the garrison of Washington in their front

I rather apprehend a renewal of the attempt on Maryland, should the river remain low for a great length of time, and should they receive considerable addition to their force

I would be glad to have Peck's division as soon as possible I am surprised that Sigel's men should have been sent to Western Virginia, without my knowledge. The last I heard from you on the subject, was, that they were at my disposition. In the last battles, the enemy was undoubtedly greatly superior to us in number and it was only by very hare fighting that we gained the advantages we did. As it was the result at one period was very doubtful and we had all we could to win the day. If the enemy receives considerable reinforcements, and we none, it is possible that I may have too much on my hands in the next battle.

My own view of the proper policy to be pursued, is, to retain in Washington merely the force necessary to garrison it, and to send everything else available to reinforce this army The railways give us the means of promptly reinforcing Washington, should it become necessary, If I am reinforced as I ask, and am allowed to take my owe course, I will hold myself responsible for the city of Washington. Several persons, recently from Richmond, say that there are no troops there except conscripts, and they few in number

I hope to be able to give you details as to late battles by this evening I am about starting again for Harper's Ferry,

G. B. McCLELLAN, Maj-Gen Comd'g

REORGANIZATION AND SUPPLIES

The work of reorganizing, drilling, and supplying the army I began at the earliest moment The different corps were stationed along the river in the best positions to cover and guard the fords The great extent of the river front, from near Washington to Cumberland, (some one hundred and fifty miles), together with the line of the Baltimore and Ohio Railroad was to be carefully watched and guarded, to prevent if possible, the enemy's raids Reconnoissances upon the Virginia side of the river, for the purpose of learning the enemy's positions and movements, were made frequently, so that our cavalry, which, from the time we left Washington, had performed the most laborious service, and had from the commencement been deficient in numbers, was found totally inadequate to the requirements of the army.

This overwork had broken down the greater part of the horses, disease had appeared among them, and but a very small portion of our original cavalry force was fit for service

To such an extent had this arm become reduced that when Gen Stuart made his raid into Pennsylvania, on the 12th of October with 2,000 men, I could only mount 800 men to follow him

Harper's Ferry was occupied on the 22d, and in order to prevent a catastrophe similar to the one which had happened to Col. Miles, I immediately ordered Maryland, Bolivar, and London Heights to be strongly fortified This was done as far as the time and means at our disposal permitted.

The main army of the enemy during this time remained in the vicinity of Martinsburg and Bunker Hill, and occupied itself in drafting and coercing every able-bodied citizen into the ranks, forcibly taking their property where it was not voluntarily offered, burning bridges, and destroying railroads.

On the first day of October, His Excellency the President, honored the army of the Potomac with a visit, and remained several days, during which he went through the different encampments, reviewed the troops, and went over the battle-fields of South Mountain and Antietam. I had the opportunity during this visit to describe to him the operations of the army since the time it left Washington, and gave him my reasons for not following the enemy after he crossed the Potomac.

On the 5th of October the division of General Cox (about 5,000 men,) was ordered from my command to Western Virginia.

On the 7th of October I received the following telegram:

Washington, D C., Oct. 6, 1862

Maj-Gen McClellan:—I am instructed to telegraph you as follows: The President directs that you cross the Potomac and give battle to the enemy, or drive him south Your army must move now, while the roads are good. If you cross the river between the enemy and Washington, and cover the latter by your operations, you can be reinforced with 30,000 men If you move up the valley of the Shenandoah, not more than 12 000 or 15,000 can be sent to you. The President advises the interior line between Washington and the enemy, but does not order it He is very desirous that your army move as soon as possible. You will immediately report what line you adopt, and when you intend to cross the river Also, to what point the reinforcements are to be sent. It is necessary that the plan of your operations be positively determined on before orders are given for building bridges and repairing railroads I am directed to add, that the Secretary of War and the General-in-chief fully concur with the President in these instructions

H W H., General-in-Chief

At this time Gen Averell, with the greater part of our efficient cavalry, was in the vicinity of Cumberland, and Gen Kelly, the commanding officer, had that day reported that a large force of the enemy was advancing on Col. Campbell at St John's Run. This obliged me to order Gen Averill to proceed with his force to the support of Col Campbell, which delayed his return to the army for several days.

On the 10th of October Stuart crossed the river at McCoy's Ferry, with 2,000 cavalry and a battery of horse artillery, on his raid into Maryland and Pennsylvania, making it necessary to use all our cavalry against him. This exhausting service completely broke down nearly all of our cavalry horses, and rendered a remount absolutely indispensable, before we could advance on the enemy.

The following were the dispositions of troops made by me to defeat the purposes of this raid

Gen Averell, then at Green Spring, on the Upper Potomac, was ordered to move rapidly down upon the north side of the river, with all his disposable cavalry, using every exertion to get upon the trail of the enemy and follow it up vigorously.

Gen Pleasonton, with the remaining cavalry force, was ordered to take the road by Cavetown, Harmon's Gap, and Mechanicsville, and cut off the retreat of the enemy, should he make for any of the fords below the position of the main army His orders were to pursue them with the utmost rapidity, not to spare his men or horses, and to destroy or capture them if possible.

Gen Crook, at that time commanding Cox's division at Hancock, en route for Western Virginia, was ordered to halt, place his men in cars, and remain in readiness to move to any point above, should the enemy return in that direction, keeping his scouts well out on all the roads leading from the direction of Chambersburg to the Upper Potomac.

The other commanders between Hancock and Harper's Ferry were instructed to keep a vigilant watch upon all the roads and fords so as to prevent the escape of the rebels within these limits

Gen Burnside was ordered to send two brigades to the Monocacy crossing, there to remain in cars, with steam up, ready to move to any point on the railroad to which Stuart might be aiming. While Col. Rush, at Frederick, was directed to keep his lancers scouting on the approaches from Chambersburg, so as to give timely notice to the commander of the two brigades at the Monocacy crossing

Gen Stoneman, whose head-quarters were then at Poolesville, occupying with his division the different fords on the river below the mouth of the Monocacy was directed to keep his cavalry well out on the approaches from the direction of Frederick, so as to give him time to mass his troops at any point where the enemy might attempt to cross the Potomac in his vicinity. He was informed of Gen Pleasonton's movements.

After the orders were given for covering all the fords upon the river, I did not think it possible for Stuart to recross, and I believed that the capture or destruction of his entire force was perfectly certain, but owing to the fact that my orders were not in all cases carried out as I expected, he effected his escape into Virginia without much loss

The troops sent by Gen. Burnside to the Monocacy, owing to some neglect in not giving the necessary orders to the commander, instead of remaining at the railroad crossing as I directed, marched four miles into Frederick, and there remained until after Stuart had passed the railroad only six miles below, near which point it was said he halted for breakfast.

Gen. Pleasonton ascertained, after his arrival at Mechanicstown, that the enemy were only about an hour ahead of him, beating a hasty retreat towards the mouth of the Monocacy. He pushed on vigorously, and near to its mouth overtook them with a part of his force, having marched seventy-eight miles in twenty-four hours, and having left many of his horses broken down upon the road He at once attacked with his artillery, and the firing continued for several hours, during which time, he states that he received the support of a small portion of Gen. Stoneman's command, not sufficient to inflict any material damage upon the enemy.

Gen. Stoneman reports, that in accordance with his instructions, he gave all necessary orders for intercepting the return of the rebels, and Col. Staples, commanding one of the brigades, states that he sent two regiments of infantry to the mouth of the Monocacy, and one regiment to White's Ford That on the morning of the 12th, about 10 o'clock he, by Gen. Stoneman's order, marched the remaining three regiments of his command from Poolesville towards the mouth of the Monocacy; that before getting into action, he was relieved by Gen Ward, who states that he reported to Gen Pleasonton with his command while the enemy was crossing the river, and was informed by him (Gen Pleasonton) that he was too late, and that nothing could be done then

Gen. Pleasonton, in his report of this affair, says

"It was at this time that Col Ward reported to me from Gen. Stoneman's division, with a brigade of infantry, a regiment of cavalry, and a section of artillery. I told him that his command could be of no use, as the enemy had then crossed the river. These are the only troops that I knew of, that were in that vicinity, and this was the first intimation that I received that any troops were endeavoring to assist me in capturing the rebels. I succeeded in preventing the enemy from crossing at the mouth of the Monocacy, and drove him to White's Ford, three miles below. Had White's Ford been occupied by any force of ours previous to the time of the occupation by the enemy, the capture of Stuart's whole force would have been certain and inevitable, but with my small force, which did not exceed one-fourth of the enemy's it was not practicable for me to occupy that ford, while the enemy was in front."

It would seem from the report of Gen. Stoneman, that the disposition he made of his troops previous to the arrival of Stuart was a good one. He stationed two regiments at the mouth of the Monocacy, and two regiments at White's Ford, the latter in the very place where the crossing was made, and the former only three miles off, with a reserve of three regiments at Poolesville, some six miles distant. Gen Pleasonton's report shows that from the time the firing commenced, until the enemy were across the river, was about four and a-half hours. Gen Stoneman states, that he started the reserve from Poolesville at about 9 o'clock, but it appears from the report of Gen Pleasonton, that it did not reach him till half-past one.

At the time I received the order of October 6th to cross the river and attack the enemy, the army was wholly deficient in cavalry, and a large part of our troops were in want of shoes, blankets, and other indispensable articles of clothing, notwithstanding all the efforts that had been made since the battle of Antietam, and even prior to that date, to refit the army with clothing as well as horses. I at once consulted with Col Ingalls, the chief quartermaster, who believed that the necessary articles could be supplied in about three days. Orders were immediately issued to the different commanders who had not already sent in their requisitions, to do so at once, and all the necessary steps were forthwith taken by me to insure a prompt delivery of the supplies. The requisitions were forwarded to the proper department at Washington, and I expected that the articles would reach our depots during the three days specified; but day after day elapsed, and only a small portion of the clothing arrived. Corps commanders, upon receiving notice from the quartermasters that they might expect to receive their supplies at certain dates sent their trains for them, which after waiting, were compelled to return empty. Several instances occurred where these trains went back and forth, from the camp to the depots, as often as four or five different times, without receiving their supplies, and I was informed by one corps commander, that his wagon train had travelled over 150 miles, to and from the depots, before he succeeded in obtaining his clothing.

The corps of Gen. Franklin did not get its clothing until after it had crossed the Potomac, and was moving into Virginia.

Gen Reynold's corps was delayed a day at Berlin to complete its supplies, and Gen Porter only completed his on reaching the vicinity of Harper's Ferry.

I made every exertion in my power, and my quartermaster did the same, to have these supplies hurried forward rapidly, and I was repeatedly told that they had filled the requisitions at Washington, and that the supplies had been forwarded. But they did not come to us, and of course were inaccessible to the army. I did not fail to make frequent representations of this condition of things to the General-in chief, and it appears that he referred the matter to the quartermaster-general, who constantly replied that the supplies had been promptly ordered notwithstanding this they did not reach our depots

The following extracts are from telegrams upon this subject.

Headquarters, Army of the Potomac, October 11, 1862

Maj-Gen Halleck, General-in-Chief, Washington:

"We have been making every effort to get supplies of clothing for this army, and Col Ingalls has received advices that it has been forwarded by railroad, but owing to bad management on the roads, or from some other cause, it comes in very slowly, and it will take a much longer time than was anticipated, to get articles that are absolutely indispensable to the army, unless the railroad managers forward supplies more rapidly"
G. B. McC Maj-Gen.

Headquarters Army of the Potomac, October 11, 1862

Maj-Gen H W. H.—"I am compelled again to call your attention to the great deficiency of shoes and other indispensable articles of clothing that still exist in some of the corps of this army. Upon the assurances of the chief quartermaster, who based his calculations upon information received from Washington that clothing would be forwarded at certain times, corps commanders sent their wagons to Hagerstown and Harper's Ferry for it. It did not arrive as promised, and has not yet arrived. Unless some measures are taken to insure the prompt forwarding of these supplies, there will necessarily be a corresponding delay in getting the army ready to move, as the men cannot march without shoes.

"Every thing has been done that can be done at these headquarters, to accomplish the desired results"
Geo B McC, Maj-Gen. Comd'g.

Headquarters, Army of the Potomac October 15, 7 30 P M, 1862

Maj-Gen H. W H, Gen-in-Chief. "I am using every possible exertion to get this army ready to move. It was only yesterday that a part of our shoes and clothing arrived at Hagerstown. It is being issued to the troops as rapidly as possible.'

Headquarters, Army of the Potomac October 15, 1862, 7 30 P M

Col R Ingalls, care Col Rucker, Quarter-Master, Washington. "Gen. Franklin reports that there is by no means as much clothing as was called for, at Hagerstown I think, therefore, you had better have additional supplies, especially of shoes, forwarded to Harper's Ferry as soon as possible"
R B M, Chief-of-Staff

Headquarters, Army of the Potomac October 16, 1862

Col R Ingalls, Care Col. Rucker, Quarter-Master, Washington Gen J. F. Reynolds just telegraphs as follows: "My quarter-master reports that there are no shoes, tents, blankets, or knapsacks, at Hagerstown. He was able to procure only a complete supply of overcoats and pants, with a few socks, drawers, and coats This leaves many of the men yet without a shoe My requisitions call for 5,255 pairs of shoes."

Please push the shoes and stockings up to Harper's Ferry as fast as possible
R. B. M., Chief-of-Staff
Headquarters, Army of the Potomac,
Camp near Knoxville, Md., Oct. 10, 1862

Col C. G. Sawtelle, Depot Quarter-Master, Washington: You did right in sending clothing to Harper's Ferry. You will not be able to send too much or too quickly. We want blankets, shoes, canteens, &c., very much.
R. Ingalls, Lt.-Col. & A. D. C, C. Q. M.
Headquarters Army of the Potomac,
Camp near Knoxville, Md., Oct 10, 1862

Capt. Augustus Boyd, Quarter-Master, Philadelphia: Shipments to Hagerstown must be made direct through, to avoid the contemptible delays at Harrisburg. If Col. Crossman was ordered to send clothing, I hope he has sent it, for the suffering and impatience are excessive.
R. I., Lt Col. & A. D. C., Chief Qr-Master.
Headquarters Army of the Potomac.
Camp near Knoxville, Oct. 13, 1862.

Capt Geo. H. Weeks, Depot Quarter-Master, Hagerstown: Has the clothing arrived yet? if not, do you know where it is? What clothing was taken by the rebels at Chambersburg? Did they capture any property that was en route to you? Have we not got clothing at Harrisburg? Send an agent over the road to obtain information, and hurry up the supplies. Reply at once.
R I, Lt.-Col. & A. D C Chief Qr.-Master.
SHARPSBURG, Oct. 10, 1862.

Gen, INGALLS,—I have just returned from Hagerstown where I have been for the clothing for this corps. There was nothing there but overcoats, trowsers, and a few uniform coats and socks There were not any shoes, blankets, shirts or shelter tents. Will you please tell me where and when the balance can be had? Shall I send to Harper's Ferry for them to-morrow? The corps surgeon has just made a requisition for 45 hospital tents. There are none at Hagerstown. Will you please to inform me if I can get them at Harper's Ferry?
FIELDING LOWRY, Capt. and Quartermaster.
HAGERSTOWN, Oct. 15, 1862

Col. Ingalls, Quartermaster,—I want at least ten thousand suits of clothing, in addition to what I have received. It should be here now.
G W WEEKS, Acting Quartermaster.
HARPER'S FERRY, Oct. 22-1862.

Gen, INGALLS, Chief Quartermaster, &c.—We have bootees 12 000 : great coats, 4,000 ; drawers and shirts are gone ; blankets and stockings nearly so 15,000 each of these four articles are wanted. ALEX. BLISS,
Captain and Acting Quartermaster.
McClellan's Headquarters, Oct. 24, 11 A M '62.

Captain D. G. THOMAS, Military Storekeeper, Washington,—Please send to Capt. Bliss at Harper's Ferry 10,000 blankets; 12,000 caps; 5,000 overcoats, 10,000 pairs bootees, 2,000 pairs artillery and cavalry boots ; 15,000 pairs stockings; 15,000 pairs drawers , 15,000 pairs pants.
The clothing arrives slowly ; can it not be hurried along faster. May I ask you to obtain authority for this shipment. RUFUS INGALLS.
Lt.-Col and A D. C., Chief Quartermaster.

HAGERSTOWN, Oct. 30.

COL. INGALLS,—Clothing has arrived this morning. None taken by rebels. Shall I supply Franklin, and retain portions for Porter and Reynolds until called for. G. W. WEEKS,
Capt. and Ass't Quartermaster.

The following statement taken from a report of the chief quartermaster with the army, will show what progress was made in supplying the army with clothing, from the 1st of September, to the date of crossing the Potomac on the 31st of October, and that the greater part of the clothing did not reach our depots until after the 15th of October.

[See next page]

Col. Ingalls, chief quartermaster, in his report upon this subject says:

"There was great delay in receiving our clothing. The orders were promptly given by me, and approved by General Meigs, but the roads were slow to transport, particularly the Cumberland Valley Road.

"For instance, clothing ordered to Hagerstown on the 7th October for the corps of Franklin, Porter, and Reynolds, did not arrive there until about the 18th, and by that time, of course there were increased wants, and changes in the position of troops.

"The clothing of Sumner arrived in great quantities near the last of October, almost too late for issue, as the army was crossing into Virginia.

"We finally left 50,000 suits at Harper's Ferry, partly on the cars just arrived, and partly in store."

The causes of the reduction of our cavalry force have already been recited. The difficulty in getting new supplies from the usual sources led me to apply for and obtain authority for the cavalry and artillery officers to purchase their own horses. The following are the telegrams and letters on this subject:

Headquarters, Army of the Potomac,
Oct. 12, 1862, 12.45 P.M.
Maj.-Gen H , Gen.-in-Chief :

It is absolutely necessary that some energetic means be taken to supply the cavalry of this army with remount horses. The present rate of supply is 4050 per week for the entire army here and in front of Washington. From this number the artillery draw for their batteries.
G. B. McC., Maj.-Gen. Com'g.

The general-in-chief, in a letter to me, dated Washington, D C., Oct 14th, 1862, replies to this dispatch in the following language:

"I have caused the matters complained of in your telegrams of the 11th and 12th to be investigated." . . . .

"In regard to horses, you say that the present rate of supply is only 150 per week for the entire army here and in front of Washington. I find from the records that the issues for the last six weeks has been 8,754, making an average per week of 1459."

1050 is the number stated in the original dispatch now in my possession, and as not only figures were used, but the number was written out in full, I can hardly see how it is possible for

Statement of Clothing and Equipage received at the different Depots of the Army of the Potomac, from the 1st of September, 1862, to the 31st of October, 1862.

Received at the Depots	From Sept. 1st to Oct. 6th	From Oct. 6th to Oct. 15th	From Oct. 15th to Oct. 25th	From Oct. 25th to Oct. 31st	Total
Drawers	10700	17000	40000	30000	97700
Forage Caps	4000	11000	19000	—	34500
Stockings	6200	22025	63200	36000	123425
Sack Coats	3000	4190	—	—	4190
Cav'y Jackets	3000	500	1250	1500	6250
Canteens	6000	10222	900	3003	29322
Flannel Shirts	6200	18325	18876	2200	45301
Haversacks	6000	12989	5000	9900	33889
Trowsers (Mounted)	4200	1000	2500	5000	12700
Boots	4200	6000	3600	20040	33840
Shelter Tents	11100	30000	9000	—	23100
Camp Kettles	2030	2100	1302	1894	3995
Mess Pans	—	—	4500	8630	8630
Overcoats (Foot)	3300	12000	14770	—	30270
Artillery Jackets	1200	500	1750	1000	4450
Blankets	—	—	3500	6500	10904
Overcoats (Mounted)	2012	1200	875	—	4384 2015
Felt Hats	2200	7300	—	—	9200
Infantry Coats	2000	12060	22500	7500	44060
Trowsers (Foot)	2000	9500	39620	25000	76120
Bootees	2000	7000	52900	—	61900
Knit Shirts	—	2655	2424	11595	16674

the telegraphic operator to have made a mistake in the transmission of the message

Headquarters Army of the Potomac,
October 14, 1862. 7 P. M.

Major-Gen. H. W. H., Commander-in-Chief:
With my small cavalry force it is impossible for me to watch the line of the Potomac properly, or even make the reconnoissances that are necessary for our movements. This makes it necessary for me to weaken my line very much, by extending the infantry to guard the innumerable fords This will continue until the river rises, and it will be next to impossible to prevent the rebel cavalry raids. My cavalry force, as I urged this morning, should be largely and immediately increased under any hypothesis, whether to guard the river or advance on the enemy, or both.

Geo. B. McC., Major-General

The following is an extract from the official report of Col Ingalls :

"Immediately after the battle of Antietam, efforts were made to supply deficiencies in clothing and horses.

'Large requisitions were prepared and sent in. The artillery and cavalry required large numbers to cover losses sustained in battle, on the march, and by diseases. Both of those arms were deficient when they left Washington.

"A most violent and destructive disease made its appearance at this time, which put nearly 4,000 animals out of service. Horses reported perfectly well one day, would be dead lame the next, and it was difficult to foresee where it would end or what number would cover the loss. They were attacked in the hoof and tongue. No one seemed able to account for the appearance of this disease. Animals kept at *rest* would recover in time, but *could not be worked*. I made application to send West and purchase horses at once, but it was refused on the ground that the outstanding contracts provided for enough ; *but they were not delivered sufficiently fast,* nor in sufficient numbers, until late in October and early in November. I was authorised to buy 2,500 late in October but the delivery was not completed until late in November, after we had reached Warrenton."

In a letter from Gen Meigs, written on the 14th of October, and addressed to the general-in-chief, it is stated, "There have been issued, therefore, to the army of the Potomac, since the battles in front of Washington, to replace losses, 9,254."

What number of horses were sent to General Pope before his return to Washington, I have no means of determining, but the following statements, made upon my order by the chief quartermaster with the army, and who had means for gaining accurate information, forces upon my mind the conclusion that the quartermaster-general was in error:

Headquarters, Army of the Potomac,
C. Q. M., Office, October 31, 1862.

Horses.

Horses purchased since 6th Sept 1862, by Col Ingalls, Chief Quarter-master, and issued to the forces under the immediate command of Major-General Geo B McClellan - - - - - - - - - - 1,200

Issued and turned out to the above force by Capt J. J. Dana, Assistant Quartermaster (in Washington)	2,261
Issued to forces at and near Washington, which have since joined this command	352
Total purchased by Col Ingalls, and issued and turned over by Capt Dana to the forces in this immediate command	3,813
Issued by Capt J J Dana, Assistant Quartermaster, to the forces in the vicinity of Washington	3,363
Grand total purchased by Col R, Ingalls, Chief Quartermaster, and issued and turned over by Capt J J Dana, Assistant Quartermaster, to the entire army of the Potomac and the forces around Washington	7,176

About 3,000 horses have been turned over to the quarter-master department by officers, as unfit for service. Nearly 1,500 should now be turned over also being worn out and diseased

Respectfully submitted,

F M, Lt.-Col & Quarter-master

This official statement made up from the reports of the quarter-masters who received and distributed the horses, exhibits the true state of the case, and gives the total number of horses received by the army of the Potomac and the troops around Washington during a period of eight weeks, as 7,176, or 2,078 less than the number stated by the quarter-master-general.

Supposing that (1,500) fifteen hundred were issued to the army under Gen. Pope previous to its return to Washington, as Gen Meigs states, there would still remain (578) five hundred and seventy-eight horses which he does not account for

The letter of the general-in-chief to the Secretary of War on the 28th of October, and the letter of Gen Meigs to the general in-chief, on the 14th of October, convey the impression that, upon my urgent and repeated applications for cavalry and artillery horses for the army of the Potomac I had received a much greater number than was really the case

It will be seen, from Col. Myers' report, that all of the horses alluded to by Gen Meigs, only (3,813) three thousand eight hundred and thirteen came to the army, with which I was ordered to follow and attack the enemy. Of course the remainder did not in the slightest degree contribute to the efficiency of the cavalry or artillery of this army, with which I was to cross the river, neither did they in the least facilitate any preparations for carrying out the order to advance upon the enemy as the general-in-chief's letter might seem to imply.

During the same period that we were receiving the horses alluded to, about (3,000) three thousand of our old stock were turned into the quarter-master's department, and 1,500 more reported as in such condition that they ought to be turned in as unfit for service, thus leaving the active army some 700 short of the number required to make good existing deficiencies, to say nothing of providing remounts for men whose horses had died or been killed during the campaign, and those previously dismounted.

Notwithstanding all the efforts made to obtain a remount, there were, after deducting the force engaged in picketing the river, but about a thousand serviceable cavalry horses on the 21st day of October

In a letter, dated October 14th, 1862, the general-in-chief says: "It is also reported to me that the number of animals with your army in the field is about 31,000 It is believed that your present proportion of cavalry and of animals is much larger than that of any other of our armies."

What number of animals our other armies had I am not prepared to say, but military men in European armies have been of the opinion that an army to be efficient, while carrying on active operations in the field, should have a cavalry force equal in numbers to from one-sixth to one-fourth of the infantry force. My cavalry did not amount to one-twentieth part of the army, and hence the necessity of giving every one of my cavalry soldiers a serviceable horse

Cavalry may be said to constitute the antennæ of an army. It scouts all the roads in front, or the flanks, and in the rear of the advancing columns and constantly feels the enemy. The amount of labor falling upon this arm during the Maryland campaign was excessive. To persons not familiar with the movements of troops, and the amount of transportation required for a large army marching away from water or railroad communications, the number of animals mentioned by the general-in-chief may have appeared unnecessarily large, but to a military man who takes the trouble to enter into an accurate and detailed computation of the number of pounds of subsistence and forage required for such an army as that of the Potomac, it will be seen that the 31,000 animals were considerably less than was absolutely necessary to an advance. As we were required to move through a country which could not be depended upon for any of our supplies, it became necessary to transport every thing in wagons, and to be prepared for all emergencies I did not consider it safe to leave the river without subsistence and forage for ten days

The official returns of that date show the aggregate strength of the army for duty to have been about 110,000 men of all arms This did not include teamsters, citizen employees, officers' servants, &c, amounting to some 12,000 men, which gives a total of 122,000 men The subsistence alone of this army, for ten days, required for its transportation 1,830 wagons at 2,000 pounds to the wagon, and 10,980 animals.

Our cavalry horses, at that time, amounted to 5,046, and our artillery horses to 6,836

To transport full forage for these 22,862 animals for ten days required 17,832 additional animals, and this forage would only supply the entire number, (40,694) of animals with a small fraction over half allowance for the time specified.

It will be observed that this estimate does not embrace the animals necessary to transport quartermaster's supplies, baggage, camp-equipage, ambulances, reserve ammunition, forage for officer's horses, etc. etc, which would greatly augment the necessary transportation.

It may very truly be said that we did make the march with the means at our disposal, but it will be remembered that we met with no serious opposition from the enemy, neither did we encounter delays from any other cause. The roads were in excellent condition, and the troops marched with the most commendable order and celerity.

If we had met with a determined resistance from the enemy, and our progress had been very much retarded thereby, we would have consumed our supplies before they could have been renewed. A proper estimate of my responsibilities as the commander of that army did not justify me in basing my preparations for the exhibition upon the supposition that I was to have an uninterrupted march. On the contrary it was my duty to be prepared for all emergencies, and not the least important of my responsibilities was the duty of making ample provision for supplying men and animals with rations and forage.

Knowing the solicitude of the President for an early movement, and sharing with him fully his anxiety for prompt action, on the 21st of October I telegraphed to the General-in-chief as follows:

Headquarters, Army of the Potomac, October 21, 1862.

Maj.-Gen. H. W. Halleck, General-in-Chief, Washington — Since the receipt of the President's order to move on the enemy I have been making every exertion to get this army supplied with clothing absolutely necessary for marching. This I am happy to say, is now nearly accomplished; I have also, during the same time repeatedly urged upon you the importance of supplying cavalry and artillery horses, to replace those broken down by hard service, and steps have been taken to insure a prompt delivery. Our cavalry, even when well supplied with horses, is much inferior in numbers to that of the enemy; but in efficiency has proved itself superior. So forcibly has this been impressed upon our old regiments by repeated successes, that the men are fully persuaded that they are equal to twice their number of rebel cavalry.

Exclusive of the cavalry force now engaged in picketing the river, I have not at present over about one thousand horses for service. Officers have been sent in various directions to purchase horses, and I expect them soon. Without more cavalry horses our communications, from the moment we march, would be at the mercy of the large cavalry forces of the enemy, and it would not be possible for us to cover our flanks properly, or to obtain the necessary information of the position and movements of the enemy in such a way as to insure success. My experience has shown the necessity of a large and efficient cavalry force. Under the foregoing circumstances I beg leave to ask whether the President desires me to march on the enemy at once, or to await the reception of the new horses, every possible step having been taken to insure their prompt arrival. G. B. McCLELLAN, Maj.-Gen Com'd'g.

On the same day Gen. Halleck replied as follows:

Washington, Oct. 21, 1862. 3 P.M.

Your telegraph of 12 M. has been submitted to the President. He directs me to say, that he has no change to make in his order of the 6th inst. If you have not been, and are not now in condition to obey it, you will be able to show such want of ability. The President does not expect impossibilities, but he is very anxious that all this good weather should not be wasted in inactivity.

Telegraph when you will move, and on what lines you propose to march.

H. W. H., Gen.-in-Chief.
Maj.-Gen. G. B. McClellan.

From the tenor of this dispatch I conceived that it was left for my judgment to decide whether or not it was possible to move with safety to the army at that time, and this responsibility I exercised with the more confidence in view of the strong assurances of his trust in me as commander of that army, with which the President had seen fit to honor me during his last visit.

The cavalry requirements without which an advance would have been in the highest degree injudicious and unsafe, were still wanting.

The country before us was an enemy's country, where the inhabitants furnished to the enemy every possible assistance, providing food for men and forage for animals, giving all information concerning our movements, and rendering every aid in their power to the enemy's cause.

It was manifest that we should find it, as we subsequently did, a hostile district, where we could derive no aid from the inhabitants that would justify dispensing with the active co-operation of an efficient cavalry force. Accordingly, I fixed upon the 1st of November as the earliest date at which the forward movement could well be commenced.

The general-in-chief, in a letter to the Secretary of War on the 28th of October, says: "In my opinion there has been no such want of supplies in the army under Gen. McClellan, as to prevent his compliance with the orders to advance against the enemy."

Notwithstanding this opinion expressed by such high authority, I am compelled to say again that the delay in the reception of necessary supplies up to that date, had left the army in a condition totally unfit to advance against the enemy, that an advance under the existing circumstances would, in my judgment, have been attended with the highest degree of peril, with great suffering and sickness among the men, and with imminent danger of being cut off from our supplies by the superior cavalry force of the enemy, and with no reasonable prospect of gaining any advantage over him.

I dismiss this subject with the remark, that I have found it impossible to resist the force of my own convictions, that the commander of an army, who, from the time of its organization, has for eighteen months been in constant communication with its officers and men the greater part of the time engaged in active service in the field, and who has exercised this command in many battles, must certainly be considered competent to determine whether his army is in proper condition to advance on the enemy or not, and he must necessarily possess greater facilities for forming a correct judgment in regard to the wants of his men, and the condition of his supplies, than the general-in-chief in his office at Washington City

ADVANCE INTO VIRGINIA

The movement from Washington into Maryland, which culminated in the battles of South Mountain and Antietam, was not a part of an offensive campaign, with the object of the invasion of the enemy's territory, and an attack upon his capital, but was defensive in its purposes, although offensive in its character, and would be technically called a "defensive-offensive campaign"

It was undertaken at a time when our army had experienced severe defeats, and its object was to preserve the national capital and Baltimore, to protect Pennsylvania from invasion, and to drive the enemy out of Maryland These purposes were fully and finally accomplished by the battle of Antietam, which brought the army of the Potomac into what might be termed an accidental position on the upper Potomac.

Having gained the immediate object of the campaign, the first thing to be done was to insure Maryland from a return of the enemy, the second, to prepare our own army, exhausted by a series of severe battles, destitute to a great extent of supplies, and very deficient in artillery and cavalry horses, for a definite offensive movement, and to determine upon the line of operations for a further advance

At the time of the battle of Antietam the Potomac was very low, and presented a comparatively weak line of defense, unless watched by large masses of troops This re-occupation of Harper's Ferry, and the disposition of troops above that point, rendered the line of the Potomac secure against everything except cavalry raids No time was lost in placing the army in proper condition for an advance, and the circumstances which caused the delay after the battle of Antietam have been fully enumerated elsewhere

I never regarded Harper's Ferry or its vicinity as a proper base of operations for a movement upon Richmond I still considered the line of the Peninsula as the true approach, but, for obvious reasons, did not make any proposal to return to it.

On the 6th of October, as stated above, I was ordered by the President, through the general-in-chief, to cross the Potomac and give battle to the enemy, or drive him south Two lines were presented for my choice 1st. Up the valley of the Shenandoah, in which case I was to have 12,000 to 15,000 additional troops; 2d To cross between the enemy and Washington, that is, east of the Blue Ridge, in which event I was to be reinforced with 30,000 men

At first I determined to adopt the line of the Shenandoah, for these reasons: The Harper's Ferry and Winchester Railroad, and the various turnpikes converging upon Winchester, afforded superior facilities for supplies

Our cavalry being weak, this line of communication could be more easily protected. There was no advantage in interposing, at that time, the Blue Ridge and the Shenandoah between the enemy and myself.

At the period in question the Potomac was still very low, and I apprehended that if I crossed the river below Harper's Ferry, the enemy would promptly check the movement by recrossing into Maryland, at the same time covering his rear by occupying in strong force the passes leading through the Blue Ridge from the southeast into the Shenandoah Valley.

I anticipated, as the result of the first course, that Lee would fight me near Winchester, if he could do so under favorable circumstances; or else that he would abandon the lower Shenandoah and leave the army of the Potomac free to act upon some other line of operations If he abandoned the Shenandoah, he would naturally fall back upon his railway communications I have since been confirmed in the belief, that if I had crossed the Potomac below Harper's Ferry in the early part of October, General Lee would have recrossed into Maryland

As above explained, the army was not in condition to move until late in October, and in the meantime circumstances had changed

The period had arrived when a sudden and great rise of the Potomac might be looked for at any time, the season of bad roads and difficult movements was approaching, which would naturally deter the enemy from exposing himself very far from his base, and his movements all appeared to indicate a falling back from the river towards his supplies Under these circumstances I felt at liberty to disregard the possibility of the enemy recrossing the Potomac, and determined to select the line east of the Blue Ridge, feeling convinced that it would secure me the largest accession of force, and the most cordial support of the President, whose views from the beginning were in favor of that line

The subject of the defense of the line of the upper Potomac, after the advance of the main army, had long occupied my attention; I desired to place Harper's Ferry and its dependencies in a strong state of defense, and frequently addressed the general-in-chief upon the subject of the erection of field-works and permanent bridges then asking for the funds necessary to accomplish the purpose. Although I did my best to explain as clearly as I was able that I did not wish to erect permanent works of masonry, and that neither the works nor the permanent bridges had any reference to the advance of the army, but solely to the permanent occupation of Harper's Ferry, I could never make the General-in-chief understand my wishes, but was refused the funds necessary to erect the field-works, on the ground that there was no appropriation for the erection of permanent fortifications; and was not allowed to build the permanent bridge on the ground that the main army could not be delayed in its movements until its completion Of course I never thought of delaying the advance of the army for that purpose and so stated repeatedly.

On the 25th of October I sent the General-in-chief the following telegram,

Headquarters, Army of the Potomac, October 25, 1862 10 45 P. M.

Maj-Gen Halleck, General in chief, Washington,—As the moment is at hand for the advance of the army, a question arises for the decision of the general in chief, which although perhaps implicitly decided by the President in his letter of the 13th, should be clearly presented by me, as I do not regard it as in my province to determine it. This question is the extent to which the line of the Potomac should be guarded, after the army leaves, in order to cover Maryland and Pennsylvania, from invasion by large or small parties of the enemy. It will always be somewhat difficult to guard the immediate line of the river, owing to its great extent and the numerous passages which exist. It has long appeared to me that the best way of covering this line would be by occupying Front Royal, Strasburg, Wardensville and Morefields, at the debouches of the several valleys in which they are situated. These points, or suitable places in their vicinity, should be strongly intrenched and permanently held, and great advantage of this arrangement would be the covering the Baltimore and Ohio railroad, and an essential part of the system would be the construction of the link of railway from Winchester to Strasburg, and the rebuilding of the Manassas Gap Railway bridge over the Shenandoah.

The intrenchment of Manassas Junction would complete the system for the defense of the approaches to Washington and the Upper Potomac. Many months ago I recommended this arrangement, in fact gave orders for it to be carried into effect. I still regard it as essential under all circumstances.

The views of the chief engineer of this army in regard to the defenses and garrison of Harper's Ferry and its dependencies are in your possession.

The only troops under my command outside of the organization of the army of the Potomac, are the Maryland Brigade, under Gen. Kenly, the 64th Pennsylvania, Col Voss; 12th Illinois Cavalry, and Col Davis's 8th New York cavalry; total, 2,894 infantry, one battery, and about 900 cavalry men. There are also two of my regiments of cavalry, (about 650 men) guarding the Baltimore and Ohio Railroad, between Hancock and Cumberland.

As I have no department, and command simply an active army in the field, my responsibility for the safety of the line of the Potomac and the States north of it, must terminate the moment I advance so far beyond that line as to adopt another for my base of operations. The question for the general in chief to decide, and which I regard as beyond my province, is this:

1st. Shall the safety of Harper's Ferry, and the line of the Potomac, be regarded as assured by the advance of the army south of the Blue Ridge and the line left to take care of itself?

2d. If it is deemed necessary to hold the line or that hereinbefore indicated in advance of it, how many troops shall be placed there, at what points, and in what numbers, and of what composition at each, and whence shall they be supplied, i. e. from this army or from other sources?

Omitting the detached troops mentioned above, and the small garrisons of Boonsboro and Frederick, the last returns show the strength of this army for duty, to be about one hundred and sixteen thousand officers and men. This includes the divisions of Stoneman and Whipple but does not include Heintzelman, Sigel and Bayard.

If Harper's Ferry and the river above are rendered fully secure, it is possible that the active army, if it spplies the garrisons, may be reduced so much as to be inadequate to the purposes contemplated; if is is preserved intact, Maryland, Pennsylvania, and the Baltimore and Ohio Railroad may be unduly exposed.

I leave the decision of these grave questions to the general in chief. I know nothing of the number of troops in Baltimore, &c.

An important element in the solution of this problem, is the fact that a great portion of Bragg's army is probably now at liberty to unite itself with Lee's command.

I commence crossing the river at Berlin in the morning, and must ask a prompt decision of the questions proposed herein.

G B McC, Maj-Gen Com

To which I received the following reply:

Washington, Oct. 26, '62, 1 35 P.M.
Maj-Gen G B McC

In addition to the command which you had when I came here, you also have the greater part of that of Maj.-Gen. Pope. Moreover, you have been authorized to use any troops within your reach in Gen Wool's department, and in Western Virginia. Gen. Banks's command is also under your direction, with the single restriction, that he is not to remove troops from Washington, until he has notified me of his orders. Since you left Washington, I have advised and suggested in relation to your movements, but I have given you no orders. I do not give you any now. The government has intrusted you with defeating and driving back the rebel army in your front. I shall not attempt to control you in the measures you may adopt for that purpose; you are informed of my views, but the President has left you at liberty to adopt them or not, as you may deem best. You will also exercise your own discretion in regard to what points on the Potomac, and the Baltimore and Ohio Railroad are to be occupied or fortified. I will only add that there is no appropriation for permanent intrenchments on that line. Moreover, I think it will be time enough to decide upon fortifying Front Royal, Strasburg, Wardenville and Morefield, when the enemy is driven south of them, and they come into our possession. I do not think that we need have any immediate fear of Bragg's army. You are within 20 miles of Lee's, while Bragg is distant about 400 miles.

H. W. H., Gen.-in-Chief.

And on the 29th I sent the following:

Headquarters, Army of the Potomac,
Oct 29, '62, 1.15 P M
Maj-Gen H W H, Washington:

On the 25th instant, I sent you a dispatch, requesting you to decide what steps should be taken to guard the line of the Potomac, when the army leaves here. To this I received your reply that I had been intrusted by the President, with defeating and driving away the rebel army, that you had given me no orders heretofore, did not give me any then, etc. Under these circumstances, I have only to make such arrangements for guarding this extended line as the means at my disposal will permit, at the same time keeping in view the extreme necessity of maintaining the moving army in adequate force to meet the rebel army before us.

The dispositions I have ordered are as follows, viz.: 10,000 men to be left at Harper's Ferry, one brigade of infantry in front of Sharpsburg, Kenly's brigade of infantry at Williamsport; Kelly's brigade, including Col Cambell's 54th Pennsylvania Infantry, at Cumberland, and between that point and Hancock I have also left four small cavalry regiments, to patrol and watch the river and the Baltimore and Ohio Railroad from Cumberland down to Harper's Ferry.

I do not regard this force as sufficient to cover securely this great extent of line, but I do not feel justified in detaching any more troops from my moving columns. I would therefore recommend that some new regiments of infantry and cavalry be sent to strengthen the forces left by me.

There should be a brigade of infantry and section of artillery in the vicinity of Cherry Run, another brigade at Hancock, an additional brigade at Williamsport, one regiment at Hagerstown, and one at Chambersburg, with a section of artillery at each place if possible. This is on the supposition that the enemy retain a considerable cavalry force west of the Blue Ridge. If they go east of it, the occupation of the points named in my dispatch of the 25th inst, will obviate the necessity of of keeping many of these troops on the river.

There are now several hundred of our wounded, including Gen Richardson, in the vicinity of Sharpsburg, that cannot possibly be moved at present.

I repeat that I do not look upon the forces I have been able to leave from this army, as sufficient to prevent cavalry raids into Maryland and Pennsylvania, as cavalry is the only description of troops adequate to this service, and I am, as you are aware, deficient in this arm.

Geo. B. McClellan, Maj.-Gen. Comd'g.

To which I received, on the 30th, this reply:

Washington, Oct 30, 1862   11 30 A M

Maj.-Gen. G. B McClellan,—Your telegram of yesterday was received late last evening. The troops proposed for Thoroughfare Gap will be sent to that place whenever you are in position for their coperation, as previously stated, but no new regiments can be sent from here to the Upper Potomac. The guarding of that line is left to your own discretion, with the troops now under your command.

H W H Gen.-in-Chief

I accordingly left the 12th Corps at Harper's Ferry, detaching one brigade to the vicinity of Sharpsburg. Gen. Morell was placed in command of the line from the mouth of the Antietam to Cumberland, Gen Slocum in command of Harper's Ferry and the line east of the mouth of the Antietam.

The orders given to these officers were as follows:

Head-Quarters, Army of the Potomac,
Oct 29, 1862   1 P M

Gen H W Slocum, Comd'g Army Corps, Harper's Ferry,—The general commanding directs that you send one brigade of your corps, to march at once to the position now occupied by Gen. F J Porter's corps in front of Sharpsburg, to watch and guard the line of the river from the ford near the mouth of the Antietam Creek to the mouth of the Opequan Creek. The officer in command will also take steps to afford proper protection to the sick and wounded in the hospitals in the vicinity of Sharpsburg and Boonsboro. The regiment now at Boonsboro' will be placed under his orders. Gen Kenly, at Williamsport, will guard the river from the mouth of the Opequan above, including the ford at the mouth of the Opequan.

The commanding general also directs that you take immediate steps to establish the remainder of your corps as follows, viz, one brigade on Maryland Heights, one brigade on Loudon Heights, with the remainder on Bolivar Heights and at Harper's Ferry. These dispositions should be made at once, so that Gen Couch can move with his corps. Please acknowledge receipt of this.

R B Marcy, Chief-of-Staff.

Head-Quarters, Army of the Potomac,
October 31, 1862

Gen G W Morell, Comd'g Upper Potomac General,—I am instructed by the commanding general to say to you, that he has selected you to perform the highly important and responsible duty of taking charge of, and commanding the troops left for the defence of the line of the Potomac River, from the mouth of the Antietam to Cumberland, as well as any other troops that may hereafter be sent for the protection of the Maryland and Pennsylvania frontier, within the limits of the line herein specified. The force which has been left to guard the line is not deemed adequate to prevent cavalry raids, but it is all that the commanding general feels authorized to detach from the army of the Potomac at the present time, and it devolves upon you to make the best use of this force in your power. You will have four cavalry regiments under your command, which should be distributed along the river, as to watch all the available fords, and give timely notice to the infantry of the approach of any force of rebels.

You will afford all the protection in your power to the Baltimore and Ohio Railroad.

You will endeavor to prevent any cavalry raids into Maryland and Pennsylvania.

You will take steps to have all the sick and wounded of our army, as well as of the rebel army, within your lines, properly taken care of, until they can be sent to general hospitals, or discharged or paroled.

You will make your headquarters at Hagerstown, and occasionally visit the different parts of your line.

You will please report promptly to these headquarters, everything of importance that occurs within the limits of your command. The three brigades now at Cumberland, Williamsport, and Sharpsburgh, including the 54th Pennsylvania Volunteers near Cumberland, will be under your command. They are commanded by Gens. Kelly, Kenly, and Gordon

Very respectfully, your obedient servant,
S W, Ass't-Adj't-General

On the 25th of October the pontoon bridge at Berlin was constructed, there being already one across the Potomac, and another across the Shenandoah at Harper's Ferry.

On the 26th two divisions of the 9th Corps and Pleasonton's brigade of cavalry, crossed at Berlin and occupied Lovettsville

The 1st, 6th, and 9th Corps, the cavalry and reserve artillery, crossed at Berlin between the 26th of October and the 2d of November

The 2d and 5th Corps crossed at Harper's Ferry between the 29th of October and 1st of November

Heavy rains delayed the movement considerably in the beginning, and the 1st, 5th, and 6th Corps were obliged to halt at least one day at the crossings, to complete, as far as possible, the necessary supplies that could not be procured at an earlier period.

The plan of campaign I adopted during the advance, was to move the army well in hand parallel to the Blue Ridge, taking Warrenton as the point of direction for the main body seizing each pass in the Blue Ridge by detachments, as we approached it, and guarding them after we had passed, as long as they would enable the enemy to trouble our communications with the Potomac It was expected that we would unite with the 11th Corps and Sickles's division near Thoroughfare Gap We depended upon Harper's Ferry and Berlin for supplies, until the Manassas Gap Railway was reached, when that occurred the passes in our rear were to be abandoned, and the army massed ready for action or movement in any direction

It was my intention, if upon reaching Ashby's, or any other pass, I found that the enemy were in force between it and the Potomac, in the valley of the Shenandoah to move into the valley and endeavor to gain their rear. I hardly hoped to accomplish this, but did not expect that by striking in between Culpepper Court House and Little Washington, I could either separate their army and beat them in detail, or else force them to concentrate as far back as Gordonsville, and thus place the army of the Potomac in position either to adopt the Fredericksburgh line of advance upon Richmond, or to be removed to the Peninsula, if, as I apprehended, it were found impossible to supply it by the Orange and Alexandria Railroad beyond Culpepper

On the 27th of October, the remaining divisions of the 9th Corps crossed at Berlin, and Pleasonton's cavalry advanced to Purcellville The concentration of the 6th Corps, delayed somewhat by intelligence as to the movements of the enemy at Hedgesville, &c, was commenced on this day, and the 1st Corps was already in motion at Berlin

On the 28th the 1st Corps and the general headquarters reached Berlin

On the 29th the reserve artillery crossed and camped near Lovettsville; the 2d Corps commenced the passage of the Shenandoah, the 5th Corps commenced its march from Sharpsburg to Harper's Ferry

On the 31st the 2d Corps moved to the vicinity of Hillsborough, the 6th Corps reached Boonsboro', the 5th Corps reached Harper's Ferry, one division crossing the Shenandoah

On the 1st of November the 1st Corps moved to Purcellville and Hamilton; the 2d Corps to Woodgrove; the 5th Corps to Hillsborough; the 6th Corps reached Berlin, one division crossing Pleasonton's cavalry occupied Philemont, having a sharp skirmish there, and at Bloomfield

On November 2d the 2d Corps occupied Snicker's Gap; the 5th Corps Snickersville the 6th Corps crossed the Potomac, and encamped near Wheatland, the 9th Corps advanced to Bloomfield, Union and Philemont Pleasonton drove the enemy out of Union, Averell was ordered to join Pleasonton The enemy offered no serious resistance to the occupation of Snicker's Gap, but advanced to gain possession of it with a column of some 5,000 to 6,000 infantry, who were driven back by a few rounds from our rifled guns.

On the 3d the 1st Corps moved to Philemont-Union, Blomfield, &c ; the 2d Corps to the vicinity of Upperville, the 5th Corps remained at Snicker's Gap; the 6th Corps moved to Purcellville, the 9th Corps moved towards Upperville, Pleasonton drove the enemy out of Upperville after a severe fight

On the 4th the 2d Corps took possession of Ashley's Gap · the 6th Corps reached Union, the 9th Corps Upperville, the cavalry occupied Piedmont.

On the 5th the 1st Corps moved to Rectortown and White Plains; one division of the 2d Corps to the intersection of the Paris and Piedmont with the Upperville and Barber's road; the 6th Corps to the Aldie turnpike, east of Upperville, the 9th Corps beyond the Manassas Road, between Piedmont and Salem, with a bridge at Manassas Gap, the cavalry under Averell had a skirmish at Manassas Gap, and the brigade of Pleasonton gained a handsome victory over superior numbers at Barber's cross-roads, Bayard's cavalry had some sharp skirmishing in front of Salem

On the 6th the 1st Corps advanced to Warrenton, the 2d to Rectortown, the 5th Corps commenced its movement from Snicker's Gap to White Plains, the 9th Corps to Waterloo and vicinity, on the Rappahannock; the 11th Corps was at New Baltimore, Thoroughfare, and Hopewell's Gaps, Sickles' division guarding the Orange and Alexandria railroad from Manassas Junction, towards Warrenton Junction, the cavalry near Flint Hill; Bayard to cut off what there might be in Warrenton, and to proceed to the Rappahannock Station.

November 7, Gen. Pleasonton was ordered to move towards Little Washington and Sperryville, and thence towards Culpepper Court House

November 8th, the 2d Corps moved half way to Warrenton; the 5th Corps to New Baltimore.

November 9th, the 2d and 5th Corps reached Warrenton, the 6th Corps New Baltimore

Late on the night of the 7th, I received an order relieving me from my command of the army

... Potomac, and directing me to turn it over to Gen. Burnside, which I at once did.

I had already given the orders for the movements of the 8th and 9th, these orders were carried into effect without change.

The position in which I left the army, as the result of the orders I had given, was as follows:

The 1st, 2d and 5th Corps, reserve artillery, and general headquarters at Warrenton; the 9th Corps on the line of the Rappahannock, in the vicinity of Waterloo; the 6th Corps at New Baltimore, the 11th Corps at New Baltimore, Gainesville and Thoroughfare Gap; Sickles's division of the 3d Corps on the Orange and Alexandria railroad from Manassas Junction to Warrenton Junction, Pleasonton across the Rappahannock, at Amissville, Jefferson, &c., with his pickets on Hazel River facing Longstreet's, six miles from Culpepper Court House, Bayard near Rappahannock Station.

The army was thus massed near Warrenton, ready to act in any required direction, perfectly in hand, and in admirable condition and spirits. I doubt whether during the whole period that I had the honor to command the army of the Potomac, it was in such excellent condition to fight a great battle.

When I gave up the command to Gen. Burnside, the best information in our possession indicated that Longstreet was immediately in our front near Culpepper; Jackson with one, perhaps both, of the Hills near Chester and Thornton's Gaps, with the mass of their forces west of the Blue Ridge. The reports from General Pleasonton in the advance, indicated the possibility of separating the two wings of the enemy's forces, and either beating Longstreet separately, or forcing him to fall back, at least, upon Gordonsville, to effect his junction with the rest of the army.

The following is from the report of General Pleasonton:

"At this time, and from the 7th inst., my advance pickets were on Hazel river, within six miles of Culpepper, besides having my flank pickets towards Chester and Thornton's Gaps, extended to Gaines's Cross Roads, and Newby's Cross Roads, with numerous patrols in the directions of Woodville, Little Washington, and Sperryville. The information gained by these parties, and also from deserters, prisoners, contrabands, as well as citizens, established the fact of Longstreet with his command being at Culpepper, while Jackson with D. H. Hill, with their respective commands, were in the Shenandoah Valley, on the western side of the Blue Ridge, covering Chester and Thornton's Gaps, and expecting us to attempt to pass through and attack them. As late as the 17th of November, a contraband just from Strasburg came into my camp and reported that D. H. Hill's corps was two miles beyond that place, on the railroad to Mount Jackson. Hill was tearing up the road and destroying the bridges under the impression that we intended to follow into that valley, and was en route for Staunton. Jackson's corps was between Strasburg and Winchester. Ewell and A. P. Hill were with Jackson.

Had I remained in command, I should have made the attempt to divide the enemy, as before suggested, and could he have been brought to a battle within reach of my supplies, I cannot doubt that the result would have been a brilliant victory for our army.

On the 10th of November Gen. Pleasonton was attacked by Longstreet with one division of infantry, and Stuart's cavalry, but repulsed the attack.

This indicates the relative position of our army and that of the enemy at the time I was relieved from the command.

ORGANIZATION AND GENERAL CONDUCT OF MILITARY OPERATIONS.

It would be impossible to participate in operations such as those described in the foregoing pages, without forming fixed opinions upon subjects connected with the organization of our armies and the general conduct of military operations.

This report would be incomplete without a brief allusion to some general considerations which have been firmly impressed upon me by the events which have occurred.

To my mind the most glaring defect in our armies is the absence of system in the appointment and promotion of general and other officers and the want of means for the theoretical instruction of the mass of officers.

The expansion of the army was so great and so rapid at the commencement of the existing war, that it was perhaps impossible, in the great scarcity of instructed officers, to have adopted any other course than that which was pursued; but the time has arrived when measures may be initiated to remedy existing defects and provide against their recurrence.

I think that the army should be regarded as a permanent one, that is to say, its affairs should be administered precisely as if all who belonged to it had made it their profession for life; and those rules for promotion &c., which have been found necessary in the best foreign armies to excite honorable emulation produce an *esprit du corps* and secure efficiency, should be followed by us.

All officers and soldiers should be made to feel that merit, that is to say, courage, good conduct, the knowledge and performance of the duties of their grade, and fitness to exercise those of a superior grade, will ensure to them advancement in their profession, and can alone secure it for them.

Measures should be adopted to secure the theoretical instruction of staff officers at least, who should as far as possible be selected from officers having a military education, or who have seen actual service in the field.

The number of cadets at the military academy should be at once increased to the greatest extent permitted by the capacity of the institution.

The regular army should be increased and maintained complete in numbers and efficiency.

A well organized system of recruiting and of depots for instruction should be adopted, in order to keep the ranks of the regiment full, and supply promptly losses arising from battle or disease. This is especially necessary for the artillery and cavalry arms of the service, which, from the beginning of the war, have rendered great service, which have never been fully appreciated by but their comrades. We need also large bodies of well instructed engineer troops

In the arrangement and conduct of campaigns, the directions should be left to professional soldiers: a statesman may, perhaps, be more competent than a soldier to determine political objects and direction of a campaign, but those once decided upon, everything should be left to the responsible military head, without interference from civilians. In no other manner is success probable. The meddling of individual members or committees of Congress with subjects which from lack of experience, they are of course incapable of comprehending, and which they are too apt to view through the distorted medium of partizan or personal prejudice, can do no good, and is certain to produce incalculable mischief.

I cannot omit the expression of my thanks to the President for the constant evidence given me of his sincere personal regard, and his desire to sustain the military plans which my judgment led me to urge for adoption and execution. I cannot attribute his failure to adopt some of those plans, and to give that support to others which was necessary to their success, to any want of confidence in me, and it only remains for me to regret that other counsels came between the constitutional commander in chief and the general whom he had placed at the head of his armies counsels which resulted in the failure of great campaigns.

If the nation possesses no generals in service, competent to direct its military affairs without the aid or supervision of politicians, the sooner it finds them and places them in position the better will it be for its fortunes.

I may be pardoned for calling attention to the memorandum submitted by me to the President on the 4th of August, 1861, my letter to him of July 7th 1862, and other similar communications to him and to the Secretary of War, contained in this report. I have seen no reason to change in any material regard the views there expressed.

After a calm, impartial and patient consideration of the subject, a subject which demands the closest thought on the part of every true lover of his country, I am convinced that by the proper employment of our resources, it is entirely possible to bring this war to a successful military issue. I believe that a necessary preliminary to the re-establishment of the Union, is the entire defeat or virtual destruction of the organized military power of the Confederates, and that such a result should be accompanied and followed by conciliatory measures; and that by pursuing the political course I have always advised, it is possible to bring about a permanent restoration of the Union, a reunion by which the rights of both sections shall be preserved and by which both parties shall preserve their self-respect while they respect each other.

CONCLUSION.

In this report I have confined myself to a plain narrative of such facts as are necessary for the purposes of history. Where it was possible I have preferred to give these facts in the language of despatches, written at the time of their occurrence, rather than to attempt a new relation.

The reports of the subordinate commanders, hereto annexed, recite what time and space would fail me to mention here, those individual instances of conspicuous bravery and skill by which every battle was marked. To them I must especially refer, for without them, this narrative would be incomplete and justice fail to be done. But I omit to tender to my corps commanders and to the general officers under them, such ample recognition of their cordial co-operation and their devoted services, as those reports abundantly vouch.

I have not sought to defend the army which I had the honor to command, nor myself, against the hostile criticisms once so rife.

It has seemed to me that nothing more was required than such a plain and truthful narrative, to enable those whose right it is to form a correct judgment on the important matters involved.

This report is, in fact, the history of the army of the Potomac. During the period occupied in the organization of that army, it served as a barrier against the advance of a lately victorious enemy, while the fortification of the capital was in progress, and under the discipline which it then received it acquired strength, education, and some of that experience which is necessary to success in active operations, and which enabled it afterward to sustain itself under circumstances trying to the most heroic men. Frequent skirmishes occurred along the lines, conducted with great gallantry, which inured our troops to the realities of war.

The army grew into shape but slowly, and the delays which attended on the obtaining of arms, continued late into the winter of 1861-2, were no less trying to the soldiers than to the people of the country. Even at the time of the organization of the Peninsular campaign, some of the finest regiments were without rifles, nor were the utmost exertions on the part of the military authorities adequate to overcome the obstacles to active service.

When at length the army was in condition to take the field, the Peninsular campaign was planned, and entered upon with enthusiasm by officers and men. Had this campaign been followed up as it was designed, I cannot doubt that it would have resulted in a glorious triumph to our arms, and the permanent restoration of the power of the government in Virginia and North Carolina, if not throughout the revolting States. It was, however, otherwise ordered, and instead of reporting a victorious campaign, it has been my duty to relate the heroism of a reduced army, sent upon an expedition into an enemy's country, there to abandon one, and originate another new campaign, which might and would have been successful if supported with appreciation of its necessities, but which failed because of the repeated failure of promised support, at the most critical, and, as it proved, the most fatal moments.

That heroism surpasses ordinary description. Its illustration must be left for the pen of the historian in times of calm reflection, when the nation shall be looking back to the past from the midst of peaceful days.

For me now, it is sufficient to say, that my comrades were victors on every field save one, and there the endurance of a single corps accomplished the object of its fighting, and by securing to the army its transit to the James, left to the enemy a ruinous and barren victory.

The army of the Potomac was first reduced by the withdrawal from my command of the division of Gen Blenker, which was ordered to the Mountain Department, under Gen Fremont. We had scarcely landed on the Peninsula, when it was further reduced by a dispatch, revoking a previous order giving me command of Fortress Monroe, and under which I had expected to take ten thousand men from that point, to aid in our operations. Then, when under fire before the defences of Yorktown, we received the news of the withdrawal of Gen McDowell's corps, of about 35,000 men. This completed the overthrow of the original plan of the campaign. About one-third of my entire army, (five divisions out of fourteen, one of the nine remaining being little larger than a brigade), was thus taken from me. Instead of a rapid advance which I had planned, aided by a flank movement up the York River, it was only left to besiege Yorktown. That siege was successfully conducted by the army, and when these strong works at length yielded to our approaches the troops rushed forward to the sanguinary but successful battle of Williamsburg, and thus opened an almost unresisted advance to the banks of the Chickahominy. Richmond lay before them, surrounded with fortifications and guarded by an army larger than our own; but the prospect did not shake the courage of the brave men who composed my command. Relying still on the support which the vastness of our undertaking and the grand results depending on our success seemed to insure us we pressed forward. The weather was stormy beyond precedent, the deep soil of the Peninsula was at times one vast morass. The Chickahominy rose to a higher stage than had been known for years before. Pursuing the advance, the crossings were seized, and the right wing extended to effect a junction with reinforcements now promised and earnestly desired, and upon the arrival of which the complete success of the campaign seemed clear. The brilliant battle of Hanover Court House was fought, which opened the way for the first corps with the aid of which, had it come, we should then have gone into the enemy's capital. It never came. The bravest army could not do more, under such overwhelming disappointment, than the army of the Potomac then did. Fair Oaks attests their courage and endurance, when they hurled back again and again the vastly superior forces of the enemy. But mortal men could not accomplish the miracles that seem to have been expected of them. But one course was left, a flank march in the face of a powerful enemy to another and better base, one of the most hazardous movements in war. The army of the Potomac holding its own safety, and almost the safety of our cause, in its hands, was equal to the occasion. The Seven Days are classical in American history, those days in which the noble soldiers of the Union and the Constitution fought an overwhelming enemy by day, and retreated from successive victories by night, through a week of battle, closing the terrible scenes of conflict with the ever memorable victory at Malvern, where they drove back, beaten and shattered, the entire eastern army of the confederacy, and thus secured for themselves a place of rest, and a point for a new advance upon the capital from the banks of the James.

Richmond was still within our grasp, had the army of the Potomac been reinforced and permitted to advance. But counsels, which I cannot but think subsequent events proved unwise, prevailed in Washington, and we were ordered to abandon the campaign. Never did soldiers better deserve the thanks of a nation than the army of the Potomac for the deeds of the Peninsular campaign, and although that meed was withheld from them by the authorities, I am persuaded they have received the applause of the American people. The army of the Potomac was recalled from within sight of Richmond, and incorporated with the army of Virginia. The disappointments of the campaign on the Peninsula, had not dampened their ardor or diminished their patriotism. They fought well, faithfully, gallantly under Gen Pope, yet were compelled to fall back on Washington, defeated and almost demoralized. The enemy no longer occupied in guarding his own capital, poured his troops northward, entered Maryland, threatened Pennsylvania, and even Washington itself. Elated by his recent victories and assured that our troops were disorganized and dispirited, he was confident that the seat of war was now permanently transferred to the loyal States, and that his own exhausted soil was to be relieved from the burden of supporting two hostile armies. But he did not understand the spirit which animated the soldiers of the Union. I shall not, nor can I living forget that, when I was ordered to the command of the troops for the defense of the capital, the soldiers with whom I had shared so much of the anxiety and pain and suffering of the war, had not lost their confidence in me as their commander. They sprang to my call with all their ancient vigor discipline and courage. I led them into Maryland. Fifteen days after they had fallen back defeated, before Washington they vanquished the enemy on the rugged heights of South Mountain, pursued him to the hard fought field of Antietam, and drove him, broken and disappointed, across the Potomac into Virginia.

The army had need of rest. After the terrible experiences of battles and marches, with scarcely an interval of repose, which they had gone through from the time of leaving for the Peninsula, the return to Washington, the defeat in Virginia, the victory at South Mountain, and again at Antietam, it was not surprising that they were, in a large degree, destitute of the absolute necessaries to effective duty. Shoes were worn out, blankets were lost, clothing was in rags; in short the army was unfit for active service, and an interval for rest and equipment was necessary.

When the slowly forwarded supplies c-us I led the army across the river renovated and refreshed, in good order and discipline, and followed the retreating foe to a position where I was confident of decisive victory, when in the midst of the movement, while my advanced guard was actually in contact with the enemy, I was removed from the command.

I am devoutly grateful to God that my last campaign with this brave army was crowned with a victory which saved the nation from the greatest peril it had then undergone

I have not accomplished my purpose, if, by this report, the army of the Potomac is not placed high on the roll of the historic armies of the world

Its deeds ennoble the nation to which it belongs. Always ready for battle, always firm, steadfast and trustworthy, I never called on it in vain; nor will the nation ever have cause to attribute its want of success, as under other commanders, to any failure of patriotism or bravery in that noble body of American soldiers.

No man can justly charge upon any portion of that army, from the commanding general to the private, any lack of devotion to the service of the United States government, and to the cause of the Constitution and the Union They have proved their fealty in much sorrow, suffering, danger, and through the very shadow of death. Their comrades dead on all the fields where we fought, have scarcely more claim to the honor of a nation's reverence than the survivors to the justice of a nation's gratitude.

I am sir, very respectfully, your obedient servant,

GEORGE B McCLELLAN,-Maj-Gen U S A.

APPENDIX A.

ORGANIZATION AND DISTRIBUTION.

The designations of the different Batteries of Artillery, both Regular and Volunteer, follow within a few pages

The following distribution of Regiments and Batteries was made as a preliminary organization of the forces at hand, shortly after my arrival at Washington.

The Infantry, Artillery and Cavalry, as fast as collected and brought into primary organization, were assigned to Brigades and Divisions as indicated in the subjoined statements.

ORGANIZATION OF THE DIVISION OF THE POTOMAC.
August 4th, 1861.

BRIGADIER-GENERAL HUNTER'S BRIGADE
23d Regiment New York Volunteers.
25th " " "
35th " " "
37th " " "

BRIGADIER-GENERAL HEINTZELMAN'S BRIGADE
5th Regiment Maine Volunteers
16th " New York "
26th " " "
27th " " "
Tidball's Battery ("A") 2d U S Artillery

BRIGADIER-GENERAL W T SHERMAN'S BRIGADE
14th Regiment New York Volunteers.
9th " Massachusetts "
De Kalb " New York "
4th " Michigan "
Hamilton's Battery ("E") 3d U. S. Artillery
Company "I" 2d " Cavalry

BRIG -GENERAL KEARNEY'S BRIGADE
1st Regiment New Jersey Volunteers.
2d " " "
3d " " "
Green's Battery ("G") 2d U S Artillery.
Company "G" 2d " Cavalry

BRIGADIER-GENERAL HOOKER'S BRIGADE
1st Regiment Massachusetts Volunteers
11th " " "

2d Regiment New Hampshire Volunteers.
26th " Pennsylvania "

COLONEL KEYES'S BRIGADE
22d Regiment New York Volunteers.
24th " " "
30th " " "
14th " " State Militia

BRIG.-GENERAL FRANKLIN'S BRIGADE.
15th Regiment New York Volunteers.
18th " " "
31st " " "
32d " " "
Platt's Battery ("M") 2d U S Artillery
Comp'y "C" New York (Lincoln) Cavalry.

COLONEL BLENKER'S BRIGADE
8th Regiment New York Volunteers
27th " " "
27th " Pennsylvania "
Garibaldi Guard, New York "

COLONEL RICHARDSON'S BRIGADE.
12th Regiment New York Volunteers
2d " Michigan "
3d " " "

BRIGADIER-GENERAL STONE'S BRIGADE.
34th Regiment New York Volunteers.
Tammany " "
1st " " "
2d " New York State Militia.

COLONEL WM F SMITH'S BRIGADE
3d Regiment Vermont Volunteers.
6th   "   Maine   "
2d   "   Vermont   "
33d   "   New York "
Company "H" 2d U. S. Cavalry.
Captain Mott's New York Battery.
COLONEL COUCH'S BRIGADE.
2d Regiment Rhode Island Volunteers.
7th   "   Massachusetts   "

10th Regiment Massachusetts Volunteers.
36th   "   New York   "
The 2d Regiment Maine Volunteers,
  2d   "   Wisconsin   "   and the
  13th "   New York   "   stationed
        at *Fort Corcoran.*
The 21st Regiment New York Volunteers,
        stationed at *Fort Runyon.*
The 17th Regiment New York Volunteers,
        stationed at *Fort Ellsworth.*

By October the new levies had arrived in sufficient numbers, and the process of organization was so far carried on, that the construction of Divisions had been effected.
The following statement exhibits the composition of the Army, October 15th, 1861.

ORGANIZATION OF THE ARMY OF THE POTOMAC

October 15th, 1861.

I.
BRIG.-GENERAL STONEMAN'S CAVALRY COMMAND.
6th U S Cavalry.
4th Pennsylvania Cavalry
Oneida Cavalry (1 Company).
11th Pennsylvania Cavalry (Harlans)
Barker's Illinois Cavalry (1 Company)

II.
COL H J HUNT'S ARTILLERY RESERVE
Battery "L" 2d U S. Artillery.
   "   "A" "   "   "
   "   "B" "   "   "
   "   "K" 3d "   "
   "   "F" "   "   "
   "   "K" 4th "   "
   "   "H" 1st "   "   (Lieut Hall)
   "   "A" 5th "   "

III
CITY GUARD, BRIG.-GENERAL ANDREW PORTER
Cavalry
Companies "A" and "E" 4th U.S Cavalry.
Artillery.
Battery "K" 5th U S Artillery.
Infantry.
Battalion 2d U S Infantry
   "   3d "   "
Company 8th "   "
   "   1st "   "
   "   Sturgis Rifles (Illinois Volunteers)

IV
BANKS' DIVISION.
Cavalry.
3d Reg't N Y Cavalry (Van Alen) 4 Companies
Artillery.
Best's Battery "I" 4th U S Artillery.
Detachment 9th N Y Artillery
Matthew's Battery "F" 1st Pennsylvania Artillery.
Tompkins' Battery "A" 1st Rhode Island.
Infantry
Abercrombie's Brig   Stiles's Brig   Gordon's Brig
12th Mass Vols   3d Wis Vols   2d Mass. Vols

12th Ind   "   9th N Y S M. 28th N.Y. "
16th "   "   29th Penn Vol. 19th " "
30th Penn. "   13th Mass. " 5th Conn. "
                                    46th Penn "
                                    28th   " "
                                    1st Md.   "

MCDOWELL'S DIVISION.
Cavalry.
2d New York Cavalry (Harris' Light) Col Davies.
Artillery,
Battery "M" 2d U S. Artillery.
   "   "G" 1st "   "
Infantry
Keyes's Brig   Wadsworth's Brig   King's Brig.
14th N Y S M,   12th N Y Vols   2d Wis Vols.
22d   "   Vols   21st "   "   6th "   "
24th "   "   23d "   "   7th "   "
30th "   "   35th "   "   19th Ind. "

HEINTZELMAN'S DIVISION.
Cavalry
1st New Jersey. Col Halstead
Artillery
Thompson's Battery "G" 2d U S Artillery.
Infantry
Richardson's B   Sedgwick's B   Jameson's B
2nd Mich Vols   3rd Maine Vols 32d Penn. Vols.
2d   "   "   "   "   "   63d   "   "
5th   "   "   38th N Y   "   61st "   "
37th N. Y   40th "   "   45th "   "
                                 Penn. Vols. (Wild Cat Reg't)

F. J. PORTER'S DIVISION
Cavalry
3rd Penn. Cav [Kentucky Cav.] Col Averell
8th   "   "   Col Gregg.
Artillery
Bat'y "E" 2nd U. S. Artillery
  "   "E" 3d   "   "   NOTE.—Transferred to
                                Sherman's Exped
Infantry
Morell's B   Martindale's B   Butterfield's B.
14th N Y Vols   13th N Y Vols   50th N Y Vols
33rd Penn   2nd Maine "   Stockton's I M R
4th Mich.   —N Y De K R   83 Penn Vols
9th Mass.   18th Mass Vol.   17th N Y Vols.
                                    25th "   "

FRANKLIN'S DIVISION.
Cavalry
1st New York Cavalry   Col. McReynolds.
Artillery.
Bat'y "D" 2nd U. S. Art'y. Hexamer's B N. Y. V.
" "G" " "
Infantry

Kearney's B	Slocum's B	Newton's B
1st N. J. Vols	16th N. Y. Vols	15th N J Vols
2nd " "	26th " "	18th " "
3rd " "	27th " "	31st " "
4th " "	6th Maine "	32d " "

STONE'S DIVISION.
Cavalry
6 Companies 3rd N. Y. (Van Alen) Cavalry.
Artillery.
Kirby's Bat "I" 1st U. S   Bunting's 6th N. Y. I B.
Vaughn's " "B" 1st R. I.
Infantry

Gorman's Brigade	Lander's Brigade
2nd N Y S. M	19th Mass Vols
1st Minn Vols	20th " "
— N. Y. Vol (Tam. R)	7th Mich
15th Mass "	Com Mass Sharpshooters
34th N. Y	

BAKER'S BRIGADE.
—— Penn Vols [1st California,]
—— " " [2nd California]
—— " " [3rd California]

BUELL'S DIVISION
Artillery
Battery "D" 1st Penn Artillery.
" "H" " "
Infantry

Couch's Brig	Graham's Brig	Peck's Brig
2nd R. I Vols.	23rd Penn Vols	13th Penn Vol.
7th Mass "	31st " "	21st " "
10th Mass "	67th N. Y. [1st L I] Vols	62d N Y V. Anderson Zou
36th N. Y Vols	65th N. Y. V (1st U S. Chass)	55th N. Y Vol

McCALL'S DIVISION.
Cavalry.
1st Penn. Reserve Cavalry.   Col. Bayard.
Artillery
Easton's Battery "A" 1st Penn. Artillery
Cooper's " "B" 1st " "
Kern's " "G" 1st " "
Infantry.

Meade's Brig	—— Brig	—— Brig
1st Rifles Penn Res	5th P R Inf.	10th P R Inf.
4th Penn. Res. Inf	1st " "	6th " "
3rd " "	8th " "	9th " "
7th " "		12th " "
11th " "		
2nd " "		

HOOKER'S DIVISION.
Cavalry.
3rd Ind Cav [8 Companies]   Lieut.-Col. Carter
Artillery
Elder's Battery "E" 1st U. S Artillery.

Infantry

—— Brigade	Sickles' Brigade
1st Mass. Vols	1st Reg't Ex Brig N Y. Vols.
11th " "	2nd " " " " "
2nd N H "	3rd " " " " "
26th Penn. "	4th " " " " "
1st Mich. "	5th " " " " "

SMITH'S DIVISION.
Cavalry
5th Penn. Cav. (Cameron Drags).   Col. Friedman.
Artillery
Ayre's Battery "F" 5th U S Artillery
Mott's 2nd New York Independent Battery.
Bart's Battery "E" 1st Penn Artillery.
Infantry

Brigade	Stevens Brig	Hancocks Brig
2nd Verm't Vols	33d N. Y. Vols	47th Penn Vols
3rd " "	79th " S M	49th " "
4th " "	6th Maine Vols	43rd N. Y "
5th " "	49th N Y "	5th Wis "

Cos "B" and "C" Berdan's Shipshooters..

NOTE.—The 47th Penn Vols and the 79th N Y S M transferred to Gen Sherman's Expedition

CASEY'S PROVISIONAL BRIGADE.

5th N. J. Vols.	—— Penn Vols (R H Reg't)
6th " "	Battalion D C Vols.
7th " "	40th Penn "
8th " "	4th N H "

NOTE.—Round Head Regiment transferred to Gen. Sherman's Expedition.

V.
GARRISON OF ALEXANDRIA.   BRIG-GEN. MONTGOMERY.
Military Governor.
—— Penn. Volunteers, (Cameron Guards)

GARRISON OF FORT ALBANY.
14th Mass Volunteers

GARRISON OF FORT RICHARDSON.
4th Connecticut Volunteers.

GARRISON OF FORT WASHINGTON.
Company 'D' 1st U S Artillery.
" 'H' 37th N. Y. Volunteers.
" 'I' " " "
" U. S Recruits unassigned.

VI.
DIX'S DIVISION, BALTIMORE.
Cavalry
Company 1 enn Cavalry
Artillery.
Bat'y "I" 2nd U S Art'y.   2nd Mass. Battery.
" — N Y Art'y.
Infantry
3rd New York Volunteers.
4th " "
5th " "
17th Mass "
25th " "
21st Indiana "
6th Michigan "
4th Wisconsin "
7th Maine "
2nd Maryland Battalion.
Reading City Guards.

APPENDIX B.

I add a Statement of the Organization and Composition of the Troops on April 1st, commencing with the portion of the Army of the Potomac, which went to the Peninsula; giving afterwards the Regiments and Batteries left on the Potomac and in Maryland and Virginia after April 1st, 1862.

TROOPS OF THE ARMY OF THE POTOMAC SENT TO THE PENINSULA IN MARCH AND EARLY IN APRIL, 1862.

I.
CAVALRY RESERVE   BRIG.-GEN. P ST G COOKE

Emory's Brigade	Blake's Brigade
5th U S Cavalry	1st U S Cavalry
6th " "	8th Penn "
6th Penn "	Barker's Squadron Ill Cav'y.

II.
ARTILLERY RESERVE   COL H J HUNT

Graham's Bat'y "K" & "G" 1st U S. 6 Napoleon [guns.
Randal's   " "E"   1st " 6   "
Carlisle's   " "E"   2d " 6 20-pds [Parrott guns
Robertson's "   2d " 6 3-in ordnance
Benson's   " "M"   2d " 6 3-in ordnance [guns.
Tidball's   " "A"   2d " 6 3-in ord "
Edward's   " "L" & "M" 3d " 6 10-pds Parrott [guns
Gibson's   " "C" & "G" 3d " 6 3-in ord. "
Livingston's " "F" & "K" 3d " 4 10-pds Parrott [guns.
Howe's   " "G"   4th " 6 Napoleon "
De Russy's " "K"   4th " 6   "   "
Weed's   " "I"   5th " 6 3-in. ord. "
Smead's   " "K"   5th " 4 Napoleon "
Ames's   " "A"   5th " 4 10-pds Parrotts } guns
                           2 Napo'n   }

ARTILLERY RESERVE

Diederick's Bat'y "A" N Y Art Btl 6 20-pd Parrott guns
Voegelie's   "   "B" "   "   " 4 "
Knieriem's   "   "C" "   "   " 4 "
Grimm's   "   "D" "   "   " 6 32-pd How

100 guns.

III.
VOLUNTEER ENGINEER TROOPS   GEN WOODBURY

15th New York Volunteers.
50th   "   "   "

REGULAR ENGINEER TROOPS.   CAPT DUANE

Companies "A," "B" and "C." U S Engineers

ARTILLERY TROOPS WITH SIEGE TRAIN

1st Connecticut Heavy Artillery.   Col Tyler

INFANTRY RESERVE (Regular Brigade)
Gen Sykes

9 Co's 2nd U S Infantry.
7 "   3d   "   "
10 "   4th "   "
5th Regt N. Y. Vols.   Col G. K. Warren.

8 Co's 10th and 17th U S. Infantry.
6 Co's 11th   U. S Infantry.
8 "   12th   "   "
9 "   14th   "   "

SECOND CORPS   GEN SUMNER.
Cavalry.
8th Illinois Cavalry   Col Farnsworth
One Squadron 6th New York Cavalry.

RICHARDSON'S DIVISION.
Artillery,
Clark's Bat'y. "A" & "C" 4th U S 6 Napoleon gns.
Frank's   "   "G"   1st N Y 6 10-pds Parrott
Pettit's "   "B"   1st " 6   "   [guns.
Hogan's   "   "A"   2d   " 6   "   "

Infantry
Howard's Brig	Meagher's Brig	French's Brig
5th N H Vols	69th N. Y. Vols.	52d N Y. Vols
81st Penn. "	63rd " "	57th " "
61st N Y "	88th " "	66th " "
64th " "		53rd Penn. "

SEDGWICK'S DIVISION.
Artillery
Kirby's Bat'y. "I" 1st U S 6 Napoleon gns.
Tompkin's " "A" 1st R.I 6 {4 10-pd Par / 2 12-pd Hoz} gns.
Bartlett's " "B" 1st " 6 {4 10-pd Par / 2 12-pd Hoz} gns.
Owen's   " "G" ——— 6 3-in. ordnance gns

Infantry
Gorman's Brig	Burns Brig	Dana's Brig
2d N Y S M	69th Penn. Vols.	19th Mass Vols
15th Mass. Vol	71st " "	7th Mich. "
34 N Y. "	72nd " "	42nd N Y. "
1st Minn. "	106th " "	20th Mass. "

NOTE.—*Blenker's Division detached and assigned to the Mountain Department*

THIRD CORPS.   GENERAL HEINTZELMAN.
Cavalry.
3rd Pennsylvania Cavalry.   Col Averell

PORTER'S DIVISION
Artillery
Griffin's Bat'y "K" 5th U S 6 10-pds Parrott
Weden's   "   "C" R.I.   — —   [guns.
Martin's "   "C" Mass   7 Napoleon Guns
Allen's   "   "E"   6 3-in ordn guns.

Infantry
Martindale's Brig	Morell's Brig	Butterfield's Brig.
2d Maine Vols	14th N Y Vols	17th N Y. Vols.
18th Mass. "	4th Mich "	63rd Penn "
22nd " "	9th Mass "	44th N Y "
25th N. Y. "	82nd Penn. "	Stockton's Mich. "
13th N Y "		12th N. Y. Vols.

1st Berdan Sharpshooters

HOOKER'S DIVISION.
Artillery
Hall's Bat'y "H" 1st U S 6 {4 10-pd Parrott / 2 12-pd How.} gns
Smith's " 4th N Y. Bat'y. 6 10-pds Parrott "
Bramhall's 6th " " 6 3-in ordnance "
Osborn's "D" 1st N Y A 4 " " "

Infantry
Sickle's Brig   Naglee's Brig   Col Starr's Brig
1st Excelsior (N.Y.) 1st Mass Vols 5th N J Vols.
2nd "   11th "   6th "
3rd "   26th Penn "   7th "
4th "   2nd N H "   8th "
5th "

HAMILTON'S DIVISION.
Artillery
Thompson's Bat'y "G" 2d US 6 Napoleon guns.
Beam's " "B" N J 6 {4 10-pd Par / 2 Napoleon} gns
Randolph's " "E" R I 6 {4 10-pd Par / 2 Napoleon} gns

Infantry
Jameson's Brig   Birney's Brig   ——— Brig
105th Pe Vols   38th N Y Vols   2d Mich Vols
63rd "   40th "   3rd "
57th "   3rd Maine "   5th "
87th N.Y. "   4th "   37th N Y "

FOURTH CORPS   GENERAL KEYES.'
Cavalry

COUCH'S DIVISION.
Artillery
McCarthy's Bat'y "C" 1st Penn. 4 10-pd Par gns
Flood's " "D" 1st " 6 " "
Miller's " "E" 1st " 4 Napoleon "
Brady's " "F" 1st " 4 10-pd Parrott "

Infantry
Graham's Brig   Peck's Brig   ——— Brig
67th N Y. Vls (1 L I) 98th Pe Vls 2d R I Vls
65th " (1 U S C) 102d " " 7th Mass
23rd Penn. " 93d " " 10th "
31st " " 62d N Y " 36th N Y "
61st " " 55th " "

SMITH'S DIVISION
Artillery
Ayres' Bat'y "F" 5th U S 6 {4 10-pd Par / 2 Napoleon} gns
Mott's " 3d N Y Bat'y 6 {4 10-pd Par / 2 Napoleon} gns
Wheeler's " "E" 1st N Y 4 3-in ordnance
Kennedy's " 1st N Y Battery 6 " " "

Infantry
Hancock's Brig   Brook's Brig   Davidson's Brig
5th Wis. Vols   2d Verm't Vol. 33d N Y Vols
49th Penn. "   3d " " 77th " "
43d N Y. "   4th " " 49th " "
6th Maine "   5th " " 7th Maine "
 6th " "

CASEY'S DIVISION.
Artillery
Regan's Bat'y. 7th N Y Bat'y 6 3-in ordn. guns
Fitch's " 8th " " 6 " " 4 "
Bates' " "A" 1st N Y Art 6 Napoleon "
Spratt's " "H" 1st " " 4 3-in ordn "

Infantry
Keim's Brig   Palmer's Brig   ——— Brig
85th Penn. Vol. 85th N.Y. Vol. 104th Penn. Vol
101st " " 98th " " 52d " "

103d Penn Vols 92d N Y Vols 56th N Y "
96th N Y. "   81st " " 100th " "
 93d " " 11th Maine "

PROVOST GUARD.
2nd U S Cavalry
Battalion 8th and 17th U S Infantry.

AT GENERAL HEADQUARTERS
2 Cos 4th U S Cav 1 Co Oneida Cav (N Y Vol)

The following troops of the army of the Potomac were left behind, or detached, on and in front of the Potomac for the defence of that line, April 1st, 1862 Franklin's and McCall's divisions at subsequent and different dates joined the active portion of the army on the Peninsula Two Brigades of Shield's division joined at Harrison's Landing.

FIRST CORPS   GENERAL McDOWELL
Cavalry
1st New York Cavalry   4th New York Cavalry
2d " "   1st Penn. "

Sharpshooters
2d Regiment Berdan's Sharpshooters

FRANKLIN'S DIVISION
Artillery
Platt's Bat'y "D" 2 1 U S 6 Napoleon guns
Porter's " "A" Mass. 6 {4 10 pd Parrott / 2 12 pd Howit's} gns
Hexamer's " "A" N. J. 6 {4 10 pd Parrott / 2 12 pd Howit's} gns
Wilson's " "F" 1st N Y Art'y 4 3-in ordnance

Infantry
Kearney's Brig   Slocum's Brig   Newton's Brig
1st N J Vols   16th N Y Vols 18th N Y Vols
2d " " 27th " " 31st " "
3d " " 5th Maine " 32d " "
4th " " 96th Penn " 95th Penn "

McCALL'S DIVISION.
Artillery
Seymour's Bat'y "C" 5th U S 6 Napoleon guns
Eaton's " "A" 1st Penn 4 " "
Cooper's " "B" 1st " 6 10-pd Parrott gns
Kern's " "C" 1st "6 {2 10-pd Parrott / 1 12-pd Howits} gns

Infantry
Reynold's Brig   Meade's Brig   Ord's Brig
1 Penn Res Rgt 3d Penn Res Rgt. 6th Penn Rgt.
2 " " " 4th " " " 9th " "
5 " " " 7th " " " 10th " "
8 " " " 11th " " " 12th " "
 1 Penn Reserve Rifles.

KING'S DIVISION.
Artillery
Gibbon's Bat'y "B" 4th U S 6 Napoleon guns
Monroe's " "D" 1st R I. 6 10-pd Parrott guns
Gerrish's " "A" N. H. 6 Napoleon "
Durrell's " Penn. 6 10-pd Parrott guns

Infantry
——— Brigade   Patrick's Brig   Augur's Brig
2d Wis Vols   20th N Y S M   14th N Y S M
6th " " 21st " Vols 22d " Vols
7th " " 23d " " 24th " "
19 h Ind " 25th " " 30th " "

FIFTH CORPS   GENERAL BANKS
Cavalry
1st Maine Cavalry   5th New York Cavalry
1st Vermont "   8th " "
1st Michigan "   Keyes's Bat Penn. Cav'y.

1st R. I. Cavalry.   18 Cos Maryland Cavalry
                      1 Squadron Virginia   "
             Unattached
28th Pa Vols 4th Reg Potomac H G (Md Vols)
WILLIAMS' DIVISION.
Artillery
Best's Battery "F" 4th U S 6 Napoleon guns
Hampton's "   Maryland 4 10-pds. Parrott guns
Thompson's "   "   4   "   "   "
Mathew's   "   "F" Penn 6 3-in ordnance   "
Cothran's "   "M' 1 N Y 6 10-pds Parrott   "
Knapp's   "   Penn.   6   "   "   "
McMahon's "   N Y   6 3-in ordnance   "
Infantry
Abercrombie's Brig   — Brig   — Brig
12th Mass Vols.   9 N Y S M 28 N Y Vs
2d   "   "   29 Pa Vols 5 Conn "
16th Ind   "   27 Ind " 46 Pa. "
1 Pot H Brig (Md Vol) 3 Wis "   1 Md.   "
1 Co Zou d'Af (Pa Vol)   12 Ind. "
                                 13 Mass."
SHIELDS DIVISION.
Artillery
Clark's Bat "E" 4th U S 6 10-pds Parrott guns
Jenk's "   "A" 1st Va 6 { 4 10-pds Parrott } guns
                         { 2 6-pds.   "   }
Davy's "   "B" 1st Va 2 10-pds Parrott guns.
Huntington's "A" 1 Ohio 6 13-pds James "
Robinson's "L" 1   6 { 2 12-p How' } guns.
                      { 4 6-p g   }
          4 Ohio Inf 1 6-p gun.
Infantry
Brigade	Brigade	Brigade.
14th Ind Vols	5th Ohio Vols.	7th Ohio Vols.
4th Ohio "	62d " "	29th " "
8th " "	66th " "	7th " "
7th Va "	13th Ind "	1st Va "
67th Ohio "	39th Ill "	11th Penn "
84th Penn "		Andrew Sharp's

GENERAL WADSWORTH'S COMMAND.
Cavalry.
1st New Jersey Cavalry,   At Alexandria.
4th Pennsylvania "   East of the Capitol
Artillery and Infantry
10th New Jersey Vols   Bladensburg Road
104th N. Y. Vols   Kalorama Heights.
1st Wis Heavy Art'y   Fort "Cass," Va.
3 Batteries N. Y. "   Forts "Ethan Allen" and
                         "Marcy."
Depot N.Y. Light Art'y Camp "Barry"
2 D C Vols   Washington City.
26th Pa "   "G" St Wharf.
26th N Y "   Fort Lyon.
93th "   "   Camp "Thomas"
94th "   "   Alexandria
88th Pa " (Detachm't)   "
91st "   "   Franklin Sq Barracks.
4th N Y Art'y.   Forts "Carroll" and "Greble"
112th Pa. Vols.   Fort "Saratoga."

76th N.Y Vols.   Fort "Massachusetts."
59th "   "   "   "Pennsylvania."
88th Pa. " (Detachm't) " "Good Hope."
99th "   "   "   "Mahan."
3d N. Y. Light Art'y Forts "Ward," "Worth'
                       and "Blenker"
107th Pa Vols.   Kendall Green.
54th "   "   "   "   "
Dickerson's Light Art'y East of the Capitol.
86th N Y. Vols   "   "   "
88th Pa. " (Detach't) "   "   "
                      { Forts "Albany," "Tel-
14 Mass. "Heavy Art'y { linghast," "Richard-
56 Penn. "   { son," "Runyon," "Jack-
                      { son," "Barnard,"
                      { "Craig," "Scott"
4th U S Art'y (Detachment) { Fort "Wash'ton"
37th N Y Vol (Detachment) { "   "   "
97th "   "   Fort "Corcoran."
101st "   "
12th Va   "
91st N Y   "
IN CAMP NEAR WASHINGTON
6th New York Cavalry. Dismounted.
10th "   "   "   "
Swain's "   "   "
2d Pennsylvania   "   "
(These troops 3,359 men, were ordered to report to Col Miles, commanding Rail Road Guard, to relieve 3,306 older troops, ordered to be sent to Manassas to report to Gen Abercrombie.)
GENERAL DIX'S COMMAND (BALTIMORE)
Cavalry
1st Maryland Cavalry. Detachment of Cavalry, Purnell Legion.
Artillery.
Battery "I" 2d U S Artillery.
   " — Maryland Artillery.
   " "L" 1st New York Artillery
2 Independent Batteries, Penn Artillery
Infantry
3d New York Volunteers.
4th "   "   "
11th Pennsylvania "
87th "   "
111th "   "
21st Massachusetts " (Detachment)
2d Delaware   "
2d Maryland   "
1st Eastern Shore Home Guards (Maryland Vols)
2d   "   "   "   "   "   "
Purnell Legion
2 Battalions ———

Note.—MR ALLEN PINKERTON was the trustworthy and efficient chief of the Secret Service Corps He is mentioned under his assumed name Mr E J ALLEN

CAPT G. A. CUSTAR, additional A. D. C and Lieutenant U. S. Cavalry, was added to the Staff of the Commanding General when on the Chickahominy

WATCHWORDS FOR PATRIOTS.

MOTTOES FOR THE CAMPAIGN, SELECTED FROM GENERAL McCLELLAN'S WRITINGS.

The true issue for which we are fighting is the preservation of the Union and upholding the laws of the general government. — *Instructions to General Burnside, January 7, 1862*

We are fighting solely for the integrity of the Union, to uphold the power of our national government, and to restore to the nation the blessings of peace and good order. — *Instructions to General Halleck, November 11, 1861*

You will please constantly to bear in mind the precise issue for which we are fighting, that issue is the preservation of the Union and the restoration of the full authority of the general government over all portions of our territory. — *Instructions to General Buell, November 7, 1861.*

We shall most readily suppress this rebellion and restore the authority of the government by religiously respecting the constitutional rights of all — *Instructions to General Buell, November 7, 1861*

Be careful so to treat the unarmed inhabitants as to contract, not widen, the breach existing between us and the rebels. — *Instructions to General Buell, November 12, 1861.*

I have always found that it is the tendency of subordinates to make vexatious arrests on mere suspicion. — *Instructions to General Buell, November 12, 1861.*

Say as little as possible about politics or the negro — *Instructions to General Burnside, January 7, 1862*

The unity of this nation, the preservation of our institutions, are so dear to me that I have willingly sacrificed my private happiness with the single object of doing my duty to my country — *Letter to Secretary Cameron, October, 1861*

Whatever the determination of the Government may be, I will do the best I can with the Army of the Potomac, and will share its fate, whatever may be the task imposed upon me — *Letter to Secretary Cameron, October, 1861.*

Neither confiscation of property, political executions of persons, territorial organization of States, nor forcible abolition of slavery should be contemplated for a moment — *Letter to President Lincoln, July 7, 1862*

In prosecuting this war, all private property and unarmed persons should be strictly protected, subject to the necessity of military operations. — *Letter to the President, July 7, 1862*

Military arrests should not be tolerated, except in places where active hostilities exist; and oaths, not required by enactments constitutionally made, should be neither demanded nor received. — *Letter to the President, July 7, 1862*

A declaration of radical views, especially upon slavery, will rapidly disintegrate our present armies — *Letter to the President, July 7, 1862.*

If it is not deemed best to entrust me with the command even of my own army, I simply ask to be permitted to share their fate on the field of battle — *Dispatch to General Halleck, August 30, 1862.*

In the arrangement and conduct of campaigns the direction should be left to professional soldiers — *General McClellan's Report*

By pursuing the political course I have always advised, it is possible to bring about a permanent restoration of the Union — a re-union by which the rights of both sections shall be preserved, and by which both parties shall preserve their self-respect, while they respect each other. — *General McClellan's Report*

I am devoutly grateful to God that my last campaign was crowned with a victory which saved the nation from the greatest peril it had then undergone. — *General McClellan's Report.*

At such a time as this, and in such a struggle, political partisanship should be merged in a true and brave patriotism, which thinks only of the good of the whole country. — *General McClellan's West Point Oration*

GEN. McCLELLAN'S
REPORT AND CAMPAIGNS.

THE ONLY COMPLETE AND ACCURATE EDITION.

By special Arrangement with Gen. McCLELLAN,

SHELDON & Co.,
Publishers, 335 Broadway, N. Y.,

Have published a

FULL AND COMPLETE EDITION OF HIS REPORT.

While going through the press, this edition was corrected by Gen. McCLELLAN. It has none of the remarkable errors which have crept into the Government edition and all the other editions that have followed the Government edition.

It also has the

"CAMPAIGN IN WESTERN VIRGINIA,"

prepared by Gen. McCLELLAN expressly for this edition. Illustrated with **Maps and Plans of Battles**, &c., prepared by Gen. McCLELLAN. One volume, 8vo. Price, $3 00.

12mo edition of the same, bound in cloth, with all the Maps, Price, $1.75. Bound in boards, $1.25.

From the Journal of Commerce.

"We regret that the Congressional edition, and other cheap editions of the Report are incomplete and inaccurate, omitting entirely some portions which present the most interesting and important views of the relations of General McClellan to the Cabinet, the army and the country The edition published by Sheldon & Company, under General McClellan's authority, is accurate"

From the Post, Chicago

"Sheldon & Co have issued their edition of General McClellan's Report on the Organization and Campaigns of the Army of the Potomac, to which is added an account of the Campaign in West Virginia, from the General's own pen. This edition is the only one which gives the main report in full, important parts of it, relating to very critical periods in the history of the Army of the Potomac, being omitted from the Congressional edition, and, by consequence, from all other editions, without exception, which are mere reprints of that. The edition published by Sheldon & Co., is complete and authentic, and is the only complete and authentic edition"

From the Boston Post.

"No man can feel that he has a copy of McClellan's Report, without a copy of this edition"

SHELDON & Co.

Have in preparation a full and complete

LIFE OF GEN. McCLELLAN,

In one volume, 12mo. It will be published at the earliest possible day

SHELDON & Co. have now ready a pamphlet edition of

GEN. McCLELLAN'S GREAT ORATION,
DELIVERED AT WEST POINT,

Embracing also a full account of all that was said and done on the occasion of the dedication of the Battle Monument. Price, 25 cents.